A HAUNTING TRAGEDY

A HAUNTING TRAGEDY

Gender, Caste and Class in the 1866 Famine of Orissa

BIDYUT MOHANTY

MANOHAR
2022

First published 2022

ISBN 978-93-90729-63-0

Published by
Ajay Jain *for*
Manohar Publishers & Distributors
4753/23 Ansari Road, Daryaganj
New Delhi 110002

Typeset by
Ravi Shanker
Delhi 110095

Printed at
Replika Press Pvt. Ltd.

To

MANORANJAN

who stood by me intellectually and even otherwise
while I completed this study

Contents

Preface 9

1. Introduction 17
2. The Political Economy of Orissa, 1860-1921 31
3. The Great Orissa Famine of 1866: The Event and the Process 74
4. Relief and Caste: Emergence of the Chhatrakhia Community 141
5. Later Famines: Social Impact and State Response 180
6. Female Mortality in Famines, 1866-1974 205
7. Gender and Class Incidence of Infectious Diseases 241
8. Gender Discrimination in Food and Health Care 268
9. Rise and Fall of Sex Ratio 293
10. Migration in the Famine Era: Gender, Caste and Class 349
11. Famine and Women, Past and Present: Some Concluding Reflections 397

Glossary 409

Index 415

Preface

This work reflects three phases of research in my academic career: doctoral research at Delhi School of Economics in the 1980s, Panchayati Raj and Women's Development during the past three decades at the Institute of Social Sciences, New Delhi and the activities around the 150th anniversary of the 1866 famine during 2014-18 with the Pipili Sanskrutika Parishad, Bhubaneswar. My participation in the Orissa Gabeshana Chakra activities in Delhi and Orissa cut through all these years. I continued to learn more about the subject and gathered more information and ideas. In this process I owe much debt to many teachers, colleagues, students, librarians, research assistants, friends and above all the Panchayat women representatives over the years. I can name only a few.

While preparing this manuscript innumerable memories crowded my mind. Initially, just after I had finished my MA from Delhi School of Economics, prominent demographer Prof. Ashish Bose of the Institute of Economic Growth, assigned me a project on migration and analyse the Census data to find out the pattern of migration both at the destination and the place of origin. While going through the various Census Reports, I noticed a lot of references to the Great Famine of 1866 and the caste Chhatrakhia. I was quite struck by the accounts of sufferings of the famine victims and decided to search for more information. I also recollected a story I had read in my childhood about a small boy Sanatan who tried to bring a fistful of rice for his starving parents but died on his way. It was included in the literature course in our school.

Professor Bose introduced me to Prof. Dharma Kumar to join her in a research project. When Prof. Dharma Kumar noticed that

I was keen on doing research she suggested that I work on the Orissa famine of 1866 and advised me to focus on the regional economic history, since Orissa had long been neglected. Based on my research report on migration, I got registered for PhD with Prof. Dharma Kumar as my supervisor. Her minute guidance and tough supervision became an asset that shaped my academic growth. I shall be ever grateful to her.

To my surprise Dharma Kumar called me one day to inform that Indian Council for Historical Research (ICHR) had a scheme to support women researchers, especially homemakers from backward regions of India and that I should apply. That four-year doctoral fellowship was a great push for my research, especially doing work in the archives in Orissa and Bengal, besides the National Archives of Delhi.

I am deeply indebted to Prof. R.S. Sharma, Chairperson, Dr. B.R. Grover, Director and Dr. P.K. Shukla, the Research Officer of ICHR who promptly attended to many of the administrative problems to facilitate my fieldwork. I am also thankful to eminent economic historian Prof. Binoy Bhusan Chaudhuri of Presidency College, Calcutta who was extremely supportive for my work. Prof. Dharma Kumar advised me to collect data from the National Archives, State Archives Record Room, National Library, District Collectorate, Board of Revenue and many places thus far unexplored by researchers for which I am ever indebted to her. When I suggested that Odia literary writings should also be studied as research material she readily agreed.

Many librarians and record room supervisors deserve my gratitude. At one point I was desperate, as the National Archives refused to issue the Famine Commission Reports because of their brittle condition. The Library attendant suggested I could issue the Famine Proceedings instead and work on them to begin with. It came as a great relief. Soon after I was fortunate to find the Famine Commission Reports in the Ratan Tata Library (RTL), my centre of work – my *sadhana peeth* – for many years.

I found RTL resources indeed a feast for me. I spent days together to go through the volumes of not only the Famine Commission Reports, but also the Annual Administration

Reports, Census Reports, District Gazetteers besides books on economic history of Europe and many other books and journals on famine. RTL in those days had no problem about funding and was undoubtedly one of the world's best libraries in social sciences. The library staff was most cooperative. Similar was the case with the Library of the Institute of Economic Growth I am ever thankful to them. The Agro-Economic Research Center too had some rare collections. The DSE-IEG complex was a wonderful place of research, full of rich resources and fellow researchers encouraging one another under the guidance of reputed scholars.

Doing research was a delight. I closely studied all the Census Reports. I have used the same quite liberally. My friends used to tease me, naming me as the Census person. I still have fond memories of that time. My contemporaries Tulsi Patel, Neelam Malhotra, Neelam Agarwal, Kulwant Kaur, Arup Mitra, Saudamine Dei, Mahendra Dev, Ashok Gulati are today prominent scholars in their own fields. My teachers Professors K.L. Krishna and Om Prakash from Delhi School of Economics helped me in many ways. I pay my special thanks to them. Professor J. Krishnamurty has been a great source of academic guidance for three decades. From my thesis period to many other occasions till today he remains a guide. I am most grateful to him.

The Delhi School list would be incomplete without mentioning the cartographer Mr. Chotu Ram of the Department of Geography and the Statistician Dr. Binod Chaudhury of IEG who helped me in preparing the maps and statistical computations. But my daily work was possible mainly because of the Delhi School Coffee House, whose staff knew who needed what at what time of the day. I must not forget the Paanwalla near Maurice Nagar Chowk for supplying me with delicious paans with high dose of tobacco. As a result, I could work for long hours. So much for Delhi School story which is full of sweet and bitter memories.

Now my stories begin on Orissa front. First of all, I began my research in the State Archives in Bhubaneswar. I hired an assistant who could take down notes on General Administration Reports and other reports. But I concentrated on the handwritten records of the famine proceedings. I must thank Dr. Nagendranath Pradhan and his family for inviting me to stay in their house during my research.

Rabindranath Sahoo and Sudhanshu Sahoo have been a part of this research work for over three decades constantly encouraging me, providing me with new source materials, especially from literary sources and above all always opening their doors for me to stay in Cuttack. I am indebted to them.

I recall my meetings with Dr. Harekrishan Mahatab former chief minister who was also a historian to discuss about the economic history of Orissa region and it was very helpful. Discussions with the famous historian Prof. Prabhat Mukherjee were extremely valuable. Sriramchandra Bhavan of Cuttack is a historic place of Oriya literature where I read the old files of *Utkal Deepika* and many other journals and those were a rich source of my research.

While staying in Cuttack during the doctoral period and later I also came across a few Chhatrakhia families who were living on the banks of the oldest canal in Jagatsinghpur. They were leading a miserable life. I went back to these areas and also visited some new areas where Chhatrakhias lived during the past decade. I am indeed grateful to all of them for providing rich material for my research.

Being totally immersed in researching on Panchayat Raj and Women's Development during the past three decades and organizing women panchayat representatives for pursuing the agenda of women's empowerment made me focus on some major aspects of poverty, livelihood and migration in different sections of society. Sometimes I had thought that the story of famine was over and we were flogging a dead horse, as one scholar put it. After working among the tribal people of Orissa and some other parts of India, I realized that the problem of food availability still persists. Because during the twentieth as well as the present century determining the causality of famine has become more complicated. Two major shifts have taken place. First the causality of famines in the present era is much more complex since the human factors as well as environmental factors interact and caused famines and food crisis. In so far as human factors are concerned one can cite the cases of African famines as well as remote areas of tribal regions. In case of Africa, famines are caused by the civil war, whereas in remote tribal areas of India the lack of infrastructural development and purchasing power prevented them to have access to food. In both the cases people died in large numbers. Even in case of tribal areas the press never highlighted the problems of scarcity of food. Hence the freedom of press is largely absent in those cases. On the other hand, the degraded environment created havoc in making the precipitation of monsoon quite erratic. Frequent drought affecting the paddy crop, wheat and other food grains create famine like situation. As in the nineteenth century, mass migration to the city or other safe places, takes place in search of jobs, drinking water, fodder for draught animals, etc. The total output falls and the marginal section of society suffers from lack of purchasing power. Of course, unlike the past, the welfare state today tries to intervene. But the arms of the state are saddled with too many duties and in the process they neglect supplying the essential articles at a subsidized rate. Sometimes the labourers lack purchasing power hence the syndrome of *dadan* labour that goes from Orissa for brick kiln factories and road construction in Andhra, Telengana and beyond. This was evident on many occasions as during my visit to Nagada in Jajpur district in 2016 or my surveys in Nuapada, Rayagada, Koraput and Mayurbhanj earlier.

Many of these issues were subject of the annual Panachayat Women's Conference that I was involved in organizing at Institute of Social Sciences (ISS) during the past three decades. I decided to integrate this experience with my research on the 1866 Famine. I am grateful to the ISS Chairperson, George Mathew who has been a steady source of support all these years. I also thank ISS staff and the Librarian for their constant help. Nirakar Beura has been an important part of my Panchayat research team for over twenty years. My sincere thanks goes to him and Banaprabha. Orissa Gabeshana Chakra friends Bijaya Bohidar, Asha Hans, Swarnamayee Tripathy, Amrita Patel, Kishor Samal and Geetanjali Dash deserve special mention.

Knowing Sri Ramesh Chandra Mohapatra, Secretary of the

Pipili Sanskrutika Parishad has been a piece of sheer good luck. He and his colleagues took me to the Pipili villages and schools and churches for fieldwork with great enthusiasm. This local history research group decided, on my suggestion, to mobilize the intellectuals researching on Orissa history, organized an important seminar and published a substantial volume on the 1866 Famine. Hats off to this fabulous group of friends.

Interestingly, I was born in a famine year 1943 and got married in a famine year 1966. I read about the Malthus theory of population during BA, where my teacher Deepak Sarangi used to talk about Malthus in a sarcastic tone. I also came across the food items that were used as famine substitutes like tender leaves of tamarind trees, ragi, leaves of drum-sticks, etc. In 1966 the famous Bihar famine and an efficient relief policy to reach out to the famine victims created a stir. K. Suresh Singh who was an outstanding officer-in-charge of the relief policy in Bihar analysed all this in his seminal book *The Indian Famine: A Study in Crisis and Change* in 1975. I also remembered that many of our friends donated money to the relief fund. This influenced my choice of research area.

When I started research, the field of economic history was experiencing many new trends. The new breed of economists and economic historians had questioned many familiar formulations of the colonial period. My teachers Dharma Kumar, Tapan Raychaudhury, J. Krishnamurty, Sukhamoy Chakravarty, Manmohan Singh and Amartya Sen and scholars like Morris D. Morris, N.S. Jodha, Michelle B. McAlpine, B.B. Chaudhuri, R.S. Rao argued and counter argued about the various aspects of the causes and consequences of the famines. I had the great fortune to interact with most of them. I acknowledge their contribution to my research with much gratitude. Their studies paid much attention to both the macro and micro history and took up cases such as Bengal, Maharashtra, south India and north India leaving out Orissa and north-east for other researchers. I have tried to fill some gap with the study of Orissa.

I wish to record my gratitude to a number of friends who were the source of constant encouragement and stood by me in difficult times. I particularly thank Geeta and Yogesh Puri, Meira and Sushil Dayal, Bulbul Das in Delhi for their support. Mark Juergensmeyer and Su Cheng our friends since the Berkeley days have been witness to my journey in India and in the US and have always extended a helping hand when needed. The Global Studies colleagues at UC Santa Barbara besides Mark, Richard Appelbaum, Richard Falk, Hilal Elver, Giles Gunn, Jan Nederveen Pieterse, Asheesh Mehta and Victor Faessel and the students I taught there have enriched my academic work in many ways during the past decade and more.

I like to record my heartfelt thanks to some people who had helped me in important ways and are no more: Gourkishore Das, Khageshwar Mahapatra, Sisir Kumar Das, Giri Deshingkar, Madhusudan Mishra and Raghunath Pradhan. Geeta and Prasanta Patnaik have been a constant source of encouragement since my Delhi School days. M.K. Premi had guided me to have access to migration data and Sabyasachi Bhattacharya to address some new issues.

The list goes on. I have left out many. I must mention my young friend Bhim Suba who helped me in finalizing tables. My friend from Delhi School days Surajit Deb helped me in checking some data for this manuscript. They deserve special thanks. Recently the famous poet Jayanta Mahapatra, writer Asit Mohanty, historians Chandi Prasad Nanda, Pritish Acharya, Kailas Ch. Das and Atul Pradhan have supplied me with important information. I sincerely acknowledge them for their help.

Last, but not the least, the sustained cooperation of my family has been very important to my work. Raising my school-going children while doing my PhD was a major challenge. Sometimes, I felt that I was not doing justice to them. Often all three of us were studying. Sometimes my husband, Manoranjan took care of them while I was in the library or out of Delhi. My father-in-law Bichitrananda who lived with us in Delhi during my research period never complained about my not being able to personally look after him adequately and was always full of encouragement for my studies. In Orissa I could leave my children in the care of my brother Sarada Charan and sister-in-law, Tilottama for extended periods in the village and spent time in archives of Orissa. My sister-in-law in Cuttack, Chiranjita and her children have been a solid support. Swami Sivachidananda always encouraged me to pursue my academic work and achieve success. In retrospect, I think it was worth it. My children Sanju and Jinee have settled very well in their own way and have always wanted their mother to continue her academic pursuits. I am very proud of them. In the recent years Sanju and Brinda, Jinee and Sangay and my grand-daughters Adya and Reeva, as well as my nephew Biswajit besides Manoranjan are the ones who have constantly pushed me to complete my various manuscripts and publish them.

The story of this work is perhaps the chronicle of any Indian woman scholar who was not daunted by the system.

BIDYUT MOHANTY

CHAPTER 1

Introduction

Why Study the Past Famines?

What is a Famine?

Let us start with the basic question as to whether famine is caused by mainly natural factors or human factors. According to the *International Encyclopedia of the Social Sciences*, 2008 'True famine is the shortage of food so extreme and protracted as to result in widespread persisting hunger, notable emaciation in many of the affected population, a considerable increase in community death rate and attributable at least in part to deaths from starvation.'[1] The *Encyclopedia* also points out that the causes of famine are always natural. Even political causes alone cannot cause famine unless they are accompanied by natural causes.

Again, echoing the same trend of thought, the *Encyclopedia Britannica*, 1997 defines famine as 'extreme and protracted shortage of food, causing widespread and persistent hunger, emaciation of the affected population, and substantial increase in death rate. The causes of famine are numerous. They can be divided into two categories, natural or physical or human.'[2] In 1970 Morris D. Morris raised the basic question, asking 'what is a famine?' He observed that the administrative staff confused between drought and famine for administrative purposes. But it should be defined in a more nuanced way. He pointed out that rainfall variability in the rain shadow areas of Gujarat could be taken as a test case of famine. In this case, he was not trying to define the concept of famine *per se*, but had wanted mainly to find out the coping strategies of the peasant community in a rain shadow area where frequency of failure of rainfall is quite well known.[3]

Amartya Sen took this discourse a step further. He observed that the symptoms of famine evident in widespread food shortage leading to deaths and starvation were significant markers, but he refused to accept the view that it is due to decline in grain output. Even if there was surplus food grains, he reiterated, there might still occur a famine, leading to large-scale deaths due to starvation and diseases. He analysed the Bengal famine of 1943 to prove his point. He noted that the symptoms of famine could occur if the entitlement in terms of command over food declined.[4] Sen's thesis on famines as entitlement failure acquired widespread support among scholars and policy-makers. But even then his view did not go unchallenged. Greenough, for example, argued that the Bengal famine also had the features of traditional famines namely, decline in food grain output.[5]

China during 1959-61 saw a devastating famine which killed millions of people – estimates vary from 16.5 to 45 million. Many factors have been advanced to explain such high number of deaths. For example, many authors attribute the causes to fall in 'aggregate food production' coupled with 'high government procurement'. Other experts, on the other hand, were of the opinion that 'inflexibility of centrally planned procurement' caused the famine.[6] They also observed that though the average availability of food was high in some regions poor food grain output caused severe scarcity which resulted in heavy mortality. Amartya Sen, on the other hand, attributed the cause of the famine in China to the absence of freedom of press. He pointed out that in India, famines of such large scale did not occur after 1966-7 because the press highlighted the event and prompt actions were taken to ameliorate the situation. On the other hand, in China the press was muffled and there was no way to know the ground reality. As a result, in spite of the availability of food, people died in large numbers.[7]

Utsa Patnaik has taken this discourse forward in her study of the Bengal famine of 1943 by observing that the decline in exchange entitlement was due to the deliberate economic policy of the colonial rulers during the Second World War. Advised by the famous economist John Maynard Keynes, the colonial rulers adopted a policy of 'profit inflation' to force the transfer of purchasing power from the people to the government in order to finance the war time expenditure. As a result, millions of people died of starvation and epidemics.[8] Patnaik's argument complements Sen's view by showing that the colonial government focused more on spending on war rather than on importing grain. Hence the exchange entitlement declined. Patnaik provided a further explanation for Sen's thesis on famine as an 'entitlement failure'.

Of course, contemporary India has not faced acute famines like those of the nineteenth century, but tribal pockets in some parts of India often faced famine-like situations. Drought-stricken areas in many parts of India presented starvation conditions and acute distress. In many parts of the world, natural calamities and war continued to present challenges. Some of the old explanations may or may not be valid but we often find the relevance of factors such as lack of infrastructure, irrigation and drinking water supply, absence of media attention, corruption and negligence of administration as being responsible for such distressing conditions. In the recent years, reports from Kalahandi, Malkangiri, and Nagda in Jajpur district of Orissa still recall familiar tales of famine conditions, even though much improvement has occurred as regards food availability, infrastructure and administrative preparedness.

In the twenty-first century, various parts of Africa were undergoing severe famines leading to heavy mortality due to starvation, malnutrition, etc. The factors are very familiar, namely, civil war, ethnic conflicts, government mismanagement, and corruption.[9] In other words, many of the factors of past famines still linger. Even though some factors may have less relevance today, the lessons from them should have abiding significance.

Orissa Famine of 1866

2016, was the 150th year of the Great Orissa Famine of 1866. To mark the occasion Anil Dhir and Ramesh Chandra Mohapatra edited the book *The Great Orissa Famine* in 2017. The famine was also known as *n'anka durbhikshya* (Famine which occurred during the Ninth Year) in Orissa because it took place during the ninth year of the reign of the Puri king. Interestingly, the famine started during the peak years of the Industrial Revolution in England, a country that depended heavily on India, its major colony for expanding its rice trade using the surplus paddy from India. Such a policy had several serious consequences, which is the subject of this study. The colonial regime's policies created widespread unemployment among weavers and salt workers, created insecurity of land tenure and had many other adverse consequences. In this situation, one million out of three million population of Orissa Division lost their lives because of starvation and epidemics. The famine of 1866 severely affected the people of Orissa with widespread impact in multiple spheres for generations to come.

The impact of the famine was so severe that it not only changed the social structure of the region but also the production relations. It led to serious efforts to evolve a system of relief administration. The new situation and the challenges it posed spurred a stream of Oriya nationalism. We have discussed at length the various impacts of the great famine in the Chapter 3.

There is a certain contemporary resonance of some of the questions raised over a century ago. We remembered the 1866 famine on its 150th year when the world was discussing the ramifications of the onset of the Fourth Industrial Revolution which relies heavily on artificial intelligence replacing much of the known forms of human labour and production processes. It is ironical that, on one side we celebrated human progress and on the other side, we still witness children of tribal areas dying of hunger and malnutrition. This happened in spite of adequate availability of food in the market. Unfortunately it is beyond the reach of many families to avail food due to lack of entitlement or purchasing capacity and also partly due to the prevailing cultural attitude! Even the supply of free or cheap food was not accessible due to lack of transportation and other infrastructure. Sometimes social habits inhibit the poor from availing food. These were familiar issues even then. Almost the same set of factors are in operation even now in the face of a vibrant democracy and an active press in India.

Scholars have raised such issues from time to time.[10] At the time of the famine of 1866 neither the institutions of democracy and welfare state nor an independent local press were present. Death of a large number children due to lack of food was a conspicuous phenomenon. This was mainly because neither the bureaucracy nor the colonial rulers in general, were familiar with the characteristics of Orissa economy or of Oriya culture. Their response was essentially based on the management norms of a colonial state.

The greatest lesson from the past famines as well as that of recent ones for the present-day policy-makers and social activists is to have primarily a deeper understanding of the immediate and long-term causes of food crisis. They must also respect the reports in the press and other sources to detect the early signals of crisis. Knowledge and sensitivity towards local customs and practices are crucial to formulate any response. Taking all these into consideration they can put in place a comprehensive, multidimensional, administrative action plan. In the modern era, availability of food at an affordable price and creating enough job opportunities for the family members so that they are able to buy food, would help minimize the impact of the food crises. Further, it would also minimize the aimless wandering and distress migration. The state has to be accountable and no modern state and its leadership can maintain a façade of legitimacy if it cannot ensure food availability to its people.

Who is to Blame?

How much blame can be put on a leader or an administrator for a major food crisis? At the completion of the 150th year of the Great Famine of 1866, many analysts put a great deal of responsibility for the Orissa famine on T.E. Ravenshaw, the then Commissioner of Orissa Division, for his failure to go by the reports from the district officials and take precautionary steps by storing food grains. However, to his defence it can be said that he was new to the region and not well acquainted with the local economy, society and customs. Moreover, as a colonial bureaucrat from England, he was wedded to the principle of laissez faire, believing that people can look after themselves in response to the market. It can also be said that his hands were tied due to the strict instructions of the higher authorities. Only after he was accosted by masses of hungry people in early August 1866, he wrote to Cecil Beadon, the Lieutenant Governor of Bengal Presidency, for sending rice to Orissa, but the latter declined his request on the ground that it would take a long time to arrange that. In this process Orissa lost one million people. Reducing the responsibility to one individual shows an inadequate understanding of what was a systemic failure. But people squarely blame him saying that he could have taken a more humane approach. Several months into the famine, Ravenshaw finally realized the plight of the people and launched many initiatives, including setting up schools, especially for girls. The medical college, teachers' training school, polytechnic and the Ravenshaw College came up soon after, on his initiative.

During this time, Fakir Mohan Senapati, the renowned Oriya novelist, wrote a powerful story called 'Rebati' narrating the plight of girls trying to get education. It was his theory perhaps that Oriya people suffered from the famine because women lacked education. Many aspects of the prevailing situation got discussed in the new Oriya weekly, *Utkal Dipika*, which fast emerged as the new forum of news and views for Oriya intellectuals. While the relevance of historical case studies of famines to the present day cannot be doubted, the vantage point from where a famine is looked at in-depth determines its value. It became more explicit from the studies on the causes of African famines in recent years. It showed that the same set of factors still operated, giving rise to famines even now. Even today, one out of seven persons go hungry in the world.[11] The reasons could be due to civil war or decline in exchange entitlement. Keeping this in view the Sustainable Development Goals (SDGs) in 2015 gave the utmost priority to end hunger by 2030.[12] In this work we have chosen the gender dimension as the vantage point to investigate the famine process. Previously, women were discriminated against. Even today their position is not much better.

Why Gender Matters

During the past famines, gender was neglected both by the policy makers and the analysts. For example, during the famine of 1866, no systematic data on gender was collected. There are only stray references regarding the mortality of women and that women were preferred at the relief centres for availing food. But it was also recorded that women could not enter these relief centres because of the unruly crowd. Men were obviously stronger and they prevented women to enter the feeding centres. However, some women were given relief at home and after the famine was officially over by the end of 1866, many women stayed back in the relief centres doing odd jobs. Further it was also reported by the press that many women became prostitutes in Calcutta. During the all-India famines of 1896-7 and 1899-1900, however, it was reported that women, particularly pregnant women, were given priority in the feeding centres.[13]

There are important official data from the Census and comments by officials, which need critical examination. Both Census commissioners of 1901 as well as that of 1911 observed that during the famine period women died less than men. The annual death rates for male and female showed that womens' death rates were lower than that of males in the non-famine years. The same trend continued in the famine years as well. Thus the sex ratio (females per thousand males) increased. They extensively wrote that women died less than men because a set of biological and sociological factors proved beneficial to them.[14] In Chapters 7 and 8 we have discussed these factors threadbare and find them less than convincing. The commissioners seemed biased in their views as Westerners.

From the gender perspective we have dealt with characteristics of Orissa economy during the period 1860 to 1921 in Chapter 2. First we have taken up the demographic situation followed by an analysis of the socio-economic features of the agrarian economy. The entire period saw frequent outbreak of famines, floods and droughts followed by epidemics like cholera and malaria, even though no other famine in the Orissa Division occurred in the same scale and magnitude as that of 1866. Famine-related epidemics continued till 1921 and the population of the Division in fact continued to decline steadily in contrast to the rest of the Indian subcontinent. At the same time, the sex ratio continued to increase as a result of sex selective distress migration as men went out in search of livelihood, leaving women behind. In the midst of all this, the land settlement took place in the region, assigning land rights to big landowners or zamindars without taking into account its effects on productivity. As a result, the peasantry suffered a lot and among them women bore the severest brunt. In the subsequent chapters specific aspects of this process have been analysed in detail. In Chapter 3 we discuss the causes and consequences of the Orissa famine of 1866. The famine was so severe that far-reaching impacts on society and the psyché of the people were visible for a long time to come. Chapter 4 deals with a particular impact of the famine on the social structure where the interface of caste, class and gender produced new social gradations and behaviour that persist to this day. In Chapter 5 we discuss the impact of the later famines that occurred in 1907-8 and 1918-19 and the partial famine of 1889, to examine whether any lessons were learnt from the Great Famine of 1866.

The question of gender vulnerability to famines is addressed in Chapters 6 to 8, to look at the validity of the claim that women had biological advantages and even some social conditioning that enhanced their capacity to face the famine conditions. In Chapter 6 we take up the evidence to see who actually died during the famine? The historical as well as the contemporary evidences show that there is no uniformity regarding the patterns of deaths. In some famines more females died then men while in others more males lost their lives. In Chapters 7 and 8 we discuss the biological and social factors affecting the death rates of males and females. There is hardly any evidence to prove that women were biologically stronger compared to men. Further, sociologically, they have always been discriminated against. It is now widely believed that the chowkidars – the village security guards – who were the main government sources of information, were biased about reporting women's deaths and hence deliberately left out the data on female deaths.

In Chapter 9 we have taken up an analysis of the trends of the sex ratio in Orissa Division during 1891 to 1921 and seek explanations in relation to the famines, droughts and floods during the period. The data were collected mostly from the various Census reports and Sanitary Commission reports. The first comprehensive census was collected in 1881. But the population statistics were underestimates. The number of females were under-enumerated. Similarly, both death and birth statistics of women were under-enumerated. However, over the years these statistics became relatively accurate. The sex ratio and women's living conditions were also related to the phenomenon of migration by men, which is discussed in Chapter 10. Large-scale out-migration of men also caused higher death rates of men due to exposure to various diseases. Since men migrated in greater number compared to women, death rate due to epidemics among men were obviously higher. Hence the sex ratio increased and for many years we continued to see larger number of women than men in Orissa. It was more due to poverty, famines and distress migration than any supposedly biological strength of women.

Relevance of Famine Studies in the Modern Global Era

Many people ask the question does famine still occur in the present world – when in a so-called 'flat world' people and countries can look after one another more easily?' To them the answer is a clear 'yes'.

Nowadays because of the vulnerability due to climate change, many parts of agricultural economies face frequent droughts, floods and other natural calamities. One notices similar kind of coping strategies, namely, dietary change, distress migration, selling of assets, and suffering from various infectious diseases, particularly by the women.[15] Tim Dyson and O'Grada have observed giving reasons as to why famines would continue to appear even in the distant future resulting in large-scale deaths. The policy makers thus must not remain complacent.[16]

One might ask about the relevance of such a study on the Orissa Famine 1866 in the twenty-first century, particularly when the world is equipped with many new resources to face such crises and with much easier modes of communication.

In more than one ways, the Orissa famine of 1866 was a manifestation of a classical famine at least in terms of intensity if not area-wise. Like the Irish famine of 1845-52 and many other classical famines, the chief cause of it was extensive crop failure followed by a failure of exchange entitlement as well as lack of efficient administration, which is an essential part of 'good governance'. On top of it, the local media was nearly non-existent. Long-term factors such as decline in the productivity of land, exploitation by the zamindars, etc., were also in operation. An astounding one-third of the total population died due to sheer starvation and epidemics within a span of just one year. This famine naturally left a deep impact on the minds of the Oriya people for generations to come. The intense suffering led to the creation of compelling famine-related literature periodically. The famine also had a deep impact on the social structure by producing new castes and creating new institutions but also shaped the behaviour of the people by generating new habits of saving and coping with scarcity. In the process Oriya cuisine underwent much change with the discovery of many new edible leaves and vegetables, which were hitherto untried. Above all, it made people conscious about not wasting precious food grains.

It also unfortunately still very important to scan through the pages of history, including the Famine Commission Report because the contemporary discourse on famines or 'famine-like situations' seeks to grapple with precisely the same set of questions relating to structural deprivation of social groups at the margins and their entitlement profile. At the same time, it is to be admitted that the population growth rate in India has started declining and the aggregate supply of food grains is keeping pace with the population growth. The share of agriculture in total work-force has also declined, though in some states it is still very high. Further there are geographical areas having a large number of Adivasis, Dalits and other poor people who live in the margins. These remote places are completely cut-off due to lack of easy transportation and are subjected to the absence of good governance. In these places agriculture is still at the subsistence level with complete dependence on rainfall. A slight fluctuation in the pattern of normal rainfall results in famine-like situation and adopting of 'safety nets' such as eating inferior grains, leaves and roots. They are compelled to dispose off their meagre assets and succumb to epidemics, finally leading to distress migration and bonded migration. People completely depend on their own produce for consumption. Lack of easy transportation facilities and purchasing power prevent the people at the bottom of the social and economic ladder there to have access to imported grains from the neighbouring places or through public outlets. Even if grains are available, people may have lost their entitlements and hence may not be in a position to buy food at an affordable price. Already, the eco-fragile regions do not get enough attention of the officials to redress their grievances on time partly because these areas are inaccessible and partly due to the frequent transfer of officials from one place to another. All these factors may sound a familiar story of the nineteenth century.[17] Further one may ask why gender? It is noticed that women and girls still get discriminated against in terms of food and health care. More girl children are malnourished and prone to various diseases even in the present era. In case of food crises they are the first ones to get affected It is particularly so if they belong to low caste and deprived communities and economically weak.[18]

Conclusion

Thus from the above analysis it is evident that famine can be described as an event and a process. It is the low caste people who suffer more. But nowadays girls are more malnourished and thus likely to succumb first.

Does famine end only in the phase of starvation deaths? Some scholars believed it to be so. But after the starvation ends epidemics related to shortage of food start. Hence duration of the famine can be described as both inclusive of starvation as well as epidemics.

However, one redeeming feature of present century 'famine-like situation' is the near absence of starvation deaths, though starvation-like conditions begin to prevail, as soon as there is inadequate rainfall and people start eating all sorts of 'famine foods' and fall prey to epidemics. The incidence of epidemics of 'classical diseases' is quite severe on the already malnourished people.

It may be worthwhile to point out at this juncture that the latest India Human Development Report 2006, has identified 8 tribal-dominated states which rank lower than the other states in terms of Human Development and Gender Development Indices. These are most vulnerable areas.[19] Similarly, the Xaxa Committee also noted that women of Scheduled Tribe population are lowest in terms of Gender Development index as well as that of Human Development index in terms of wealth, education and equal opportunity for livelihood.[20]

Like the 'Letter to the Statesman on starving poor' published on 2 May 1866 giving details on the famine conditions, which saved many lives during the Orissa famine of 1866, the role of *a constructive* press *is also very* important. It can highlight the distress situation, incidences of epidemics and also the increased number of migration to other states. The migrants have very little bargaining strength. After being highlighted by the press, the administration quickly takes some action. The present-day dealing with famine-like situations shows the continuity of the same bureaucratic mentality of the officers, particularly those working in the remote areas. The same trend of continuous transfer of officials, particularly during the drought situations, leads to utter confusion and duplication or nullification of the previous officer's orders. They are less familiar with the ground reality while dealing with the affected people in remote areas. Hence the action taken is either delayed or inadequate and by that time a lot of loss of life has already ocurred.

This book will not only shed light on the pages of history but will also serve as a possible perspective for policy and action for the government agencies and civil society members to deal with the famine-like situations and minimize the sufferings of the people by taking precautionary measures well in advance.

Notes

1. *The International Encyclopedia of the Social Sciences.* 'Famine', New York, The Macmillan Company, 2008, pp. 322-3.
2. *The New Encyclopaedia Britannica.* 'Famine', vol. 4, London, The New Encyclopaedia Britannica, 1997, p. 675.
3. Morris D. Morris, 'What is a Famine?', *The Economic and Political Weekly,* 9(2), 2 November 1970, pp. 1855-63.
4. Amartya Sen, *Poverty and Famines: An Essay on Entitlement and Deprivation*, New York, Oxford University Press, 1982, pp. 39-44.
5. Paul R. Greenough, 'Indian Famines and Peasants in Indian Famines: The Case of Bengal in 1943-44', *Modern Asian Studies*, 14(2), 1980, pp. 205-35.
6. Xin Meng, Nancy Qian, and Pierre Yared, 'The Institutional Causes of the Great Famine of China 1959-1961', *Review of Economic Studies*, 82(2), 2015, pp. 1568-1611 https://www0.gsb.columbia.edu/faculty/pyared/papers/famines.pdf
7. Amartya Sen, op. cit., p. 81.
8. Utsa Patnaik, 'Profit Inflation, Keynes and the Holocaust of Bengal 1943-44', *Economic and Political Weekly*, 53(42), October 2018, pp. 33-43.
9. Andrey Korotayev, Malkov Artemy and Daria Khaltourina, *Introduction to Social Dynamics: Secular Cycles of Millennial Trends*, Moscow, USSR, 2006.
10 Bob Currie, *The Politics of Hunger in India: A Study of Democracy, Governance and Kalahandi's Poverty*, Chennai, MacMillan India Ltd., 2000.
11. https://www.foodaidfoundation.org/world-hunger-statistics.html
12. http://www.undp.org/content/dam/undp/library/corporate/brochure/SDGs_Booklet_Web_En.pdf
13. *Famine Relief Code Bombay Presidency 1927* edition, p. 22.
14. *Census of India 1901*, pt. 1, p. 118, *Census of India*, 1911, pt. 1, p. 212, Appendix, pp. 220-2.
15. Basant Sahu, 'Household Drought Coping, Food Insecurity and Women in Orissa', *Economic and Political Weekly*, 53(17), 28 April 2018, pp. 70-9.
16. Tim Dyson and Cormac O' Grada (eds.), 'Introduction', *Famine Demography: Perspectives from the Past and Present,* New York, Oxford University Press, 2002, pp. 1-18.
17. Manoranjan Mohanty, 'Orissa Famine of 1866: Lessons for the 21st

Century', in Anil Dhir and Ramesh Mahapatra (eds.), *The Great Famine Orissa Famine 1866, N'Anka Durbhikhya*, Bhubaneswar, Amadeus Press, 2017, pp. 70-83.

18. Suranjita Ray, 'Beyond the Conventional Understanding of Famine: A Study of Kalahandi', *Journal of Rural Development,* 34(4), October-December 2015, pp. 567-88.
19. Mohanty, op.cit.
20. https://www.drishtiias.com/summary-of-important-reports/xaxa-committee-on-tribal-communities-of-india

CHAPTER 2

The Political Economy of Orissa, 1860-1921

Introduction

The impact of British rule on the society and economy of India during the nineteenth century has been a matter of much debate among scholars. One view, mostly using the experience of the Bombay Presidency, highlighted the beneficial aspects of the colonial policies. On the other hand, the counter-perspective mainly took the situation that developed in the Bengal Presidency and stressed the devastating consequences of the British policies that caused enormous miseries to the people.[1] Indeed the Bombay Presidency did prosper due to the extensive cotton cultivation. Cotton was used as raw material by the colonial rulers to send back home and the Presidency felt the warmth of the limited growth. On the other hand, the Bengal Presidency languished under Permanent Settlement of the land and the zamindars squeezed the tenants to the maximum, leaving them no incentive to produce more. The whole of Orissa, including the Orissa Division, which was directly governed by the British, belonged to the second category. On the whole, there is no doubt that colonial rule initiated certain processes in the economy, society and polity that had long-term consequences. Development of infrastructure, including railways, irrigation facilities, and other steps led to commercialization of agriculture, expansion of markets and monetization of the rural economy.[2] However, their effects were uneven for different areas and sections of the people.

Orissa Division, 1860-1921

The British had colonized four districts of Orissa Division, namely Cuttack, Balasore, Puri and Angul, in 1803 (see Map 2.1). It remained under the Bengal Presidency till 1912, after which the region became a part of the Province of Bihar and Orissa. In 1936, Orissa became a separate province comprising the Oriya-speaking

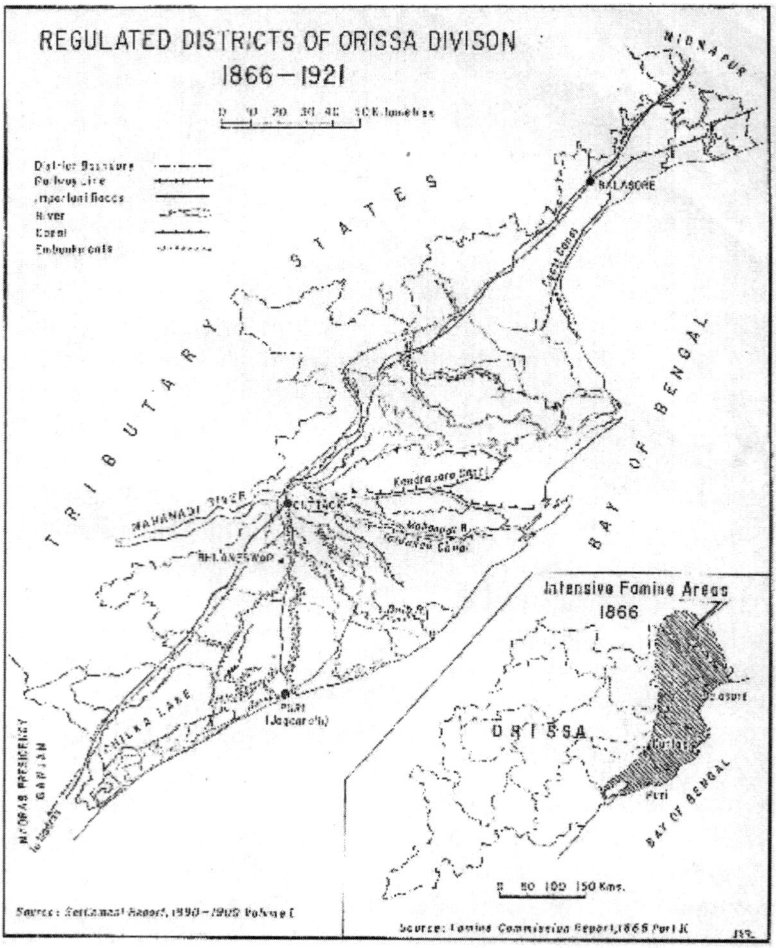

Map 2.1

areas of the Orissa Division and some princely states. (In our analysis however, we have omitted Angul district owing to paucity of data.) This region was not only poorly governed by the British administration but even basic facilities of communication were not developed for a long time and it was continuously being used as a source of revenue extraction.

Unlike the other parts of the Bengal Presidency, Permanent Settlement was not introduced in Orissa at one go. Instead, a series of temporary land settlements were carried out on an experimental basis till 1822. In each successive settlement, the land revenue continued to increase. The colonial rulers were not conversant with the local language and had employed Bengali officers who too were unfamiliar with the local situation. These settlements continued to raise the revenue thus causing hardships to the cultivators who were tenants. The zamindars too were unhappy with this trend as they found it difficult to collect the required revenue from the tenants. The increase in land revenue led to decline in the area under the *thani raiyats* (permanent cultivators) and increased the number of *pahi raiyats* (temporary cultivators). In order to increase the revenue, the rulers suspended the system of giving rent-free lands to different sections of the society against the various services they rendered for rulers or social and religious institutions. As for example, the *paiks* or the local militia were both cultivators and soldiers as well. They were given rent-free holdings to perform those duties, that is, to maintain peace in the area as well as cultivate land during peace time. But under the new dispensation their land was no longer rent-free. This was a major reason for their alienation and dissatisfaction with the colonial rulers. Subsequently, it led to the Paik Rebellion of 1817, which may be considered to be the first major anti-colonial uprising in India.[3] That event led to initiation of another form of land settlement in that area. It was known as *raiyatwari* settlement, where land was owned by the *raiyats* (farmers) who paid revenue directly to the colonial government.

Along with this, salt monopoly was introduced which made local production and marketing of salt very uncompetitive. To further complicate the situation, the rulers were interested only in collecting land revenue and neglected their duty providing good governance to the people. They did not, for example, maintain the river embankments which was very crucial for saving the winter rice, the main crop of coastal Orissa, from floods. In addition, the Orissa Division was devoid of any form of communication with the rest of India till 1901. The region was linked to Calcutta by a muddy road on which it was very difficult to traverse during the rainy season. Of course, there were some small and reasonably large ports such as Chandbali, Dhamara, False Point and Gopalpur. But those were open only when there was no rain or storm. These ports were used extensively to export rice from Orissa from 1860 to 1865 but could not be used to import rice when it was needed badly during the rainy season of 1866, the peak period of the famine. In other words, by the time of the great famine of 1866, Orissa's economy was at its worst. It is no wonder that the suffering was so acute that its experience became the reference point for formulating a famine relief policy for India.

After the famine was over, the government of course started many ad hoc developmental works such as canal irrigation, construction of roads, railway lines, etc. But the canal works were stopped half way through and did not cover Khordha and some other parts of the division. The cultivators of the Khordha subdivision having the *raiyatwari* settlement would have benefited directly from it. Perhaps, since the *paiks* of Khordha had rebelled against the rulers, they did not want to improve their economic condition by introducing the canal system. Ostensibly, the canal works were abruptly ended because it did not earn any revenue unlike the case of the Madras canal. In contrast to the Orissa Division, the Madras Presidency had a *raiyatwari* system of land revenue. Each peasant was responsible for paying land revenue to the government. In such a system, the peasants could irrigate their land and increase their productivity.

The situation during the post-famine period was relatively better since Orissa was gradually recovering from the ravages of the famine. It is indicated by the growth of population in the region. Fortunately, devastating famines like that of 1866 never occurred in subsequent decades, though in other parts of India people did suffer greatly in the famines of 1876-7, 1896-7 and

1899-1900. Only the District of Puri was affected partially in the famine of 1896-7. After 1900, Orissa Division did undergo a series of local food crises followed by outbreaks of epidemics like cholera, dysentery, malaria and influenza till almost 1921. As a result, unlike other parts of India, Orissa suffered from population loss even in 1931 and did not enjoy the dividend of growth of population which the rest of India experienced.

Orissa under the colonial rule did not feel any visible impact of the Industrial Revolution in Europe. Even though canal irrigation was introduced, it did not reach the areas that needed it most. Hence there was no crop diversification. It was partly due to the specific requirement of water for the winter rice only when rainfall is scanty. Moreover, the tenants did not have any interest to take water from the canal since that would have meant an increase in revenue payable to the zamindars. Moreover, even though the railroads linked Orissa in 1900 with Calcutta, it did not increase Orissa's rice export as Orissa produced only coarse rice, the demand for which had declined. However, due to the railways the migration rate from Orissa to Calcutta increased considerably because of frequent crop failures and epidemics. In that sense, the railroads provided a safety net to escape from hunger and starvation. Thus Orissa's economy demonstrated the classic case of colonial misrule evident in decline in agricultural production, shrinking number of cultivators and even decline in the general population. Orissa experienced high mortality due to a series of localized famines and epidemics, and high magnitude of out-migration.

In so far as capital formation was concerned, there was hardly any industrialization in Orissa Division except a few small-scale units of handicrafts and filigree works. Some went to Calcutta to work in the jute mills. But most of them worked in the unorganized sector.[4] In other words, Orissa's economy symbolized the typical case of colonial extraction that pauperized the general population in the colony.[5]

Physical Configuration of Orissa Division

For our study it is relevant to keep in mind the geo-physical character of the region in the nineteenth century. The post-

Independence construction of dams and irrigation projects, have considerably changed the ecology. But due to climate change and the type of development activities which have gone on in the recent decades, some of the natural conditions of vulnerability still prevail. Being deltaic, Orissa Division has long been vulnerable to both droughts and floods. The total area of the division was 9,098 sq. miles or 14,642 sq. km. The canals, embankments and railways in fact accentuated the problem of floods. The three districts of the division – Cuttack, Balasore and Puri – lie between the hills and the Bay of Bengal and are situated on the deltas of five rivers, namely, Subarnarekha, Burabalang, Baitarani, Brahmani and Mahanadi, and their tributaries. Of these five rivers, the last three pose great problems of floods. Chilika Lake, comprising an area of 310 sq. miles or 803 sq. km, is situated in Puri district and was constantly a flood threat to Puri, because it is linked with the Bay of Bengal and sometimes it used to get blocked because of sand bars at the mouth.

The Division can be broadly divided into three distinct regions: the hilly region, the salt tract between the coast and the Bay of Bengal and the arable tract. The arable tract is rich with silt, extremely fertile and the most densely populated. The arable land can again be divided broadly into three parts:

1. A fully protected area in terms of drought and floods, limited to Cuttack and South Balasore. Land value was naturally the highest here.
2. Semi-protected areas, which were protected only from floods.
3. Unprotected areas marked by annual flooding.

The problem of floods was very acute in all the three districts, for three reasons. The first was the variation in the sea level due to the south-east monsoon; almost all the large floods owed their origin to this. The second was the steady northward littoral sand drift. This drift tends to form bars across the mouth of rivers from south to north, sometimes 25 to 30 ft high above sea level, and it blocks the entry of the rivers into the sea. Third, as a result of the drift the deltas of these rivers are short. In rivers like the Ganges and the Indus the deltas are situated about 644 km from the sea, but the deltas of Mahanadi and other rivers are little more than 80 km long.[6]

Several parts of the three districts have been vulnerable to floods and droughts. For example, in Puri, three-fourths of the total area of the district were prone to floods. In Cuttack also the vulnerability was high, because the lowlands formed 70 per cent of the total cultivated area.[7] In Balasore, on the other hand, the proportion of highlands was larger, but in case of heavy rainfall or heavy flood, the highlands are unable to compensate for the loss of crops in the lowlands. However, when the rainfall is deficient the lowlands produce enough crops to compensate for the loss of crops on the highlands.[8] Balasore had another peculiar feature – almost all the *thanas*, except Bhadrak, contained some hilly, some sandy and some fertile land.[9]

During the nineteenth century and in the early parts of the twentieth century all the three districts were subjected to frequent floods; major floods occurred in all the three rivers in 1859, 1872, 1892, 1896, 1911, 1919 and 1920.[10] (Floods also occurred in 1866 and 1907 which were famine years as well.) Even in 1919, at least 25 per cent of each district was left unprotected. This land was not cultivated in most years.[11] Thus the vulnerability to floods deeply affected the life and economy of these districts.

The Agrarian Scene

The principal occupation of the people of the division was agriculture. In 1901, 64 per cent of the total population depended on agriculture,[12] in 1911, 74 per cent[13] and in 1921, 69 per cent.[14] In other words, the people's dependence on agriculture continued for a long time. The main crop was rice.[15] There were three types of rice – *biali* (autumn rice), *sarad* (winter rice) and *dalua* (spring rice) of which the winter rice was by far the most important.[16]

The Settlement Report of 1906-9 records the predominance of winter rice right through the end of the nineteenth century.[17] For example, it was pointed out that one of the *parganas* of Puri continued to devote 91 per cent of its area under the winter rice in as late as 1909. This also meant that dependence on mono crop made the rice-cultivated areas more prone to famine situation throughout the nineteenth and twentieth century.

To avert risk, cultivators could adopt several minor strategies within the prevailing cropping pattern. One was to sow different varieties of crops having different times of maturity in the same plot of land, some of which could resist floods while some others resisted drought conditions. Hunter wrote, 'In order to provide against the uncertainties of the season, the husbandmen sow the species which require flooding or those that will not suffer from it as well as those that will flourish with but a moderate rainfall.'[18] On the other hand, Maddox stated that in Khorda subdivision the *raiyats* concentrated on a type of winter rice which was more risky but also more prolific than the other kinds.[19] Besides, *raiyats* also sowed different crops such as pulses and summer rice after the floods, to minimize the losses of rice due to floods. In this way there was a small measure of diversification.

The *raiyats* of Banki Government Estate, which was extremely flood prone, had adopted a cycle of crops starting with autumn rice followed by winter rice and thereafter going for *rabi* crops and finally sugar cane.[20] The Flood Committee Report of 1928 also observed that the cultivators in the unprotected area transplanted paddy several times, sowed *rabi* and *dalua*, as well as used to send one member of the family to Calcutta.[21] But, as we shall see later, these cropping strategies often failed in coping with famine conditions.

Cash Crops in Orissa Division

Cash crops such as jute, cotton and sugar cane that were cultivated in different parts of Bengal Presidency, Madras Presidency, and Bombay Presidency did prove to be a lucrative crop for the cultivators. Cultivators benefited especially when the prices of these cash crops increased. But the same did not happen in this part of the Bengal Presidency, the Orissa Division. According to one estimate, in 1901, Bengal supplied the entire jute required in the world market.[22] In this both the zamindars and the tenants were benefitted. So much so, that in Rangpur district, Bengal Presidency, not less than 30 per cent of the total land was devoted to jute cultivation. Similarly, a lot of unclaimed land was reclaimed in Gorakhpur, UP to cultivate sugar cane. Cash crops in the Bombay Presidency also led to increase in income of the cultivators and they in turn could buy rice.[23] This explained the decrease in the incidence of famines in that region after 1900.

The absentee zamindars staying in Calcutta kept on demanding various types of cess, leaving no incentive for the Orissa cultivators to experiment with cash crops. On the other hand, the landlords raised their own income through moneylending and rent and showed no interest in improving farming.[24] Besides, the government also did not invest much in the permanently settled areas, compared to other parts of the country. This lack of interest in investment by the government was evident since the canal network did not cover the entire division, particularly the Khordha subdivision, where the land remained arid. Further, it seemed that Orissa possessed only a limited amount of land under the early rice, which was actually suitable for cultivation of jute. Similarly, the railroad connected only the district headquarters of Cuttack, Balasore and Puri, leaving the remote areas untouched.

However, the development of irrigation facilities and railroads and the response to price stimulus did lead to a small degree of diversification of cropping pattern. The main cash crops of Orissa Division were cotton, betel leaves, jute, tobacco and sugar cane. It must be noted that the cultivation of cotton decreased during the period of our study.[25] It was grown generally on homestead lands irrigable from a tank or canal or in the rich alluvial soil by the riverside. The outturn per acre was only 1 maund of cleared cotton, which yielded Rs. 20 in gross income in 1890-1900.[26] The gross income of paddy per acre was also Rs. 20 in the same period.[27]

Betel leaves are a very lucrative crop, but the total area under this was only 100 acres in 1890-1900. The net income of betel leaves was Rs. 131 per 0.58 acre of land for eighteen years from the second year of the plantation.[28]

Maddox noted that the cultivation of jute was limited to the irrigated tract of Cuttack during 1890-1900 and in many places it was replacing cotton. The area under jute was 900 acres in 1890-

1900. The areas suitable for jute according to Maddox were mostly homestead land and sometimes riverside land which were also suitable for early rice.[29] After the introduction of the railways, the cultivation of jute increased but not significantly.[30]

The Banking Enquiry Committee Report of 1929-30 reported that the gross return of rice per acre was Rs. 35 and Rs. 120 for fibre (including jute and cotton) in Bihar and Orissa respectively.[31] But the peasants did not switch over to jute, probably because the area under early rice was limited,[32] the area on which jute can be grown, and second, because the problems of floods and droughts had continued till 1931. This explanation finds some support from the fact that the area under jute had increased in the irrigated part of Cuttack between 1890 and 1915.

Maddox had reported that tobacco was an important cash crop and some *raiyats* depended on it to pay their rent. But the area under cultivation was only 3,400 acres limited to some riverside *parganas* of Cuttack. The gross income of tobacco planted in 0.04 acres of land was Rs. 150 per year in 1890-1900.[33]

Maddox has not given the figures for the area under sugar cane cultivation, though he noted that it needed plentiful water supply and one acre of sugar cane yielded Rs. 250 worth of molasses.[34] The area under sugar cane was small in all the three districts.[35]

Thus cultivation of winter rice remained the principal crop of Orissa Division even after the introduction of canal irrigation and railways, unlike that in western India. Thus, contrary to the western Indian situation, Orissa did not experience much expansion of cash crops or any large-scale modernization of agriculture and remained prone to food crisis.

Extension of Cultivation

Statistics of extension of cultivation in the settlements in the period 1836-43 and 1890-1900 concealed the various fluctuations due to many factors. There was a depression in price level just after the first settlement which continued till 1855. Heavy demand for Orissa rice from other parts of India had its effect on the market. Moreover, the heavy loss of population due to the great famine of

1866, and a steady recovery of the population between 1872 and 1891 had their effects. According to Maddox, the area under cultivation between the two settlements increased by 32 per cent in Cuttack, 40 per cent in Balasore and 23.4 per cent in Puri.[36]

We do not have firm data on the population of Orissa Division till 1872. But the Census statistics for the decades 1872-81 and 1881-91 showed the following percentage variation of population (Table 2.1).[37]

This spurt in population was partly due to recovery from the famine of 1866 and partly due to improved enumeration.[38] Up till 1891, the extension of cultivation had kept pace with the growth of population. In the next two decades, cultivation did not grow even though the population grew less rapidly. For example, it was observed in the revision settlement report of 1906-12 that the area under cultivation fell short of the growth of population though the area under settlement was slightly larger than that of the settlement of 1890-1900[39] (see Table 2.2).

No settlement was done in the decade between 1911 and 1921. Floods and droughts resulted in famine conditions in most of the years in the decade. It is likely that the area under cultivation fell more sharply than the population, which decreased by 2.11 per cent in Cuttack, 7 per cent each in Balasore and Puri, in the decade 1911-21.[40]

The next settlement was done in 1922-32 (in the same area as the Provincial Settlement 1890-1900).

This showed that the area under cultivation increased by 5.5 per cent in Cuttack, 9 per cent in Balasore and 4.5 per cent in Puri between 1890-1900 and 1922-32.[41] The rate of increase in Balasore

TABLE 2.1: PERCENTAGE VARIATION OF POPULATION STATISTICS, 1872 TO 1891

	1872-81	*1881-91*
Cuttack	+ 16.3	+ 7.8
Balasore	+ 22.7	+ 5.0
Puri	+ 15.4	+ 6.4

Source: Census of India 1891, pp. 119-24.

Table 2.2: Variations in areas under cultivation and population between 1891 and 1911

Subdivisions	*Percentage variation in cultivation, 1891-1911*	*Percentage variation on population, 1891-1911*
Cuttack	+ 2.9	+ 8.6
Kendrapara	+ 5.8	+12.9
Jajpur	+ 4.7	+ 5.2
Balasore	+ 5.7	+ 8.6
Bhadrak	+ 0.29	+ 2.9
Puri (Sadar)	+ 0.4	+ 8.4

Source : Final Report on the Revision Settlement of 1906-1912, p. 22.

was higher because land was reclaimed in the coastal portion of Balasore. Some of the land speculators from Midnapur, Bengal had come to Balasore and were reclaiming land near the sea belt by erecting embankments. The speculators known as *chakdars*, paid low fees initially to reclaim a portion of land.[42] But the soil was not very productive and the success of crops depended greatly on the absence of floods. In Puri district, 25 per cent of the best land of Sadar subdivision went out of cultivation because of constant floods after 1900.[43] On the other hand, the area under cultivation had increased in Khordha subdivision and the intensity of cultivation had increased as the *raiyats* had switched over to settled cultivation from *jhum* (shifting) cultivation.[44] But the land in Khorda subdivision was not very fertile and only one crop, e.g. winter rice, was produced, as we have already seen. During this period, 1891-1931, the percentage variation of the population of Cuttack was +13.5, and +10.2 in Puri, whereas in Balasore it was negative (–0.6).[45]

The area under cultivation had fluctuated after 1900. For example, the area under cultivation increased by 5 per cent between 1891 and 1911 but also increased only by 5.5 per cent between 1891 and 1931 in Cuttack. In Balasore also the area under cultivation had increased by 3 per cent between 1891 and 1911 and increased by 9 per cent between 1891 and 1932. It was only in Puri that the rate of increase in the area under cultivation was marginally higher in 1891-1931 than in 1891-1911. Thus the extension of cultivation between 1891 and 1921 could not keep pace with the increase in population in Cuttack and Puri but had outstripped the growth of population in Balasore. The population of Balasore, however, was not growing rapidly because of floods, droughts and epidemics.

Yield Per Acre

If we consider the factors of agricultural deterioration due to flood and drought problems after 1900 and expansion of cultivation to inferior lands, it is likely that the yield per acre declined in Orissa Division after 1900. Both Blyn[46] and Narain[47] pointed out that the downward drift of yield had started since 1911 in Greater Bengal, which included Orissa Division. In this scenario, the role played by an important institution, the Jagannath Temple in Puri, which directly affected the society and economy of Orissa Division, needs special attention.

Role of Jagannath Temple in the Orissa Economy

Jagannath Temple is situated in Puri district and influenced the economy, polity and society of Orissa Division in general and of Puri district in particular, and does so even today. Unfortunately, not much systematic research has been done on this aspect focusing on the past history.[48] Pilgrims came from all parts of India to visit the Jagannath Temple. They stayed for a few days and during the Car Festival in June-July, spent a minimum of three days in Puri. They also visited many other temples in and around Puri. Each day the temple's kitchen cooked food for thousands of people. The kitchen has 125 hearths to cook food using the wood fuel. These pilgrims who came here did not cook for themselves since the temple provided them with food at a cheap rate. They also took home dry offerings of food for their relatives. The temple owned considerable amount of land which were being cultivated by different persons in surrounding villages as a kind of tenants (called *sebayats*) in exchange for their services to the temple, including supply of necessities of daily rituals such as flowers, different types of wood, Indian basils, earthen pots, sandal paste, rice, pulses and vegetables, etc. The priests were given rent-free land to serve the deities daily. Some other suppliers of provisions were also given land on long-term lease for their services. But on festival days, which were numerous (it is said in Oriya that Lord Jagannath celebrates thirteen festivals in twelve months) the temple needed more of everything, including cooks, helpers, etc. The pilgrims also needed lodging houses, helpers and other necessities during their stay.

W.W. Hunter, the Scottish historian, who represented the prevailing Victorian attitudes (the conviction that work is a duty which is good for the soul) towards the British subjects was assigned to write the Statistical Account of Bengal Presidency in 1870s. He observed that 'The devotion of centuries has long ago made Jagannath a very wealthy god'.[49] But he admitted that it was difficult to estimate the temple income accurately. The income from land in 1876-7 was Rs. 3,10,000, which was equivalent to 30 per cent of the total government revenue of Rs. 10,41,910 in 1870-1.[50] The annual rent roll of the monasteries connected with the temple amounted to Rs. 2,70,000 and direct land revenues from the land of the temple cultivated by its tenants came to be Rs. 40,000 thus Rs. 3,10,000 in all. The other main source of income came from the pilgrims. The pilgrims offered gold, silver and even landed property profusely, of which there is no accurate estimate. The total annual value of these offerings was estimated by some experts, though Hunter did not name them, to be Rs. 7,00,000. Hunter, however, felt this estimate to be excessive. In turn, he himself had given another estimate which was based on the pilgrim tax collected by the British government. The gross sum of pilgrim offerings was estimated on the assumption that the pilgrims paid twice the sum of pilgrim tax to the temple.[51] So Hunter estimated, after the abolition of pilgrim tax, the value of pilgrim offerings to be Rs. 2,70,000 and the total annual income of Jagannath Temple to be Rs. 6,80,000 or 65 per cent of the total gross revenue of Orissa Division in 1870-1.[52]

In 1906-7, O'Malley, the writer of Gazetteer of three districts of the Division, gathered from the temple manager that the temple received an average annual income of Rs.1,39,586 from all sources in the three years 1903-4 to 1905-6. It amounted to 11 per cent of the total government revenue of 1906-8.[53] The decrease in proportion was partly real and partly due to the method of calculation. It was partly real because the Puri Sadar Subdivision in which the temple land was situated had become more flood-prone after 1900, so the temple lost revenue. O'Malley, however, did not include the rent-rolls from the *maths* (monasteries) which was included earlier. The annual average expenditure for the same period amounted to Rs. 92,569.[54]

In so far as the number of pilgrims was concerned, Hunter observed that a large number of pilgrims from north and south India used to come to Puri, though no trustworthy statistics were available on the correct number of pilgrims. We only get a broad range of figures. A gentleman who had spent his entire lifetime in Puri, according to Hunter, had estimated that between 50,000 and 3,00,000 pilgrims visited Puri every year. Hunter wrote that the number of pilgrims was 1,00,000-2,00,000 per year.[55] O'Malley was of the opinion that the annual number of pilgrims visiting Puri by rail was 3,00,000 in 1901, 3,31,000 in 1904 and 2,45,000 in 1905 respectively. The average duration of their stay was three days but many of them stayed longer.[56] Perhaps after the introduction of the railways the duration of stay might have been reduced.

Hunter estimated the number of employees of Jagannath Temple as 20,000 men, women and children directly and indirectly, or 3 per cent of the total population of Puri district in 1872.[57] Apart from the temple, there were many *maths* (monasteries) which were also a part of the system, providing services to the temple. These religious institutions had landed properties which were mostly given rent free. These *maths* employed large number of persons to carry out various activities relating to the temple. But it was difficult to assess the economic significance of those since the government did not keep any records.

The Jagannath Temple also influenced the economic structure of Cuttack and Balasore indirectly, at least before the introduction of railways, since pilgrims used to come from Calcutta through

Cuttack and Balasore. There were a number of shelters to provide food and lodging to the pilgrims on their way to Jagannath Temple.[58] Besides, the pilgrims also visited the other sacred places of Balasore and Cuttack. As will be seen later, the temple influenced the food habits of people of the region in fundamental ways.

But first let us have a close look at the population trends.

Orissa's Demographic Situation from 1872 to 1921

Orissa Division like the rest of India suffered from fluctuations in population due to famines, floods and epidemics, from 1872 till 1921. After that the population of India started growing, but Orissa's population started growing only after 1931. Incidentally, the First Census of 1872 was not a complete one. The first complete Census took place only in 1881. In that decade, the population of India increased by 0.9 per cent followed by 9.4 per cent in the next decade. The increase was minimal, amounting to 1.0 in the decade of 1891-1901. The following decade was relatively free of widespread famines and so the population showed an increase of 6.4 per cent. However, again, the next decade had witnessed a severe influenza epidemic in 1918-19 and its impact was felt at the population level. It grew only by 0.9 per cent in the entire decade.[59]

In contrast, Orissa Division's population received a severe blow in 1866, though various estimates showed that it was around three million, just before the famine struck the Division. The famine claimed around one-third of the population. We have discussed about it in Chapter 3. But in 1872 the total population caught up to three million again.[60] Of course, the part of the reason for increase was rapid recovery from the great famine but a part of it could be due to an underestimate of the population before the famine since there was no systematic counting of population before 1872. We have also discussed the increase or decrease of population in relation to increase of area under cultivation. In this section, the increase or decrease of population would be shown in relation to the prevalence of famine and epidemics and their well-beings. Table 2.1 showed the decadal variation of population in the range of 23 to 15 per cent, between 1872 and 1881. It came down to a range of 8 and 5 per cent in the next decade. An increase was noted in 1901 and was in the range of 8 and 6 during the decade.[61] Orissa, unlike the rest of India, did not suffer from the famines of 1896-7 and 1901 or from the plague. But the next two decades experienced a series of floods and famines including that of 1907-8. The following decade was no better. Orissa experienced a series of floods, droughts and yet another famine in 1918-19 which got compounded with the great influenza and cholera epidemic. The population did not grow much.

But interestingly women outnumbered men throughout the study period. The sex ratio (females per thousand males) for example, increased from 1,037 in 1901 to 1,086 in 1921.[62] The same pattern is seen in all the three districts. The increase was due to two factors, namely, increase in migration of males, and high mortality due to famines, epidemics and to some extent the underestimation of female mortality. Each of these factors has been discussed in a later chapter. But the most important point to note is that the sex ratio kept on increasing in the successive censuses which is unusual when seen against the trends in the recent period.

The earlier Census Commissioners wrote extensively regarding the social systems such as marriage, dowry, their occupational involvement, which throw light on the socio-economic facets of the local inhabitants. So it will be worthwhile to discuss some of those issues briefly though we have analysed this in some detail in later chapters. For example, the Census Commissioner, in 1891, observed that almost all the castes had females outnumbering males. Widow remarriage was common except in the high caste groups of Karans and Brahmins. Further, child marriage was not practised even in the high castes such as Karans, Khandayats and Brahmins. Incidentally, the caste groups like the Chasas and the poorer sections of Khandayats were peasant castes who also practised bride price. A sub-caste of Brahmins also had the practice of bride price. In fact, women outnumbered men in occupational categories like grain trade, rice parchers and cotton spinners, etc. (Table 2.3).

The reasons for the visibility of women's work could be cul-

Table 2.3: The Sex ratio by Castes in Orissa Division and by Occupation in Bengal Presidency in 1901

Name of Castes, Orissa Division	*Sex ratio (0-5)*	*Names of occupation in which female dominate (Bengal Presidency)*	*Sex ratio, 1891*
Brahmins	1,952	Dhobas	1,079
Karans	1,078	Grain dealers	1,034
Khandyats	1,078	Rice pounders	2,435
Chasas	1,018	Grain parchers	2,195
Gurias	1,045	Cow keepers, labourers	1,340
Bauris	1,020	Cotton spinners, labourers	6,371
Pans	1,023	Na, Labourers	NA
Kandaras	1,028		

Sources: For caste and sex ratio please see: T*he Census of India 1901: The Lower Provinces of Bengal and Their Feudatories,* vol. V1A, pp. 192-267. For occupation and sex ratio please see, *The Census of India: The Lower Provinces of Bengal and Their Feudatories,* vol. 3, p. 285.

tivation of rice, which required back bending intensive labour, particularly during transplantation and weeding and only women could do it. Second, as Luddden had observed, the burden of debt compelled the small farmers and agricultural labour to allow the women and children to work in the field.[63]

Table 2.3 gives the sex ratios of different high and low castes in Orissa and that of different female-dominated occupations for the Bengal Presidency as a whole. But some of those caste groups are specific to Orissa only. For example, the castes Karans, and Khandayats as well as Chasas are specific to Orissa Division. All three castes used to get intermixed as soon as the lower castes improved their economic conditions. In the caste hierarchy, Karans were next to Brahmins. Next in order were the Khandayats and then came Chasas. Both Chasas and Khandayats were engaged in cultivation along with a section of Brahmins. The Karans were mainly engaged as writers of the court. But poorer members of the caste depended on cultivation. As soon as the Khandayats and Chasas became well off, they claimed themselves as Karans and tried to adopt dowry practices instead of bride price.

As regards the sex ratio of the female-dominated occupations, it is noticed that women were engaged mostly in grain-related occupations and also spinning thread. Activities such as dealing in grains, parching and pounding of rice, etc., were taken up not only by the women of peasant castes but also from other service caste members. The women of weaving caste spun cotton to make thread. In other words, women's economic contributions were pretty visible in the context of Orissa. Along with that Orissa experienced a series of religious movements such as Jainism, Buddhism, Bhakti movement, which preached gender equality. Further, the fact of having a large tribal population where gender relations were relatively less unequal, must have influenced the attitude towards women in general in Orissa. In other words, the kind of problems faced by the women of Punjab and Haryana due to land policy during colonial rule as pointed out by Oldenburg was absent in Orissa.[64] At the same time, it should be observed that women were uniformly discriminated against. Biswamoy Pati observes, women agricultural labourers got lower wages as compared to men. Similarly, male labourers sometimes got a piece of land for performing labour regularly, but women did not.[65]

Land Revenue and Land Tenure Systems in Orissa Division

Types of Settlements

Unlike the other divisions of Bengal Presidency, Orissa Division was not permanently settled, except for a part of north Balasore consisting of 1,21,276 acres or 9 per cent of the total area which was permanently settled in 1793 along with other parts of Bengal. It was transferred from Midnapur to Balasore in 1868. The total revenue paid to the Government was Rs. 34,835.

In addition there were 21 permanently settled estates within the three districts. They were called Kilajat Estates and consisted of 1,668.05 sq. miles or 20 per cent of the total area of the three districts. These estates were subjected to the same kind of civil and criminal laws as that of other parts of the three districts.[66] These estates were situated on the sea shore or on hill sides. The estates on the sea shore concentrated on salt manufacturing and cultivation of rice was subsidiary in those areas. The population of these areas suffered most severely during the famine of 1866. We have discussed this in some detail in the next chapter. The rest of the area, which comprised 1,55,540 sq. km, was under temporary settlement. Out of this, Khorda Estate, with an area of 2,590 sq. km or 17 per cent of the total area was settled on a different system,[67] known as the *rayatwari* or *khas mahal* system. Initially, the *raiyats* of Khorda were treated as tenants and were assessed very heavily. But by the year 1836, a comprehensive settlement was made and the *raiyats* were given full occupancy rights. The distinction between *thani* and *pahi raiyats* was abolished. They were also given the right to dispose of their land if they wished.[68]

In 1836-43 a detailed settlement was completed in Orissa Division. The settlement of 1836-43 was to expire in the year 1865-6, but was extended for another 30 years because of the severe famine of 1865-6. S.L. Maddox, the Settlement Officer, conducted the next settlement in the decade 1890-1900. It was again revised in 1901-12 and 1922-32. Thus one notices that even though Orissa was a part of Bengal Presidency, the settlement system was a mix of permanent settlement system, temporary settlement and also *raiyatwari*. But the land revenue continued to be fixed afresh from time to time unlike that of Bengal where permanent settlement was the predominant system. This fluidity was a great deterrent for the peasant community in Orissa to take any initiative to improve the productivity of the land.

Types of Land Tenure

Maddox classified the classes or categories of people who possessed land or derived income from it as follows.[69]

1. The so-called 'proprietors' who were directly responsible for payment to the state, the revenue of the land which they owned. They were known as zamindars or *malguzars*.

2. Tenure holders with quasi-proprietary rights under the zamindars were known as *muquaddams*, *padhans* (*pradhans*) and *sarabarakars*.
3. Those who possessed revenue-free holdings, their land was free of revenue in perpetuity. They were known as *lakhiraj* or *bahaldars*.
4. Holders of resumed revenue-free tenures or *bazyaftidars*, who were the relatives of the zamindars and kings.
5. *Jagirdars*, who were persons who held some land free of rent for the services they rendered to the zamindar, king or temples.
6. Purchasers of wasteland, reclaimed and now settled there were known as *kharidadars*.
7. Resident cultivators, who had the right to hold land at a rent fixed for the terms of settlement, known as *thani raiyats*.
8. *Pahi raiyats*, who did not have the occupancy rights as the *thani raiyats*, but paid lower rent than them.
9. Tenants or sub-tenants of categories 4 to 8.
10. *Chandina* or that category of shopkeepers, artisans and labouring households who did not own any agricultural land, but paid rent for their homestead land.

Of these categories, the most significant ones were the zamindars as the powerful intermediaries between the state and the peasant, and the *thani* and *pahi raiyats* who were largest in number. We shall discuss these two categories in some detail in the following section.

The list clearly shows that multiple layers of land rights, control and obligation as well as a system of extraction and exploitation were steadily put in place over an already existing unequal traditional agrarian structure during the early decades of colonial rule.

ZAMINDARS

The word 'zamindar' was coined during the Mughal period and was equivalent to a *bhuiya* under the indigenous kings. Zamindars were responsible for collection of revenue. Later on the Marathas also adopted the word 'zamindar'. In 1803, the British too accepted the same word.[70] However, zamindars were not comparable to the zamindars of Bengal.[71] Most of the highly valued estates in Orissa passed into the hands of Bengali speculators in Calcutta between 1804 and 1818 because of the 'Sunset laws' imposed by the British. These zamindars won the auction biddings for Orissa estates easily because not many from Orissa could be present to deposit their revenue before sunset when the time period ended, after which their land was auctioned. According to B.B. Chaudhuri, 51.6 per cent of the 3,000 proprietors of the settlement of 1804 were dispossessed between 1804 and 1818.[72] The factors responsible for this were the decline in salt trade and depreciation of the local currency, *cowries* because the revenue was now demanded in silver.[73]

Apart from the fact that Oriya zamindars could not deposit their rent on time since the court was situated in Calcutta and the information did not reach them on time. As a result the land used to get auctioned at a low price and were bought by the Bengali zamindars.

This situation caused resentment among the people of Orissa and it led to the first anti-colonial uprising in Orissa known as the Paik Rebellion, in the year 1817 against the British rule. The uprising of course, was suppressed but the revenue system of Khordha, the origin of the uprising, was converted into the *raiyatwari* system of land revenue settlement wherein the government dealt directly with the cultivators for revenue collection. However, other areas in Orissa Division were not affected by this arrangement.

A conspicuous characteristic of the zamindars of Orissa Division was the relatively small size of their estates. Maddox noted that in 1890-1900 the average size of the estate was 263 acres in Cuttack, 678 acres in Balasore and 1079 acres in Puri.[74] Between 1906 and 1912 the Settlement Officer of Orissa observed that the petty proprietors were numerous in south Balasore and north Cuttack.[75] The average size of the estate had come down to 138 acres in Cuttack in 1933 from 1890-1900.[76] The average size of the estate was perhaps still smaller if one realizes that each estate was held by a number of proprietors.[77] Perhaps because the average size of the estates was small, the zamindars did not take much interest in the improvement of agriculture. As we will see later, the zamindars hardly availed of land improvement loans. They also imposed several kinds of cesses over and above the rent. The problem of cess was so acute that almost all the reports on land revenue administration and also the general administration reports of 1866 to 1921 mentioned it.[78] Maddox, for instance, listed 14 types of illegal cesses which were collected by the zamindars of Balasore on different occasions. The cesses were often as high as two *annas* per rupee of the rent.[79] The zamindars could exert such illegal cesses partly because the *pahi raiyats* had not got occupancy rights till 1890-1900 and the population was growing rapidly just after the famine of 1866. It is important to note that the zamindars belonged mostly to the higher castes. For example, Brahmins constituted 27 per cent, Karans 22 per cent and Kayashthas 28 per cent respectively.[80] Interestingly, Karans are also known as Kayashthas. Perhaps Maddox confused them with Khandayats. Further, it is also mentioned that Khandayats became sub-proprietary tenure holders.

THE RAIYATS

As referred to earlier, there were two types of *raiyats* – *thani* and *pahi*. The distinction between two types of *raiyats* was that the *thani raiyats* had occupancy rights, the right to plough the best land of the village and were exempted from house tax. *Pahi raiyats* on the other hand, did not have any occupancy rights over the land. Their rent kept increasing from time to time. [81]

Thani raiyats generally paid higher rents than the *pahi raiyats*. In fact, it was so high that during the famine of 1866, the *thani* rents could not be paid and the *thani raiyats* deserted their land and ran away looking for alternatives. Often they returned to the same area and tried to be taken back as *pahi raiyats*.[82] As a result, by 1890-1900, the settlement area under *thanis* had decreased considerably. In Cuttack, for example, the area decreased by 62 per cent, in Puri by 66 per cent and in Balasore by 43 per cent.[83] Simultaneously, the area under *pahi* cultivation had increased by 47 per cent, 94 per cent and 104 per cent in Cuttack, Puri and Balasore respectively. The area under *pahi* cultivation increased in spite of the increase in *pahi* rents because of population pressure, stability of labour supply and rising agricultural prices.

Many official reports indicated that the average size of the holdings probably decreased between 1866 and 1931. For example, Hunter reported that in Balasore the average size of a holding was 8 acres in 1870.[84] In 1888, the Dufferin Commission Report observed that the average area of a *raiyat's* holding in Orissa was approximately 3 acres and the proportion of *raiyats* who had 3 acres or below was 70 per cent of the total number of *raiyats*.[85] In 1928, the Royal Commission on Agriculture reported that the net or effective size of holdings amounted to 6 acres throughout Orissa.[86] The Banking Enquiry Committee had estimated the size to be 4 to 5 acres in the same period.[87]

This historical account gives more insights into the origins of small peasant agriculture in Orissa, which is the main characteristic of rural Orissa even in the twenty-first century. In order to ascertain the actual size of the holdings, a census was conducted in 76 villages, scattered all over Balasore district, in 1912. Altogether there were 7,752 families owning 31,569 acres of land. The distribution was as follows. The more prosperous *raiyats* had an average holding of 6¼ acres but the size of the family was larger than that of the marginal *raiyats*, whose families were smaller and the average size of the holding was below 2 acres. Altogether, 59 per cent of the families held 91 per cent of the land and a similar pattern was noticed in Puri also.[88]

INDEBTEDNESS OF THE *RAIYATS*

With the growth of money economy, moneylenders also emerged in different parts of Orissa to meet the growing needs of the peasants. The rent had been monetized and there were fluctuations of price in the market. In order to meet those demands, the peasants started borrowing from the moneylenders and became indebted to them for their entire life.[89] The *raiyats* of Orissa were heavily indebted to the local moneylenders and the zamindars. According to some reports the moneylender did not deprive the *raiyats* of their land.[90] Hunter in 1870 noted that half of Cuttack's *raiyats* were heavily indebted either to the local moneylenders or to landlords[91] but he did not mention the amount of debt or the rate of interest. In Puri, he also reported that 'The cultivators, as a class are deep in debt to the landholders, who make advances of money and rice to them.'[92]

Maddox, who discussed the budget of an average *raiyat* having 3 acres of land, was of the opinion that the *raiyat* would face a deficit of 5 *maunds* of rice per year to cover his subsistence needs unless his land was fully irrigated. The expenses on marriages or in bad seasons had to be met from the earnings of his sons who served as labourers. In case of drought or floods, *raiyats* with 3 acres of non-irrigated land had to borrow from the moneylender. Maddox concluded that they 'would not ... in all probability ever again be clear of debt.'[93]

Kingsford, the Assistant Settlement Officer of Balasore, also shared similar view when he remarked on the indebtedness of the *raiyats* and wrote that the moneylenders were either the zamindars or proprietary tenure holders, though they were not very hard creditors. Even though the *raiyat* had to pledge a piece of land, the zamindar did not dispossess him of his land.[94] But B.B. Chudhuri has pointed out that the agricultural labourers were also recruited from the smaller peasantry because of decrease in the size of the holdings. As a result, they had to supplement their income by working for others. He has referred to the situation in Puri district of Orissa in 1908 to show that the social base of agricultural labourers had changed.[95] The small size of the holding of the *raiyats* could be due to the natural growth of population as well as due to mortgage of part of the holding. But as we have seen earlier, the population of the district was not growing rapidly. On the other hand, risks from floods, etc., had been a constant factor. So it is probable that at least one factor which contributed to the small size of the holding was indebtedness and mortgage and eventual sale of the part of the holding. Even though the cultivators had benefited by the price rise in the early decade of the twentieth century, they were still indebted to moneylenders and zamindars. The zamindars of Orissa generally used to have granaries from where they used to lend paddy to the cultivators at the rate of 25 per cent interest in kind, recoverable at harvest time.[96] Eighty per cent of the *raiyats* were in debt in Cuttack in 1906.[97] The *Puri District Gazetteer* observed in 1929: 'There is heavy indebtedness among the agricultural population, the cultivators being in debt both to their landlords and to professional moneylenders.'[98]

This historical account is important because the farmers of Orissa in the twenty-first century are still suffering from indebtedness, even though a lot of initiative have been taken by the state to provide credit from various sources. The self-help groups, cooperatives and the agricultural banks have provided many channels of credit. But as the stark cases of farmer suicides in recent years show that borrowing from moneylenders is a major source of distress of farmers in Orissa and in many other parts of India.[99] The situation in Orissa in the colonial times showed how small peasant agriculture in subsistence conditions created this vulnerability and how some of these conditions still persisted.[100]

AGRICULTURAL LABOURERS

Finally, there is another important category, namely, agricultural labourers, who were the first to succumb to famine. The Famine Commissioner of 1866 had noted that this category was somewhat larger in Orissa Division than in other divisions.[101] Maddox also pointed out that daily labourers were the worst sufferers during the famine years because they spent whatever they earned and did not have any savings. They also did not migrate to distant places to earn a livelihood. Perhaps it was true of the period (1890-1900) when Maddox wrote. But after the introduction of railways they also migrated to Calcutta and other distant places. Much depended on their knowledge of such places where work would be available.

Maddox wrote that farm servants were better off than the agricultural labourers because the master did not forsake them until he himself was reduced to the 'last strait'. Farm servants formed 2.5 per cent of the total population and day labourers 5 per cent.[102] Incidentally, the agricultural labourers were recruited mostly from the Dalits, Bauris and the poorer Chasa caste (a farming caste generally in the OBC cluster). Ironically, farm servants, who were actually bonded labourers with the zamindars, got some subsistence support from their farm owners whereas the agricultural labourers who were technically 'free' in the labour market and not tied to any one farm were the ones who suffered.

Social Composition of the Buyers of Land and the State of Agriculture

The Maddox Report pointed out that the majority of the buyers of land belonged to the category of 'others'. Table 2.4 depicts the percentage share of different buyers of land during that period.

It seemed that the land was transferred from cultivators to non-cultivators comprising personnel in various services in the colonial administration including new professionals. Thus Orissa's economy could be characterized as 'feudal as well as semi-feudal'.[103] This process was accentuated every time there was a famine or any such distress condition. There was yet another trend of non-cultivating classes owning land and leasing it out for cultivation – a process that continues even now. This was one of the major source of impoverishment in Orissa.

While the restructured land system created vast conditions of vulnerability, the colonial regime's policy on trade and commerce made it complicated and worse.

TABLE 2.4: STATUS OF PURCHASERS

	Money lenders	*Landlords of the holding*	*Raiyats*	*Others*	*Area sold in acres*
Cuttack Thani	40	44	103	312	774.87
Others	41	80	123	312	606.94
Balasore Thani	19	–	73	45	388.09
Others	100	–	446	108	876.69
Puri Thani	104	–	247	1025	–
Others	646	5	3,423	913	5,326.61

Source: Maddox Report, vol.1, p. 328.

Decline of Salt Manufacture since 1860

Till 1860-1, the year of abandonment of the salt monopoly, the revenue derived from the sale of salt constituted the single largest source of revenue for the state. It was much higher than land revenue.[104] Even as late as 1870-1, the revenue from the sale of salt constituted 48 per cent of the total revenue in Puri and 30 per cent of the total revenue in Balasore.[105] The average quantity of salt produced per year during 1853 to 1860 – the period of salt monopoly – was two million maunds.[106]

The workers involved in salt manufacture were paid 5 annas per maund of salt initially, which was increased to 6 annas in the year 1860-1.[107] The salt manufacturers, in turn, employed working parties of *molongis* who were paid at the rate of 2 to 3 annas per day.[108] Salt manufacture continued from December to June in Balasore and from March to June in Puri in the coastal parganas.[109] So the agricultural labourers and small *raiyats* got additional employment and income during the off season.[110] The salt industry employed 26,000 workers in various activities in 1860-1.[111] Besides the above, boatmen, tailors and carpenters also got employment because salt was exported in country-made boats, using sails.[112]

The Orissa salt, however, could not compete with Madras-made salt and the cheap Liverpool salt.[113] So the British government decided to discontinue the manufacture of salt in Orissa in 1860-1. The land used for the manufacture of salt was again converted into paddy fields. However, the additional employment in agriculture could not fully compensate for the loss of income from salt manufacture, because the reclaimed lands were less fertile. Simultaneously, the export earnings out of salt trade declined drastically. But the medium of payment had become monetized and it was difficult for the tenants as well as the zamindars to make payments since they required more of *cowries* (local currency) to convert into silver.

The decline of salt trade also had an impact on the employment situation as the alternative off-season employment for the local people disappeared. Orissa's maritime trade was flourishing till 1800, after which it declined because of the trade policy of the colonial rulers. The trading commodities consisted of textile products, filigree work, precious stones, etc., to Java as well as Bali and other parts of Indonesia.[114] Coupled with that, the monetization of currency (from *cowries* to currency) led to a kind of great depression in the economy of the region between 1820 and 1850. At the same time, the revenue collectors were collecting rents mercilessly, leading to local revolts in many places.[115] The economy it seemed was indeed getting ready for the great famine!

Embankment, Canals and Railways and Their Impact, 1866-1921

In 2002, Rohon D'Souza had argued that eastern India was transformed over 150 years ago 'from a flood-dependent agrarian regime to a flood-vulnerable landscape' by the British colonial rulers.[116] Indeed he proved to be right.

After the massive flood of 1866, a committee was set-up to review the embankment conditions of Orissa Division. It was found that there were about 820 km of government embankments and 399 km of *zamindari* embankments in Cuttack.[117] It was reported that the latter embankments were inefficient in controlling the floods and should be reconstructed. But nothing was done till 1894. Another committee was set-up to ascertain the facts during the settlement. It was reported that during 1890-1900 the total length of embankments in Orissa was 1,559 km out of which it was decided to abandon embankments amounting to 599 km and to retain 962 km.[118]

Again, it was decided in 1896-7 that the government should maintain 758 km of embankments situated on the banks of big rivers; these protected an area of 2,652 sq. km (28 per cent of the total area) and another 465 km were maintained for canals in Cuttack.[119] Thus only 29 per cent of the area was fully protected, leaving the other portions of Cuttack district semi-protected or unprotected. In Balasore and Puri there were no government embankments. In the meantime, Chilika Lake was silting up and had to be deepened at a very high cost. Reservoirs that were to be constructed to prevent flooding needed money and were not built.

In other words, the government shirked from its duty of maintaining the embankments even though they were very important for the stability of agriculture.[120]

The government also wanted to construct a network of canals in Orissa Division as early as 1860 on the Madras model. In fact, the East India Irrigation Company did start the work of construction as early as 1863.[121] But the company went bankrupt and it was sold to the government. Another company called Orissa Undertaking was started in 1869. It planned to irrigate 15,00,000 acres of land, which would yield a profit ranging from 9 per cent to 21 per cent from additional revenue. However, though as much as £ 12,00,000[122] had been spent there was hardly any progress on irrigation.[123]

It is well known that the introduction of canal irrigation and the coming of railways did not lead to either diversification of the agrarian economy or substantial rise in wages and income in Orissa Division. This has been documented not only by the British officials but also reconfirmed by several scholarly studies which showed that unlike their many positive effects in the Punjab, United Provinces and Maharashtra, in Orissa they did not have that kind of catalytic effect because of the lack of other necessary initiatives.

Maddox reported that by the end of 1895, the government had already spent Rs. 26 million but most of the canals were in Cuttack, and only a small portion in South Balasore. Maddox pointed out that the Orissa canals did not repay the investment in them.[124] The water charge was only Rs. 1.5 per acre. The maximum area irrigated between 1869-70 and 1898-9 was 1,70,399 acres or 17 per cent of the total cultivated area during 1890-1900.[125] Based on a series of enquiries which were conducted between 1883 and 1899, Maddox came to the conclusion that 'there is nothing to show that irrigation has caused any great rise of rent rates or extension of cultivation, though it has affected, to some extent, the nature and number of the crops grown on the irrigated areas'.[126] The yield per acre of irrigated land was 13½ maunds in contrast to 12 maunds in unirrigated land.[127] He also observed that the experts who had designed the Orissa canals on the model of the Madras canals had perhaps forgotten that Orissa got 60 inches of rainfall whereas Madras received only 40 inches.[128] Other reasons for canal water system not being successful in Orissa Division were listed by Whitcombe, included the 'absence on the part of the cultivators of any demand for the water, local tenurial conditions (that placed) the Oriya peasant at the zamindar's mercy, depriving him of any incentive to increase his productivity by irrigation or any other means'.[129] Similarly, the objective of the coastal canal (it was known as coast canal though it ran through the coast) was to connect Calcutta with Orissa Division for navigation. But it did not earn much revenue and so it was practically closed down after the coming of the railways.

The Bengal-Nagpur railway connecting all the three districts with Calcutta and Madras was opened in 1899.[130] The main item sent by rail was rice. Due to the railways, the traffic and trade through waterways declined.[131] However, railways did not lead to diversification of crops. It has been pointed out by scholars such as Ludden[132] and McAlpine[133] that introduction of canal irrigation and railways led to diversification of cropping pattern in the Punjab and Uttar Pradesh, as a result of which peasants had enough cushion to tide over the impact of famines.

McAlpine has elaborated in great detail how the introduction of rail roads led to the expansion of the market and farmers could trade cash crops for getting food from elsewhere in times of scarcity. Their income in the process had increased and they were less vulnerable to famines. One wonders as to why this phenomenon did not take place in Orissa Division which continued to be famine-prone till 1921, in spite of the introduction of railways and canal irrigations. As mentioned earlier, the explanation lies in the nature of land tenure and specificity of the soil. However, in the rest of India the construction of railroads did raise money wages during 1890-1900.[134] But with the coming of railways, as we will see later, the volume of emigration increased in Orissa.

Coming to the ecological impact of all these developmental works, there is some substance in the argument that the intensity of floods had increased considerably after 1900 because of the blockages caused by embankments of different kinds to water flow.[135]

The Flood Committee Report of 1928 noted that people in the unprotected areas felt that they had frequent floods due to embankments and canals. But the experts, while admitting that point, felt that the benefits of irrigation area in terms of surplus rice exceeded the cost of having floods. They also felt that one day the costs would exceed the benefits.[136] The impact of embankments and resultant water-logging on the disease profile in Orissa Division has not been sufficiently studied. But there is evidence to show that deaths due to malaria increased after 1900 in the region. The Census Superintendent of Bengal, Bihar and Orissa in 1911 commented extensively on water-logging and malaria in Bengal Presidency in general and Orissa Division in particular. He quoted Major A.B. Fry, I.M.S. to the effect that if Cuttack was not malarial prone in 1911 it was because '... the amount of existing infection has not reached a numerical value high enough to cause widespread epidemics. The supply of anopheline mosquitoes has certainly in places reached the numerical value and I shall not be surprised to find a heavy epidemic occurring in the near future.'[137] Moreover, Puri district which was free of malaria till 1908, had started witnessing malaria epidemics after that, which may have been due to the added embankments and railways.[138]

Vulnerabilities Old and New in Orissa's Agrarian Economy

Impoverished Peasantry, Unsettled Ecology

Thus the people of Orissa Division experienced a steady process of impoverishment and ecological dislocation due to a combination of frequent changes in land relations and construction of infrastructure without consciously linking them to the local needs.

Orissa Division was located in an area which is deltaic and is cramped between the hills and the Bay of Bengal and is served by five great rivers which created problems of floods and droughts.

The peasants were growing mainly rice, with minor adjustments like switching over to a different variety of rice or to pulses to minimize the loss of crops due to floods and droughts. Even though a network of canal irrigation was created, and the railroads linked Orissa Division to Calcutta, cash crops were not introduced except in some pockets of irrigated areas because of the risks involved. There was indeed some extension of the area under cultivation, which kept pace with the growth of population till 1900, but not thereafter. Twenty-five per cent of the area had become unfit for cultivation in each district in 1919 because the intensity of floods had increased. The area under cultivation had also increased but the soil was of poor quality. So it is possible that the yield per acre was declining from 1911.

Orissa's *zamindari* estates were smaller in size than in Bengal. Again, some of the big zamindars were absentee landlords, who did not take much interest in improving agriculture and extracted different kinds of cesses from the tenants. Since the size of the holding was small – on an average 3 to 6 acres between 1877 and 1928 – and with uncertain conditions of floods and droughts, the *raiyats* had to depend on the zamindars and moneylenders for grain loans at high interest – the rate of interest was 25 per cent per annum for the entire period. Even though the zamindars and moneylenders did not dispossess the *raiyats* of their land completely, the status of the *raiyats* had changed for the worst.

The manufacture of salt, which used to give additional employment to the *raiyats* of Orissa Division in the off seasons, declined sharply after 1860. As one will see in the next chapter, by 1866 Orissa's economy was in a condition of multiple vulnerabilities, at the time of the severe famine. The famine occurred when Orissa was utterly unprepared to meet any kind of disaster. Besides, the delay in land settlement led people to keeping the land fallow in the fear of having to pay increased rent after settlement. Coupled with that, the administrative set-up was not familiar either with the local culture or peculiarity of the climatic conditions. The administrators, including Commissioner Ravenshaw, were newly appointed along with Bengali officers. They did not have much stake in local development.

The Jagannath Temple in Puri played a special role in the life and economy of the people. The temple earned very large sums of money from pilgrims from all over India, and was itself a large employer of different kinds of labourers, in addition to creating a market for various goods and services. But the earnings of the temple priests were not spent in any productive use since much of it was spent in festivities.

Add to all this the effects of the embankments, which complicated the situation further. As noted earlier, Orissa Division also had a network of embankments for protection from floods and also a number of new canals, particularly in Cuttack. Some of them were maintained by the government and some by the zamindars. By 1896-7 it was decided to keep certain embankments which would protect the canal areas of Cuttack and some portions of fertile area of the district as well. But the other areas were left vulnerable to floods. No attempts were made to build reservoirs or deepening the mouth of the Chilika Lake as protection measures. The embankments constructed for the purpose of railways and the deep holes created to raise the rail lines increased the frequency of floods. This in turn created salination, water-logging and made the region more malaria-prone. Thus, the agrarian political economy of Orissa Division, particularly the colonial measures made the people extremely vulnerable to disasters.

Notes

1. Michelle B. McAlpine, *Subject to Famine: Food Crisis and Economic Change in Western India.1860-1920,* Princeton, University Press, 1983, rpt. 2014. For opposite view see, Dadabhai Naoroji, *Poverty and Un-British Rule in India*, London, S. Sonnenchein, 1901, rpt. 1962, Publication Division, Government of India, B.B. Chaudhuri, 'Movement of Rent in Eastern India 1793-1930', *The Indian Historical Review,* 11(2), January 1977, pp. 346-8.
2. Biswamoy Pati, *Resisting Domination: Peasants, Tribals and the National Movement in Orissa, 1920-1950,* New Delhi, Manohar, 1993, p. 14.
3. Orissa State Archives, *The Paika Rebellion: A Documentary Study*, Bhubaneswar, Orissa State Archives, 2017. In fact the Paika

Rebellion completed 200 years in 2017 and led to its observance with lot of fanfare throughout Orissa.

4. Proceedings of 34 Annual Session of Orissa History Congress, *Growth of Industrial Working Class in Colonial Orissa, 1900-1947*, Bhubaneswar, Orissa History Congress, 2013, pp. 128-32.
5. Subash Chandra Barik, *British Economic Policy in Odisha: A Study in Historical Perspective 1803-1947*, Calcutta, Punthi Pustak, 2013.
6. Irrigation No.4741/XC-6-27 I, Resolution, subject; Appointment of a Committee to enquire into the flood problems of Orissa dt. 25 November 1927. 'Orissa Flood Committee Report 1928', Government Press, pp. 8-9.
7. W.W. Hunter, *Statistical Account of Bengal, 1877*, vol. 18, Trubner & Co., London, p. 147. See also *Cuttack District Gazetteer* 1933, p. 81.
8. Hunter, *A Statistical Account of Bengal*, op. cit., vol. 18, p. 325.
9. *Census of India, 1911*, vol. 5, pt. 1, p. 21.
10. *Floods in Orissa Rivers during 1955 and 1956, Final Report*, Bhubaneswar, Government of Orissa, Revenue (Special Relief) Department, 1958, p. 41.
11. This information was provided by the government in response to Gopebandhu Das, who asked whether considerable areas of the coastal districts of Orissa were left unprotected by the embankments. *Proceedings of the Bihar and Orissa Legislative Council*, 28 November 1919, p. 405.
12. *Census of India, 1901*, vol. 6, pt. 1, p. 490.
13. *Census of India, 1911*, vol. 5, pt. 1, p. 562.
14. *Census of India, 1921*, vol. 7, pt. 1, p. 254.
15. The main source of data on cultivation are the Settlement Reports and the Agricultural Statistics of India. Since the former was done with much care and periodically, we have relied more on it. However, since the objective of the settlement was to fix the rent, *raiyats* might have concealed or abandoned some area under different crops just before the settlement, but the extent of such concealment is unknown. The Agricultural Statistics have been used to cross-check the settlement report. The data for the Agricultural Statistics were collected through cadastral survey so those data were more accurate in Orissa Division than those of other parts of Bengal Presidency. *Agricultural Statistics of India 1901-1902 to 1905-1906*, vol. 1, p. 115.
16. According to Maddox, *sarad* rice is sown in June-July and reaped in November-January, *biali* rice is sown in May-June and harvested

in August and September, and *dalua* rice is sown in November-December and harvested in March.

17. Malabika Chakrabarti, *The Famine of 1896-7 in Bengal: Availability or Entitlement Crisis,* New Delhi, Orient Longman, 2004. She observed that in the famine of 1896-7 Orissa Division escaped lightly except some parts of Puri, but other parts of Bengal Presidency suffered greatly. She has tried to establish the linkage between winter rice crop and intensity of the famine. According to her, areas depending on winter rice only suffered a great deal.
18. Hunter, *A Statistical Account of Bengal,* vol. 18, p. 100. In the case of Balasore also *raiyats* concentrated on several varieties of coarse rice which would grow in state of the 'unseasonableness of rainfall', ibid., p. 290.
19. *Maddox Report 1890-1900,* vol. 1, para 127. Also see, GOB/REV/AGRI/FP, June 1901, No. 2549; From Collector of Puri to Commissioner, Orissa Division. Dt. 7 November 1900. GOBO/Judicial/LSG, F/2, Flood No. 802; From Commissioner, Orissa Division to the Secretary, 17/18 September 1919.
20. *Final Report on the Resettlement of Banki Estate 1917-1920*, 1921, Orissa, Board of Revenue, p. 28.
21. *Flood Committee Report 1928,* op. cit., pp. 14-15.
22. David Ludden, *An Agrarian History of South Asia,* Cambridge University Press, Cambridge, 1999.
23. Michelle B. McAlpine, 'Death, Famine and Risk: The Changing Impact of Crop Failures in Western India, 1870-1920', *Journal of Economic History*, 39(1), March 1979.
24. Ludden, op. cit.
25. It was reported by Maddox that 'Cotton ... is said to be less largely cultivated than in former years...' *Maddox Report 1890-1900*, vol. 1, para 151. S.L. Maddox, *Final Report on the Survey and Settlement of the Province of Orissa (Temporary Settled Areas) 1490-1900*, vol. 1, Calcutta, Calcutta Secretariat Press, 1900, para 152.
26. Ibid. The area under cotton declined between 1900-1 and 1920-1 in all the three districts. The area under cotton was 7,300 acres and it came down to 2,500 acres in Cuttack. In Balasore it decreased from 2,700 acres to 500 acres during the same period. Quoted in Agricultural Statistics for respective years.
27. *Maddox Report 1890-1900*, vol. 1, para 152.
28. Ibid.

29. Ibid.
30. In Balasore, for example, the area under jute rose from 2,800 acres in 1898-9 to 4600 in 1901-2 but in 1930-1 it had decreased to 2,800 acres again. In Cuttack on the other hand, the area under jute increased from 5600 acres in 1901 to 23,200 acres in 1915-16. After 1915-16 there was a declining trend and in 1930-1 the area under jute was 18,200 acres. But it never increased beyond 1.77 per cent of the total net cultivated area in Cuttack. In Puri jute was not cultivated. *Agricultural Statistics of India for Respective Years*. The statistics were collected for the years 1901-2, 1915-16 and 1930-1.
31. *Banking Enquiry Committee Report on Bihar and Orissa 1929-30*, vol. 1, Calcutta, Central Publication Branch, 1930, p. 12.
32. Dharm Narain had also observed that the area under winter rice was very 'specific' to the rice cultivation in Bihar and Orissa Provinces and the influence of price on such areas 'relatively small'. Dharm Narain, *The Impact of Price Movement on Areas Under Selected Crops in India 1900-1939*. Cambridge, Cambridge University Press, 1965, p. 120.
33. *Maddox Report 1890-1900*, vol. 1, para 136.
34. Ibid., para 150.
35. In 1901-2 the area under sugar cane plantation was 4,500 acres in Cuttack and 2,700 acres in Puri. (*Agricultural Statistics of India 1902-05-06*, pp. 156-7). But the area under sugar cane declined to 2,900 acres in Cuttack and to 2,400 acres in Puri in 1920-1. *Agricultural Statistics of India 1920-21*, pp. 186-7.
36. Balasore experienced the greatest increase because a lot of cultivable area was thrown out of cultivation after the great cyclone of 1831-2. It was reclaimed later on. (*Maddox Report 1890-1900*, vol. 1, para 505.)
37. *Census of India, 1891*, vol. 3, pp. 119-24.
38. *Census of India, 1901*, vol. 6, pt. 1, pp. 97-9.
39. In the settlement of 1890-1900, the temporary settled areas amounted to around 5,000 sq. miles. *Maddox Report 1890-1900*, vol. 1, para 1. But the area under the revision settlement of 1906-12 was 5206 sq. miles. The revision settlement included temporarily settled area, revenue free estates, Killa Madhupur, Darpan, Aul and Khandaiti Mahal of Khurda. Khurda Estate was not included. J.F.W. James, *Final Report on Revision Settlement of Orissa (1906-1912)*, 1914, Bankipore, Secretariat Book Depot, p. 1.

40. *Census of India, 1921*, vol. 7, pt. 1, pp. 43-5.
41. W.W. Dalziel, 1934, *Final Report on the Revision Settlement of Orissa (1922-32)*, Patna, Government Press, p. 14.
42. Ibid., p. 96.
43. *Puri District Gazetteer 1929*, p. 174.
44. In fact, the process of settled cultivation from shifting cultivation had begun in the later nineteenth century and had continued. *Puri District Gazetteer 1908*, (rpt. 1984), p. 154.
45. *Census of India, 1921*, vol. 7, pt. 1, p. 76.
46. Blyn noted that there was a negative trend of 0.06 per cent per year in acreage between 1906-7 and 1945-6 in greater Bengal, which included Orissa Division. (George Blyn, *Agricultural Trends in India: 1894-1947: Output, Availability and Productivity*, Philadelphia, University of Pennsylvania Press, 1966, pp. 138-9, 174.)
47. Dharm Narain pointed out that the total sown area of Bihar and Orissa declined between 1900 and 1931. Dharm Narain, *The Impact of Price Movements*, op. cit., pp. 128-9 and 139.
48. Nowadays of course many scholars have started working on different aspects of the temple. One of the important resource book is Hermann Kulke, Anncharlott Eschmann and Gaya Charan Tripathi (eds.), *The Cult of Jagannath and the Regional Tradition of Orissa*, New Delhi, Manohar, 2014.
49. Hunter, 1976, *Statistical Account of Bengal, Puri and the Orissa, Tributary States*, vol. 19, 1977 rpt., Delhi, Concept Publishing Company, p. 54.
50. Incidentally, the temple did not pay revenue to the state. The comparison with total revenue is only an indication of the wealth of the temple.
51. Even though Hunter felt the figure Rs. 7,00,000 was excessive, he quoted an Indian historian who pointed out that the Muslim rulers used to collect Rs. 1,00,000 as pilgrim tax, thereby implying that the pilgrims carried more than the amount paid as tax. Hunter himself had given a lower estimate of pilgrim tax as collected by the government. He assumed that pilgrims gave twice the amount of pilgrim tax to the priests. By 1876, the pilgrim tax was withdrawn. So the pilgrims did not have to part with that much. From this he concluded that the pilgrims must be paying not less than three times the pilgrim tax. This amounted to Rs. 3,70,000. There is a flaw in his analysis. For example, he had confused between the offerings to priests and the offerings to Lord Jagannath. In practice

the income of *pandas* from the pilgrims is very different from that to Jagannath Temple. But even then, the point that he was trying to make was valid, i.e. the income of the temple from the pilgrims was substantial.

52. Hunter, *Statistical Account of Bengal*, op. cit., vol. 19, pp. 56-7.
53. *Puri District Gazetteer 1908* (rpt. 1984), p. 124.
54. Ibid.
55. Hunter, *Statistical Account of Bengal*, vol. 19, pp. 66-7.
56. *Puri District Gazetteer*, 1908, p. 116.
57. Hunter, *Statistical Account of Bengal*, vol. 19, p. 557.
58. John Beams, *Memoirs of Bengal Civilian*, 1961, Delhi, Manohar, 1981 (1st pub. 1961), pp. 195-6. Incidentally, there is a road called Pilgrim Road in Cuttack town through which pilgrims used before the coming of the railways.
59. Davis Kingsley, *The Population of India and Pakistan*, Princeton, Princeton University Press, 1951. p. 27.
60. H. Beverley, *Report on the Census of Bengal, 1872,* Calcutta, Bengal Secretariat Press, 1872, p. 118.
61. *Census of India 1901*, Bengal, Bihar and Orissa, Tables, vol. V1A, p. 6.
62. Kanaklata Devi 'Causes of Declining Sex Ratio in Orissa: An Analysis', *Journal of Family Welfare,* 49(1), June, 2003, pp. 42-9.
63. Ludden, op. cit.
64. Veena Oldenberg, *Dowry Murder: Impact of a Cultural Crime,* New Delhi, Oxford University Press, 2003.
65. Pati, op. cit., p. 8.
66. K.C. Jena, *Land Revenue Administration in Orissa during the Nineteenth Century,* Delhi, S. Chand & Co., 1968.
67. Khurda had settlements in 1836 and 1880, *Maddox Report 1890-1900*, vol. 1, pt. 1.
68. K.C. Jena, *Land Revenue Administration in Orissa*, pp. 139, 149.
69. *Maddox Report 1890-1900*, vol. 1, Para 255.
70. G. Toynbee, *A Sketch of History of Orissa from 1803 to 1828*, Calcutta, Prafulla, 2005, pp. 36-7.
71. Baden-Powell, *Land Systems of British India,* vol. 1, Delhi, Oriental Publishers, 1974 (1st pub. 1892), p. 568.
72. Binoy Bhusan Chaudhuri, 'Eastern India', in Dharma Kumar (ed.), *Cambridge Economic History of India,* vol. II, Cambridge, Cambridge University Press, 1981, p. 96. Hereafter, *CEHI II.*
73. Ibid., p. 95.

74. *Maddox Report 1890-1900*, vol. 1, Para 269.
75. *Settlement Report 1906-12*, p. 38. Also see, *Banking Enquiry Committee Report 1929-30. Bihar and Orissa*, vol. 1, pp. 10-11.
76. *Cuttack District Gazetteer*, 1933, p. 182.
77. Hunter pointed out that the effective size of each estate was even smaller in Balasore because each estate was held by several proprietors. W.W. Hunter, *Statistical Account of Bengal*, op. cit., vol. 18, p. 293. Also see B.H. Baden-Powell, *Land System of British India*, vol. 1, Orient Longman, 1995, p. 569.
78. *Land Revenue Administration Report, Bihar and Orissa 1914-15*, p. 6. Also see, *Land Revenue Administration Report, Bihar and Odisha 1915-16*, pp. 15-16.
79. *Maddox Report 1890-1900*, vol. 1, para 266. The Famine Commissioner in 1866 made similar remarks.
80. Biswamoy Pati, 1993, *Resisting Domination: Peasants, Tribals and National Movements in Orissa 1920-1950*, New Delhi, Manohar, p. 6. Also cited in Sushanta Kumar Bag, 'Agrarian Problem, Peasants and National Movements in Orissa' published in *Indian History Congress Proceedings*, vol. 68, pt. 1, 2007, pp. 944-64.
81. They also had the right to use trees on their plots.
82. The Famine Commissioner observed that after the settlement of 1836-43, the *thani raiyats* 'had been really paying more than the value of their assessable land.' *FCRO 1866*, pt. 1, Para 44. Also see, *Maddox Report 1890-1900*, vol. 2, para 11.
    Also see, B.B. Chaudhuri, 'Eastern India', op. cit., *CEHI II*, p. 134.
83. Chaudhuri, 'Movement of Rent in Eastern India 1793-1930', *The Indian Historical Review*, 11(2), January 1977, pp. 346-8.
84. Hunter, *Statistical Account of Bengal*, op. cit., vol. 18, p. 293. Also, according to Hunter, 50 per cent of the area in Cuttack and 60 per cent of the area in Balasore was below 10 acres, thus indicating that the majority of *raiyats* were holding below 10 acres. Ibid., p. 293.
85. GOI/REV/AGRI/FP, Dec. 1888, Nos. 1-24, 'Dufferin Commission Report'. Also see, Baden-Powell, *The Land Systems*, op. cit., p. 478.
86. *Royal Commission on Agriculture in India: Evidence Taken in Bihar and Odisha 1928*, vol. 13, London, His Majesty's Stationery Press, 1928, p. xxvi.
87. *Banking Enquiry Committee Report on Bihar and Orissa 1929-30*, vol. 1, Calcutta: Central Publication Branch, 1930, p. 11.
88. *Revision Settlement Report, 1906-12*, p. 38.

89. Pati, op. cit., p. 15.
90. *Cuttack District Gazetteer, 1933,* p. 145.
91. Hunter, *Statistical Account of Bengal*, vol. 18, p. 106.
92. Ibid., vol. 19, p. 96.
93. *Maddox Report 1890-1900,* vol. 1, para 187.
94. Ibid., Para 189. Also, the members of the Banking Enquiry Committee had interviewed the *raiyats* of the protected and unprotected areas of Cuttack and Puri. Invariably they found that most of the *raiyats* were indebted to the local zamindars and moneylenders. They paid 25 per cent rate of interest on paddy loans. The usual months of borrowings were August and October, *Banking Enquiry Committee Report, 1929-30*, vol. 1, pp. 41-52.
95. B.B. Chaudhuri, 'Eastern India', op. cit., p. 167.
96. *Puri District Gazetteer 1908*, p. 178.
97. *Cuttack District Gazetteer 1906*, p. 126.
98. *Puri District Gazetteer 1929*, p. 199.
99. B.B. Mohanty and Papesh Kumar Lenka, 'Small Farmers Suicide in Orissa', *Economic and Political Weekly* 54(22), June 2019, pp. 51-9.
100. Fanindam Deo, *Roots of Poverty: A Social History,* Bhubaneswar, Amadeus Press, 2009, pp. 13-280.
101. *FCRO 1866*, pt. 1, para 50.
102. *Maddox Report, 1890-1900*, vol. 1, para 193.
103. J.K. Mahapatra and Urmi Mala Das, 'Agrarian Transition and Social Development in Orissa', *The Indian Journal of Political Science*, April-June 1993, pp. 293-4.
104. J.K. Samal, *Orissa Under the British Crown, 1858-1905*, New Delhi, S. Chand & Company, 1977, p. 84.
105. Hunter, *Statistical Account of Bengal*, vol. 19, p. 156 and vol. 18, p. 345.
106. *Rundall's Report, 1883*, para 14. Quoted in Samal, *Orissa Under the British Crown*, p. 90.
107. *Bengal Administration Report, 1860-61*, p. 31.
108. Hunter, *Statistical Account of Bengal*, vol. 18, p. 336.
109. Ibid., vol. 18, p. 336 and vol. 19, pp. 336 and 152 respectively.
110. B.B. Chaudhuri, 'Movement of Rent in Eastern India, 1793-1930', *The Indian Historical Review*, III(2), January 1977, p. 343.
111. G. Rundall, *Report of Manufacture of Salt in Orissa, 1883*, para 6 quoted in J.K. Samal, *Orissa Under British Crown*, op. cit., p. 90.
112. Senapati wrote extensively on the decline of the salt industry in

Balasore and how it had supported different types of labourers, and his uncle was a contractor who had undertaken to supply country boats for the export of salt, and employed a large number of tailors and carpenters. F.M. Senapati, *Atma Charita 1843-1919*, Cuttack, Friends Publishers, 1981, p. 13.

113. Liverpool salt was sold at Rs. 65 per 100 *maunds*. Orissa salt was sold at Rs. 83 per 100 *maunds*. *Salt Administration Report 1860-61*, para 8.
114. Lalatendu Das Mohapatra, *Commerce in Orissa 1600-1800,* Jagatsinghpur, Prafulla Pathagar Publication, 2010.
115. Ludden, op. cit.
116. Rohan D'Souza, 'Colonialism, and Nature: Debating the Origin of Mahanadi Delta's Hydraulic crisis (1803-1928)'. *Economic and Political Weekly,* 37(13), 30 March 2002, pp. 1261-72.
117. *Maddox Report 1890-1900,* vol. 1, para 22.

Similar figures for Balasore and Puri were:

	Government	*Zamindari*
Balasore	74 miles	not available
Puri	none	257 miles.

118. *Maddox Report 1890-1900*, vol. 1, para 22.
119. *Puri District Gazetteer 1929*, pp. 186-7.
120. B.B. Chaudhuri, *Peasant History of Late Pre-colonial and Colonial India,* New Delhi, Pearson Longman, 2008, p. 224.
121. Quoted in Elizabeth Whitcombe, 'Irrigation', *CEHI II*, p. 694.
122. The Sterling-rupee exchange rate was 1:10 in 1877.
123. Whitcombe, 'Irrigation', *CEHI II*, p. 702.
124. *Maddox Report, 1890-1900*, vol. 1, para 104.
125. Ibid., vol. 1, para 108 and 10.
126. Ibid., vol. 1, para 111.

Ibid., para 109.

127. *Cuttack District Gazetteer 1933*, p. 111.
128. Whitcombe, 'Irrigation', *CEHI II*, p. 700.
129. *Cuttack District Gazetteer 1933*, pp. 169-70.
130. Ibid., p. 169. Also see, *Puri District Gazetteer 1929*, p. 212.
131. *Census of India 1901*, vol. VI, pt. 1, p. 100.
132. David Ludden, *An Agrarian History of South Asia*, Cambridge, Cambridge University Press, 1999, p. 188.
133. Michelle B. McAlpine, 'Dearth, Famines and Risks: The Changing

Impact of Crop Failures in Western India , 1870-1920', *The Journal of Economic History*, 39(1), March 1979, pp. 143-57.

134. Maddox reported in 1890-1900 that the coast canal of Balasore had deleterious effects on the local population and it did increase the intensity of floods in certain areas. *Maddox Report 1890-1900*, vol. 1, para 48.
    A committee set-up in 1924 to go into the matter (flood) reported that it was not due to various embankments but due to deforestation in the catchment area. *Cuttack District Gazetteer 1933*, p. 101.
135. *Flood Committee Report 1928*, p. 13.
136. *Census of India 1911,* vol. V, pt. 1, p. 72.
137. *Puri District Gazetteer 1929*, p. 137.
138. Ibid.

CHAPTER 3

The Great Orissa Famine of 1866
The Event and the Process

Introduction

The Orissa famine of 1866 was one of the most important events in the economic history of not only Orissa but India as a whole. It is evident from the accounts of W.W. Hunter and C.E. Buckland, who had devoted a lot of attention to the various dimensions of the great famine.[1] Recent works by economic historians too have provided much insight into the causes and consequences of the famine, reflecting new issues which arose in course of research and theoretical debates on the subject.[2] Many of them took the Famine Commission Report of 1866 or the Famine Commission Report of 1880 as serious reference points while a few others took note of literary and other sources of social history to reconstruct some of the propositions. In this work we take both kinds of sources for understanding the nature of this historical episode.

Before the great famine of 1866, Orissa had undergone several minor famines, many of them after the onset colonial rule in Orissa in 1803. Noteworthy among them were the famines of 1806, 1808, 1809, 1817, 1828, 1836, 1837 and 1842.[3] But apart from acknowledging the occurrence of the famines and mentioning the years, no causal explanations were offered in the official reports. Before we take up the major dimensions of the great famine of 1866 let us keep in mind how the Famine Commission Reports summed up its causes:

1. Failure of rain,
2. The imminent expiry of the 30-year land settlement thus resulting in insecurity of the land holding system,
3. Considerable increase in the export of rice.

The prolonged impact of the Great Depression, which had set in just after the land settlement in 1835 lasted till 1840 due to the following reasons:

1. indifference of the bureaucracy,
2. poor state of communications,
3. absence of a dynamic trading class, and
4. preoccupation of the zamindars with maximizing their own profit, no matter how adversely it affected the peasantry.

The above list of causes may be comprehensive, but is analytically inadequate as it mixes up policy measures that had structural consequences with administrative steps for the specific situation. It gives nearly similar salience to long-term and short-term causes, explanations and processes. The centrality of some of the policy measures which had long-term effects gets lost in this kind of account. It has been pointed out, for example, that the closure of salt manufacture in 1861 threw an additional 26,000 people out of occupation and they turned to agriculture because of the colonial salt policy.[4] Further the weavers were rendered jobless because the colonial rulers imported cheap cloths and sold them in the local market. That is why some experts have tried to trace the causes of the famine of 1866 to factors which were in operation for a long time. The productivity of land was declining because of heavy rent, poor condition of cattle, lack of manure, irrigation and rotation of crops. As mentioned above, it was also observed that the salt manufacturers and weavers depended solely on agriculture because they were thrown out of their occupation. Their traditional economic activity became less remunerative because they could not compete with the imported goods.[5] Coupled with that, the maritime trade, which was flourishing till 1800 declined during the colonial rule because of their new trade policy.[6]

Another structural aspect was the nature of land tenure, which was also responsible for the occurrence of the famine. The land settlement was going to be over in 1866. So the zamindars were apprehensive of the increase in the volume of rent by the colonial administration of Bengal Presidency. Hence the zamindars tried to keep vast acres of land fallow so that they did not have to pay rent on it. That the nature of land settlement was one of the long-term causes of the famine is evident from the fact that Khordha subdivision which was under permanent settlement did not suffer from the famine so intensely.[7] The experts while analysing various tribal revolts against the colonial rulers pointed out the effects of an alien land revenue administration which compelled the tribal people to use money instead of *cowri* which was the traditional medium of exchange for paying the rent. Their earlier pattern of exchange of various commodities was replaced by a new, unfamiliar system often leading to auctioning of their land to Bengali landlords. The introduction of currency notes had the same kind of impact as modern-day demonetization since nobody had enough money to carry on trade. Additionally, the landlords introduced cash crops for earning greater profit forcing the peasants and others to work as farm labourers for them. Whatever crops the tribals produced was collected from them in the form of rent. Further, the money-lenders also lent them money, now at a higher rate of interest in the changed conditions and contributed to the process of turning them into paupers. Therefore, it is important to classify and carefully analyse the various kinds of factors, which cumulatively led to the occurrence of famines in 1770, 1866, 1872-4, 1892, 1897, 1907-8 and 1918-19 causing heavy mortality and migration in the Bengal Presidency.[8]

The Orissa famine of 1866 affected an area of 1,04,221 sq. km with an estimated population of 1,18,55,543. It was interesting to note that the famine affected the areas where only Oriya people were living. It was also estimated that about 8 per cent of the total population died within one calendar year. The Orissa Division was the region most severely affected by this famine. It had an area of 19,816 sq. km and an estimated population of three million on the eve of the famine of whom at least 27 per cent died.[9] Besides the enormous mortality, it had generated many fundamental changes in economic and social structure and the social and economic behaviour of people of the region.

The famine of 1866, therefore, deserves an in-depth treatment, even though the kind of detailed official data available for later famines were not collected on this famine, which was the worst of them all. Nevertheless, there is a mass of data of varying degrees of reliability which, we have used. No doubt, we have relied a lot on the government proceedings, Census reports, Famine Commission reports and other government data. But at the same time we seriously look at the Oriya press reports, autobiographies and biographies of contemporary figures and also literary works including poetry and fiction and even folk memory. It should be pointed out that the main drawback of the data from official sources was its *post facto* character – those were collected after the famine was over. So it was difficult to capture what was actually happening in the villages.

Immediate as well as Long-term Causes of the Famine

Let us go into the causality dimension in a little more detail and keep in mind the distinction between immediate and long-term causes of the famine. Whereas decline of grain output due to the failure of rains and the increased export of rice were among the immediate causes, the insecure land relations due to temporary settlement was the long-term, structural factor making the vast peasantry highly vulnerable.

Output Decline due to Rain Failure

From October 1865 onwards there was no rain in Orissa Division and this was a major factor in leading to crop failure. At least 4 inches of rain either in October or in subsequent months is absolutely necessary for the maturity of crops in the un-irrigated area.[10]

In fact, throughout 1865 the rainfall was scanty in the entire lower provinces of Bengal Presidency. There was plenty of rainfall before the sowing started but rainfall stopped entirely in the middle of October, it was the time, when winter paddy required it most. In other words, the distribution of rainfall during the agricultural cycle was irregular.[11]

Hence the immediate and an important cause of the famine of 1866 was the output decline or a drastic fall in the volume of grain production due to rain failure. It was seriously compounded by an entitlement decline or sudden reduction in the purchasing capacity of the people. Something like the latter day demonetization in 2016 took place at that time, replacing the medium of exchange from *cowries* (the prevalent form of money used by the common people) to currency notes which were not familiar to the people. This set of factors was made even more complicated by the policy of the colonial administration to increase grain exports. All this was happening in an atmosphere of the expanding practice of the *laissez-faire* policy of the British government, which as a matter of policy decided not to do anything to check the price rise.[12] While these immediate factors caused the distress situation for the vast number of people, there was the absence of adequate relief, which intensified people's sufferings.

As discussed elsewhere, there were two estimates regarding the extent of output decline, one by the Commissioner of Orissa, T.E. Ravenshaw as of 1 November 1866 and another by the authorities of Famine Histories of 1885. According to the Commissioner, the aggregate output was just enough to feed an estimated population of 2.5 million in the year 1865-6, i.e. nearly the whole population. In spite of that, famine occurred because the zamindars and traders hoarded their grain stocks. The authors of the *Famine Histories* noted that the output had declined by two-thirds, to the extent of leaving one million without food at the rate of 0.5 *seer* per day for a year. Incidentally, in 1880 a Commission was set-up to review the famine situation in India. It was published in three parts.[13]

The available data was not adequate so as to enable us to decide who was right. But judging from references in the official records to 'total crop failure', 'not an ear of corn' was there, etc., it appeared that the authors of *Famine Histories* were perhaps nearer the truth. We shall return to this issue shortly with a few more details.

Export of Rice

In so far as the amount of rice export was concerned, the context was the considerably increased demand for coarse rice from the US because of the Civil War (1863-5) there. The data on exports given below may be actually an underestimate. First of all, it showed only the extent of export through three ports. It did not take note of the amount, which got exported on road by pack bullocks. It would not be an exaggeration to point out that a fair amount of rice got exported, particularly from the ports of Balasore. It continued to increase till 1863-4 after which it declined slightly. The amount exported from the other two districts was not that significant.

In fact, it is worth noting the similarities between the Irish famine with that of Orissa famine of 1866. Before the colonial rulers entered Ireland, the peasants used to cultivate different types of crops such as rice, corn, pulses, and vegetables. Once the colonial rulers entered, they tried to introduce the cultivation of potatoes on a massive scale. The production was so high and remunerative that the peasants resorted to cultivating only one crop and forgot the traditional safety net of diversification of cropping pattern.[14] Similarly in Orissa the export of rice increased so much that the peasants got lured and started producing rice forgetting the traditional practice of sowing multiple grains. In other words, Orissa shifted more towards the monocropping system and became more vulnerable to the vagaries of weather.

The recorded export of food-grains increased to an unprecedented level in the year 1864-5, leaving little for storage for 1865-6 (see Table 3.1). The Telugu-speaking trading caste business people, described in one account as ‘the energetic Telenga Koomtees’ of the Madras region, had entered Orissa in a big way to buy up grain. A French company also exported through False Point in Cuttack. In fact, Orissa rice was so much in demand that even a ‘roadstead’ port like Puri and False Point in Cuttack had started exporting substantial amounts since 1860-1. Coupled with the export, the absentee landlords from Calcutta had already sold off their annual produce just after getting their share. That in turn

TABLE 3.1: TOTAL AMOUNT OF RICE EXPORTED FROM ORISSA (1860-5)

Units: maund

Years	*Balasore (maund)*	%	*Cuttack (maund)*	%	*Puri (maund)*	%	*Total (maund)*	*Actual Total (maund)*	*Difference (maund)*
1860-1	3,50,074	76.59	23,049	5.04	83,936	18.36	4,57,059	4,57,059	0
1861-2	3,27,504	73.73	60,880	13.71	46,780	10.53	4,44,164	4,35,164	9,000
1862-3	4,07,622	90.76	86,986	19.37	4,816	1.07	4,49,134	4,99,424	-50,290
1863-4	5,20,052	94.64	29,464	5.36	0	0.00	5,49,516	5,49,516	0
1864-5	8,06,576	86.03	72,128	7.69	58,824	6.27	9,37,528	9,37,528	0
Total	24,11,828	85.00	2,72,507	9.60	1,94,356	6.85	28,37,401	28,78,691	59,290

Sources: Report of the Commissioners appointed to enquire into famine in Bengal and Orissa, vol. 1, pt. 1, p. 47.
Reproduced in *Orissa Famine (Na'anka): A Documentation of Primary Sources*, Orissa State Archives, Bhubaneswar, 2016, p. xvii.

must have depleted the stock even further. It was estimated that export of both paddy and rice had increased by more than 500 per cent between 1855-6 and 1864-5. In the year, 1865-6, the export of grain continued though at a reduced rate.[15] The phenomenon of export of rice again occurred even at the time of the famines of 1876-8, 1896-7 and 1899-1900.[16] The Bengal famine of 1943 was no exception.[17]

In so far as the long-term causes of the famine were concerned, as discussed in the previous Chapter 2, Orissa was undergoing a temporary land settlement which was to be over by 1865. The zamindars and the peasants kept the lands fallow so as to be assessed at a low rate.

Further, just after the land settlement in 1835 the Great Depression had set in and lasted till 1840. The *thani* peasants were assessed very highly before the Depression. After that they found it very difficult to pay the land revenue.[18] Hence the peasants had no incentive to produce more since the zamindars used to squeeze them to the maximum. Besides, the absentee landlords took minimal interest to improve the quality of land except collecting the produce and selling those off at the earliest.

As mentioned earlier, this situation made the masses of tenants and agricultural labourers highly vulnerable to distress conditions; as the zamindars themselves were temporary title-holders. Further the fertility of soil was declining because of non-profitability of cultivation due to lack of irrigation, and good quality manure, and poor condition of the bullock population. There was a lack of motivation all around. But still more and more people started depending on agriculture because, as mentioned before, the colonial government's import policies on salt as well as clothes had robbed them off employment opportunities in those sectors.

Estimates of Output

Let us take up the issue of output decline in some more detail, as this is a crucial dimension of food scarcity and famine.

To estimate agricultural output we require figures of area under cultivation as well as yield per acre. Since systematic data were not collected on those aspects we do not have any reliable figures. But two estimates are available on output and output decline.[19]

Ravenshaw had estimated the area under cultivation in 1865-6 to be 2,246,056 acres; 1,797,645 acres in temporarily settled area and 449,411 acres in the permanently settled area.[20] This estimate was perhaps an underestimate to the extent that it was prepared by the overworked Deputy Collectors in the midst of famine work. Also the *raiyats* had kept some lands fallow in the year 1865, because of the 30 year settlement was to expire in that year and the zamindars and *raiyats* wanted to avoid the increase in the rate of assessments.[21]

On the other hand, the *Famine Histories* used the replies received by the Deputy Collectors in 1867 given by the landholders and put in the area under cultivation in 1865-6 at 2,424,000 acres,[22] which was higher than Ravenshaw's estimate. This latter estimate was perhaps more accurate than the former because the settlement was postponed till 1890 and there was no immediate reason for concealment of area under cultivation by the zamindars.

Standard Yield

According to Ravenshaw the standard yield per acre was 20 maunds of paddy, the best lands producing 30 maunds and the worst lands 10 maunds. In 1890-1900 when the second extensive settlement was done, Maddox pointed out that the standard yield per acre was 12 maunds of rice or 19 maunds of paddy in non-irrigated areas, ascertained after a large number of experiments.[23] So if we judge the estimate of standard yield of Ravenshaw, it seems that it was higher than that of Maddox because he had taken the non-irrigated area only.[24]

The authors of the *Famine Histories* had assumed that the average outturn of an acre would be 14 maunds of clean rice taking bad quality and good quality of land together.[25] As we have seen while discussing Ravenshaw's estimate, *Famine Histories* estimate of outturn of crops would be over-estimates if we accept the Maddox estimate to be correct.

Condition Factor

As was noticed earlier even the faulty system of ascertaining the extent of crop failure was absent in case of the famine of 1866. On top of it, the members of the Board of Revenue had 'set their face against any kind of enquiry' because they felt that they were not going to grant any remission in revenue.[26] The Famine Commissioners had observed in their remarks that Ravenshaw had assumed that half the crop was saved.[27]

It seems that the assumption of Ravenshaw regarding condition factor was an overestimate, which will be discussed in some more detail later. Besides, the Famine Commissioners also felt that way. In their support they had cited the witnesses who felt that the crop was from 7/8 to the total production of the current year in different parts.[28]

In this case the authors of *Famine Histories* had accepted the estimate of the Famine Commissioners of 1866 on the loss of crops to be correct, namely that 1/3 crop had been saved.[29] Perhaps this was nearer the truth, because of several other reasons as well. First, the figures for the distribution of rainfall indicate that in many places the main crop was a total failure (see Table 3.2). Second, officers and others who were present on the ground gave reports,

TABLE 3.2: MONTHLY DISTRIBUTION OF RAINFALL (IN INCHES IN THE YEAR 1865)

1865	*Cuttack*	*Balasore*	*Puri*
May	7.4	11.55	13.0
June	8.1	4.25	5.6
July	12.2	5.9	4.3
August	7.7	8.25	5.6
September	7.5	9.30	5.2
October	0.0	0.30	0.0
November	0.0	0.0	0.0
December	0.8	0.0	0.0
Total	51.4	52.6	36.3

Source: FCRO 1866, pt. 1, paras 57 and 58.

which corroborate this. The eyewitness accounts of the crop of the high lands in 1865-6 were full of statements mentioning, 'total failure' of crops[30] and that 'even the cattle did not touch the straw.'[31] The Collector of Balasore reported that in the western part of Balasore, there was very little grain worth cutting. In south Balasore also 'the grains when thrashed proved to be all husks' and the grain was but a small portion of what came from the field during the year.[32]

Mr. Barlow, the Collector of Puri, who had visited the salt tract of Puri in the month of December 1865, also found total failure of crops in the salt tract of Puri district. He had made an extensive tour of the district.[33]

The crops of the salt tracts of other districts besides Puri, were also likely to have failed. Even though the land was not fertile, the farmers shifted to rice cultivation in this area after the abolition of salt manufacturing by the colonial regime. The crops of these lands were entirely dependent on rainfall for their survival. Since the rains failed in October 1865, the crops of this area too would have failed.

The crop yield of the low lands were also likely to have been poor, as the moisture content of the soil even of the low lands, would have been insufficient for the main rice crop to mature.[34] Thus we find that the output of the main rice crop was probably very low on the uplands and in the salt tracts, and below normal in the low lands. So, it can be argued that the estimate of *Famine Histories* was nearer the truth, i.e. only 1/3 of the total crop production could be saved in 1865-6.

Consumption, per capita Requirements

Of per capita consumption, Ravenshaw's estimate, i.e. 14/16 *seer* (14 units out of 16 units of one *seer*) seems to be high.[35] He had not given any reason for assuming such high requirements per day. The Famine Commission of 1866 had also discussed the per capita consumption requirement. According to the Commission, the quality of food given depended very much on 'circumstances'. For example, they pointed out that when there was some doubt regarding the occurrence of famine and the government did not want to be liberal, rice should be given in such amount in which people could subsist. But when the famine is severe, the government should be more liberal. (The Famine Commissioners of 1866 were critical of the diet of prisoners in Bengal Jail, which was prescribed to be 14/16 *seer* for non-labouring prisoners and an additional one unit of *seer* for the labouring prisoners. These amounts were too liberal they felt. This standard was thought to be appropriate since a starving Irishman could survive on ¾ *seer* of bread or half *seer* of biscuits.) Finally the Commission recommended that labourers who were not doing any hard labour should be given half *seer* of rice and some pulses or fish or some 'clarified butter'. Incidentally, the Commissioners also reported that throughout the famine of 1866, the opinion regarding the amount of food required varied between ¼ of a *seer* and half *seer*. The Board of Revenue, however, maintained that ¾ of a *seer* was required, according to the Commissioners.[36]

W.W. Hunter had accepted ¾ *seer* with some pulses for the labouring class and for non-labouring class he had recommended 10/16 *seer* per day.[37] Maddox on the other hand, had accepted the views of the authors of *Famine Histories*, i.e. 10/16 *seer* per day.[38]

Recently, a controversy has been raised regarding the per capita consumption requirement and we have discussed the concept of 'requirement' at some length in Chapter 8. Here it may suffice to say that ½ *seer* cereal would yield 1,600 calories and it would be sufficient for famine victims to subsist, provided they did not do any labour. At the initial stage, however, the victims would lose 25 per cent of their body weight. They would continue to thrive provided the surroundings were clean and they received medical aid.[39] Keeping this discussion on Ravenshaw's estimates in mind we may now turn to the authors of *Famine Histories* and see how they dealt with this question.

The authors of the *Famine Histories* had assumed 11/16 *seer* of rice per person per day during normal times, which they pointed out, would be reduced to ½ *seer* during the famine period.[40] This assumption seemed reasonable in the light of the above discussion. But estimates of both the authorities had limitations relating to the variables used by them. Let us discuss these limitations before going into the estimates of food availability given by them. Later on we will incorporate the adult unit instead of uncorrected population totals to see whether the food availability decline was still substantial to warrant such magnitude of deaths.

Adult Units

It should be noted that neither Ravenshaw nor the authors of *Famine Histories* converted the population totals into adult units. So, for purposes of converting the estimated population of 1865 to adult units, we have taken Maddox's method, i.e. the assumption that a family consisted of two adults and two children or four adult units.[41] The reason for taking Maddox's figures is that the Census 1872 was too close to the famine[42] and the average figure of 1881 had come at a time when Orissa Division was recovering from the famine of 1866. Thus, according to the above conversion ratio using Maddox's method, Ravenshaw's estimated population would be around 2 million and that of *Famine Histories*, 3 million.

Incidentally, no data on such important aspects as storage and seed requirement was available.[43] But the quantity of exported grains was given separately, though its impact on availability was not discussed by these authorities. Ravenshaw indirectly justified the export of rice from the Orissa Division by pointing out that the region had produced surplus rice in normal years.

Now if we convert the population totals as given by Ravenshaw and the authors of *Famine Histories* into adult units the estimates of population requiring the same amount of food would be less. Still, Ravenshaw's estimates would have some deficit of food grain (1 million tons) and the estimated deficit of the authors of *Famine Histories* would be somewhat more (Table 3.3). But the main point to be emphasized here is that Ravenshaw wanted to show that the rice crop did not fail to such an extent as to warrant a declaration of famine in Orissa. In fact, implicitly he kept on assuming that there was plenty of stock in the Orissa Division. But the authors of *Famine Histories* pointed out that the output decline in Orissa did warrant to declare a famine. Coupled with the loss of crops, neither the revenue nor the rent of November 1865 was remitted

TABLE 3.3 ESTIMATES OF FOOD AVAILABILITY IN THE FAMINE OF 1866

Categories	*Ravenshaw's Estimate*	*Famine Histories' Estimate*
Normal area	2, 247, 056 acres	2, 424, 000 acres
Standard yield	10 maunds of clean rice[44]	14 maunds of clean rice
Normal output	22.5 million maunds of clean rice	33.9 million maunds of clean rice
Population in 1865 Adults	2.5 million 2 million	3.7 million 3 million around
Consumption requirement	6 maunds of clean rice per person per year	6 maunds of clean rice per person per year
Normal requirement of the population	15 million maunds of clean rice	22.2 million maunds of clean rice
Surplus	7½ million maunds of clean rice	11.7 million maunds of clean rice
Area under[45] rice in 1865-6	Same as above	Same as above
Condition factor in 1865-6.	½	⅓
Total output in 1865-6	11.25 million maunds of rice	11.3 million maunds of rice
Consumption requirement	Same as above	½ seers per day of 4.6 maunds per person per year
Sufficiency of output in 1866	4.25 million deficient	7 million maunds of clean rice was deficient in 1865-6

Sources: GOI/Home/Public, January 1867, No. 958 from Commr OD to the Secy. BR, GOB, dt. 1 November 1866; *Famine Histories 1885*, pp. 42 and 45; None of the authors took into account the requirement of seed. According to Maddox, one acre of land required 1 maund of paddy: *Maddox Report 1890-1900*, vol. 1, para 187.

and the zamindars and *raiyats* had to sell their harvest produce at a price which was much lower than the prices of other times of the year.[46]

Expectations and Anxieties during Times of Price Rise

All the series on prices during this period showed that prices rose considerably within a span of 11 months. (Information on retail price of rice was available from several sources.) The Famine Commission, 1866 had consulted all the available official sources and had brought out a weekly series on prices starting from last week of October 1865 till the end of December 1866. Another series of prices of paddy, rice and other substitutes of rice and cotton was available for selected years, namely 1860, 1865, 1866 and 1867 from the Inundation Committee Report, 1869. *Famine History* (1885) also published a monthly price list for the above period. Finally, *Utkal Dipika*, the first Oriya weekly, also published some information on prices from August 1866 onwards.

The main limitation of all these lists was that they were underestimates. First, the price lists were collected from the district headquarters only. Nobody knew as to what was happening in the rural areas. Second, the series on annual average retail price as well as that of Inundation list on prices showed that prices rose to the highest level in the year 1866 compared to 1860. In addition, the second series also showed that the prices of the substitutes of rice moved in the same direction as that of rice. Next year, the prices of substitutes fell more sharply than that of rice. The *Utkal Dipika* list on prices showed that prices of rice started declining after October 1866. Taking October 1865 as the base period, it was noticed that the average weekly price of rice rose by more than twice in Puri, but by more than four times in Cuttack and Balasore by October 1866. The monthly price series also showed the same phenomenon. But the supply did not expand sufficiently. In June 1866, it was pointed out by the Department of Public Works that much of the money allotted to it could not be spent because people did not accept wages but demanded food[47] (see Table 3.4). The fact that people did not accept money but demanded rice instead, showed

TABLE 3.4: APPROXIMATE PRICE OF COMMON RICE IN POORE (PURI), CUTTACK AND BALASORE GIVEN IN *SEERS* PER RUPEES FROM OCTOBER 1865-DECEMBER 1866

	Poore	*Cuttack*	*Balasore*	*Average*
Latter part of October 1865	8-13	8-15	11-16	12
Week ending 13 November 1865	8	12	15	11⅔
Week ending 27 November 1865	11²⁄₄	10²⁄₄	16	12⅔
Week ending 11 December 1865	12	11¼	16	13¼
Week ending 28 December 1865	14	14	14	14
Week ending 8 January 1866	13²⁄₄	14	13	13½
Week ending 15 January 1866	12²⁄₄	12	13	12½
Week ending 29 January 1866	8¾	11¼	10	10
Week ending 5 February 1866	8¾	9½	11	9¾
Week ending 19 February 1866	8½	9	9	9
Week ending 5 March 1866	8¼	9¼	9½	9
Week ending 19 March 1866	8¼	9¼	10	9⅙
Week ending 2 April 1866	7½	7½	7½	7½
Week ending 16 April 1866	7¾	6¼	8½	7⅓
Week ending 30 April 1866	6¼	6	8	6¾
Week ending 7 May 1866	6¼	6¼	8	7
Week ending 14 May 1866	6¾	6	8	7
Week ending 18 May 1866	6	4¾	6	5½
Week ending 4 June 1866	6	4¾	6½	5¾
Week ending 18 June 1866	5¾	4	5½	5
Week ending 25 June 1866	5¾	4	5	5
Week ending 2 July 1866	6¼	4	5	5
Week ending 16 July 1866	5¾	4½	5½	5¼
Week ending 30 July 1866	5½	5	4¾	5
Week ending 6 August 1866	5½	5½	4½	5⅙
Week ending 20 August 1866	5¾	5	3⅛	4⅝
Week ending 3 September 1866	5½	5	5	5⅙
Week ending 17 September 1866	7⅝	6	6	6½

Week ending 1 October 1866	7¼	7	7	7⅙
Week ending 15 October 1866	7¼	7	9	7¾
Week ending 25 October 1866	7¼	8¼	9	8⅙
Week ending 5 November 1866	0	8	11	9½
Week ending 19 November 1866	0	13¾	17	15⅜
Week ending 3 December 1866	0	15	20	17½
Week ending 17 December 1866	0	10¾	19	14⅞
Week ending 31 December 1866	0	12	15	13½

Source: Orissa Famine (Na'anka): A Documentation of Primary Sources, Orissa State Archives, Bhubaneswar, 2016, XVII, p. 31, nos. 30-1.

that the series constructed by different authorities had underestimated the extent of price rise.

The members of the Board of Revenue as well as the Commissioner of Orissa Division suspected that the village *mahajans*, zamindars and 'agriculturists' had stored some rice throughout the famine period but did not part with it at any cost, since they kept it for their own immediate use or for their dependents.[48] This is supported by the heavy export of rice which started again from Balasore to Calcutta and from Puri to Ganjam in February 1867.[49] Similarly, pack bullocks had started arriving from Balasore to the coastal parganas of Cuttack district, which had suffered most during the famine of 1866. So much so that the Assistant Collector of Cuttack reported to the Collector of Cuttack that he had come across 2,000 to 3,000 pack bullocks at a time being lead towards the coastal parganas. Each bullock was carrying one maund of rice. These bullocks were coming from southwest Balasore.[50] It is true that the movement of grains occurred at least partly because of the new crop, but some of it appears to have come out of past stock.[51]

One reason why zamindars did not part with their stocks was lack of easy communications. Second, transactions in grain were regulated at a 'customary rate', which obviously they could not change overnight. Third, as the Famine Commissioner had also pointed out, the grain traders, including zamindars and *mahajans* were supposedly 'timid' and 'liable to panic'[52] and these fears were further heightened by the fact that the priests of the Puri temple had predicted three years of famine in Orissa Division.[53] (This judgement was unfair to the trader and others, as we shall see argue later.)

Again, the law and order situation deteriorated during the famine period. Food riots broke out, especially in Puri. The Collector of Puri had asked for special enforcement of police to deal with the food riots. This would have made the zamindars and grain dealers more apprehensive. Early in October 1865, all the grain shops of Cuttack town were closed down but were re-opened again the next day. Panic closings were repeated again later. Ganjam district, which depended on Orissa Division for rice, also experienced similar panic closure of shops. Ravenshaw explained this phenomenon as being due to 'connivance among the dealers' in Cuttack.[54] He had advised the Collector not to interfere since he was confident that the market forces would take care of the situation.[55] However, the Famine Commissioners of 1866 pointed out that the traders did not collude but there was a spontaneous move at the prospects of the crop even though it looked as if they had conspired.[56]

Though the Famine Commission blamed the local dealers for not taking risks, they realized the immense problems which the transport bottleneck had created for private traders. The seaport of Balasore remained closed for country boats in the monsoons.[57] Second, the land route from Midnapur was a muddy road, and during the rainy season it was impossible to cart rice on this road.[58] Moreover, an unprecedented flood in August 1866 in Orissa made things worse.

However, there were some exceptions, given the limited transport facilities. Some traders in the borders of Ganjam and Puri did respond to the price rise and sent rice to and fro through Chilika Lake.[59] Some of the traders even tried to bring rice from western Orissa through the flooded Mahanadi.[60] But it was not enough to bring down the prices. Due to this and other factors, the social environment was full of tension.

Crimes and Protests

Famine-time incidents of violence and protests have an interesting pattern, which may have diverse manifestations and consequences. But they tell more than the records of the time may seek to convey.

Some scholars believe that Indian people were so docile that they never agitated in the wake of the severe famines during the British regime, though interestingly, according to the *Encyclopedia Britannica* the first signs of imminent occurrence of a famine is increase in crime rate[61] and aimless wandering of the people. Many cite the case of the Potato Famine in Ireland in 1845-9, where out of 8 million people about one million people died and a large number emigrated. It is also true that large-scale thefts, arson, etc., took place during that period, but it did not result in rebelling against the government or the Queen's country.[62] In India's case, O'Grada observed that the increase in crime rate was the first signal of the famine. He was referring to the later day entries in the India Famine Code, 1880. The offence had a distinct feature, namely, food snatchings, and looting of shops, granaries and the like. Notably, the looters were mostly women and children. In case of the famine of 1942-3 in Russia, the looters were men and women from all age groups. Stalin dealt with them heavily by putting many of them to death. In an earlier instance of a famine in 1332 in France, the criminals were also convicted and dealt with a heavy hand.

O'Grada, however, noted that the relationship between famine and crime rate was not linear. People often resigned to their fate in the phase of starvation because they were too emaciated and weak to make demands for food. For example, the starving poor completely surrendered to their fate during the Bengal Famine of 1943. But in the Ethiopia famines of 1972-3 and 1985-6, when the government failed to provide relief, it led to the overthrow of the regime.[63] In recent decades, famines of that magnitude may have been rare in South Asia, though famine-like situations appear in many areas and children and women suffer from acute malnutrition partly due to shortage of food. But in case of Africa, famines continue to occur frequently due to political conflicts, ethnic strife, civil wars and rivalry between autocratic rulers, resulting in political crimes and mass starvation.[64]

As with the case of the Irish Famine, it would appear that people in Orissa during the famine of 1866 too did not revolt against the government. Based on government reports and the accounts in the contemporary press, one may rule out mutiny-like events and nor did people blame the government for the food shortage. Rather they blamed it on their fate. It is also to be noted, as discussed in the next chapter, it were the priests of the Jagannath Temple who looted the famine victims by luring them into the temple with the promise of serving them rice. After giving them their first meal, they kept all their ornaments and threw hot water on them to evict the relief-seekers from the temple compound.

However, minor revolts against zamindars did break out, according to some reports. If we collate them, it would seem as protests against the regime as well the local zamindars. In several cases, the rioters burnt down the granaries of the zamindars, 'making them paupers', as some reports put it. Ramakhoy Chaterjee, the Deputy Collector of Puri district, reported that there were a large number of shop lootings, snatchings of sacred offerings from the temple, and burning down of granaries in March and April 1866, just after the harvest.[65] Commissioner Ravenshaw reported the same thing for Balasore as well. Further, he also noted that the crimes started occurring from April 1865 onwards when the first pinch of scarcity was felt. In Mayurbhanj, a princely state under the Orissa Division, riots broke out due to food scarcity. Therefore, Ravenshaw quickly finished writing his note on the Divison and hurriedly left for Mayurbhanj.[66] It is noteworthy that two different currents of nationalist feelings emerged out of the Irish and Orissa cases. The Potato Famine in Ireland led to the alienation of the people and paved the way for the rise of Irish nationalism against British rule. In case of the people of Orissa, the 1866 famine triggered currents that laid a strong foundation for Oriya nationalism and finally Orissa (and Sindh) became the first states in British India constituted on the basis of language in 1936.

Role of Press

In 1990, Amartya Sen highlighted the role of a free press in preventing large-scale deaths and other serious consequences during famines and pointed it out as a positive factor in liberal democracies.[67] For instance, the famine of 1958-60 in China resulted in more than 30 million deaths because of the lack of a free press, which could have spread the information on food scarcity and there would have been perhaps national and international steps to move supplies of food grains from other parts of China or from outside. Since every People's Commune was pursuing the policy of producing adequate grains for its own consumption, under the policy of self-reliance, they tried to manage the food crisis all by themselves and miserably failed. Even though there are disputes regarding the number of famine deaths – ranging from 3 to 30 million – the fact that millions died in the 1950s in a country where an agrarian revolution had succeeded, was a blot which cannot be forgotten in history.[68] Subsequent famines in the world in Sub-Saharan Africa, especially Ethiopia and Somalia, and the war-riven regions in other parts of Africa such as Sudan, got quick publicity in the world press, resulting in many voluntary agencies such as the Disaster Relief International (DRI) appearing on the scene along with the United Nations. Today, electronic media and satellite communications have made it possible for the world community to come to the aid during any distress situation in any part of the world.

The press not only publicizes scarcity of food grains, but more importantly its unavailability to particular sections of a population, because in a liberal democracy the government is supposed to have a social commitment to look after all sections of the society, which may not necessarily be the case of a dictatorial polity. Unfortunately for Orissa, the local press was almost completely absent during the colonial period. Hence the government of Bengal Presidency, of which Orissa was a part, was unaware of the ground reality and the gravity of the situation. In February 1866 the Deputy Magistrate of the Relief Committee did write a strong official appeal to the newspaper, *Patriot* published from Calcutta, on 5 March 1866, urging people to send money for relief. A similar appeal was printed in April 1866 in the newspaper *Englishman*, also published from Calcutta.[69] But both these appeals were meant for raising contributions for the relief operation. These appeals did not describe the magnitude of the famine. It was only on 2 May 1866 that the *Englishman* carried a heart-wrenching appeal in the form of a letter narrating the magnitude of the suffering, which shook the English rulers in England. The caption of the letter was 'Starving Poor of Orissa'. Apart from that the press in London, the US, Australia and New Zealand also started reporting about the famine in India. Most of them continued to report about the sufferings of the people and made scathing attacks on the administration till 1867. Some of the press correspondents found it difficult to report about the famine from such long distance, hence they began setting up local offices in India. The correspondents had some idea about the Irish Potato Famine and they thought that there would be an inevitable pattern. But when they actually saw the magnitude of the sufferings of the famine victims in Orissa, they realized the extent and dimensions of the damage and started critiquing the colonial administration. One press reporter even wrote that a man killed all his family members just to get rid of hunger. Besides, cases of cannibalism were also reported.[70] It was because of the press attack that the colonial rulers became concerned about their faults and went overboard and formulated major new policies to address future famines. They mobilized resources, spent money for relief and became so careful that in the 1874 Bihar famine, not a single life was lost.

There was no local newspaper till September 1866 when the *Utkal Dipika*, an Oriya weekly began to be published from Cuttack. By that time the intensity of the famine was over, at least officially. The *Utkal Dipika* carried vivid details about the famine situation in many areas, including the pitiable condition of the famine migrants to Calcutta.[71] In other places too many vernacular presses reported the famine deaths. These reports publicized the failure of the administration in containing the famine. In response, the colonial government decided to regulate and curtail the freedom of expression by enacting the Vernacular Press Act in 1878.[72]

Role of Government

Government imports were needed badly to dampen prices and make food grains available. Unfortunately, the members of the Board of Revenue in Bengal Presidency and of course Commissioner Ravenshaw were so much committed to the ideology of *laissez faire* that they did not wish to interfere with the operation of the market forces. The Famine Commission devoted considerable space in its Report to narrate the actual situation as to how the members of the Board were satisfied with just giving orders to collect price data; how the Lieutenant Governor (sitting in Calcutta!) declined to interfere with the market prices, and how the Board members declined to import rice as late as June 1866.[73]

Finally, in June 1866, the Board agreed to import rice. But by then the rainy season had set in and the sea had become rough, so the import of rice had become more difficult. There was only one muddy road linking Calcutta with Puri where only bullock carts could move. Some traders did try to bring paddy but those got wet because of the heavy rain. Moreover, when some stock did arrive, the starving people literally snatched them away and devoured them immediately without even cooking it. This led to many deaths. On the whole, the Famine Commission blamed the Board of Revenue and the Lieutenant Governor of Bengal as well as the Commissioner of Orissa Division for not taking proper action in time.[74]

Relief Policy

There was no systematic famine code to regulate the administration of relief in the famine of 1866. Here it should be recollected that Britain had encountered an intense famine in Ireland, which lasted for four years from 1845-9 in which nearly a million people died of starvation and a million more emigrated from Ireland. But the colonial rulers did not seem have learnt any lesson from it.[75] In case of India, the Orissa famine was so intense that it had no parallel at that time. At the same time, we must note that there was a famine in 1860-1 in Doab where around 2 million people had died.

Even though there was no clearly formulated famine relief policy, still the administration of relief was guided by certain considerations. The first and foremost consideration, and we have referred to it repeatedly for good reasons, was the adherence to the *laissez faire* principles of Adam Smith, according to which, the market would take care of demand and supply of rice by adjusting prices. Coupled with that, the administrators were also influenced by Thomas Malthus' principle of population, which predicted inevitable doom, unless the growth rate of population was checked.[76] Hence, as Ira Klein has pointed out, 'Millions of lives were sacrificed in the 19th century because the pull of humanitarianism on the government was not so strong as the claims of Malthusianism and Social Darwinism.'[77] Thus the administrators tried to keep the cost of relief as low as possible.[78] Another factor which influenced the administration of relief, was the Poor Law in England meant to reduce the cost of looking after the poor.[79] So they kept debating whether people needing relief should work to earn wages.[80]

Being influenced by all these factors, the administrators did not start relief measures, except in Puri, till May 1866. When it did start, the main thrust of relief policy was the reliance on normal work projects of the Department of Public Works. The mode of payment was money wages. Later on, those who were fit enough, were employed in light labour. The nature of work ranged from excavation of canals to construction of embankments and roads.[81] Piece-rate was adopted. Gangs of relief workers consisting of able-bodied persons used to be formed to complete certain tasks. After the completion of that task, wages were distributed equally among the individual members of the gang. Hence the weak, women and children were not admitted to the gangs. The irony was that women and children needed relief the most more than the able-bodied persons, most of whom migrated elsewhere.[82]

A person used to get 3 *annas* per day as wage in the public works.[83] Let us find out whether a family of four adults (though at that time the number would have been more) could have subsisted or got their minimum calorie requirement with that amount of wage in May 1866. On 7 May 1866, rice was selling at the rate of less than one and a half paise per *seer* which rose to two paise per *seer* in the month of June. So a person who was getting three *annas* would be able to get little more than one *seer* at the first instance and later on he would be able to get 5/8 of a *seer* per day only. But four adults required minimum two *seers* of rice to survive.[84] In addition, prices were only notional. Thus it could be concluded that the money wage was below subsistence. As we will see later, general labourers fled from work as it did not provide them with subsistence.

Similarly, the distribution of gratuitous relief was not guided by the physical needs of the famine victims but was mostly guided by the number of recipients and total quantity of grain available at that moment. Hence the most needy people often could not get relief if they came late or if the able-bodied persons elbowed them out effectively.[85] That relief was never adequate is also evident from the comments of the Famine Commission of 1866:

> And that, in truth, it was not caste nor caste prejudice that was the main cause, as we think very evident from the fact that it is stated on all hands that by far the greatest loss of life has fallen on those lower castes who had least caste prejudice, whose manner of life least unfitted them to avail themselves of public relief and who were most accustomed to labour.[86]

Lower caste people were the largest number of those who had died during the famine. But other caste groups too suffered casualties. We shall discuss this later in this chapter. Some aspects of the relief policy will be taken up in the next chapter for a detailed analysis, despite some overlapping.

The government finally did import rice from Burma. Some amount of wheat was imported as well. But people were accustomed to eating only par-boiled rice and the Burmese rice was not par-boiled; several people died after eating this rice due to bowel complaints. Similarly, in the relief camps, not only the amount of relief was inadequate but food was served under very insanitary conditions leading to the outbreak of cholera epidemics. Further, even though wheat was imported, there were no flour mills to grind it. Besides the Oriyas were not in the habit of eating *roti* made from wheat flour. The starving people were served raw rice in many relief camps. Since they were starving, they could not wait to cook them and ate them raw and fell sick and many died of starvation. Post-mortem of bodies showed that their stomachs were full of raw rice! The living conditions of the relief camps were not hygienically satisfactory. The camp tents were pitched on places such as the damp ground of Puri beach. The inmates of the camps were forced to sleep on straw mats. As a result, many famine victims died of fever and pneumonia in large numbers. Thus the relief policy was neither adequate nor people-friendly.

Different Estimates of Mortality

The mortality data is unreliable because nobody actually knew the population figure before the famine and how many were dead or missing during the famine period. (The first population Census took place only in 1872.) Moreover, no on-the-spot enquiry was done during the famine. Still, two important estimates are available on mortality: estimates of the Deputy Collectors which were submitted in July 1867, and that of the authorities of the *Famine Histories, 1885.* They are worth discussing here briefly because scholars working on the famine of 1866 have generally accepted one or the other.[87]

In 1867, there were some efforts to collect statistics on famine deaths. The deputy collectors visited places where half the population was estimated to have died. Besides, the zamindars were asked to fill up forms regarding the population, mortality and emigration. When in doubt, the Deputy Collector went to check the statistics compiled by the agents of the zamindars but they too had to depend on the same agents for collection of data on the ground. According to the enquiry conducted by the deputy collectors, the population of Orissa Division was higher by 15,000 in 1865 than the previous estimate given by the Famine Commissioner of 1866. Accordingly, the mortality figure was also raised to 8,09,564 or to 27 per cent approximately.[88] Even this was an underestimate as will be seen presently. The break up of mortality by each district was 29 per cent for Cuttack, 32 per cent for Puri and 33 per cent for Balasore.[89]

The authors of *Famine Histories* stated that the 1867 enquiry

TABLE 3.5: STATEMENT SHOWING MORTALITY IN PURI DISTRICT (EXCLUSIVE OF KHORDHA)

Name of Pargana (A)	*No. of Inhabitants before the famine (B)*	*No. of persons after the famine (C)*	*No. of person dead (D)*	*Person dead in percentage (E)*	*No. of persons counted (C+D)*	*Difference in Actual No. (F)*	*Percentage Difference (G)*
Malood	3,329	1,818	1,617	48.57	3,435	106	3.09
Budgercote	3,813	1,947	1,896	49.72	3,843	30	0.78
Pegh. Parricood	10,235	4,433	6,802	66.46	11,235	1,000	8.90
Manikpatana	6,104	1,027	4,477	73.35	5,504	-600	-10.90
Chowbeescood	28,654	9,727	18,927	66.05	28,654	0	0.00
Seerae	11,384	3,966	7,418	65.16	11,384	0	0.00
Rahan	48,182	20,663	27,519	57.11	48,182	0	0.00
Limbhal	41,896	37,896	4,000	9.55	41,896	0	0.00
Kotrahang	30,889	27,889	3,000	9.71	30,889	0	0.00
Puschimdoaee	18,326	16,828	1,498	8.17	18,326	0	0.00
Poorboodoaee	13,829	8,395	5,434	39.29	13,829	0	0.00
Kotdes	93,424	53,603	39,821	42.62	93,424	0	0.00
Banchas	10,067	5,781	4,286	42.57	10,067	0	0.00
Uttuis	13,447	7,561	5,886	43.77	13,447	0	0.00
Antorodh	20,683	10,663	10,020	48.45	20,683	0	0.00
Asturung	2,293	746	1,548	67.51	2,294	1	0.04
Kurlo	10,920	5,233	5,687	52.08	10,920	0	0.00

Kodhar	14,102	6,622	7,480	53.04	14,102	0	0.00
Marichipur	7,449	3,222	4,227	56.75	7,449	0	0.00
Domarkband	2,445	6,832	913	37.34	7,745	5,300	68.43
Total	4,01,501	2,34,145	1,67,356				
Actual	3,91,471	2,34,852	1,62,456		3,97,308	5,837	
Difference	10,030	-707	4,900	46.86			

Note: The no. of inhabitants before the famine do not correspond to exact numbers. This anomaly can be due to distress migration because of famine.

Source: Compiled by the police up to October 1866; put in by Baboo Ramakoy Chatterjee, Deputy Collector. Orissa Famine (Na'anka) 1866-7, A Documentary of Primary Sources. Orissa State Archives, Bhubaneswar, June 2016, p. 174.

had underestimated the 1866 mortality. They pointed out that when the survivors were put at 20,86,000 in 1867, the absolute number of deaths was put at 8,09,561. When the figure for the survivors was raised to 27,00,000; the death figure should also have been raised by the same proportion. Thus, it should have been at least one million or 27 per cent.[90]

It is likely that even the estimate of famine mortality done by the authors of *Famine Histories* was too low because they had considered only the *starvation phase* of the famine which continued till the end of 1867, but they had not considered mortality beyond 1867. If we include the *epidemic phase* of the famine which invariably followed the famine (especially Indian famines), the death rate would not have come back to the level of non-famine years till 1868, on a conservative estimate. It might have even continued longer. Moreover, the authors of *Famine Histories* assumed that most of the emigrants would have come back. But the experience of later famines showed that the emigrants were more exposed to infection than the native population and thus ran the risk of death almost in the same proportion as that of the native population, if not greater. For both these reasons it appears that the mortality rate during the famine of 1866 would have been higher than one million.

That the famine mortality rate was an underestimate will be clear if we consider Table 3.5 above. The table clearly shows that the death rates varied from 68 to 10 per cent of the population of the Parganas of Puri district. Of course, one may argue that the data reflected the micro picture. But it revealed many things. For instance, the *chowkidars* who were responsible for collecting the data might have omitted to count many dead bodies who had died due to cholera epidemic and they always omitted to count women and girl children who had died. Later on the police might have given the guestimates only. So based on the above table, one may argue that there was a strong possibility of underestimation of deaths and migration. Table 3.6 shows the percentage of deaths in Orissa Division.

TABLE 3.6(A): PERCENTAGE DISTRIBUTION OF DEATHS

Number of deaths among agriculturists which were predominantly *pahi raiyats* and who also worked as labourers	10,262	4.5
Bona fide labouring class	11,262	4.8
Artisan classes	13,681	5.8

Source: GOI/Home/Public, January 1868, nos. 21-2, pt. A; 'Final Report on Mortality during the Late Famine'.

TABLE 3.6B : DISTRIBUTION OF TOTAL FAMINE DEATHS AND CLASS COMPOSITION OF DEAD VICTIMS IN THE DISTRICTS CUTTACK, PURI AND BALASORE IN 1866 FAMINE

	Total Deaths	*Cultivators*	*Labourers***	*Artisans*
Cuttack	3,78,009	1,83,887 (49)*	94,346 (25)	99,776 (26)
Puri	2,13,944	1,01,895 (48)	73,734 (34)	36,333 (17)
Balasore	2,17,608	1,32,997 (61)	39,288 (18)	39,795 (18)
Total	8,09,561	4,18,779 (51)	2,09,368 (26)	1,81,414 (22)

Notes: * Figure in parentheses are percentages.
** The figures under this head leave out the labourers who died in Puri town (4,908) and those who died in Balasore town (3,411) and those coming to Balasore town from other places (2,117).
Source: Same as Table 3.6(A).

Famine, Sex-Differential Mortality and Out-migration

We shall discuss the above aspects in subsequent chapters in some detail. Here we shall mention these dimensions briefly to give a fuller picture of the 1866 famine.

The Revenue Secretary to the Government of Bengal remarked that the old and young died in larger numbers in 1866.[91] The Sanitary Commission of 1868 stated that the famine had affected the aged, sickly and the infirm in particular.[92] Again, Hunter pointed out in 1872 that the rural population would enter a famine as a 'frigate goes into battle, cleared of all useless and inefficient member'.[93] That meant children, women and the old and the sick were left behind to meet their fate.

The evidence of sex-differential mortality is not fully reliable. A clergyman named Buckley who was very active during the famine, had set-up several orphanages and recruited many orphans during the famine. He reported to the Commissioner that the boys of the orphanage looked healthier than the girls, and also had a lower death rate.[94] The experience of adults was apparently different. The Commissioner of Orissa Division noted the observation made by the Collector of Balasore that more males than females had disappeared. Four women came to the relief centres for every one man.[95] Again, according to the Famine Commissioner of 1866, 'The very old of both sexes have probably succumbed. But there remain a large number of elderly women who have survived by the aid of public relief....'[96]

Hunter, on the other hand, gave a very different picture of famine mortality in the Hugli (Bengal district) relief centre. There the recorded death rate of women and children (of both sexes) was higher than for men (Famine migrants of Orissa flocked to Hugli on their way to Calcutta).[97]On the basis of the slender evidence available, it appears that the male death rate was not higher than the female death rate in every age group in 1866. The famine of 1866 had occurred at a time when Orissa Division was quite isolated. Still it did generate a lot of mobility, though no accurate figures were available.

The emigration statistics for the famine of 1866 were collected in June and July 1867, along with the statistics of mortality. As mentioned earlier, the zamindars were given forms to fill up information on the emigration statistics along with death statistics. The data on emigration related to the number of emigrants who had left at the beginning of the famine and interestingly did not include distress migration during the various stages of the famine of 1866.[98] According to the authorities, nearly, 4 per cent of the estimated population of 1865 of Orissa Division had emigrated during the famine period.[99] If distress migration were included then the figure would be much more.

It should be noted that the Famine Commissioner did not take into account migration and the resultant deaths which occurred in the aftermath of the famine. A large number of Chhatrakhias could not tolerate the insult of losing their caste status and migrated to the British colonies overseas to join occupations such as the cultivation of sugar cane and rubber plantations in Southeast Asia, Mauritius, Burma, Guyana, Fiji, etc. They were mostly agricultural labourers, small cultivators and artisans from Orissa. Since they were the first timers going overseas and were not aware of the hardships of a sea voyage, many died on the way. There also occurred epidemics in the ships and took a heavy toll, of which we do not have the exact figures.[100] We have discussed these aspects in a systematic manner in the chapter on migration.

Occupational Structure of Famine Victims

In one respect the famine of 1866 was different from the other famines in Orissa. In this famine the *raiyats* (small farmers), agricultural labourers and artisans all died in large numbers. Some of the small zamindars and relatively well-to-do *raiyats* were also affected to some extent. (In later famines of Orissa Division only marginal *raiyats* were affected along with agricultural labourers and weavers.) Tables 3.6a, and 3.6b show that the largest number of deaths was among the cultivators, reflecting two facts: the percentage of cultivators to total population was high; second, the cultivator category may have contained a category of *raiyats* who had uneconomic holdings and hence hired themselves out as labourers but were included as *raiyats*. To this extent the distinction between marginal *raiyats* and pure agricultural labourers is blurred.

We give below a large number of case studies from official investigations during and after the famine of 1866 and some reports of missionaries and private records in addition to the other official data. Despite the lack of systematic and reliable information, we can still get a clear idea about the class and caste dimension of famine mortality from these sources.

The Famine Commission of 1866, however, concluded that

the calamity had affected all classes of people but the agricultural labourers and artisans suffered more than the *raiyats.* The Commission observed that *raiyats* suffered more because of the indirect effects of the famine, but the other two classes suffered from both direct and indirect effects of famine. 'But in other respects the testimony is universal that the calamity of the famine fell with, by far the greatest severity on the wage labourers, the agricultural labourers, coolies and small artisans. Among the latter [included were] the weavers, already plying a declining trade.'[101]

Other references by collectors and missionaries also showed that the *raiyats*, agricultural labourers and artisans suffered greatly from the famine. For example, a small sample survey of 55 houses in a village near the town of Balasore had been conducted in 1866 to ascertain the impact of famine and cholera on different castes from October 1865 to October 1866 (Table 3.7). Cholera was already rampant in the first phase of the famine till June but after the heavy rainfall in July both fever and cholera played havoc. The last column 'Gone', can be interpreted as emigrated or dead. The Collector stated that the villagers themselves were not sure whether those people had died or emigrated. Of course, the sample is very small, but it still sheds interesting light on the caste incidence of the famine.

The famine affected different castes differently. The most affected caste was the lower backward caste Bhumibehera, in whose case the loss was 100 per cent, next to them was another cultivating caste Kodal. Both the castes were small cultivators and had few assets. Next in the order of suffering were the weavers. The pastoral caste Goala, of course, would suffer during the famine, because cattle were badly affected by the scarcity. But it is surprising that in this village the Dalit agricultural labourers or Kandaras, and the professional beggars did not suffer much. We have no figures on them for deaths or out-migration. The number of agricultural labourers, it is true, was so small in number that the situation in this one village proves nothing. But the professional beggars were more numerous, and the report on them having survived is puzzling since one would expect private charity to dry up during the famine. It might have happened that they went to the

TABLE 3. 7: STATEMENT SHOWING THE EFFECTS OF THE FAMINE AND CHOLERA ON BHASKARGANJGE VILLAGE NEAR BALASORE TOWN BETWEEN 1865 AND OCTOBER 1866

Caste or Class	*Persons in 1865*	*Persons Gone in 1866*	*Per centage in parenthesis*	*Occupation*	*Remarks*
Kodal	34	22	12 (35)*	All small cultivators	Of these 3 persons lived together in one house and left together most probably to Calcutta
Gaur	25	20	5 (20)	Pastoral Caste	–
Kandara	4	4	0	Landless labourers	–
Raju	16	13	3 (19)	Cultivators	–
Khandait	30	25	5 (17)	Cultivators	–
Karan	13	12	1 (8)	Petty revenue officials	–
Teli	32	29	3 (9)	Oil presser	–
Tanti	58	46	12 (21)	Weavers	–
Maganta	31	31	0	Professional Beggars	–

(contd.)

TABLE 3.7 (contd.)

Caste or Class	*Persons in 1865*	*Persons Gone in 1866*	*Per centage in parenthesis*	*Occupation*	*Remarks*
Musalmans	17	13	4 (24)	–	They lived together and migrated to Midnapur
Christians	31	28	3 (10)	–	Altogether there were five households, there deaths which had occurred among them were either due to dysentery or cholera and not starvation.
Bhumibehera	3	–	3 (100)	Not known	All of them lived together and the villagers did not know whether they had died or migrated
Total	346	294	52 (15)		

Note : * Figures in parentheses are percentages.

Source: GOB/Home/Public, 11 October 1866, no. 350, from the Collector, Balasore to the Commissioner, Orissa Division.

nearby Balasore town which was *en route* the pilgrim city, to beg and thus might have survived. The sample survey in contrast to official statistics showed that the death or migration rate of small cultivators was more than that of the labouring population.

While analysing the reasons for excessive deaths among the labouring class, one of the Deputy Collectors of Cuttack who visited a group of *parganas* nearer the city of Cuttack had included the *pahi* (migrant) *raiyats* also. The *pahi raiyats* incidentally depended partly on the proceeds of wages. The death rate among these *raiyats* were also very high.[102]

Ravenshaw pointed out that in the localities in Cuttack such as Kujang and Aul, where the famine was very acute, the mortality was estimated to be 50 to 60 per cent of the poorer classes, and only one-eighth to one-tenth of the richer classes.[103] The majority of the agricultural labourers and artisans belonged to the poorer class. He also noted that the famine hit most the Bauris, Tantis, Doms and Chasas, who did not have any reserve of money or grain to fall back upon.[104] In 1872, W.W. Hunter, the Scottish historian and a member of the ICS, wrote that most of the salt manufacturing landless labourers, who were from the castes of Chasas (peasant caste), Keutas (fishermen caste), the Dalit castes Bauris and Kandaras (also agricultural labourer castes) and Irikas, were swept away by the famine of 1866 and so much so that workers for salt manufacturing had to be later imported from the Madras Presidency.[105]

Rev. William Miller, who had lived for 20 years in Orissa as a missionary before the famine of 1866, gave evidence that the Bauri and other lower castes died in greater numbers than the upper castes for two reasons. First, the government relief was not adequate, so much so that the lower castes,who went to relief centres died in greater number for various reasons discussed elsewhere. Second, the Bauris and other lower castes lived hand to mouth on daily wages whereas the *raiyats* had other assets like bullocks and brass vessels to sell before they became paupers.[106]

As pointed out earlier, in 1867, the Deputy Collectors had gone to the worst affected *parganas* to verify the death figures given by the zamindars. One of them pointed out that there was a great loss of life among the artisans in Hariharpur *pargana* in Cuttack district. In one village alone about 600, principally weavers, had died.[107]

The deputy collector of Cuttack had visited another group of 15 *parganas* situated within a range of 1 to 24 miles from the post office of the city of Cuttack. The deaths were only 15 per cent, considerably less than in other *parganas*, but here too labouring and artisan castes died in greater proportion than the other castes. He gave the mortality figures and percentage distribution of deaths on the basis of that visit.

The Deputy Collector also identified the 'bona fide labouring class' as Panas, Kandaras, Bhois – all Dalit castes and Sabars – the Adivasis. These were the castes who, according to the official, came in hundreds to steal the horned cattle and also used some of them for meat. They were in fact, he said, the original cultivators of the soil now turned into labourers.[108]

The Deputy Collector also pointed out that the above *parganas* were near the city of Cuttack. Since the people of the city required the services of manual and skilled labourers, they were attached to those *parganas*. But he did not explain the link between the excess number of artisans and the disproportionately high mortality. Perhaps, at the onset of famine, their regular employment channels had dried up before those of the other groups and hence the excessive number of deaths. The deputy collector also pointed out that in certain villages in those *parganas* the weavers died 'in hundreds'.[109]

In Khorda subdivision of Puri, in the biggest government estate where the relief work had started earlier, the lower classes suffered terrible mortality. The deputy collector wrote that the small *raiyats* died in large numbers as they did not have sufficient food storage, having sold whatever stocks they had. But the maximum number of deaths occurred among the labouring class. He reported that many of them had little patches of land, but the chief source of their income was wages in kind or cash. They did not have enough stocks of grain to support themselves. Their source of income had dried up because of crop failure. So the labouring classes, mainly Bauris, were the earliest and the most numerous victims of the famine. The clusters of huts of Bauris were desolate along the coastal villages. He pointed out that the poorer class of artisans also suffered severely. They too were dependent on their daily earnings, but at the time of famine their services were not needed. He included fishermen, weavers and carpenters among the artisans.[110]

Similar reports also came from the worst affected *parganas* of Balasore.[111] Thus the victims of the famine were from all occupational categories, except the very substantial *raiyats* and bigger zamindars. Among them the agricultural labourers, artisans and small *raiyats* – a high proportion from Dalit castes – suffered most.[112]

Reasons for such Suffering

Fall in Wages of the Labourers

It might be argued that money wages were very rarely paid and were confined to the towns. But on the eve of crop failure, employers may have switched from kind to cash payment. The collector of Balasore wrote in April 1866 that the agricultural labourers did not receive their payment in the form of paddy due to scanty crop of the previous season in some areas at least.[113] Besides, the wages on public works and irrigation works at a later stage of the famine were paid in cash. We have some scattered data on actual money wages, i.e. the wages paid to the coolies by the salt contractors and wages paid by the public works. On 6 December 1865 the Collector of Puri, had visited the salt tracts. There he found that the salt contractors had employed some dozens of coolies and about 40 carts to carry salt to the coast. He mentioned that each cart was getting 7 *annas* per 100 maunds of salt but each coolie was getting two paise only. So he suggested that the daily wages should be raised to four paise. However, it is not known whether the wages were in fact raised. Even if it were raised, at current prices it would just suffice for one meal per person per day. It was also reported that the coolies would rather collect *saag* (edible green leaves) and eat rather than carry salt for a meagre wage.[114] There is no data on the price of the cattle feed or the adequacy of the cartman's wages.

Most likely the price of cattle feed had increased during the famine period because of the bad quality of the straw, so the cartman must have spent more on cattle feed in order to keep the cattle fit. At the same time, he had to spend more to maintain himself in the face of the price rise.

The wage paid in the famine relief works as well as by the irrigation company was also below subsistence, especially during the intense phase of the famine. (Later on the Commissioner of Orissa pleaded that even the daily money wage rate of three *annas* was not enough and recommended that it should be raised to eight *annas*. He argued that the current rate was sufficient during a period of prosperity but not enough when prices were so high.[115] At the price ruling during May, it may have been sufficient for one meal but in June or July 1866 it would not have been sufficient for even one meal.

That the money wage paid by the public works department was below subsistence was also evident from the reports given by both the superintending engineer of Cuttack and the executive engineer, Balasore Division, in May 1866. The Executive Engineer wrote that the coolies and the carpenters fled from public works as they were unable to obtain any rice for consumption at the high rate of Rs. 8 per maund or 5 *seer* a rupee, which was the market rate in Bhadrak subdivision of Balasore.[116] The superintending engineer of Cuttack Circle also supported this view.[117] The officiating superintending engineer, Cuttack Circle, also wrote that the work on Puri Road was progressing slowly as it was difficult to procure rice; he indicated that the daily wage was below 4 *annas*.[118] The irrigation company on the other hand had employed a large number of people from January 1866 to June 1866, and the company was paying the wage partly in kind and partly in cash.[119] For some time the company even served cooked rice to the workers.

Before the famine, a brick-laying worker was able to buy more than 6 *seers* of fine rice with his daily wage of approximately 3 *annas*. But in November 1865 he could purchase barely 2 *seers* of rice with his daily wage. This should be read keeping in mind the fact that the official list on prices tended to underestimate the extent of actual price rise. Thus even the skilled labourers could not maintain themselves with the prevalent rate of wages in the famine of 1866.

We have evidence from the executive engineer of Kathjori division who told the Famine Commission that the first death from absolute starvation that came under his observation occurred about 20 November 1865. It was a case of a bricklayer drawing Rs. 6 per month. He had a large family to feed and was unable to provide for them. According to him, during February and March there were a great many deaths even among people who were drawing ordinary pay.[120] This was in spite of the fact that the irrigation company had introduced a famine allowance per person drawing less than Rs.10 per month, starting from December.[121]

Decline in Employment Opportunities for Agricultural Labourers

Agricultural labourers received their wages in kind. There is no systematic data on agricultural wages though scanty references indicate that the daily wage rate was 3 *seers* of fine rice during the harvesting season and less than that during the rest of the year.[122] This was sufficient for a family of agricultural labourer, as long as the labourers got employment opportunities. But the amount diminished substantially during the famine for the following reasons. First, the workers from salt manufacture competed for jobs as agricultural labourers after 1860.[123] Second, in 1865, the harvest failed by two-thirds; so the labour requirement for harvesting would have fallen.[124] The decline in employment opportunities was also evident form Anant Das's diary. He wrote that his father, an agricultural labourer, did not get any work and deserted his family in the early months of the famine of 1866.[125] Third, thatching of houses, which was an annual phenomenon also did not take place in full swing perhaps because of inadequate and bad quality of straw.[126] It would also have required a fewer labourers. Many families would have deserted their houses in search of food. Moreover, since the area under summer rice was not very significant, the loss of employment resulting from fewer acres of summer rice would have reduced the employment to some extent.

Previously, in March and April, the relatively well-off *raiyats*, *zamindars* and to some extent the *raiyats* just below the well-off ones, used to make annual contracts with the agricultural labourers for the next year's agricultural operations.[127] During the famine year of 1866, *raiyats* with less grain would not have entered into contracts. Lastly, it was noticed that the area under rice cultivation had declined in the agricultural year of 1866-7, because of lack of agricultural implements.[128]

On the whole, the employment opportunities of the agricultural labourers had shrunk, so they became one of the first victims of the famine along with other labourers.[129] That the agricultural labourers had become unemployed and had suffered from deprivation was also evident from the sudden spurt of crime and grain dacoity. The dacoits belonged to lower castes such as Bauri, Kandara and Pan and the bulk of the agricultural labourers came from those castes.[130]

Thus, the money wage could not keep pace with the rising prices, even though the wage on public works was raised from 2 to 3 *annas*. Moreover, the public works were limited to towns and government estates. The agricultural labourers who were paid in kind suffered a lot because of lack of employment. Hence general labourers and agricultural labourers were the first ones to die of hunger.

Raiyats *who Suffered in the Hands of Zamindars*

One category of small *raiyats* who had no occupancy rights over land suffered almost as much as the agricultural labourers. The other *raiyats* having occupancy rights did somewhat better, though they also suffered.[131]

As mentioned earlier, the first one was known as *pahi raiyats* and the second one was known as *thani*. The *pahi raiyats* took land on market rent. Generally, the market rent was so high that hardly any margin was left with them. Hence at the onset of the famine they fled and wandered here and there.

The rents paid by *thani raiyats* were very high and they also cultivated some land at *pahi* rent (the market rent) to make ends meet, so they could hardly save grain for scarcities. Besides, the unprecedented flood of August 1866 had washed away the standing early rice crops and also some winter rice in the low-lying area. This was a direct loss to the cultivators, small and big alike. Moreover, the zamindars continued to collect the rent due in November 1865 and April 1866. They acted ruthlessly and took away whatever scanty crops the *raiyats* had, saying that they had to pay revenue to the administration. From those who were unable to pay the rent, the zamindars took away cattle, and even tore away their roofs. Further the zaminders also collected various kinds of cess leaving scanty saving with the *raiyats*. The government received numerous petitions about this. The deputy collector conducted enquiries and found that these allegations were true in Cuttack.[132] Similarly, in another tributary mahal, Bisenpur, the new zamindars had entered into a series of law suits to enhance the rent. The accumulated rent was demanded in 1865. In the mean time, the harvest had suffered. In yet another mahal, Kujang, the tenants suffered greatly because the zamindar himself was indebted. There only a small portion of land was cultivated in 1866, and three-fourths of the crop was lost.[133] Thus, the zamindars had aggravated the economic condition of *raiyats* in certain parts of Cuttack.

In many cases, the zamindars were also hard hit. But they had stocks of grain to fall back upon. In desperate conditions people attacked and burnt down the grain stores of zamindars making some of them paupers as a result of the food riots during the famine.

In some places, such as the salt tracts, where agriculture was uncertain, the small *raiyats* suffered along with the agricultural labourers. For example, when the Collector of Puri visited the salt tract in December 1865, he noted that some cultivators who used to pay Rs. 10 to 20 as total revenue were found begging in public places.[134]

In November 1866, the Commissioner, who had submitted a summary report on the economic conditions of the entire division, described a similar situation in Cuttack also. For example, he wrote that people had sold cattle, roofs, doors and also proprietary right of land to obtain food. He mentioned that in Jajpur subdivision,

1,240 sale deeds of land had been executed during 1866 as against 479 deeds of sale in 1865. In 1866 *raiyats* subsisted on government rice only.[135] The intensity of the distress was also shown by the caste of the women and children who were working in the public relief programmes, the Commissioner added. He pointed out that the women and children of Brahman (Brahmins), Khandaits (land-holders), Mohanti (writers /professional caste) and Goala (pastoral caste) did not work on the roads before the famine because of caste prejudice. But during the famine they started doing light labour for wages. Their number exceeded 2,000. Later on, in the same report, the Commissioner also quoted the deputy collector of Khorda, the biggest government estate, who reported that the number of deaths of the agricultural labour castes, namely, Hadi, Dom, Bauri and the Lohars, were the largest. Next came the chasas (cultivators, land and agricultural owners and labourers), Goalas and Tantis (weavers).[136]

J.C. Geddes, the special Collector who was employed during the famine period, also observed the 'distressed condition' of the *raiyats*, though he did not distinguish between small and big *raiyats*. He had toured different parts of the division. He wrote that the agricultural class had lost three crops in two years. First of all, the rain failure in 1865 also destroyed the early crops as well as the winter crop. The *raiyats* had consumed their seeds and had also disposed of everything and had become destitutes.[137] Finally, a zamindar of Balasore who was examined by the Famine Commissioner said that many *raiyats* of zamindars also died and their land was left untilled.[138] According to the Inundation Committee (1869), 18 small estates which were paying revenue of Rs. 1,065 in aggregate had been sold between 1855 and 1867 compared to 11 between 1842 and 1854.[139] In other words, some of the small zamindars were also affected by the famine because they could not realize revenue.

Distress of the Weavers

Weavers have got a special mention in the accounts of this famine, in addition to the artisans, because they were going through an economic decline earlier too. The weavers as a class were facing serious difficulties because of stiff competition from imported cloth, even before the famine had set in, at least in two tracts of Orissa Division: Bhadrakh subdivision and Puri Sadar. Ravenshaw noted that many weavers (Tantis) were worryingly asking about government policy. Their weaving was becoming unremunerative, but due to caste prejudice they could not be engaged in any other occupation.[140] In a similar tone, Harrison, a Junior Secretary in the Government of Bengal, pointed out that weavers were suffering to the extent of saying that the local officers should tell the leaders of their caste that competition was driving them away from the market and hence they should take up some other occupation.[141]

At the onset of the famine of 1866, the weavers suffered along with the salt manufacturers whose income had declined because of the closure of salt manufacturing units by the government. There was no direct reference to the fact that demand for cloth had further fallen during the famine period. But the price series provided by the inundation committee showed that the price of raw cotton was lower than the price of rice, indicating thereby a fall in demand for cloth.[142] Even when the famine was over, the weavers continued to suffer.[143] So the cotton relief programme which started during the famine continued for a long time.[144]

Situation of the Fishing Community

In parts of Orissa in 1866, the fishing community, according to some observers, prospered during the early part of the famine. Thus, the Collector of Puri wrote in his diary that he visited the *kewt sahi* (the lane of fishing community) in the worst-affected area of Puri (Satpara, Malud, Parikud, Tua, etc.) and found that they were not emaciated. The explanation he offered was that the shallow water of Chilika Lake afforded ample fishing. Where such opportunity did not exist, they died, even in Puri.[145] This was in December 1865.

However, in Balasore, the Collector reported that the fish workers suffered intensely from drought as well as floods as they were very poor.[146] They were living on the bank of the river

Subarnarekha. There is no information about the fish workers in Cuttack. The condition of the fishing community of Chilika was probably an exception, since the shallow waters of Chilika not only had enough fish but also supplied a lot of green leaves to the nearby inhabitants. No other place had this combination.

Hunter, however, wrote in 1873 that the fishing community did not suffer from the famine of 1866 but the boating community had suffered, as the export of grain came to a standstill.[147]

The autobiography of Anant Das sheds very interesting light on the behaviour of the *pandas* (Brahmin priests). He found that the *pandas* of Puri Temple profited greatly.[148]

We shall take up this and related issues in subsequent chapters.

Who were the Famine Victims?

Morris D. Morris, a renowned economist, noted that the land-holding cultivators suffered the least during the famine period, they had land and other assets. They disposed of their assets to overcome the crisis. N.S. Jodha, on the other hand, contradicts him partially, saying that instead of maintaining the current consumption level, the peasants try to preserve the capital assets for future production. But both of them agree that they took rational decisions.

However, in case of the Orissa famine of 1866, it was noticed that both cultivators and also zamindars were targets of food riots. In the process, the rioters destroyed their granaries and turned the zamindars into paupers. Food riots do take place even now in case of acute shortage of food. Farmers usually save some capital asset for future production. For example, many cultivators preserved the seeds to plant them in the next season though they did sell their utensils and ornaments during the famine period. Some of them even sold their ploughs and cattle. Thus the peasants may be rational, but the type and extent of coping strategies they adopt depend on the nature and degree of the crisis.

As mentioned earlier, the Famine Commission of 1866 noted that the agricultural labourers were the most affected group. Next in order were the fisher folks, though, as noted earlier, in some stretches they survived because of availability of plenty of fish. But a survey conducted during the Bengal Famine of 1943 showed that fisher folks suffered the most. May be it was peculiar to the Bengal famine. Or it may be connected to the fact that the government had put severe restrictions on the movement of boats as a part of its war policy against Japanese invasion.

Greenough[149] has discussed at length the coping strategies of the service castes, namely, artisans, sharecroppers, carpenters, etc., and how all of them depended on the landlords during the crisis period. He drew attention to the phenomenon of patron-client relationship which continued to prevail even in famine time because of a kind of moral binding. However, it should be noted that such relationships may work in case of mild droughts and other scarcity situations, but as soon as the deficient rainfall occurs, they usually decide to retrench labour or not renew the annual contract with them. This is particularly true in case of subsistence agriculture. However, it should be noted that the moral binding vanishes as soon as severe drought is imminent.

On the whole, people from practically all castes and occupations suffered during the famine. But the degree of suffering was relatively less for the *raiyats* and middle and large zamindars and it was worst for agricultural labourers, weavers and other artisans, besides the boating community. Due to Chilika Lake, the fisher folks did not suffer in parts of Puri. Most of the sufferers belonged to the lower castes or Dalit communities.

Long-term Consequences of the Famine

In many ways, the famine of 1866 brought about fundamental changes in Orissa. While large-scale out-migration went on due to the scarcity conditions, the loss of population in the region also attracted streams of immigrants till 1891. Declining trends in birth rate continued till 1891. As pointed out earlier, the sex composition of the famine victims was not collected by the officials; but going by references in literary sources we learn that more women than men died during the famine. It is also mentioned that a large number of women became prostitutes. A new caste called Chhatrakhia, or those who ate in the relief kitchens was born. People from all castes were subsumed under this caste which was regarded as low caste.[150] We shall discuss it in some detail in the next chapter. But some mention is warranted here.

The *Utkal Dipika* wrote that many people had kept the destitutes of this 'caste' as servants but they did not touch even water served by them. As a result, the servants felt demeaned. The *Utkal Dipika* pleaded for the destitutes to be readmitted to their former castes as they had done *prayashchit* (repented) for having eaten in the relief centres.[151] Some social reformers tried to 'purify' those people and readmit them into their former castes. The 'pundits' of Calcutta and Puri were consulted, but the caste prejudice was so strong that at first the Puri pundits did not approve the proposal. On 11 April 1868 the *Utkal Dipika* again reported that as a result of the efforts of Sri Bichitranand Das, a social leader, the zamindars agreed to resettle the Chhatrakhias and the villagers also wanted to readmit them to their respective castes. The Chhatrakhias were supposed to give a feast to their relatives and make some offerings to the goddess of the village in order to be taken back to their respective castes. The *Utkal Dipika* also hoped that gradually all the outcastes would get readmitted to their caste, and regretted that similar measures could not be taken up for the orphans who had gone to the missionaries for food and shelter.[152]

Unfortunately all outcastes were not readmitted to their former castes. Chhatrakhias are found even today in Cuttack, Puri and Balasore. In Cuttack, for example, they are settled on the embankments of the government canals, suggesting that they had also worked at the canal site during the famine period.[153] The recorded numbers are very small, however. In 1901 there were 488 males and 775 females belonging to this caste.[154]

The missionaries took charge of many children orphaned during famine.[155] The *Utkal Dipika* reported that there were 8,000 orphans in the care of the missionaries. It commented that they should not be converted to Christianity. It also reported that many prostitutes took care of the orphan minor girls.[156] Fakir Mohan Senapati also wrote about this: 'Nothing was permanent. The famine was over. The year after that some children as well as some adults were wandering here and there. The Hindu "society" boycotted them as Chhatrakhia. But the missionaries recruited them and enthusiastically made them educated.'[157]

The most lasting, long-term impact of the great famine was the nascent birth of Oriya nationalism. The shock of the great disaster made many Oriyas think about the condition in which the Oriyas were living. An important theorization of the impact of colonial rule in India also emerged from this historical tragedy. In fact, the idea of Drain Theory got formulated taking Orissa famine as the test case. Dada Bhai Naoroji wrote extensively about the Drain Theory using the sufferings during the Orissa famine at the national level. Earlier, Karl Marx had narrated about the colonial extraction from India and the process of destruction of local industries. Naoroji explained how India as a colony was getting sapped in the form of excessive export of natural resources. Based on an understanding of the Orissa famine, he illustrated the drain of wealth from India and demanded an end to British rule.[158]

Changes in Production Relations

There were some important changes in the revenue system which were perceived differently from different vantage points. W.W. Hunter, the Scottish historian, wrote that due to the famine the ancient land system 'had become less unequal' in some places. He wrote that rents were determined according to the caste rank in the Parikud *pargana* of Puri where a Hindu *raja* had been installed. For example, a Brahmin used to pay less than what other castes paid for the same kind of land. After the famine, the rents had become uniform. He also pointed out that money rent was converted into produce rent after the famine of 1866 in this *pargana*.[159] Actually, these were essentially done for administrative convenience of the colonial regime.

After the famine, the area under *thani* cultivation declined. A large number of *raiyats* had lost their rights to their land. In 1890-1900, it was found out that the areas under *thanis* had declined by 62 per cent in Cuttack, 66 per cent in Puri and 43 per cent in Balasore between 1836 and 1896.[160]

Many *raiyats* had deserted their lands during the famine; the *raiyats* were readmitted as *thanis* if they could prove that they had held *thani* land rights by inheritance or had purchased from the landholders at the last settlement recorded in the *khatians*.[161]

Up to 1866 the occupancy rights were not freely transferred, but within one year, i.e. in 1866, 1,240 deeds of sale of land had been executed in Jajpur subdivision alone. Many rent-free holdings also changed hands. The work of the registration office also expanded.[162] Hunter reported an increase in the sale of land in Balasore during 1866.[163] Many Brahmins had transferred their rights in revenue-free lands and maintained themselves with other works during the famine in Puri.[164] Emigration and mortality reduced the supply of labour and hence had weakened the bargaining power of the zamindars immediately after the famine, compared to the pre-famine period. The land was not tilled in many places in 1866 due to factors such as shortage of labour and seeds. So it is possible that for the purpose of resuming farming, the zamindars reduced the *pahi* rent. There is no data on this. In some places the zamindars wanted to resettle the outcastes which indicated that they needed *raiyats* as well.[165]

Organization of Agriculture

The immediate result of the famine of 1866 was that the area under cultivation diminished for want of cultivators and labourers. According to Hunter, the area under salt manufacture that was turned into rice fields was also not cultivated again. Looking at the Orissa Division as a whole, in Balasore, the extent of fallow land had increased so much that it took nearly 10 years for the area under cultivation to come back to the pre-famine level.[166]

The other important change was the introduction of canal irrigation. Originally it was introduced to act as a safety net against floods as well as droughts. Further the government wanted to link Orissa with Calcutta and Madras Presidency in order to overcome the communication and transportation problems that they faced during the famine. This proposal was mooted after the heavy floods of 1855, but only after the 1866 famine the work was entrusted to the East India Irrigation Company.

Once completed, the irrigation facilities did provide some protection to crops in case of rain failure especially in Cuttack district. But for various reasons to which we cannot go into here, the *raiyats* of Orissa could not take full advantage of the facilities to adequately diversify the cropping pattern. Even to this day, the cropping pattern has not yet been adequately diversified. On top of it, the area under paddy crop is declining in recent times. It explains the high poverty ratio in present-day Orissa. It is high time that the planning had become bottom up.[167]

Post-Famine Wages and Prices

The post-famine money wage rates increased as a result of two factors: decline in the number of labourers due to famine mortality, and the heavy expenditure on public works, which were carried out in all the three districts in the form of repairing embankments and construction of roads and canals. Surprisingly, the agricultural wages in kind did not change at all. Money wage was generally paid in towns. The Board of Revenue decided to pay more to the labourers in the public works as the supply of labourers had diminished. But the money wage could not influence the real wage in the agricultural sector, perhaps because it was fixed by custom and even the influence of famine was not strong enough to change the rate of real wage. The most striking long-term impact of the famine was that the officers coming to Orissa Division were now familiar with the tragedy of this famine. As we will see in Chapter 10, one of the officer remarked that Orissa could avoid the tragedy of the famine 1866 in 1921 because people had migrated to Calcutta.

Overview

Thus overall, it can be said that the famine of 1866 that took a massive toll of life and caused large-scale misery to people, was seriously linked to the processes of decline in agricultural output and the trend of decline in the income of many classes of people. The recorded prices rose four to five times compared to the pre-famine years but were not very much higher than the neighbouring famine-affected districts like Midnaapur and Ganjam. So the private traders were not tempted to import grain into Orissa. The Board of Revenue of Bengal, to which Orissa was attached, was also strongly opposed to government imports on the principle of non-interference with the market, in spite of earnest requests from the district collectors, and later even from the commissioner. This went on till the month of June 1866 after which Orissa was cut off from the outside world as it did not have any good roads connecting it to Calcutta and Madras nor any good ports which could be utilized during the rainy season. The unprecedented floods in the month of August 1866, which submerged vast areas of low-lying land for a varying period of four days to a month, also intensified the sufferings of the people. Thus within a period of six months, i.e. from April to September 1866, a large number of people died of sheer starvation. On a conservative estimate more than a million people had died out of the total population of 3.7 million of Orissa Division, though a firm estimate is not possible for want of data.

People from all classes of people died during this famine but the small *raiyats* and agricultural labourers and people from the lower castes suffered maximum deaths. The causes of death were starvation and epidemics of cholera, smallpox, and dysentry.

The famine had a deep impact on the social behaviour of people in Orissa Division. It created a new class called Chhatrakhia which exists even today. It produced a new vocabulary and added many new words to the Oriya language. Also added to Oriya cuisine. Many new items consumed out of scarcity leafy vegetables continue to be eaten by people. It also brought some significant changes in the tenurial relations and the organization of agriculture. Orissa received some attention from the Bristish Raj after it had lost more than a million people. A steamer service was opened in 1871 and roads were constructed linking Orissa to Calcutta and Madras. A canal system was also built in its aftermath. Labourers got additional employment in the public works, canal works and finally in railroad construction, till about 1900. Above all, a new consciousness of Oriya nationalism emerged in the wake of the cataclysmic experience of this famine.[168]

The intense suffering in the famine of 1866 had shaken the revenue officials and the relief policy adopted in the famine of 1866 formed the template for policy response towards the later famines in India. So when the probability of a Bengal-Bihar famine of 1873-4 was apprehended, the revenue department officials tried to save as many people as possible. Accordingly, 'They set about making preparations with the utmost energy to carry out relief measures on a scale and with a thoroughness which had never been equaled before'.[169] As a result, there was not much loss of life during the famine of 1873-4.[170] Many experts felt that the experience of the 1866 Orissa Famine laid the ground for a Famine Code which was eventually formulated in 1880. But there was a catch. Between formulation and execution of the policy, many factors arising from the evolving state and society shaped its implementation which mattered a lot.

Notes

1. W.W. Hunter, *A Statistical Account of Bengal*, vols. 18 and 19, 1877, rpt. 1977, New Delhi, Concept, pp. 142-50, 148-73 and 328-34. Also C.E. Buckland, *Bengal Under the Lt. Governors Being a Narrative of the Principal Events and Public Measures during Their Periods of Office: 1854 to 1898*, 2 vols., New Delhi, Deep Publications, 1901 rpt., 1976.
2. S.D. Choudhuri, 'Bengal Famine: Misfortune of Imperial Schema' https://www.academia.edu/38989565/Bengal_Famine_of_1943-.Misfortune_or_Imperial_ Schema?email_work_card=view-paper; also see https://www.theguardian.com/world/2019/mar/29/winston-churchill-policies-contributed-to-1943-bengal-famine-study Also see Utsa Patnaik, who argued that the Bengal Famine 1942-3 was the result of Keynsian policy to squeeze the level of consumption to finance the Second World War. https://www.newcoldwar.org/profit-inflation-keynes-and-the-holocaust-in-bengal-1943-44/

3. Famine Commission Report of Orissa (FCRO), 1866, ed. State Archives, *Orissa Famine: Na'nka (1865-66)*, Bhubaneswar, Government Press, 2016, p. xv.
4. J.K. Samal, *Orissa Under the British Crown*, New Delhi, S. Chand and Company, 1977, pp. 1-27.
   Prabhat Mukherjee, *History of Orissa in Nineteenth Century*, Bhubaneshwar, Utkal University Press, 1964, pp. 355-96. Also see, G.C. Patnaik, *The Famine and Some Aspects of the British Economic Policy in Orissa: 1866-1905*, Cuttack, Vidyapuri, 1980, pp. 16-54.
5. Jagabandhu Acharya, 'Oriya Migrant Labourers: An Exploratory Study of the Agrarian Conditions Leading to Creation of an Industrial Labour Force during the Late Nineteenth and Early Twentieth Century', M. Phil thesis submitted to Jawaharlal Nehru University, 1976, pp. 76-86.
6. Lalatendu Das Mohapatra, *Commerce in Orissa 1600-1800*, Prafulla Pathagar Publication, Orissa, 2010.
7. H.C.B.C.R. Raban, offg. Collector to the Commissioner, Cuttack Division, no. 297, 15 June 1867.
8. Chandi Prasad Nanda and Hermann Kulke (eds.), *Rethinking Local History and Identity Politics: Locating Kurmi Community in Orissa*, New Delhi, Manohar, 2015, p. 34.
9. L. Visaria and P. Visaria, 'Population 1757-1948', in Dharma Kumar (ed.), *Cambridge Economic History of India*, vol. 11, Cambridge University Press, 1982, p 529 (hereafter *CEHI*).
10. Maddox wrote that 'it is evident that well-distributed rainfall of 40 inches with no less than 4 inches in October is sufficient to secure the crop, though for a bumper crop at least 50 inches with 8 inches in September and 6 inches in October is needed'. *Maddox Report 1890-1900*, vol. 1, para 107.
11. Famine Commission Report, vol. 1, pt. 1, para 47.
12. The details of the factors as well as of tables have been discussed in Bidyut Mohanty, 'Famine and Its Impact on Agrarian Structure in Orissa Division 1866-1921' unpublished thesis submitted to Delhi University, 1988, Appendices 8.1 to 8.3, pp. 469-506.
13. Report of the Indian Famine Commission, pts. I, II, III, *Famine Histories*, London, Eyre and Spottiswoode, 1880.
14. V. Suganya and B. Padmanabhan, 'The Famine Eviction, Destitution and Survival Migrants', in V.Sangitha, B.J. Geetha, K. Sindhu, S. Bhupathi and S. Snekha (eds.), 2019. http://www.languageinindia.com/2019 retrieved from Academia Edu.

15. The Famine Commissioner reported that a large amount of grain was exported through Chilika to Ganjam and further but there were no figures on such export. *Orissa Famine Commission Report 1866,* pt. 1, para 47 (hereafter *FCRO 1866*). The figures of export by sea are therefore less than the actual total export.
16. Tim Dyson, *A Population History of India: From the First Modern People to the Present Day*, New Delhi, Oxford University Press, 2019, p. 139.
17. Churchill's policies contributed to 1943 Bengal famine – Study. https://www.theguardian.com/world/2019/mar/29/winston-churchill-policies-contributed-to-1943-bengal-famine-study
18. B.B. Chaudhuri, 'Eastern India,' in Dharma Kumar (ed.), *CEHI*, vol. II, p. 134.
19. Ravenshaw incidentally had given the estimate of output of 1866-7 by taking the normal area under cultivation, condition factor of 1865-6 and population of pre-famine year of 1865 to show that if the famine had killed off one-fourth of the population, the estimated output would be adequate to feed the remaining population. So he did not adjust the consumption requirements. GOI/Home/Public, January 1867, no. 958, From Commr. OD to the Secy BR, dt. 1 November 1866.
20. Ibid.
21. Evidence given by G.S. Roy, editor of *Utkal Dipika* and Abkari Writer in Cuttack Collectorate, 'Famine Commission Report,' pt. II, p. 87. Also see, *Utkal Dipika,* 10 November 1866. Also see, Moral and Material Progress Report, 1866-7, p. 70.
22. 'Ravenshaw's Report on 1 November 1866'. One maund = 40 standard *seers.*
23. *Maddox Report 1890-1900,* vol. 1, para 136. Incidentally Maddox had assumed that the conversion ratio between paddy to rice was 8:5. Ibid, But the authors of *Famine Histories* and Ravenshaw had assumed 2:1 as will be evident from the text. The popular notion of the conversion ratio is 2:1 between paddy and rice.
24. The Inundation Committee on the other hand has assumed that the average yield per acre was 17 maunds of paddy taking the Division as a whole. *The Inundation Committee Report, 1869*, p. 24.
25. *Famine Histories 1885*, p. 42.
26. *FCRO 1866,* pt. I, para. 118: Also see, GOI/Home/Public, June 1867, no. 146; Minute by Governor-General of India, dt. 20 April 1867.
27. *FCRO 1866*, pt. 1, para. 112.

28. Idem.
29. *Famine Histories, 1885,* p. 42.
30. GOI/Home/Public, February 1867, no. 119; Extracts from the diary of the District Superintendent of Police, Puri from 20 to 25 November 1865 of the lower part of Chilika and Banpur in Puri, dt. 20 to 25 November 1865.
31. Fakir Mohan Senapati, *Atma Charita* (Oriya), Cuttack, Cuttack Student Store, 2014, p. 31.
32. *FCRO 1866*, part 1, para 112. Also it was reported in land Revenue Administration Report of 1865-6 that the rain had stopped early in October and moisture content was too low to bring the paddy into maturity and in most part of the Division the paddy withered away. GOI/Home/Public March 1867, no. 136; Extracts from the Administration Report of Orissa 1865-6.
33. GOI/Home/Public, January 1867, no. 309; Extracts of Mr. Barlow's diary through Satpara, Parikud and Malud for 4 to 15 December 1865, dt. 29 December 1865.
    Mayadhar Mansingh wrote about Anant Das who wrote that his father used to get paddy mixed with weeds in the year 1865, indicating that the quality of paddy was not good in that year. Mayadhar Mansingh, *Durbhikya* Oriya, Cuttack, New Students Store, 1955, p. 62.
34. 'Ravenshaw's Report on 1 November 1866'.
35. Ravenshaw had taken 2/3rd of a *seer* in Cuttack weight which is higher than the standard measure the ratio being 10/16: 13/16. So we have converted that measure to standard measure which becomes equivalent to 14/16 *seer*. Hunter, *Statistical Account of Bengal,* vol. 19, p. 145.
36. *FCRO 1866*, pt. 1, para 86.
37. W.W. Hunter, *Famine Aspects of Bengal Districts 1872*, London, Trubner & Co., 1874, p. 53.
38. *Maddox Report 1890-1900,* vol. 1, p. 133.
39. Passmore, R., 'Famine' in *Encylopedia Britanica,* vol. 9. Chicago, William Benton, 1969, p. 59.
40. *Famine Histories, 1885*, p. 42.
41. *Maddox Report 1890-1900,* vol. 1, para 187.
42. The average size of the household was 5.3 in 1872.
43. Barlow pointed out that the *raiyats* though starving had stored seeds. '*Barlow's Diary through Chilika*'. Maddox pointed out, 1 maund

of paddy is required for an acre. *Maddox Report 1890-1900*, vol. 1, para 187.

44. Since Ravenshaw had used the Cuttack region weight measure throughout his estimate of output and since his objective was to show that there was just sufficient production in the year 1865-6, which comes out of his analysis, we have not changed the scale, except mentioning the fact that the per capita consumption requirement and yield per acre were on the excessive side.
45. In fact, Ravenshaw as well as the authorities of *Famine Histories* did not distinguish between the cultivated area under cultivation in non-famine years on the eve of the famine. They assumed a lower condition factor on the eve of the famine year. As we have seen earlier, the area under cultivation would have decreased because of the fear of higher assessment. At the same time there was a heavy demand for Orissa rice. So perhaps the area under cultivation did not decrease much.
46. *FCRO 1866*, part 1, para 113.
47. GOI/Home/Public, February 1867, no. 37; From the Commissioner, OD to the Secretary, GOB, 28 May 1866.
    Also see, GOI/Home/Public, February 1867, no. 1878; From the Secretary, GBO to the Secretary, BR, GOB, 20 June 1866.
    Also see, GOI/Home/Public, February 1867; no. 89; From the Honorary Secretary to the British Indian Association to the secretary, 28 June 1866.
48. GOI/Home/Public, February 1867, no. 1878; From the Secretary, GOB to the Secretary, BR, GOB, 20 June 1866.
49. GOI/Home/Public, March 1867, no. 495; From the Collector Balasore to the Commissioner, OD, 12 January 1867.
    Also GOI/Home/Public, March 1867, no. 602; From Collector, Puri to the Commissioner, OD, 14 January 1867.
50. GOI/Home/Public, June 1867, no. A5; From the Assistant Collector to the Collector of Cuttack, 2 April 1867.
51. Ravenshaw pointed out that price had fallen in Balasore in the month of December 1866, because of release of old stock. GOI/Home/Public, December 1866, no. 4868B; From the Secretary, BRLP to the Secretary, GOB, 10 November 1866. But the lower prices could be due to the arrival of new crop in the market, though there was no reason for zamindars and *raiyats* to dispose of the new crop because they were exempted from paying *kists* in November

1866 and also for later period, GOI/Home/Public, February 1867, no. 534. From the Secretary, GOB, to the Secretary, BR, GOB, 19 February 1867.

52. *FCRO 1866,* pt. 1, para 86.
53. *FCRO 1866,* pt. II, p. 58. Also see, GOI/Home/Public, June 1867, no. 144; Minutes of Lieutenant Governor of Bengal.
54. GOB/Home/Public, June 1866, no. 262; From the Magistrate, Puri to the Commissioner of OD, 8 June 1866, reproduced in Correspondence and Papers , p 51.
55. GOI/Home/Public, February1867, no. 407; From the Commissioner to the Secretary, GBO, 27 October 1865.
56. *FCRO 1866,* pt. 1, para 86.
57. Hunter, *Statistical Account of Bengal,* vol. 18, p. 337.
58. *FCRO 1866,* pt. 1, paras 196 and 200.
59. *FCRO 1866,* pt. III, p 254. Also see the evidence given by Babu Latchna Patur, a Ganjam merchant who traded in rice from Ganjam and the evidence was given by Goopee Pander, FCRO 1866, pt. II, p. 19.
60. GOI/Home/Public, July 1867, no. 1090; From the Deputy Commissioner, Sambalpur to the Commissioner, OD, 20 May 1867.
61. Passmore, R., 'Famine' in *Encylopedia Britanica,* vol. 9, Chicago, William Benton, 1969, p. 59.
62. https://en.wikipedia.org/wiki/Great_Famine_(Ireland)
63. Cormac O. Grada, 2009, *Famine: A Short History,* Princeton, Princeton University Press, pp. 52-5.
64. Alex Deb Waal, *Famine Crimes : Politics, and Disaster Relief Industry in Africa,* Indianapolis, Indiana University Press, 1997.
65. *FCRO 1866,* pt. II, reproduced in Government of Orissa, *Orissa Famine: A Documentation of Primary Sources,* Government Press, 2016, p. 173
66. From T.E. Ravenshaw, Officiating Commissioner of Cuttack Division to the Secretary to the Government of Bengal (no. K, dated 2 May 1866) reproduced in *Orissa Famine,* ibid., p. 603.
67. Amartya Sen, 'Individual Freedom as a Social Commitment', *New York Review of Books,* 14 June 1990.
68. There are conflicting views regarding the role of press and famine mortality. Sen attributes 30 to 40 million deaths to absence of press, but Peter Nolan has an opposite view to express. Of course, Sen replied after that. Recently Frank Dikotter has attributed 40 million deaths in China because the press was muted. It is also important to learn that even the publicity given by a local press could draw the

attention of BBC regarding the sale of child and starvation deaths in Kalahandi in 1985. Other than the Prime Minister Rajiv Gandhi came to visit the poorest district of Orissa. Manoranjan Mohanty, 'Orissa Famine of 1866: Lessons for the 21st Century', in Anil Dhir and Ramesh Ch. Mahapatra (eds.), *The Great Orissa Famine, 1866: Na'nka Durbhikya,* 2017, Bhubaneswar, Capital Press, pp. 70-83.

69. *FCRO 1866*, pt. 1, reprinted in *Orissa Famine: A Documentation of Primary Sources,* Orissa State Archives, Government Press, Bhubaneswar, 2016, pp. 51, 61 and xxi.
70. Anil Dhir, 'Death in Every Paragraph: Reportage of Orissa Famine 1866 in English Press', in Anil Dhir and Ramesh Mohapatra (eds.), *The Great Orissa Famine, 1866: Na'nka Durbhikhya,* Amadeus Press, Bhubaneswar, 2017, pp. 133-44.
71. Ibid., p. 867.
72. Dhir and Mohapatra, 2017, p. 142.
73. GOI/Home/Public, February 1867, no. 1878. From the Secretary, GOB, to the Secretary, BR, GOB, 20 June 1866.
74. *FCRO 1866*, pt. 1, pp. 238-91.
75. Tim Dyson, *A Population History of India: From the First Modern People to the Present Day,* New Delhi, Oxford University Press, 2019, p. 79. The author writes that the first severe famine of 1769-70 occurred during the Company rule in Bengal whose population was around 30 million. It was caused by extensive crop failure. The Company was so indifferent that instead of administering relief it decided to raise the land revenue. Nobody knew as to how many people died of starvation. In local language it is known as *Chaitter Mannontor*. Bengali nationalist Bankim Chandra wrote a famous novel known as *Anand Math* where the hero incited the local people to revolt against the colonial rule.
76. S. Ambirajan, *Classical Political Economy and British Policy in India*, Delhi, Vikas Publishing House, 1978, p. 77.
77. Ira Klein, 'When Rains Failed: Famine, Relief and Mortality in British India', *Indian Economic and Social History Review*, 21(2), 1984, p 189.
78. L. Brennan, 'The Development of the Indian Famine Codes, Personalities, Politics and Policies', in B. Currey and G. Hugo (eds), *Famine: As a Geographical Phenomenon,* Holland, D. Reidel Publishing Company, 1984, p. 92.
79. The Poor Laws were a system of relief for the poor which existed in England and gradually developed over years. Finally the Law got codified in 1557-98. https://navigator.health.org.

uk/content/poor-law-amendment-act-1834-also-known-%E2%80%98new-poor-law%E2%80%99-received-royal-assent-14-august-1834?gclid=EAIaIQobChMI8bjHu_664gIVUg4rCh2Z-7Q41EAAYAiAAEgLC7_D_BwE

80. Klein, op. cit.
81. Quoted in H. Srivastava, *The History of Indian Famines 1858-1918: The Development of Famine Policies,* Agra, Sri Ram Mehra, 1968.
82. *Famine Histories*, p. 48.
83. *FCRO 1866*, pt. II, Evidence no. 43, p. 56.
84. According to the Famine Commission of 1866, minimum relief should constitute half *seer* of rice, some vegetables and some ghee per person to maintain himself. *FCRO 1866*, pt. I, para 86. Reginald Passmore has also pointed out that a person requires half *seer* of cereal (which yields 1600 calories) to survive. But his body weight will be reduced by 25 per cent. If he does hard work and he will not survive. R Passmore, 'Famine' *Encyclopedia Britannica,* vol. 9, William Benton, Chicago, 1969, p 59.
85. *Famine Histories 1885,* p 48. Also see, *Utkal Dipika,* 29 September 1866.
86. *FCRO 1866*, pt. 1, para 313.
87. A.M. Loveday for example, has quoted the estimate of the Famine Commission of 1866. A.M. Loveday, *The History and Economics of Indian Famine,* London, G Bell and Sons, 1914, p. 51.

    B.M. Bhatia on the other hand has quoted the estimate of the Famines Histories 1885.To the one million deaths in Orissa he has added another three lakh deaths for the rest of the portion of the famine tract. B.M. Bhatia, *Famines in India: A Study of Some Aspects of the Economic History of India 1860-1965,* rpt. 1963, Bombay: Asia Publishing House, 1967, pp. 68-9.

    Visaria and Visaria have accepted slightly higher figure than that of given by the Deputy collectors. Vasaria and Visaria, 'Population', *CEHI* II, p. 529.
88. *Report of the Indian Famine Commission 1880,* pt. III, *Famine Histories,* Eyre and Spotitswood, London, 1880, p 45. It was also pointed out by the deputy collectors that the percentage loss total estimated population amounted to 29 in Cuttack, 32 in Puri and 34 in Balasore respectively. The word 'lost' meant both missing and dead. Ibid., n. 2, p. 45.

    The Board of Revenue had revised the mortality figure of 1867 by 4805. GOI/Home/Public, January 1868, no. 1801 M; From

Secretary, BR to the secretary, GOB, 8 November 1867.
Maddox, the settlement officer had reduced the mortality figure to half a million. *Maddox Report 1890-1900,* vol. 1, para 195.

89. *Orissa Famine: A Documentation of Primary Sources,* State Archives, Bhubaneswar, 2016, p. xxv.
90. *Famine Histories, 1885,* p. 45.
91. GOI/Home/Public, January 1867, no. 3202, from the Secretary, GOB to the Secretary, GOI, 5 December 1866.
92. *Sanitary Commission Report of Bengal 1868*, p. 410.
93. W.W. Hunter, *Famine Aspects of Bengal Districts 1872*, Simla, Government Press, 1873, p. xxxi.
94. GOI/Home/Public, January, 1867, no. 958; from the Commissioner, OD to the Secretary, BR, 1 November 1866.
95. Ibid.
96. *FCRO 1866,* pt. I, para 13.
97. W.W. Hunter, *Statistical Account of Bengal,* vol. 3, D.K. Publishing House, Delhi, 1876, rpt. 1973, p. 365.
98. The Collector of Puri reported that roadside deaths among the 'aimless wanderers' were not included. GOI/Home/Public, January 1868, nos. 21-2, pt. A from the Collector of Puri to the Commissioner, OD, 15 June 1867.
99. GOI/Home/Public, January 1868, nos. 21-2, pt. A. Also see, *Utkal Dipika*, 18 August 1868.
100. Anil Dhir, ' Chhatrakhais: The Emergence of a New Caste', in Anil Dhir and Ramesh Ch. Mahapatra (eds.), op. cit., pp. 113-26.
101. *FCRO 1866,* pt. I, para 76.
102. The Deputy Collector also wrote that 10/16 of the 'agriculturists' (*raiyats*) were *pahi raiyats.* GOI/Home/Public, January 1868, nos. 21-2, pt. A, 'Final Report on the Mortality Caused by the Late Famine in the District Cuttack.'
103. GOI/Home/Public, January 1867, no. (b): 'Summary of the Operations since August 7, 1866', presented by the Commissioner of Cuttack Division.
Also, E.W. Molony, the Special Famine Commissioner wrote in 1867 that labour as a class had been reduced in number in the last famine, so much so that it was difficult to procure labour in Puri. GOI/Home/Public, July 1867, no. 485, from the Special Famine Commissioner to the Secretary to the Orissa Famine and Orphan Relief Committee, Calcutta, 17 May 1867.
104. Bauri, Dom-agricultural labouring castes, Tanti-mainly weavers,

Chasas-cultivating castes but some of them lived as labourers because of small landholding. GOI/Home/Public, January 1867, no. 958. From the Commissioner, OD to the Secretary, BR, 1 November 1866.

105. W.W. Hunter, *Orissa: On the Vicissitudes of an Indian Province under Native and British Rule*, 2 vols., vol. 1, London, Smith and Elder, 1872, p. 44.
106. *FCRO 1866*, pt. II, Evidence no. 24, p. 26.
107. GOI/Home/Public, 4 January 1868, nos. 21-2, pt. A; Commissioner, OD to the Secretary, BR, 22 July 1867.
108. Thus out of death rates among the agricultural labourers, the *pahi raiyats* were higher than the average of 15 per cent. GOI/Home/Public, January 1868, nos. 21-2, pt. A; from the Commissioner, OD to the Secretary BR, 24 July 1867.
109. Ibid.
110. GOI/Home/Public, January 1968, nos. 21-2, pt. A; From the Collector, Puri to the Commissioner, OD.
111. Ibid.; From the Collector, Balasore, to the Commissioner, OD. Also Hunter wrote that 'Day labourers were formerly a numerous class in Balasore but they suffered severely in the famine of 1866, and are now few in number.' Hunter, *Statistical Account of Bengal,* vol. 18, p. 297.
112. Ravenshaw observed that 'The greatest mortality was among labouring classes and artisans. The raiyats certainly suffered much less, the poorer raiyats more, but I am not in a position further to classify the raiyats in regard to mortality,' *FCRO, 1866*, pt. II, p. 73.
113. GOI/Home/Public, March 1867, no. 107; from Collector of Balasore to the Commissioner, OD, 2 April 1866.

    Also, the Deputy Collector wrote that the customary employment of labourers which ensured them food and security dried up at the onset of famine, so there was great mortality among them; GOI/Home/Public, 4 January 1868, nos. 21-2, pt. I, Final Report on the mortality in Cuttack district during the last famine.

    A report on the famine in Madras Presidency during 1896-7 shows that wage rate was paid in cash and not in kind during the famine in Ganjam. The cash wages could not keep pace with the price rise in Ganjam as well as in Bellary. Dharma Kumar, *Land and Caste in South India: Agricultural Labour in Madras Presidency during the Nineteenth Century,* Cambridge, Cambridge University Press, 1965, p 146.

114. GOI/Home/Public, February 1867, no. 308; Barlow's Diary through Chilika Tracts in December 1865, submitted to the Commissioner of Cuttack division on 29 December 1865.
115. GOI/Home/Public, February 1867, no. 1701; From the Commissioner, OD to Secretary, GBO, 4 February 1867. Also see, *Famine Histories 1885*, p. 46.
116. GOI/Home/Public, February 1867, Telegram from the Superintending Engineer, Cuttack to Colonel Nicolis, 26 May 1866.
117. GOI/Home/Public, February 1867, no. 179 w; extracts from Executive Engineer of Balasore to the Superintending Engineer, Cuttack circle, 19 May 1866.
118. GOI/Home/Public, February 1867, no. 2466; from Superintending Engineer, Cuttack circle.
119. According to Anant Das the wage rate in the Irrigation Company was two *annas* and half *seer* of rice. His brother had started working in the canal in order to support both of them. Mayadhar Mansingh, *Durbhikshya* (Oriya), p. 53.
120. *FCRO 1866*, pt. II, Evidence no. 43, p. 50.
121. Ibid, Evidence no. 51, p. 60.
122. Hunter pointed out in 1876 that the agricultural labourers were paid in kind 6.5 *seers* of paddy or little over three *seers* of rice per day; the wage had not changed since 1850. The hardest times for the agricultural labourers were September, October and November. Hunter, *Statistical Account of Bengal*, vol. 18, p. 110, vol. 19, pp. 97-8. *Maddox Report (1890-1900)* on the other hand pointed out that the labourers were paid wages in kind, in two *seers* to 2.5 *seers* of rice. The labourers who were engaged throughout the year also were remunerated in kind but the rate varied from subdivision to subdivision. For example, it varied from two *seers* in Kendrapara subdivision in Cuttack to $1^5/_8$ *seers* in Bhadrakh. *Maddox Report 1890-1900*, vol. 1, p. 132.
123. It was reported in the minutes of Schalch, the junior member of BR, that population were attracted to the SE and SW portions of Puri district, the salt manufacturing area. After the stoppage of salt manufacture the number of people had become higher than the capacity of the soil to support. Thus they perished in great number. GOI/Home/Public, January 1867, no. 5694; From Secretary, BR to Secretary, GBO, 27 December 1866.
124. There is no direct evidence to show that employment opportunities had declined in the famine of 1866, but there was some evidence

for the later famine which was not so severe as the famine of 1866. It seems likely that a similar kind of adjustment would have been made during the famine of 1866. For example, the parganas near Chilika Lake had suffered from drought in June and July 1878. Immediately the raiyats got scared, and started doing their own work for which they ordinarily used to hire labourers. In the process they saved grains which would have been paid as wages. GOB/ Rev/Agri/ FB. July 1879, no. 1406, From the Commissioner, OD to the Secretary, GOB, 10 July 1879.

125. Mayadhar Mansingh, *Durbhikshya,* p. 65.
126. N.N. Pradhan wrote that it was heard that as a result of loss of crops, straw houses could not be thatched. N.N. Pradhan (ed.), *Introduction to Gangadhar Granthabali* (Oriya), Cuttack, Dharm Grantha Store, 1978, p. 23.
127. N.N. Banerjẹe, *Report on the Agriculture of the District Cuttack,* Calcutta,Secretariat Press, p. 47. Also, *Maddox Report (1890-1900),* vol. 1, pp. 136-7.
128. It was reported by the Commissioner, OD that one-eighth of the cultivable land was lying fallow because of death and want of seeds. From the experience of later famines, it can be inferred that the cultivation migh have hampered due to deaths of the bullock population. *Source:* GOI/Home/Public, January 1867, no. 958; From the Commissioner, OD to Secretary, BR, 1 November 1866. Also *FCRO 1866,* pt. II, Evidence nos. 76 and 81, pp. 100 and 103.
129. Senapati also wrote that by the end of 1865 the labourers had already disposed of their belongings, such as brass utensils, and deserted their homes. Husband, wife, father and son did not see each other. They begged from door to door. But there was nobody even for giving alms. Senapati, *Atma Charita (Oriya),* p. 31.
130. *Police Administration Report 1866,* p. 47. Also *FCRO* 1866, pt. II, Witness given by additional judge, examined on 12 January 1866, pp. 89-90.
131. Hunter pointed out that of those who sought relief and got it a very large proportion of them died. Those who had sought relief were from the lower castes, who did not have caste prejudice and who did not mind working, yet they were the people who died in large number. W.W. Hunter, *Statistical Account of Bengal,* vol. 18, New Delhi, Concept Publishing House, 1973, p. 171.

     The additional judge who was examined in Balasore said that *raiyats* with land came last to the relief centers. *FCRO,* 1866, pt. II, p. 90.

132. GOI/Home/Public, January 1868, nos. 21-2; pt. A: From the Commissioner, OD to the Secretary, BR, 24 July 1867.
133. Ibid.
134. GOI/Home/Public, February 1867, no. 308; G.N. Barlow's diary through Satparah, Parikud and Malud for 4 to 15 December 1865 submitted to the Commissioner of Cuttack Division on 29 December 1865.
135. GOI/Home/Public, January 1867, no. 958; From the Commissioner OD to the Secretary, BR, 1 November 1866. Also see, Mansingh, *Durbhikshya*, p. 4.
136. GOI/Home/Public, January 1867, no. 958; From the Commissioner, OD to the Secretary, BR, 1 November 1866.
137. GOI/Home/Public, March 1867, no. 1675: Special Collector to the Commissioner, OD, 2 February 1867.
138. *FCRO 1866*, pt. II, Evidence no. 81, p. 103.
    Also the Assistant Magistrate, Balasore was examined on 22 January 1867 wrote 'Of those who do little cultivation, say under five acres, one-eighth or one-ninth of them had died. Of the better class of cultivators comparatively few would have died. In many places, the lower class of people ran away', *FCRO* 1866, pt. II, Evidence no. 86, p. 106.
139. *Inundation Committee Report 1869*, p. 23.
140. GOI/Home/Public, June 1867, no. 621 3/4; From the Commissioner, OD to Secretary, BR, GOB, 14 May 1867.
141. GOI/Home/Public, June 1867, No 2282; From the Junior Secretary, GBO to the Secretary, BR, GBO, 14 June 1867. Also see, GOI/Home/Public, July 1867, no. 2676; From Junior Secretary, GOB to the Secretary, GOI, 14 July 1867.
142. Demand for cloth had fallen in Ganjam; From the Acting Collector of Madras to the Chief Secretary of GOM, 13 August 1866, reproduced FCRO, 1866, pt. III, p. 56.
143. 'Throughout Bhudrukh the purely agricultural classes were well off and non-agriculturists, especially weavers and coolies had difficulty in purchasing the grain as the ryots were withholding the grain.' GOI/Home/Public, June 1867, no. 496; From the Commissioner, OD to Secretary BR, 30 April 1867.
144. GOI/Home/Public, July 1867, no. 2676; From the Junior Secretary, GOB to the Secretary GOI, 4 July 1867.
    Also GOI/Home/Public, July 1867, no. 394; From special Famine Commissioner to Secretary. Orissa Famine and Orphan Relief Committee, Calcutta, 3 May 1867.

Also, Srivastava has pointed out that the famine of 1866 had affected all classes of people. Elsewhere as in Bihar, the effect of the famine of 1866 was felt on professional beggars, helpless and infirm, petty village artisans, agricultural labourers and noonias. In Madras presidency, non-agricultural classes, persons of fixed low salaries and raiyats of Ganjam had suffered. Hari Sankar Srivastava. *The History of Indian Famines 1858-1918: The Development of Famine Policies*. Agra, Sri Ram Mehra, 1968, p. 80.

Cotton relief is a special kind of relief, which used to be given to the weavers and *purdanashin* women who did not come to regular relief centres due to caste prejudices. In particular weavers were given thread to weave cloth. This cloth was taken back by the government to be distributed among other needy people and the weavers were remunerated. In case of *purdanashin* women they were given cotton to be converted into thread for which they got remuneration.

145. 'Barlow's diary'.
146. The Collector wrote the entire pargana Kismatnapu which was inhabited by fishermen was depopulated. GOI/Home/Public, January 1868, nos. 21-2, pt. A, 4 January 1868; From the Collector of Balasore to the Commissioner, OD, 16 July 1867.
147. Hunter, *Famine Aspects*, Government Press, Simla, 1873, p. xx.
148. The *pandas* (priests) of the temple invited the people who had ornament and persuaded them to deposit with them (*pandas*) so that nobody would steal them. They also promised them a full meal everyday. Besides, the *pandas* also promised to return the ornaments as soon as conditions became normal. Many believed in this and deposited their ornaments. But after that the pandas used to beat them up and drive them away. Mansingh, *Durbhikshya,* p. 55, *Cuttack District Gazetteer*, 1906, p. 52.
149. Paul R. Greenough 'Indian Famines and Peasant Victims of Bengal Famine 1943-44', *Modern Asian Studies* 14(2), 1980, pp. 205-35.
150. Also the Collector of Puri wrote that he stopped all the gratuitous relief to outcastes in Malud of whom there was a large numbers. In Cuttack and Puri. There were many such women who had been turned out of their caste for having accepted government relief in the great famine of 1866. They all worked in Cuttack and in the town of Puri, but did not work in Bajrakot, Malud and Parikut, GOB/Rev/Agri, October 1878, no. 635; From the Collector, Puri to Commissioner, OD, 2 April 1878.

151. *Utkal Dipika,* 31 August 1867.
152. *Utkal Dipika,* 18 January 1968.
153. Even nowadays there is a market in Cuttack city which is known as Chhatra Bazaar in which the relief centres were opened. WE have given brief description about the location in the Chapter 4.
154. *Census of India, Bengal Report, 1901.* vol. 5, pt. 1, p. xxxiii.
155. Anant Das wrote, the missionaries not only recruited the orphans but also members of other castes whom he saw in the orphanage. Mayadhar. Mansingh, *Durbhikshya,* p. 91. Also, 'The Famine Orphans of Orissa'. T*he Indo-European Correspondence,* vol. 11, no. 13, 10 March 1867, Calcutta, p. 171. *The Christian Spectator,* vol. 1, no. 7, January 1872, Calcutta, p. 278 in John Brown (ed.), *The Centenary Volume of the Baptist Missionary Society 1792-1892.* London, 1872, p. 260.
156. *Police Administration Report of Bengal 1866,* Appendix II, p. 4. Also *Utkal Dipika,* 12 February 1867.
157. F.M. Senapati, *Atma Charita,* p. 35.
158. Prakash Mishra, 'Dadabhai Naoroji: The Theory of Drain', in Dhir and Mohapatra (eds.), *The Great Orissa Famine,1866-Na'anka Durbhikhya,* pp. 289-300.
159. W.W. Hunter, *Orissa 1872,* vol. 1, p. 33. B.B. Chaudhuri has pointed out that produce rent is paid in places where the agriculture outcome is uncertain. 'Where cultivation was uncertain, inferior crops grown and the yield low, the peasants usually paid rent in produce.' B.B. Chaudhuri, 'Eastern India,' *CEHI* II, p. 124. It is possible that the salt tract parganas of Parikud and Malud had shown instability in the face of the famine hence the money rent was converted into produce rent. Later on this salt tract did face recurrent famines.
160. '. . . and in the famine years of 1866-7 very large numbers were forced to throw themselves on the mercy of zamindar. Some abandoned their lands and fled, and came back later on to be readmitted as *pahi raiyats*; others gave up their *thani pattas* in return for advances; others no doubt-though of this there is less record – were removed altogether from their lands on failure to pay their rents.' *Maddox Report (1890-1900),* vol. 1, para 32. Also B.B. Chaudhuri has pointed out that the decline took place because of the agricultural depression which had set in just after the settlement of 1836-40 and then the famine. In both these situations the rent proved to be excessively high, compelling the thani peasants to 'relinquish their holdings.' B.B. Chaudhuri, 'Eastern India', p. 134.

161. *Maddox Report (1890-1900),* vol. 1, para 417.
162. GOI/Home/Public, January 1867, no. 958; From the Commissioner, OD to the Secretary, BR, 1 November 1866, p. 31.
163. W.W. Hunter wrote: 'In the famine year (1866) 360 such transfers by sale and mortgage were duly registered being more than one-third of the total number registered in the eleven years 1864 to 1874'. Hunter, *Statistical Account of Bengal,* vol. 18, p. 315.
164. GOB/Rev/Agri, August 1878, no. 1931; From the Collector to the Commissioner, OD, 16 August 1878.
165. GOI/Home/Public, January 1867, no. 958; From the Commissioner OD to the Secretary BR, GOB, 1 November 1866. In many places the homestead lands remained vacant on the ground that all the members of the family had died in the famine. It was believed that having houses on those place might lead to similar consequences!
166. Hunter, *Statistical Account of Bengal,* vol. 18, pp. 300-1.
167. Srijit Mishra https://ideas.repec.org/p/ind/igiwpp/2009-006.html
168. Dr. Ganeswar Nayak, *Development of Transport and Communication in Orissa, 1866-1936,* New Delhi, Anmol Publisher, 2001.
169. *Report of the Indian Famine Commission 1880,* pt. 1, 'Famine Relief', pp. 15-16.
170. Tim Dyson, op. cit., p. 134. In fact, Dyson writes that a major crisis occurred in Bihar during 1874-5 and Richard Temple effectively dealt with the situation by importing food grain from Burma. But the same Richard Temple handled the victims of Madras famine of 1876-8 in a stern manner providing very small quantity of ration to the victims. Because the over enthusiastic response during the Bihar famine of 1874 led to severe criticism at the level of the higher officials. As a result total mortality rose to 5.6 million during the Madras famine 1876-8. As a reaction to this the Nationalists like Ramesh Chandra Dutt and Dadabhai Naoroji strengthened their position of criticizing the colonial rule, pp. 135-7.

    But the fact of the matter is that the intense sufferings of Orissa people during the great famine of 1866 made a deep impression on many officers they repented the loss of one lakh people within such short span of period. However, it is to be noted that Richard Temple handled the Madras famine so strictly that it was also known as Temple famine.

CHAPTER 4

Relief and Caste
Emergence of the Chhatrakhia Community

Introduction

All great famines have produced serious consequences in the social, economic and political spheres. Unavailability of food coupled with 'shifting exchange entitlements' or loss of purchasing capacity, of a vast magnitude population are bound to affect society as a whole.[1] In fact, the role of food in the history of humanity determines the nature of the cultural processes in the development of ethnic and regional identity.

It is true that the societal responses try to minimize the impact of these consequences by assimilating some of the effects. However, famines are so severe that the scars created by such events remain visible even after decades or centuries of their occurrence. It is particularly so in an agrarian society. The scars haunt a society eternally. For example, the Great Irish famine of 1845-9 still remains a part of the folk memory of the people there. It had a massive impact on demography, society and economy.[2] The famous painting, titled 'Potato Eaters' is a grim reminder about the devastating impact of that famine. It was painted by Vincent Van Gogh much later. But he got the inspiration from that event. Both the great famines also shaped the birth and growth of nationalism both in Ireland and Orissa since both were neglected by the then rulers, namely, Great Britain.[3]

In Orissa, after the famine was officially declared over in November 1866, new social groups had emerged in the region. Chhatrakhia was the most conspicuous among them. As mentioned earlier, these were the people who ate in the public relief centres and were regarded as outcastes by the other caste groups. Some experts hold the view that since these people came from a number castes they should be called a community. But similar processes led to the formation of many other castes in history such as Khaṇdayats who were soldiers and did farming in peace time or Kshatriyas who were warriors. In fact, the formation of outcastes and in some cases, attaching a stamp of inferiority on a social group has many parallels in India. The Kurmis in Bihar too suffered the same kind of indignities.[4]

Famine experience of people and the responses of the state and various private organizations in providing relief gave rise to many social trends. In this chapter we shall look at a few specific dimensions of this process, especially caste formation and cultural currents generated in the wake of the famine, in some detail. It should be noted that those who tried to escape from the label of Chhatrakhia, became either Christian converts or adopted Alekha Dharma, also known as Mahima Dharma, a non-Brahmanic religious stream popular among the tribals and Dalits. More on this later in this chapter. Here we shall analyse the processes of formation of such groups and their attempt to overcome the stigma attached to that and the effort to cope with the new situation. We do this also by referring to the thought currents triggered by the famine experience reflected in Oriya literature. As discussed in the previous chapter, agricultural labourers, artisans[5] and Santhals[6] of the princely areas died in large numbers due to the famine.[7]

The Relief Administration and the Caste Question during the Famine of 1866

Relief and Caste in Government Relief Centres

It is important to note that the colonial regime had no systematic famine relief policy giving guidelines for administering relief. As mentioned earlier, Orissa was in effect cut-off from the outside world in July 1866 due to floods. Rice could only be imported in the month of September. But by then much suffering and mortality had already taken place. [8] Rice was so scarce and the wages were so low that people refused wages in cash. Besides, the famine sufferers were physically too weak to undertake any hard work. Actually only one organization, an irrigation company, was offering wages in kind. But it was operating in Cuttack district only.

Apart from the government relief, which formed a major source, non-government sources such as religious institutions, zamindars, and the above-mentioned irrigation company were engaged in giving some relief.

When we closely look at the relief administration both by the government and by private initiatives we get a view of not only the nature of sustenance support it provided but also its impact on the social structure and social process. So it will be worthwhile to discuss as to how exactly the relief administration was done.

Actually, the government was indifferent towards providing gratuitous relief till April 1866 though a committee was formed in Puri district at the initiative of the Collector before that. The members of the committee collected local subscriptions and started giving cooked food in Puri as early as December 1865. But the Orissa Division Commissioner took an adverse view of it and prohibited such distribution of food in February 1866[9] thinking that it would have a disruptive effect on the functioning of the market. The ideology of free market economy operated even in such a situation! In June 1866, however, the government finally approved the composition of the relief committee having a mix of official and non-official members. The activities of the relief committees consisted of distribution of cash, helping the re-opening of houses of poor people (known as Poor Houses), organizing relief in villages, sale of rice in specific places, giving advances for the purchase of seed grains, and also 'special relief for respectable women, weavers and orphans', as a report put it.[10] Among these, the opening of poor people's houses and managing the feeding centres formed the main activities of the committees. However, the government kept on interfering with the functioning of the committees and the import of food grains to monitor its effect on the market.

A closer look at the operation of the feeding centres will give us an idea about the social dynamics at play, especially about caste rigidity and the cracks in it.

From April 1866 onwards the committees started buying rice from zamindars and merchants at a lower rate than the market rate. Cooked rice was distributed to the needy persons. Later, the committee could not use the money to buy rice because of non-availability of it. Hence gratuitous relief could not be given in adequate quantity till June 1866. Relief centres were extended to the interior parts of Cuttack district, including places like Taldanda and Kendrapara, where the irrigation company had started canal work. At this point, the irrigation company took rice from the committee to provide it as wage to the famine victims who worked in the canal construction work. They could perform only light work because of their poor physical health.

The maximum number of feeding centres were opened in September 1866. There were 43 feeding centres in Cuttack, 22 in Balasore and 23 in Puri. In Cuttack, on an average, 32,000 persons were served daily of which 13,449 persons did light labour while the rest were fed free. In Puri, on the other hand, the average number of persons given relief food was much less than those of Cuttack, namely 9,012 of whom 4,853 were given light work, as of September 1866. But the numbers continued to increase till November.[11]

In the beginning, the relief committees were reluctant to distribute cooked rice to the famine-affected people as they felt that in a caste-ridden society, eating cooked food in a public kitchen may be problematic by itself. Incidentally, the purity and pollution of cooked food was determined in terms of the status of the caste in a tradition-bound society. So a Brahmin would not eat cooked food served by persons from any other caste. Even Brahmins from one sect would not take food cooked by a person from another sect. Among tribes also, the Santhal tribe refused food cooked by Brahmins. But the situation demanded public action on this. Since people were wandering from place to place in search of food and work, the relief committees started serving cooked food to whoever came to the centres. Brahmin cooks were initially not employed in the feeding centres but later on there were Brahmin cooks, but members of other castes also served the food. Further the centres were distributing food by making them sit in a row irrespective of their castes. Interestingly, people of high caste in the beginning tried to avoid such 'polluting' arrangements and somehow managed without going to the centres. Many of them went even to distant places to eat to hide their caste identity. In some places, caste prejudice was so intense that many high caste people decided to die of starvation rather than eat at the relief centres.[12]

It was after noticing such caste behaviour that the relief committees decided to distribute raw, uncooked rice to the affected people. Many committee members, however, thought that those who were in need would come to these centres irrespective of any caste.[13] But distribution of raw rice had its own problem. People were so famished that they started eating uncooked raw rice and died due to toxicity. As mentioned earlier the government imported rice from Burma. But it was not parboiled rice which was commonly eaten in Orissa. At some stage, they also imported wheat without realizing that Orissa did not have any flour mills. Thus the famished people ended up eating raw rice. A medical doctor Jackson who conducted autopsy on several cadavers of famine victims found raw rice in their intestines.[14] It should be noted that for the first time, the Orissa Famine Commission Report mentioned the expression 'starvation deaths'. But surprisingly, later reports omitted this expression completely.

In each of these centres, shelters were also provided to the famine-affected people. In Puri, for example, it was decided to move the famine victims to a camp on the strip of sand that separates the sea from the town.[15] But these camps were so damp that it was impossible for them to live there. The straw beds for sleeping were never changed, and new batches of famine victims slept on the same straw beds. (It is important to note that during the period of the Great Famine of Ireland, similar conditions led to the dreaded infectious disease typhus which claimed thousands of lives.) In Puri many of those who stayed in the camps suffered from fever and pneumonia with a few succumbing to them.

Cuttack being the capital of Orissa Division at that time, received a lot of attention. Rows of houses were hurriedly constructed in a place now called Chhatra Bazar (literally meaning relief market) where the victims were settled. These houses were ill ventilated and people had to literally crawl to enter them. In Balasore district, on the other hand, regular roadside rest houses for pilgrims or *dharmshalas,* which were used to accommodate pilgrims travelling to Puri, were converted into temporary shelter houses for the famine victims.[16] As mentioned earlier, a mud road linking Calcutta to Puri called Jagannath Sadak passed through Balasore. During the famine period, some river embankments got constructed using famine labour. It is mentioned in some reports that many people had feared that since they were kept in enclosures and were vulnerable, they would be taken for sacrifice at the site of embankments.[17] All kinds of rumours spread during the famine. Because of a common feeding centres, famine victims from various castes came in contact with each other. They shared the same sleeping area. Rumours were also rife that the government would force them to eat food cooked by Muslims (Mohammedans in local parlance). Thus there were enough conditions created around the famine relief centres which made people to lose or loosen their caste identity. Many caste-conscious persons tried to avoid going to the relief centres as long as they could. The caste dynamics continued to play thereafter carrying the mark of 1866.

In Ganjam district, then a part of Madras Presidency, a lot of people suffered from the famine in 1888-9. The relief seekers were so desperate that they barged in to snatch food from the relief centres. They were also termed derogatively as 'Chhatrakhias'. By then the term had acquired a clear meaning. In this case, the low caste people wanted to take raw rice. But the Deputy Collector directed that separate relief centres should be set-up for high caste and low caste people which were at miles apart. They set-up a separate kitchen for Muslims as well. A note made by the Additional Collector mentioned that in one estate where the government had started a free kitchen, only for orphans. The Collector pointed out that he compelled the high caste people to come to the relief centres, but they fled to the forest instead. The high caste people did not even accept the raw rice distributed by the government.

Thus caste consciousness was so entrenched that most of these famine victims reached the shelter houses or the relief centres only at the last stage when they found no other alternative. Many of them died after having a meal or two due to dysentery or cholera. The government employed several sweepers to take away the dead bodies. They were given some money for each body. According to one report, out of sheer greed sometimes those sweepers killed many of the disabled victims who could not defend themselves to claim the money.[18] Another problem was the long distance between the shelter houses and some of the villages. So they had to walk long distances to come to the feeding centres. This disrupted their daily life. Therefore, in later famines more emphasis was placed on providing relief centres in the village itself.

Interestingly, in the Madras Famine of 1876-8 people also did not like to stay in shelter houses because of similar reasons. Rumors were afloat that the government wanted to convert them to Christianity or would send them overseas. Many problems in relief administration were reported during that period. In some cases, even physically weak persons were drafted for relief projects involving hard labour. The shelter houses remained in darkness due to severe shortage of lamp oil. It made it easy to steal whatever valuables the inmates had. Even ration tokens were not spared. Hence the practice of having relief centres in shelter houses was abandoned and village relief centres became the norm.[19]

Organizationally, the relief centres in Orissa Division were chaotic and living there was described as 'demoralising and debasing to the extreme'.[20] The government officials, including the Divisional Commissioner, had no idea regarding the conditions prevailing in these centres. Once while supervising one of them the Commissioner was shocked to see the deplorable condition of the shelter houses in Cuttack. There was similar situation in other districts too.[21] Incidents relating to two such centres, namely, Taldanda Canal area and Lal Bag (in Cuttack district) have been discussed in great detail in the document Famine Proceedings. For example, how Kirkwood, the Assistant Collector of Cuttack, handled thousands of famished victims when they begged for food and surrounded him in Taldanda. A stampede often broke out when people tried to get some grains. In another incident, the guards resorted to violence, in order to control the famine victims in the Cuttack relief centre. The incident was criticized in an editorial of *Utkal Dipika*.[22] As noted earlier, the relief centres were situated at a distance of 5 to 10 km away from their villages. Food was distributed simultaneously in all the centres so that the same person did not eat in more than one centre. The victims used earthen pots and torn cloth and sometimes banana leaf to eat their food. They were served watery dal and cold rice. No effort was made to give them hot, and fresh, nutritious food.[23] Besides, the amount of food served was not adequate to nourish them back to health.

The number of persons to whom food was served also depended upon the quantity of rice available. If rice was in short supply, relatively able-bodied persons were denied food and asked to go for work, though it was known that no work was available.[24]

Interestingly, the colonial officials put down their detailed comments on how caste rigidity operated at the time. As has been mentioned in Chapter 3, the members of low caste came in large numbers as they did not have any caste restriction. The truth was that there was not enough food to meet the demand. People were too famished to take heed of the caste restrictions and people of all castes shared food together.[25]

Relief and Caste in the Private Initiatives

Private initiatives to help the famine victims came from three different quarters: religious institutions such as missionaries, temples and *maths*; the zamindars and East India Irrigation Company. We have some data on each of these aspects, though systematic quantitative data is not available on either of them. In any case, these private initiatives were not enough to save the famine victims from starvation. Then, as well as now, large-scale disasters, coping strategies, relief organizations and long-term preparedness require central role of the state; the role of the civil society and corporate sector may just supplement it. In case of the 1866 famine and in subsequent occasions, the government tried to trivialize the role of private players. As a result, the official famine account did not mention adequately about their contribution. Besides, the zamindars too have not left any record of relief work provided by them. We give here an account taking threads from various sources. That is how, for example, we know that most of those who ate in the relief centres set-up by the missionaries were converted to Christianity and were regarded as outcastes in contrast to those who were fed by the temples or zamindars, and so remained in the same caste fold.

A. MISSIONARIES

The missionaries started coming to Orissa soon after the British established their control over the region. Some accounts mention that they were struck by reading the accounts of Dr. Buchanon (1806) on the Car Festival of Lord Jagannath and particularly the instances of self-immolation of some of the devotees in front of the chariot. The missionaries started preaching in Orissa in a systematic way from 1822 onwards after setting up some churches.[26]

The missionaries' relief activities during the 1866 famine in Cuttack, Puri and Balasore led many people, especially orphans, to convert to Christianity. A hamlet was expanded to accommodate a large number of orphans in Cuttack. The area of this settlement was 200 acres. The inmates were taught how to cultivate land scientifically. A school was also established for these children. Other settlements were set-up in Puri district to rehabilitate the famine-affected people. In these cases they were taught to weave cloth. The Famine Commission Report 1866 observed that the famine of 1866 left behind a large number of helpless orphans and the missionaries took charge of them all.[27] A large number of children were resettled in Jalleswar, Shantipore and Balasore. Similarly, Fakir Mohan Senapati in his autobiography, lamented that after the famine was over many orphans were seen to be wandering as there was nobody to take care of them. The Christians took them to their fold and converted them to Christianity. Biswamoy Pati talked at length regarding their hopes and despair which they felt after leaving the mother religion.[28]

How the missionaries started looking after the orphans in

Cuttack and initiated them up to Christianity is narrated in an autobiography of a convert named Anant Das. According to him, his brother had already warned him to not eat in government feeding centres. But he was desperately so hungry that he joined the line in the feeding centre to have some food. While having food, a priest of one the churches looked for orphans among them to admit in their orphanage. Anant lied that he was an orphan, who was on the look out for his brother and thus ended up in the orphanage. Soon, his brother also followed suit.[29] Clearly, conversion was not a preferred option in the prevailing social milieu. After the famine, the local press like *Utkal Dipika* and *The Hindu Patriot* pleaded with the authorities to reinstate the orphans to their original religion. But the government did not pay any heed to their voice nor did the caste society persist on this issue.

B. ROLE OF JAGANNATH TEMPLE AND THE *MATHS*

It is worth noting that the important temples like the Jagannath Temple in Puri and Lingaraj Temple in Bhubaneswar[30] had a long-standing practice of offering cooked food to the deities as a part of the daily rituals. Hunter reported in 1876 that at the time of the Car Festival in Puri, food used to be cooked in the temple kitchen for 90,000 devotees and at other festivals for 70,000 persons.[31] In other words, mass scale cooking inbuilt in the temple complex.

A unique feature of the Jagannath Temple is the sanctity that people associate with its offerings. The cooked food offered to devotees is known as *mahaprasad* – meaning 'the great offering'. Hunter wrote that a poor outcaste person knew that there existed such a sacred city where people from high caste and low caste could eat together. Once the rice is offered to the God, it becomes sacred. Outside the main gate called Singhadwar or the Lion Gate, thousands of people congregated to partake of it both low caste and high caste.[32]

Further, the Car Festival which attracts thousands of devotees is seen by many as an occasion which blurs caste and class distinctions since everybody has an equal right to pull the ropes of the chariot in which Jagannath, Balaram and their sister Subhadra take a 1.9 mile journey from the temple to the Gundicha *ghar* – another temple where the maternal aunt of the deities is worshipped. Similarly, the *Lakshmi Panchali,* read out while worshipping Goddess Lakshmi, preaches the idea of equality across castes. The story goes in the *Lakshmi Purana* that once Goddess Lakshmi went to the house of an untouchable woman (*chandalini*), and granted her a boon and accepts her offerings as the Goddess is impressed by her sincerity of her worshipper. But this action of Lakshmi antagonizes her husband, Lord Jagannath who on the prompting of his elder brother Balaram, throws her out of the temple and declares her an outcaste. In protest, she exposes their claim to universality and equality and takes revenge, by making them starve for twelve years. Finally, both the brothers apologize to her and get some food served by Lakshmi at her separate abode. I have analysed the *Lakshmi Purana* story in some detail in comparative perspective in another book, *Lakshmi the Rebel: Culture, Economy and Women's Agency,* discussing the interaction between caste, economy and culture from a gender perspective.[33] In other words, the Puri Temple had been playing (and still plays) an important role in shaping the socio-economic life of the Oriya people. As mentioned in Chapter 2, the temple employed many categories of people to perform the daily chores of the temple rituals. Moreover, traffic on the pilgrim road from Calcutta to Puri served an economic function providing many opportunities to various kinds of workers to serve the pilgrims en route.

Thus the Puri Temple had played a major role in organizing famine relief activities. But as for the arrangement of distribution of food in relief centres during the famine period, it is to be noted that the power of management of the temple vested with the queen of Puri, since the king was a minor. It turned out that, as the official records put it, she was not an efficient manager of the temple affairs.[34] But how important was the role of the tmple and the Puri king is known from the fact that the famine of 1866 is popularly known as *N'anka Durbhikhya*, meaning the famine that occurred in the ninth year (Anka) (in the royal almanac) of the king of Puri.[35]

However, in the beginning of the famine, the temple and the

maths or monasteries did open relief centres till the month of May. There is an interesting dimension to this. That the monasteries had sold paddy to the East India Irrigation Company and the government during the period was evident from the piles of silver coins discovered recently in Puri.[36] But after the initial phase, the official relief committee took charge since temple relief was not adequate. Later, in October 1866, the committee bought 15,000 maunds (one maund = 40 *seers*) of paddy from one of the monasteries at a rate lower than the prevailing one.[37] There were reports of starving people snatching the food offerings being carried by the temple workers.

On the other hand, there were also instances where the priests of the temple instead of helping, cheated the relief seekers, on the pretext of giving them cooked food and took away valuables from them in exchange.[38]

Everyday the temple kitchen cooked rice for thousands of pilgrims. After cooking they used to strain the cooked rice and channelled the starch water from the boiled rice (locally called *peja*) into a particular open drain leading to the river. During the famine, people thronged there in large numbers just to have that gruel from the drain, which was in some way nourishing no doubt, but would obviously lead to infection because of the unhygienic conditions.

C. THE EAST INDIA IRRIGATION COMPANY

The experiment of private investment in construction of canals was taken up in Madras and Orissa, and the East India Irrigation Company was set-up in 1862.[39] As mentioned earlier, it paid wages in grains and attracted more labourers in comparison to other public works.

The Company employed people between January and June and stopped its work during the rainy season when people needed work most. September onwards the Irrigation Company started paying raw grain for light labour in canal work.[40] But only Cuttack district people benefited from it.

D. ROLE OF ZAMINDARS

On the eve of the famine of 1866 most of the zamindars were absentee landlords and their estates used to be managed by petty clerks and *gumastas*.[41] Further, some of them had disposed off the year's produce just after the harvest, depleting the stock meant for the local people to buy.

Economic historians of famine such as B.M. Bhatia, discussing the context of the famines had pointed out that the old social organization in India had been already disrupted by the middle of the nineteenth century. The new, propertied class refused to recognize the social obligations due from them. In this situation the absentee landlords compelled the *raiyats* to pay rent and engaged agents for collection. The moneylenders took full advantage of the situation and amassed a great deal of wealth. They lent money only to the persons having landed property. Again some of them kept moveable and non-moveable assets under mortgage in lieu of paddy.[42]

However, not all zamindars were indifferent. On the eve of the famine, a group of zamindars pleaded with the government for rent remission but were not successful. Some zamindars in Balasore had started relief centres and small dispensaries to treat the cholera patients. In Puri the zamindar of Parikud estate exhausted almost all his resources to feed the famine-stricken people.[43] Similarly, one of the zamindars of Kendrapara subdivision by the name of Narendra donated his assets to save the famine victims. In this area, a saying from that era which is still in vogue is that the 'God' Indra rules in the heaven and Narendra ruled on the earth'.[44]

Thus, from the above narrative, it is evident that the contribution of private charity was inadequate to meet the devastating situation created by the intense famine. Hence, the affected population flocked to the shelter houses howsoever inhuman they were and to the feeding centres set-up by the government.

Caste, Class, Age and Gender of the Relief Seekers

The type of data available on the caste, class, household size, etc., of the relief seekers in the Bengal Famine of 1943,[45] is not available for the great Orissa famine of 1866. But enough is available to suggest that the first batch of people coming to the feeding centres were from low caste, mainly Dalits, such as Kandaras, Pans and Bauris. They were agricultural labourers and were first to be affected by the famine.

Moreover, there are records about incidents of 'grain robbery' by the people of these castes which was apparently rampant during the famine. Prisons were full of these petty thieves who happily admitted to having committed robbery.[46] In prisons they were assured of lenient treatment for their acts.

However, the reports say that the low caste people did not come in large numbers to regular construction work site was because of unfavourable working conditions there at the initial stages. The Famine Commissioner, 1866 wrote that the work was done through petty contracts as the famine victims were 'totally unfit' for the work.[47] Unfortunately, the Famine Commission did not mention in what way they were unfit. Perhaps the famine victims were famished and undernourished and thus lacked energy to do hard construction work such as digging or carrying heavy loads. Though since the construction work was done through the contractors on a piecemeal payment basis famished people were unable to carry on such hard work. As a result, they could not take much advantage of this source of earning. Besides, these construction works were done in far-off places.

There were other problems as well. To begin with, the feeding centres were located in the district headquarters. The famine-affected people had to walk long distances in large numbers to reach there and many of them collapsed and died en route owing to exhuastion and hunger. Hunter, quoting the Famine Commission reports that more than the caste prejudice, the unsanitary conditions of the feeding centres made people avoid going there till very late. The situation worsened after the floods of August 1866. The food was cold and flies hovered over the food. People carried broken pots or banana leaves to eat on. Only when both the floods and drought occurred, that the *raiyats* including those who had occupancy rights, had no alternative but to land in these feeding centres.[48]

They went to the centres somewhat later than the lower caste people because they had some stored grains to fall back upon. Anant Das wrote that though they belonged to the cultivating caste they were landless. Even so, his mother could get some rice by husking paddy and his father would gather edible roots for eating. Finally, his father deserted them leaving behind his mother, four sons and three daughters. Das went in search of his maternal uncle with the hope of food. Even though, he reached the village where his uncle lived he could not find him and out of sheer desperation went to the feeding centre.[49]

The famous Oriya writer, Mayadhar Mansingh [50] in the preface of his book *Diary of Ananta Das*, wrote the narratives of the famine of Orissa, 1866 as heard from his grandmother and other elderly persons of his village who had experienced the event first hand. His area, Parikud, an island on Chilika Lake, was one of the worst affected areas in 1866. He wrote that his family had mortgaged their utensils and ornaments with a trader and bought *ragi* to be eaten in a gruel form during the famine period. As he belonged to a cultivating caste (Chasa or Khandayat) and possessed a few acres of land they could somehow tide over the crisis. As a result, his family did not get disintegrated.

As we have seen, the weavers were badly affected because of the lack of demand for their products. The fishing community was adversely affected in areas where the catch was not available. So many weavers and *keuta* (fishermen) went to the feeding centres.[51] Some poor Brahmins also ate in the feeding centres. The Assistant Collector of Puri reported that in a prosperous Brahmin village, out of a total population of 309 persons, 92 had died. However, the Commission felt that many of the missing persons would have emigrated and would be back again.[52] In another village, the Assistant Collector found that out of the 28 households there only two survived.[53]

Therefore, on the whole, it seemed that the agricultural labourers belonging to low castes such as artisans, and fishing community were the first victims of the famine to approach the feeding centres. The latecomers to the feeding centres belonged to the cultivating caste as well as other high castes. They survived the onslaught of the famine relatively well initially.

That people from the landed and cultivating caste came to the relief centres is also evident from an English poem written by Jayanta Mahapatra titled *My Grandfather*. He records that his grandfather's parents died of starvation though they belonged to the landowning peasant caste. During the famine his grandfather was wandering in the streets when a chowkidar employed by the missionaries spotted him and brought him to the orphanage there. His grandmother also experienced a similar situation. They became Christians and rebuilt their lives later. It may be mentioned that their grandson, Jayanta Mahapatra became a famous poet whose creations reflect the history of Orissa and the confluence of world traditions. The moral sentiments of the Bible are as much visible in his poetry as those of the great Indian epics, *Ramayana* and *Mahabharata*.[54]

Unfortunately, there is no systematic data available regarding the impact of the famine on the old and young people. But the Famine Commission, 1866 reported that the relief committees showed preference for old women and young boys in providing relief.[55] The government declared the famine to be over by November 1866 when new crops started to arrive in the market, even though the epidemics still raged. The relief centres had to feed a number of old women and children. At this critical time, trying to arrange caregivers for the needy was very important. The missionaries took care of many children while many people adopted some young boys but not girl children. Sex preference in the patriarchal society was thus abundantly clear. Prostitutes adopted some of the girl children, many of who grew up to be sex workers.[56] In Cuttack alone there were 130 minor girls. The government took steps to rescue them from the brothels and settle them in female orphanages. But the older women remained in that profession. In so far as the other old women were concerned they had to be supported by the relief centres since they had no other place to go.[57] Even though information is very scanty, it shows that relatively more women and children than men came to the feeding centres after the famine was declared as over. At the same time, it is to be noted that during the peak period of the famine, women and children were edged out because men crowded the centres and women were somewhat scared to stand alongside the men in the feeding centre queue. But it is somewhat commendable that women who had never crossed the threshold of their house were found doing odd jobs in the relief centres like cooking, spinning, etc. and other social jobs. This began a new trend in the occupational structure as well.

New Trends in the Social Order

During this period, social events like marriages and other ceremonies relating to birth and death were deferred. Contrary to the conventional practices of abstaining from eating non-vegetarian food during the eleven days' period of mourning, people ate non-vegetarian food even during this period. Similarly, other death rituals such as offering feasts to blood relations, placing rice meals as the offering for the departed soul everyday for ten days at the backyard, were also not observed. The notion of purity and pollution with regard to cooked food thus got altered to some extent. Ananta Das in his diary mentions that people even stole cooked food from the kitchens of unknown people to appease their hunger. During normal time it would be considered blasphemous.

Mansingh, whose grandparents suffered during the famine, pointed out that the survivors of the famine narrated to him various incidents relating to these aspects. There were even instances where mother and father snatched food from their children's mouths. Desertion of family was rampant. Instances of cannibalism are also recorded.[58] Many people migrated overseas. It included a sizeable number of Chhatrakhias who felt guilty to go back to their village after having eaten at the relief centres during the famine. It was one of the reasons for the break down of many families as well. Many of the migrants died *en route*, on road or ship and many never returned.[59]

Formation of a New Caste

As mentioned earlier, a new caste called Chhatrakhia, came into existence consisting of those who ate in the public relief kitchen during the famine. Originally they came from all castes. As indicated earlier, among the Chhtrakhias, some were Christian converts and others were identified as of Alekha Dharma and some neither. In the Census of 1891 the Commissioner wrote that 488 males and 775 females reported themselves as Chhatrakhias.

Let us look at some aspects of this new social group.

First, formation of outcastes was nothing new in the context of Indian famines, particularly after the introduction of the British rule. K. Suresh Singh quoted Buchanan to show how a new caste was created during the Bengal Famine of 1770. The members were called Saryuriyas. Originally they were Hindus but later on they ate cooked food made by 'impure hands' during that famine. After a lapse of almost one hundred years, during the Doab famine of 1861 again, the affected people were reluctant to go to the shelter houses or eat in the feeding centres set-up by the government, for fear of losing their caste. They belonged to North-Western Provinces then consisting of Uttar Pradesh, Punjab, Rajasthan and a few other areas.[60] Similarly, during the famine of 1866, a similar caste was formed in Bihar also, who came from Kellar and Sundi and lived by begging. This caste was still found to exist in 1901, according to K. Suresh Singh.[61]

In case of Orissa, however, it created a major social problem. It is not known if the creation of the sub-castes created any such anomaly in other regions. Referring to J.C. Geddes (1874) on the intensity of the caste problems in the aftermath of the famine, K. Suresh Singh observed that recovering caste identity was one of the major social problems. This was because a large number of persons became 'irreclaimable outcastes' since they ate in the feeding centres during the famine. In the process, it disrupted the entire social fabric. Families were split, children got separated from their parents, etc.[62]

Geddes quoted *Manusmriti* which says that in times of acute hunger it was not a sin to eat whatever is available while referring to the procedure laid down by the Orissa priests to face such situations, which allowed many discretions. Still, a distinct caste of Chhatrakhia got formed either due to lack of understanding about the nature of the feeding centres or inability of the poor to pay for the purification ritual as prescribed by the Brahmin priests. Interestingly, on the one hand, the other caste groups who were looked down upon as untouchables maintained their original, hierarchical caste identity among themselves.[63] This was true even of the migrants who found it difficult to shake off the insult heaped upon them, but at the same time maintained the distinction of high and low caste groups among themselves at the place of their migration.[64] In other words, Chhatrakhia, even as a new depressed caste, was a cluster of differentiated social groups. This explains the rigidity of the Indian caste order on the one hand, and the flexible way it negotiates with social and economic pressures on the other.

It may be recalled here that members of all castes shared cooked food offered at the Jagannath Temple without altering their caste order. In fact, the practice of people from various castes eating *mahaprasad* (offering made to Jagannath) or *abhada* (as the cooked rice is called) from the same earthen pot is permitted as having the sanction of the Jagannath religious order. But at the same time during the famine, eating of cooked food together in the feeding centres turned them into Chhatrakhias. In other words, the people of Orissa looked down upon the feeding centres opened by the government. This approach also affected the land rights of these people. It became a handy tool for the zamindars to evict the *raiyats* who had become a Chhatrakhia. Despite the fact that they had occupancy rights, the zamindars now replaced their tenure with another set of people. Brahmin priests too took advantage of the situation to earn some money in the crisis period by performing elaborate purification rituals of the Chhatrakhias to readmit them to their original castes.

The *Utkal Dipika* wrote that many people had kept the destitutes of the Chhatrakhia caste as servants in their homes but would not touch even water served by them. As a result, the servants felt humiliated. The *Utkal Dipika* argued that these destitutes should be readmitted to their former castes as they had 'repented' their act of having eaten in the relief centres.[65]

In fact, a couple of social reformers tried to purify those people so that they were readmitted into their former castes. The *pundits* of Calcutta and Puri were consulted, but the caste prejudice was too strong to persuade them. At first the Puri *pundits* did not want to readmit them to their respective castes. But the efforts continued. On 11 April 1868, the *Utkal Dipika* again reported that, as a result of the efforts of Bichitranand Das, a social worker, the zamindars had agreed to resettle the Chhtrakhias in their territory and the villagers also agreed to readmit them to their former castes. But the Chhatrakhias had to perform some rituals of readmission before that. They were expected to throw a feast for the villagers and make some offerings to the goddesses of the village. Bichitranand Das published a booklet containing the procedures of getting readmitted and requested the zamindars to get it distributed in the weekly markets. The *Utkal Dipika* also hoped that gradually all the members of the outcastes would be readmitted. The magazine regretted that similar measures could not be taken for the orphans who were taken by the missionaries.[66] It showed the prevailing sentiments against religious conversion.

During the famine period, land transactions increased considerably. The *raiyats* had to mortgage their land for food and later left their villages.[67] But the *raiyats* having occupancy rights lost that right if they deserted it during the famine. The government had announced that the *raiyats* would be restored their occupancy rights if they could show any proof of their ownership. After the famine period they came back to their native place due to the attraction of their land. But the Brahmin priests and the upper caste landlords resisted the *raiyats* (belonging to the cultivating castes) to get back their occupancy rights. In some cases, the zamindars welcomed them as share-croppers for the same piece of land. Thus the famine condition significantly altered the land relations, and the lower castes, even the cultivating caste peasants lost their occupancy rights and many of them became sharecroppers. The phenomenon of the massive proportion of landless rural labour that continued for the next century and more had its origin partly in this experience in Orissa.

Risley, the Census Commissioner of Bengal Presidency in 1901 noted that Chhatrakhias first came to be noticed in the 1881 Census. This caste was divided into two sub-castes or strata – upper and lower. The upper strata consisted of those who were originally Brahmins, Karans (Kayasthas), Khandayats, and Goalas. The members of these groups could inter-marry. The lower sub-caste or strata comprised castes ranking below these in the social order. He also noticed that inter-caste marriages between the lower and upper strata was not possible. He commented that 'It can hardly be doubted that much social misery must have been endured before the people adopted a situation so entirely at variance with the principles in which they had been brought up, and that for one who became a Chhatrakhia, many died of want.[68]

Again, in the 1901 Census, the number of Chhatrakhias was recorded as 488 males and a much larger number of 775 females.[69] It might be due to the fact that more women went to the relief centres and after the famine was over they found it to be more difficult to get readmitted to their original caste order. And also more men migrated to different places near and far in search of work and food.

In 1933,Cousins wrote in the Gazetteer of Cuttack in a similar vein and provided some details of the social practices associated with the Chhatrakhia caste.[70]

Interestingly, the word Chhatrakhia was only a one time creation but it has lived for ever. It was created for the first time during the famine of 1866 to refer to those who ate in the *chhatra* (relief centre). In the subsequent famine proceedings we do not find any mention of Chhatrakhias. It was probably because the strong resentment against the relief centres had declined. One could argue that the intensity of famine in Orissa Division had diminished also, which was partly true. But the famines of the twentieth century did result in heavy mortality and public relief centres were in operation. The administrators took care of caste feelings by carefully organizing the forms of relief. Generally they began giving relief in the form of raw rice. It may also be the case that the collectors and other officers who were collecting data on later famines perhaps did not collect any data on this aspect.

The cultural impact of the Chhatrakhia phenomenon can be seen in many spheres. Terms like 'Chhatrakhia', 'go to Chhatra', etc. became part of the vocabulary of abuse in Oriya. As we have noted in Chapter 3 even, now Cuttack city has a huge wholesale market for selling and buying vegetables, known as Chhatra Bazar. This was the place where a public relief centre was located. The people who came to dig the canal ate in this relief centre. Recollecting the origin of Chhatra Bazar, Rajendra Prasad Das wrote that the place is known as Chhatra Bazar depicting the fact that relief was distributed during the famine of 1866. But people have distorted the name as Chhatra Bazar, according to him, implying that people committing petty crimes were living there.[71] Till mid-1960s one could notice rows of tiny houses having no proper ventilation except small doors where the famine victims were settled near the bazar. Over the years that area has become prime property. Thereafter, the well-to-do would identify themselves as Khandayats, Karans or Rajputs. Now they live in three colonies called Shankarpur, Balabhadrapur and Dhiasahi in the broad area of Chhatra Bazar. The inhabitants of these respectable colonies get angry if they are referred to as residents of Chhatra Bazar.

Yet another impact of the famine was the settlement of tribals in the same colony as the non-tribal people. Since the famine victims in the region became physically weak and could not perform hard labour, the government brought the tribals from the interior forest areas to dig the canals. So one sees the beginning of tribal settlement in the coastal areas of Orissa from this time.

As mentioned in the previous chapter, many new words were coined. For instance a word called *N'nkia* referring to a person as famished as those who had starved during the famine of 1866 – came into vogue in Oriya language and continues to be used till today. It now also means a certain kind of behaviour comparable to that of a famine destitute. These terms are frequently heard in remote rural areas. Also, in the course of the famine and its aftermath, a large variety of new dishes made entry into Oriya cuisine which was already rich due to the numerous Puri temple items and dishes from different regions and groups of the region, especially from the multiple festivals celebrated by the people. (For example, the food cooked in the Temple is heavily spiced with black pepper, which perhaps had travelled here along with Adi Shankara from Kerala, who established religious centres in various parts of India, including one at Puri.) The famine-stricken people in the forests and coastal areas, tried out in desperation, with great risk ate leaves, stems, roots, vegetables and fruits which were hitherto never tried before. Some of the delicious, yet simple dishes of today's Oriya cuisine owe their origin to the otherwise tragic 1866 famine. In fact, in a way, the famine cuisine has shaped the taste buds of Oriyas.

Christian Converts

K. Suresh Singh has documented how people got converted during different famines in nineteenth-century India. He believed that this was the background against which the governments of Rajasthan, Orissa and Madhya Pradesh made laws after Independence, banning the conversion of tribals by the Christian missionaries through 'allurements' and 'enticements?'.[72] In this context he has also referred to the famine of 1866. It is to be noted that among the Christians there was a clear-cut division between those who got converted because they ate in the free kitchens – popularly called *bhaata* (or rice) Christians and other native Christians. The latter group looked down upon the former group because they got converted for food only.[73] There were other categories of Christians also. They were, known as in colloquial language as Lady Christians, Paddy Christians, Hen Christians and Pen Christians. Paddy Christians, thus known for eating rice in the relief centres. Lady Christians were so-called due to marriage with a Christian. Hen Christians because they had dined with the Sahibs, and Pen Christians because they had got education. We have already referred to cases where the missionaries played an active role and took charge of the orphans and established various settlements. Some of those settlements exist till today.

Conversion to Alekha Dharma

A section of Chhatrakhias adopted a religion called Alekha Dharma to escape the ostricization by the society.[74] In Orissa the mystic poet Bhima Bhoi, a blind and tribal preacher, was the founder of this Dharma, though an Alekh Swamy who came from the Himalayas in 1864 preached about it first. Bhima Bhoi was a non-believer of the Hindu pantheon of gods and did not believe in caste system. In 1867, *Utkal Dipika* published accounts of Alekha Dharma or Mahima Dharma as a new Dharma prevalent in the princely estates. It also reported how low caste members were getting converted to Mahima Dharma.[75] In 1873, the Brahmins became agitated and decided to ostracize those who would adopt the Mahima Dharma.[76] In 1881, a group of Mahima Dharma disciples comprising men and women wanted to destroy the idols of Jagannath, Balabhadra and Subhadra in the Puri Temple. But the *pandas* and the police prevented them from doing so.[77] Thus Mahima Dharma fought against casteism and idol worship. So it was but natural that some of the Chhatrakhias would have adopted this religion.

As Ishita Dube has observed in her study, Mahima Dharma did pose a challenge to the authority of the king and the priest in the nineteenth century. This religion rejected caste rule and commensality and was not in favour of acquiring any property. But slowly this character of the religious community changed and the followers of this Dharma fell prey to the temptation of acquiring property. In the process Alekha Dharma lost many of its challenging characteristics.[78]

Adopting Brahmo Samaj

By 1866 the Brahmo Samaj movement had already began to be spread in Bengal and had reached Orissa. The 1866 famine gave a boost to this movement because it too challenged the caste order. By 1891 the movement had spread far and wide though it was restricted to the urban elite. The members of the Brahmo Samaj tried to bring radical changes in Indian thought and traditional culture.[79]

Famine and Oriya Literature

Any severe famine impacts not only the psyché of the people and the fabric of society but also affects the cultural realm, especially literature and the arts. Margaret Kelleher has analysed a few novels in connection with the great Irish Potato Famine of 1846 as well as the famine literature on the backdrop of the Bengal Famine of 1943. She observed that there has been what she described as 'feminization of the famines', because the authors of many of the novels created images in which women and children of the lower classes became objects of pity, commodification or gratification for the high-class hero who proved to be their saviour. She further noted that this kind of depiction is a modern phenomenon as well.[80]

In the case of the famine of 1770 in Bengal, Bankim Chandra Chattopadhya created the inspiring novel, *Anandamath*, to generate patriotism.[81] Similarly, assessing the impact of the Bengal famine of 1943-4 many novels, plays, films and poems were written reflecting the contemporary period of war, impact of Industrial Revolution and patriotism. Recently, Mandira Ghosh in her book on Bengal famine has elaborated quite vividly the impact of the Bengal famine when, according to her, many women entered the flesh trade to earn their livelihood.[82] The Bengali film *Ashani Shanket* (Distant Thunder) was made by the famous filmmaker, Satyajit Ray based on the above famine. It showed how the famished migrants in the end marched forward towards a lost horizon.

The famine of 1866 was no exception. We have already mentioned that many new terms got coined during that famine signifying the severity of the famine. Besides *n'ankia*, other terms like, *ranka* (excessive anxiety to get something), etc., came into existence. In order to gauge the continuity of the impact of the 1866 famine, Oriya dictionary at three points of time (1932-6), 1968 and 1983 were consulted.

In 1932-6, Gopal Chandra Praharaj compiled the monumental Oriya dictionary called *Bhasha Kosha* in six volumes for the first time. He devoted one and a half page just to the above words. Despite some repetition, let us note the meanings he gave to these terms. He pointed out that Chhatrakhia caste was created for the first time during the famine of 1866 because they ate in the government relief centres. The word *n'ank* has been defined as the famine that occurred in the ninth year of the rule of Puri king where about eight lakh people died. *N'ankia* refers to persons reduced to a skeleton for want of food. Chhatrakhia, he informed, show the exploitation of women during the famine period. These were women who ate in the relief centres and took to prostitution later on. In addition, he wrote that some Chhatrakhias converted to Christianity while others remained as Hindu and were known as Rajputs and Chhatris, etc.[83]

In 1967, Shridhar Das (a well-known educator), compiled *Naba Abhidhan* (New Dictionary). He had consulted the volumes written by Praharaj. But he defined Chhatrakhias as those who ate in the free kitchens but did not mention the origin of the word. In other words, he sought to minimize its pejorative connotation.

As regards to *n'ankia,* he reproduced the observations made by Praharaj.[84]

In 1983 Nrusingh P. Mishra revised the Oriya Dictionary. He repeated the observations made by Praharaj in so far as *chhatra-khia* was concerned,[85] but ignored the word *n'ankia* completely perhaps, to avoid reference to a dark period of Oriya history. Thus it is interesting to see how the impact of the famine of 1866 still persists in the minds of the Oriya people. However, attempts have also been made from time to time, to recast the memory of the great tragedy. For example, the later dictionaries did not devote much space to words like 'chhatrakhia' 'ranka', nor 'n'ank'. Krishna Ch. Kar compiled an Oriya dictionary in 1966 which was reprinted in 2008. It defined *n'ank* as the ninth year of the king of Puri and denotes the occurrence of the famine of 1866. Apart from that he does not give any other information. But the most curious point to note is the statement that the word 'ranka' was created during the famine period to reveal that people were so famished that they behaved crazily at the sight of food. Besides dictionaries, Oriya novelists, and poets also wrote many novels based on the theme of the above famine. We turn to these next.

Fakir Mohan Senapati (1843-1918), the father of Oriya short

story, was an eyewitness to the famine of 1866. He narrated vividly the horrors of the famine in his autobiography, giving details on the phenomenon of Chhatrakhias and Christian converts. For example, he observed that women were so emaciated that even the signs of motherhood were not visible.[86] This kind of references are however lacking in the official reports.

Even though in the aftermath of the famine, Orissa experienced a number of developmental activities, we have not come across any famine-related stories till 1933. Just after that we find that two authors wrote four novels to describe the events as well as the traumatic experience of the Chhatrakhias. In both the cases the character of a famine victim had changed in a qualitative manner. Sanatan is a famous case written in the form of poetry and fiction in many versions. In the earlier versions he had died while trying to get food to save the lives of his parents. Later Sanatan symbolized the famine victim who does not die and continues his search of food. In fact, he rebels against the system and tries to change the social order. Let us now discuss two famous novels written by Kalindicharan Panigrahi dealing with this theme.

Actually, till 1936, Panigrahi was known as a romantic writer. After that he was influenced by socialism and his writings took up progressive ideas. Both the novels *Muktagarhara Khyudha* (Hunger in Muktagarh) and *Amar Chita* (Eternal Pyre) were written after 1936 and both were based on the background of the famine of 1866.

To put it briefly, the author shows how Shubhakanta, king of a princely estate, Muktagarh, was quite oppressive because of the circumstances in which he was born and brought up. But a change of heart occurred when he saw the sufferings of the people in the famine of 1866 and decided to spend his entire money and estate to help the famine victims. Sanatan, a Brahmin youth, who was instrumental in changing his heart, was no longer depicted as a person who died of hunger due to lack of food. In this novel, Sanatan rebelled against a Brahmin moneylender and killed him because he did not lend rice to the poor. In this account, the moneylender also exploited women. Sanatan was tried under colonial law and was sentenced to death and the king Shubhakanta was deported to Kalapani, because he was a close friend of Sanatan.[87] Sanatan, the poor Brahmin boy, instead of becoming a symbol of sacrifice as was the case in earlier writings who died trying to save his father, now turned into a rebel in this story.

The character of Sanatan resurfaced again in a short story written by the poet Lakshmikant Mahapatra in 1936. Sanatan's character seemed to have become immortal since he peeps into the literary world in the form of a myth, frequently at a later stage. Prasanna Kumar Mishra wrote a poem searching for a myth which drives Oriyas to survive in spite of famine, floods and cyclones. He noticed that Sanatan provided the human values for which he sacrificed his life. He wrote this in the preface of his poetry collection titled *Sanatan in the Truck Carrier as a Labourer.* The allusion is to the phenomenon of distress migration that persisted in the poverty-stricken Kalahandi-Bolangir region even in the twenty-first century. So for Mishra, Sanatan did not die of starvation but rather led the struggle for the entire Oriyas to get rid of the socio-economic obstacles people faced in life.

Godabarish Mahapatra (1886 to 1956), reputed poet and satirist of Orissa, depicted yet another picture of the suffering of the 1866 famine. In his short story titled 'Ebe Madhya Banchichhi' (He Lives On) he narrates the experiences of the people of his village who ate freely in the relief centre, where food was distributed free. He rued the fact that the great nation of Oriyas having so many achievements in the previous centuries had turned into a nation of beggars overnight due to the famine. The author also noted the fact that in spite of hunger, many Oriyas didn't eat in the relief centres and preferred to die rather than eat there. This story was written during the freedom struggle to arouse the nationalist sentiments of the Oriya people.

The character of Sanatan crops up again and again in Radhamohan Gadanayak's poems. In 1945 he wrote a poem 'Mari Nahi, Se Te Marana Jayee' (Not Dead, He has Conquered Death). The same poem titled now as 'Sanatan' was published in the Oriya journal *Jankar* in 1959. Commenting on the poetry collection of Gadanayak, Chintamani Behera described the character Sanatan as representing the inner soul of the famished people of the entire N'anka period of Orissa.

The origin of the character Sanatan, is quite revealing. Originally, the English writer L.H.G.D. Turnbull's book of short stories titled *Golden Deeds of India* contained the story of Sanatan, under the title 'The Faithful Heart'. Based on that story the Bengali writer Narendra Dev wrote 'Many Days and Many Tales'. Further, based on the same theme yet another longish poem was published in the Oriya journal, *Utkalika*. The title of the poem was 'He Just Fell Down on the Roadside'. It was written by the same author as above. In both cases, the picture of Sanatan kept on haunting the readers. Both Ramakrishna Nanda and Radhamohan Gadanayak took the depiction of the Sanatan story by Narendra Dev forward and wrote their powerful poems in Oriya.[88] According to Surendra Mohanty, yet another book titled *Hunger* depicts various facets of hunger including that of Sanatan.[89]

Another popular novelist, Kanhu Charan Mohanty, also wrote two novels on the background of the famine of 1866. The first one is *Ha Anna* (O' Rice) narrating the stages of deprivation due to the famine suffered by a relatively prosperous cultivator's son Jagu Pradhan. Jagu had lost everything in the food riots. He got refuge at last through the private relief initiative provided by a Mahant of Puri. The novel mentions instances of cannibalism and narrates various kinds of sufferings, including exploitation of women by the Mahant. There is a glimmer of romance in the story as Jagu along with other famine victims took shelter at a *math* where he met his childhood love Uma. There is also an interesting dimension to the story where through the hero, the author questions the existence of god.

Another novel by Kanhu Charan, titled *Shasti* (Punishment), narrates how it was literally a punishment inflicted upon the persons who had eaten in the public relief centres by the society during the famine. Here Sanatan alias Sanei Parida, the son of a relatively well-to-do cultivator leaves his village after selling his land to another co-cultivator at a throwaway price. After the famine is over he comes back to his village but is considered a Chhatrakhia and regarded as an untouchable. However, nothing is lost, he was told, if he could throw a feast for the villagers as well as to the village deity. His lady love Dhobi, the daughter of the co-cultivator to whom Sanei's land was sold and who had got married somewhere else, had become a widow during the famine period, helped Sanei Parida to get readmitted to the caste-fold secretly. Later on, however, Dhobi refused to marry him on the grounds of social norms and Dharma. Incidentally, the cultivating caste allowed widow remarriage and Dhobi's mother kept on requesting her husband to get her married to Sanei. Sanei gets frustrated and decides to rebel against the society and started living with persons from other castes and religions. He also married a Chhatrakhia woman who was a mother of a child. These acts of Sanei further infuriated the village priest and the relatively more prosperous cultivators of the village. They try to ostracize him again. But Sanei leaves his newly constructed house, land, and other assets and along with his wife and a few friends in dignity before they can punish him further.[90]

In his preface to *Ha Anna*, Kahnu Charan Mohanty wrote that he had a first-hand experience of a severe famine that occurred in 1915-16 in one of the princely states. In 1933 he went through three volumes of the Famine Commission Reports (1866) and wrote the first novel on the background of the famine. The novel *Shasti,* even though describing the experience of Chhatrakhias just after the famine of 1866, was written in 1945 and not immediately after the first novel.

In both the cases, the hero belonged to the cultivating caste. But Sanei Parida voiced a rebellious note against the social norms and leaves the village. Jagu Pradhan on the other hand, succumbs to the fury of the famine and is rescued by his beloved who is not from his own caste.

As mentioned earlier, Jayanta Mahapatra, eminent Orissa poet pointed out that his grandfather Chintamani became a convert to Christianity during the famine of 1866 since he ate in the public relief centres. Based on his experience, Mahapatra wrote an English poem entitled 'Light of a Mad Person'.[91] Mahapatra also revealed that because of his religion he was discriminated against and was the chief reason he remained an introvert throughout his life.

The Present Scenario

Now we present a reflective discussion on the phenomenon of Chhatrakhia and its contemporary status in Orissa. It is based upon interviews with some members of the Chhatrakhia caste as well as interaction with some anthropologists of Orissa.

After a lapse of one hundred and fifty years, one would have expected this group of people to be completely integrated with their other caste members. Unfortunately, the scar is still visible. Two such clusters are still located in Cuttack district. About 3,000 households are still living in Chhatra Bazar. Similarly, about 500 households are still located on the either sides of the Taldanda and Patamundai canals. (It may be recalled that the Irrigation Company had recruited labourers to dig up canals and paid them in kind during the famine. Later on the relief committee also sold rice to the famine victims and distributed cooked food to the starving people in these areas.) Some of these households are located near Machhagaon canal also. Majority of them have adopted the surnames of the Khandayat caste. It could be due to the fact that majority of the survivors of the relief centres were from the cultivators' castes (Khandayats and Chasas) who came much later to such feeding centres.

Second, the caste Khandayat means swordsman or headman of a *khand*. In ancient times these people acted as peasant militia during the war times and became cultivators in the time of peace. So people from both high and low caste got recruited to this caste. In the nineteenth century as well as early twentieth century there has been considerable inter-caste mobility between Karanas (Kayasthas), Khandayats and Chasas (cultivating castes) in terms of marriage alliances. In fact, in the 1931 census, many Chasas returned themselves as Khandaits (spelt thus then).[92] Since the Khandayat caste recruited members from different castes in the past it is not surprising that majority of the Chhatrakhias adopted the surnames of Khandayats or that of cultivating castes. Of course, it does not mean that they did not adopt any other surnames.[93] The main occupation of these households is still agriculture and to some extent also trading. Some of them are wholesale dealers of vegetables, some are employed as mechanics, etc. They themselves have tried to move upwards in the caste hierarchy by acquiring some wealth. On a rough estimate, at least 60 per cent of the inhabitants of Chhatra Bazar have *pucca* houses. Some of them have become successful in business and services. Their sons and daughters have been married off in the Khandayat families. In one case at least the daughter of a Chhatrakhia is married off to an IAS officer.

However, their social behaviour is still reflective of the stigma of having eaten in relief centres attached to them by the society. They react violently, and become intolerant and abusive to others at the mere sound of the word 'Chhatra' (it is an abuse word in Oriya language now).[94] It may be noted that the Communist Party of India had recruited many members from this locality and had a pocket of influence there for a long time, reflecting its commitment to the cause of the downtrodden classes.

The reasons for such reaction by them after a lapse of 150 years can be sought in the characteristics of Orissa economy. It is still mainly agricultural. In 2011 the urban share of the population was only 17 per cent. In terms of poverty ratio about 50 per cent of the population live below the poverty line, though the share has come down slightly but still remains higher than the national average. Given the above characteristics it is no wonder that caste rigidity still prevails though its grip is loosening slowly.

Overview

The famine of 1866 caused nearly one million deaths due to starvation and epidemics. After importing rice much later, the government launched relief work and started distributing cooked food in lieu of work in the common feeding centres. It also built makeshift shelters near the feeding centres. These measures had many serious, long-term consequences which are recorded in official documents, press reports and literature.

The caste prejudices were too strong in an apparently tolerant society (due to the presence of a tolerant culture associated with Lord Jagannath and multiple religious and tribal cultural traditions coexisting for a long time). People who ate in those relief centres were branded as outcastes and called Chhtrakhias. After the famine was over, they were not welcome back in their original village and were denied to get back their land rights.

The government settled them near the relief centres and on both sides of the main canals. Some of them adopted Christianity, others joined Mahima Dharma which challenged Hinduism. Social reformers tried very hard to readmit them to their respective castes. But the efforts failed miserably.

Even after a lapse of one hundred and fifty years we still find the scars of the famine on the society since the Chhtrakhia caste still exists. Though majority of them have prospered and moved on economically. The society still perceives them as the product of the famine and they are still looked down upon. This attitude has made them intolerant and to some extent violent. Some of the women members of this caste avoid using the word 'Chhatrakhia' and said that they were helpless victims of the deeds of their ancestors.

The rigidity of caste system still persists in Orissa perhaps because of the low degree of urbanization and being predominantly agricultural and backward. However, it is important to note that in spite of the suffering no social movement has yet emerged to ameliorate the fate of the community. There are many instances where social leaders have rebelled and tried to educate themselves to climb the ladder of economic prosperity. But the Chhatrakhia members are mostly poor and still struggle for their daily existence. Hence, they silently bear the brunt of the insults.

The great famine of 1866 had widespread ramifications on Oriya society, economy and polity. Politically, the landlords tried to gain control over the *raiyats* by displacing them from their land and tarnishing their image as Chhatrakhia. Socially, not only a new caste was formed which still exists but also members of many families died and many families broke up or got separated. Besides, Oriya language got some new words into their dictionary. In addition, the scope of Oriya cuisine got expanded. Last but not the least, the famine created an opportunity to work towards a unified Oriya state which fructified only in 1936.

Notes

1. Amartya Sen, *Poverty and Famines: An Essay on Entitlement and Deprivation,* Delhi, Oxford University Press, 1986.
2. Cecil Woodham Smith, *The Great Hunger: Ireland 1845-49,* London, Harper and Row and Penguin Books, 1962 https://en.wikipedia.org/wiki/Great_Famine_(Ireland)
3. At this point a comparison can be made between the Kurmi community and Chhatrakhias, which Nanda and Kulke (eds.) have analysed in their writings on the former community. According to them, Kurmis suffered from various famines. They also suffered from the 'culture of silence' or *nirbakization* for generations together. They would articulate their dissenting voices by writing their autobiographies and playing leadership role in the freedom struggle. They acquired such powers because of access to education. In case of Chhatrakhias, on the other hand, such culture of silence could not rise because of lack of access to education. They still suffer from the past indignities silently. Nanda and Kulke (eds.), 2015, p. 61 referred in the notes, Chapter 3.
4. Ibid.
5. Sen, *Poverty and* Famine, op. cit., p. 39.
6. While analysing the famine mortality of Bengal Sen noticed that these were the communities who suffered most.
7. Chandi Prasad Nanda and Hermann Kulke (eds.), op. cit.
8. B.M. Bhatia, *Famines in India: A Study of Some Aspects of the Economic History of India (1860-1965),* Bombay, Asia Publishing House, 1967, p. 67.
9. From the Commissioner, Orissa Division to the Collector, Puri, no. 375, 5 February 1866. Bengal Revenue Proceedings, February 1866.
10. Harishankar Srivastava, *The History of Famines and Development of Famine Policy, 1858-1918*, Agra, Sriram Mehra and Co., 1968, p. 68.
11. W.W. Hunter, *A Statistical Account of Bengal, Puri and Feudatory States,* vol. 19, New Delhi, Concept, 1876, rpt. 1976, p. 150.
12. However, as we have noticed in Chapter 3 Hunter (1876, rpt. 1976) observed that if there were caste prejudices then the low caste members would not have gone to the relief centre. In fact, the truth was that there was acute scarcity of food!
13. Ibid. But Ramakhoy Chatterjee the Deputy Magistrate and Deputy Collector, Puri in his evidence before the Famine Commission

was of the opinion that initially the feeding centres had employed Brahmin cooks but afterwards, cooks belonging to other castes were employed. *Famine Commission Report of Orissa, 1866* (*FCRO, 1866*), pt. 2. Evidence given by Ramakhoy Chatterjee. Again even though food was cooked by the Brahmin cooks, it was distributed by the members of other castes. Mayadhar Mansingh, *Durbhikhya* (Oriya) Cuttack, New Students Store, 1955, p. 82. Autobiography of Anant Das a famine victim was first published in a journal called *Prabhat* in August 1937. It was a mouthpiece of the Christian community at that time. At a later stage, late Mr. Mayadhar Mansingh an eminent Oriya writer published Anant's biography in the form of a book: *Durbhikhya*. Unfortunately, we do not have access to the original biography. We heavily depend on the description of the story as done by the above author.

Later on the acting Collector of Ganjam pointed out during the 1888-9 famine that the relief centres should employ Brahman cooks. Because Ganjam also had many Oriya people and according to him they were more conservative than Telugus. Thus the separate kitchens were set up for high and low caste people apart of at least 1 km away. There was a separate kitchen for the Muslims also. We have mentioned about this in the Chapter 3.

14. *FCRO, 1866*, pt. 1, para. 312.
15. Hunter, *A Statistical Account*, vol. 19, 1876, rpt. 1976, p. 147.
16. Ibid., vol. 18, pp. 330-1, p. 167.
17. Mansingh, *Durbhikya*, 1955, p. 75. In fact, there are folk stories in Oriya which narrate that people are sacrificed at the site of the embankments to prevent it from collapsing.
18. Ibid.
19. Srivastava, *Indian Famines*, 1968, pp. 148-9.
20. Hunter, *A Statistical Account*, op. cit., vol. 19, p. 171. In 2018 I visited the Settlement in Pipili. One of them narrated the story of the great famine and how his own great grandfather was converted to Christianity.
21. Srivastava, *Indian Famines*, 1968, p. 73. The experience of Ireland during the famine of 1845-9 was repeated again in case of Orissa. The famished victims continued to stay or migrated in the relief centres sleeping on the same set of straw and suffered from typhus since the fleas multiplied continuously. Woodham-Smith, *The Great Hunger: Ireland 1845-49*, 1962, London, Hamish Hamilton. Of course, Orissa did not have typhus but the cholera germs were

there since people would be passing stool on the bed itself. Hence the new persons would have been contacted with the diseases as well. These conditions would have prevailed *en route* to Calcutta.

22. Jagannath Prasad Das, *Desha, Kala, Patra* (Oriya), Cuttack Student Store, 1992, p. 126.
23. In 1897 also the sanitary conditions of the poor houses were very bad. Batches after batches of famine victims continued to eat on the same leaves and rice and *dal* used to look black because of excessive number of flies. The food was served cold. On the top of it the victims never washed their hands due to lack of water. Nor did they take bath. Thus living in an insanitary conditions must have led to epidemic diseases. *Source: Indian Famine Commission Report 1901*, Appendix, vol. 3, Evidence of witnesses in Central Provinces, Civil Surgeon, Nimar district.
24. Hunter, *A Statistical Account,* vol. 18, op. cit., pp. 170-1.
25. Mansingh, *Durbhikhya,* 1955, pp. 81-2.
26. P.K. Patra, *The History of Baptist Missionary Society and its Activities between 1822 and 1942*. Cuttack, The Orissa Mission Press, 1943, pp. 11-13.
27. Ibid.
28. Biswamoy Pati, *Identity, Hegemony, Resistance: Towards a Social History of Conversion in Orissa, 1800-2000,* Bhubaneswar, Three Collective Essays, 2003
29. Mansingh, *Durbhikhya,* 1955, p. 91.
30. Unfortunately, we do not have any data on the role of Lingraj Temple, though it is as famous as the Puri Temple.
31. Hunter, *A Statistical Account,* vol. 19, op. cit., p. 66.
32. Ibid., pp. 42-3.
33. Bidyut Mohanty, *Lakshmi the Rebel: Culture, Economy and Women's Agency*, New Delhi, Har Anand, 2019.
34. Das, *Desh, Kala and Patra,* 1992, p. 45.
35. Prabhat Mukherjee, *History of Orissa in the 19th Century,* Bhubaneswar, Utkal University, 1964, p. 359.
36. Oral evidence.
37. Ibid.
38. Ibid.
39. Mansingh, op. cit.
40. Hunter, *A Statistical Account,* vol. 18, op. cit., p. 156.
41. B.B. Chaudhuri, 'Eastern India', in Dharma Kumar (ed.), *Cambridge Economic History of India,* 1984, p. 96.

42. B.M. Bhatia, *Famines in India,* 1967, p. 111.
43. Das, *Desh, Kala and Patra,* 1992, pp. 86 & 238.
44. Interview with the local people.
45. Paul R. Greenough, *Prosperity and Misery in Modern Bengal,* New York, Oxford University Press, 1982, pp. 187-8.
46. *FCRO, 1866*, para 242.
47. Ibid.
48. Ibid., pt. 1, para 76.
49. Mansingh, *Durbhikhya,* 1955, p. 67.
50. Ibid., p. 4.
51. *FCRO, 1866*, pt. 1, para 76.
52. Hunter, *A Statistical Account,* vol. 19, op. cit., p. 149.
53. Ibid., p. 150.
54. http://vjha26.blogspot.com/
55. *FCRO, 1866*, para 309.
56. Mohanty, 'Famine and its Impact', 1988.
57. *FCRO, 1866*, pt. II, para 13-14.
58. The *Utkal Dipika,* 11 August 1966.
    Also Mansingh, *Durbhikhya*, 1955, p. 4.
    As students, we also read one poem on Sanatan which was written by the famous writer late Ram Krishna Nanda. On my enquiry, he revealed that he read that story in a supplementary textbook in the English course prescribed in Patna University. But he could not recall the author's name nor the title of the book.
59. Anil Dhir 'The Chhtrakhias: The Emergence of a New Caste', in Anil Dhir and Ramesh Mohapatra (eds.), *The Great Orissa Famine 1866: Na'anka Durbhykshya*, Bhubaneswar, Amadeus Publication, 2017, pp. 126-32.
60. K.S. Singh, 'Famine, Nationalism and Social Change: The Indian Scenario'. *Indian Historical Review,* 14 (1 & 2) (June-January 1987-8), p. 199.
61. Ibid., p. 202.
62. Ibid., p. 201.
63. Ibid., p. 202.
64. Dhir and Mohapatra, op. cit.
65. *The Utkal Dipika,* 18 January 1868.
66. Ibid., 11 April 1868. Anant Das's brother wanted to take him to Puri Temple to get the purification done. Mansingh, *Durbhikhya*, 1955, p. 92
67. Mohanty, 'Famine and its Impact', 1988.

68. Quoted in K.S. Singh, 1987-8, p. 202.
69. *Census of India, 1901, Bengal, Bihar and Orissa Report,* vol. 6, Report, part 1, p. 415. Also quoted in K.S. Singh, 'Famine, Nationalism', 1987-8, p. 203.
70. E.R.J.R. Cousins, *Bihar and Orissa District Gazetteers: Cuttack,* Patna, Government Press, 1933, p. 66.
71. Rajendra Prasad Das, *Smritire Cuttack* (Oriya), Bhubaneswar, Aam Orissa, 2019, p. 66.
72. K.S. Singh, 'Famine, Nationalism', op. cit., pp. 198-9.
73. Ibid., p. 198.
74. Ibid., p. 202.
75. Das, *Desh, Kala and Patra,* 1992, pp. 371-3.
76. *The Utkal Dipika*, 6 September 1873.
77. Ibid., 26 March 1881.
78. Ishita Banerjee Dube, 'Taming Traditions: Legalities and Histories in Twentieth-Century Orissa', in Gautam Bhadra, Gyan Prakash and Susie Tharu (eds.), *Subaltern Studies,* vol. 10, Delhi, Oxford University Press, 1999, pp. 98-125. Incidentally I visited the ashram of Mahima Gadi in 2017. The women devotees were quite keen to take money from us on the pretext that they were living from hand to mouth!
79. B.C. Das (ed.), *Life and Culture in Orissa,* Cuttack, S. Publisher, 1978, pp. 154-5; also see Naba Kishore Das, 'Orissa and Cultural History and Linkages with South-East Asia: A Critique', *International Journal of Cross Cultural Studies* 2(1), June 2016, p. 37. https://www.mukpublications.com/resources/IJCCSvol. 2no.1(2016).1.pdf
80. Margaret Kelleherm, *The Feminization of Famine: Expression of the Inexplicable*, Ireland, Cork University Press, 1997.
81. https://en.wikipedia.org/wiki/Anandamath
82. Mandira Ghosh, *Impact of Famine of Bengal on Bengali Literature,* New Delhi, Blauynske Publishing, 2014.
83. Gopal Chandra Praharaj. *Purnnachandra Oriya Bhasakosh* (A Lexion of the Oriya language), Cuttack, The Utkal Sahitya Press, 1933-4, vols. 3 and 4, pp. 2764 & 4071.
84. Shridhar Das, *Naba Abhidhan* (New Dictionary), Cuttack, Grantha Mandir, 1967, pp. 302 & 462.
85. Nrusingh P. Mishra, *Manorama Sankhipta Oriya Abhidhan* (Manorama short Oriya Dictionary), Cuttack, Manorama Publishers, 1983, p. 322.

86. Fakir Mohan Senapati, *An Autobiography*, Cuttack, Friends Publishers, 4th edn., 1917, rpt. 1981, pp. 29-35.
87. Kalindi Charan Panigrahi, *Muktagarhra Khudhya and Amarchita* in *Kalindi Rachana-chaya* (Oriya) (Collected Works of Kalindi), vol. 2, Cuttack, New Students Store, 1974 pp. 1-314. As is mentioned earlier in the footnote 49, Sanatan became a symbol who did not die for a handful of rice but rebelled.
88. Asit Mohanty in Dashrathi Das, Sudersan Acharya, Debendra Kumar Das and Gaurang Charan Dash (eds.), *Sahitya Kosha*. Bhubaneswar, Aam Orissa, 2018, pp. 686-90.
89. Surendra Mohanty cited in ibid.
90. Kahnu Charan Mohanty, *Ha Anna* (in Kahnu Charan Granthavali), pt. II, Cuttack, Granth Mandir, 1933, rpt. 1962; *Shasti,* ibid., pt. 4, Cuttack, Grantha Mandir, 1945, rpt. 1966, pp. 1-255.
91. 'Autobiography' of Jayanta Mahapatra by Research Edu, pp. 1-27.
92. *Bihar and Orissa District Gazetteer, Cuttack District,* 1933, p. 61.
93. There are instances of families with other surnames such as Chhatrakhia carpenter or Chhatrakhia who worked as carpenter.
94. In a personal communication Dr. K. Suresh Singh, the chief editor of *People of India,* series informed the author that he did not locate a single Chhatrakhia in Orissa. So it did not appear in his list. Actually no one ever introduced himself or herself as belonging to Chhatrakhia caste.

CHAPTER 5

Later Famines
Social Impact and State Response

Introduction

Famines occurred several times in the successive decades in Orissa after the 1866 famine due to a combination of factors such as weather failure, unfavourable government policy and lack of people's capacity to cope with scarcity, among other things. We have analysed the cases of famine during the next fifty years taking advantage of the available census data as well as official reports and that of the press. The objective here is to examine whether the policy interventions significantly changed the impact of the famines on various social groups.

As mentioned above after the great famine of 1866, the Orissa Division experienced series of famine conditions six more times: 1888-9, 1891-2, 1896-7, 1900-1, 1907-8 and 1918-19. They were officially described as 'scarcity' or 'distress' in the agricultural parlance, except in a couple of cases. In case of 1896-7, the rest of India suffered from severe famine, but Orissa was spared, except Puri district. Further, in case of 1888-9, a partial famine was declared and remission of rent was granted. The government declared famine both in 1907-8 and 1918-19. But in other cases, the output declined, death rates rose due to epidemics of infections diseases like cholera and dysentery, which became rampant, but officially it was not declared a famine situation. The government declared those either as 'distress' or 'scarcity' situation. The distinction between 'distress' and 'scarcity' and 'famine' is that in case of the former two, the government is not obliged to start relief work, but in case of famine, the government is bound to do so. Since census operations had started in 1872 and more systematically in 1881, we have some data on the impact of these distress situations on various social groups. Except for the year 1891-2 of which no data is available, we find that on all other occasions the poorer classes, namely, agricultural labourers, marginal *raiyats* and to some extent weavers of the unprotected areas, were the most affected sections. In this chapter we analyse the composition and the adaptability pattern of famine or distress victims of three famines, namely, 1888-9, 1907-8 and 1918-19, which will give us an idea about the pattern of the social impact of famines. Further, in 1896-7 and that of 1900-1 famines, it is important to note that the entire Bengal Presidency was under the grip of a severe famine on both occasions. Their impact on the Orissa Division was relatively less. It was perhaps because she was still recovering from the severe consequences of the 1866 famine in terms of population pressure.

We will now take up the case of each famine and try to see whether there was any change in the evolving scenario as far as the various castes and class groups were concerned and what were the continuing features.

Famine of 1888-9[1]

Plight of the Agricultural Labourers

In 1888-9, because of deficient rainfall, the *raiyats* especially in Khorda subdivision (including Puri), sowed so-called inferior crops such as ragi (*mandia*), *swam*, *kulthi*, etc., to a greater extent than normal.[2] These crops required less water and also less labour. But their market value was less than that of rice. These cereals served them well to meet the consumption needs, but could not meet other essential needs such as buying supplement food and clothes, paying rent to the zamindars, etc. As usual, the agricultural labourers suffered the most. Opportunities for them to work in the fields declined sharply. Employment in public works was meagre and wages were low. We have many accounts of this situation given by officials.

Maddox, the Settlement Officer, observed that 'the lot of the day-labourer is rather hard in Orissa as it is in many other parts of India. Spending what he earns from day-to-day, he has very little to pawn or sell in times of distress, and is, therefore, the first to succumb, unless constantly watched and provided with work within his easy reach.'[3]

Describing the 'scarcity' condition in Khorda in 1887-8, the Collector of Puri wrote that irregular rainfall in June and July immediately created apprehension in the mind of cultivators and they scaled down the fieldwork. As a result, the day labourers who mainly depended on the fieldwork, suffered a lot.[4]

While employment opportunities declined in the agricultural sector, the wage rate in the public works did not allow the labourers to buy more than 1.85 *seers* of rice, per day in the month of June 1888. This was at the rate of 22 *seers* per rupee and 1.53 *seers* per day in the month of March 1889 at the rate of 16⅜ *seers* per rupee in Puri.[5] But the basic requirement of an able-bodied person was on an average ¼ of a *seer* of rice per day, and he had at least three more adults at home.[6] So his daily earnings were not sufficient to maintain him and his family. Moreever, if an able-bodied and strong labourer could earn only 1½ *anna* in the public works,[7] the enfeebled labourers must have earned much less. In fact, the wage rate paid in public work was so low that whenever the labourers got some other job they fled from the relief work. Further, availing only rice for consumption was not enough, one needed oil, salt, and vegetables and some animal or non-animal protein for physical sustenance, besides clothes and shelter. In other words, paying very low wages and extracting hard work from the labourers in fact prove our argument that the rulers followed Darwinian and Malthusian polices till at least 1900, as Ira Klien has observed.

The agricultural labourers of Khorda subdivision were paid a semi-starvation rate even in normal times. They were recruited mostly from the tribals and Scheduled Castes such as the Savars and also Bauris.[8] They constituted 15 per cent of the total population of Khorda in 1872.[9] Even in normal times these agricultural labourers had to meet their food requirements by supplementing their agricultural wage with the sale of forest produce, eating forest products, and also by adopting shifting cultivation. But these activities were banned until 1889.[10] Incidentally, the Forest Law was first formulated in 1865. Since the timber products were very lucrative and brought lot of revenue for the colonial rulers, they banned the forest dwellers to use any of those products. This situation led to considerable resentment and several uprisings and also created a backdrop for the rise of nationalism. At the same time, Ramachandra Guha writes that tribals had control over the forests since they acted as the watchdog of those resources.[11] During the famine year 1889, perhaps the law was relaxed for them to collect the forest produce locally as is reported in the Annual Administration Report 1889. But the supply of wild edibles might have dwindled during the famine years due to lack of moisture. Besides, forest products like firewood may have lost their markets during the scarcity. Thus, the labourers of Khorda resorted to eating wild fruits, roots, a wide range of leafy vegetables and fish from the Chilika Lake. [12]

The agricultural labourers were the first to feel the pinch of scarcity. [13] As in the case of the 1866 famine, the salt manufacturers and fishermen also suffered, because of the decline in the salt trade and in sea-borne trade in Puri.[14]

The *raiyats* too suffered, though the officials did not report on this. As Maddox wrote, 'In bad years, payment of rent and loans will not leave the cultivator enough to eat, and he will probably borrow again in June or July, enough to carry him on till the end of the year.' [15]

Further with regard to the condition of the weavers, we have brief mention of it in official reports. The revenue proceedings on famine were silent on their conditions. But in general, Maddox observed that 'the most helpless class among the artisans are the weavers, who, living from hand to mouth with a scanty income, and having little or no connection with cultivation, seriously suffer in famine'.[16] However, there was some mention of relief to the weavers in the year 1887-8. The weavers were given thread spun by the distressed women and subsequently cloth was collected from the weavers. This generated a little income for the weavers and the *purdahnashins* (women in veils). But the total amount of cotton relief in monetary terms was a paltry sum of Rs. 17-12-3 pies in 1887-8.[17] Unfortunately, the conditions of other women and children were not discussed in these accounts, though they were the most vulnerable and first one to succumb during the distress period.

The Famine of 1907-8: The Pattern Continues

The same pattern of adaptation on the part of *raiyats* and sufferings of agricultural labourers, small *raiyats* and weavers continued in the famine year of 1907-8 and 1918-19 for which relatively more data are available.

Agricultural Labourers

Payments to agricultural labourers continued to be made in kind in normal periods and the same pattern continued even during the famine period. But the employment opportunities now diminished because of crop failure. Fewer labourers were needed to reap the harvest or for any other agricultural activities in 1907-8. In fact, this trend continued over the decade of 1901-11.[18] Besides, as in earlier famines, the quality of the straw would not have been good, and it is probable that many people would not have thatched their houses that year (1907-8), thus further reducing employment opportunity for labourers. On top of it, the *raiyats* would not have been able to make the annual contract with the labourers, thereby deepening their woos.

This situation was clear from the official correspondences. The Under Secretary to the Government of Bengal sent two notes on 6 December 1907 – one relating to famine relief operations in Cuttack and the other about a conference on famine in Orissa – to the Lieutenant Governor of Bengal, to the Commissioner of Orissa Division, and the Collector of Cuttack. He noted therein: 'The landless labourers, infirm and beggars in the affected area are already feeling the pinch of scarcity. There is now little demand for labour and private charity has almost ceased.'[19] The harvesting of bumper crops in the protected areas also did not generate much employment for the labourers of the famine-affected areas. Therefore, the Under Secretary to the Government of Bengal had written to the Collector of Cuttack on 10 December 1907, advising the desirability of opening relief works in the famine-affected areas. The Under Secretary questioned that when the labourers from famine areas could migrate to Calcutta, why could they not work in the protected areas? But there was perhaps some truth in the Collector's submission.[20] Logically however, one can argue that the Under Secretary failed to understand that the job created in the protected area was perhaps just enough for the local labourers and they would resent outsiders since it might depress the prevailing wage rate.

In the post-1866 period, there was an increase in the area under cultivation of pulses and summer rice,[21] which generated a little additional employment. This was the case in the affected areas of Cuttack in the famine years of 1907-8. But in Balasore and Puri, as the share of these crops to total crops was insignificant, the employment opportunities were almost nil.[22] The *bhadoi* crop comprised mainly of early rice and *mandia* (ragi); *aghani* crops consisted of winter rice, and *rabi* crops including spring rice and pulses.[23] The plight of the people was narrated vividly in the note of the Commissioner of Orissa Division to the Collector of Balasore. He wrote that the landless people of Cuttack were eating tops of raw jute plants,[24] tender banana leaves and other rubbish, and cholera epidemic had broken out.[25]

Famine of 1907-8 and the Press

We have already mentioned that only *The Statesman* published from England, had published a news item titled 'Starving Poor' about the 1866 famine, and from there the colonial rulers came to know about the great tragedy in Orissa. In contrast however, by the end of the nineteenth century, many Indian newspapers and weekly magazines were published in the local languages as well as in English and their correspondents had access to the famine-affected areas to file field reports. They reported extensively about the sufferings of the people in the famine-affected areas. Thus, in November 1907, a representative of *The Statesman* from Calcutta, toured the affected areas extensively and published a series of articles in the newspaper, just after the floods. Gopabandhu Das who was the Secretary, Students' Relief Committee, Cuttack, had also published a series of news items in the *Utkal Dipika* about the 1908 famine, based on investigations by students, who had toured the affected areas of Cuttack district in April 1908. Both the reports mentioned that the labouring classes were eating substitutes for rice and as a result cholera had broken out and had become an epidemic.

Gopabandhu Das wrote that the people of low castes such as the Panas, Kandaras and Gokhas were eating wild berries instead of rice.[26] In a later report he wrote that the people were eating raw dates, brinjals, raw mangoes and various kinds of leafy green vegetables which generally grew in paddy fields after the harvest (locally known as *muthi sag*).[27] *The Statesman* also wrote that people were fighting with each other over edible tree bark and were eating roots, *madaranga sag* (a leafy green vegetable which grows near the ponds or any other damp place), etc.[28] The local press alleged that starvation deaths were occurring in the famine-affected areas. That labourers from the low castes were the victims of famine was also evident from the Collector of Cuttack's report since only low caste people such as Panas and Kandaras came to the relief kitchen and were fit for the test relief work to find out if that could provide wage labour to the affected people.[29]

The Collector of Cuttack however, tried to refute the allegations of starvation deaths though he agreed with the reports that people were eating substitutes like edible roots or tree bark and wild *sag*, in lieu of rice, but he argued that this was not unusual in flood-affected areas. He also wrote that *madaranga sag* was tasty.[30] It was true that even in ordinary times, the labouring class ate these vegetables but only as a side dish: it did not replace rice completely as it in 1907 and 1908 and in other famine years. Incidentally, politicians and bureaucrats have continued to hold such views for over a century as was evident when a chief minister of Orissa described eating of ants in Kalahandi in scarcity situation as a delicacy in 1985. This gained a lot of notoriety in the press and he was severely criticized. Of course, tribals do eat ants, rats and other things which are not acceptable in non-tribal modern society, but given a choice between good rice and ants they will certainly prefer rice. Thus as in earlier famines, the agricultural labourers were the first ones to be severely affected by the food shortage and the accompanying epidemics.

Raiyats

The *raiyats* of the unprotected areas, which formed the major portion of the Orissa Division, experienced a series of crop failures. It culminated in a more than 40 per cent decline in output in the year 1907-8 in the temporarily settled areas, in the three districts. Data are not available for the permanently settled areas, but it is likely that they also suffered from famine because they were situated in flood- and drought-prone areas. After the floods in August 1907 there was no hope of re-sowing the winter rice, which occupied a major portion of the total cultivated area. *Raiyats* tried to minimize the loss of output by extending the area under pulses and summer rice. The pulses were affected by insects because of excessive flood water. Extension of cultivation of spring rice was not possible due to the non-availability of lowlands. There was also little facility for irrigation.

Even at the subdivision level, the retail prices of rice rose by more than 100 per cent in the year 1907-8 as compared to the base period 1903. The *raiyats* of Balasore with 6 acres of land or less (i.e. the majority of *raiyats*) could not have gained much out of the price rise because they did not have enough marketable surplus. Their condition remained vulnerable even after the suspension of land revenue.[31]

The *raiyats* could also take loan under the Land Improvement Loans Act XIX of 1883 and the Agriculturists Loans Act XII of 1884. Under the former Act, landowners were allowed to take advance in normal as well as famine times, in order to improve the productivity of land and to generate employment. The latter act was meant for small *raiyats* with holdings between 2 and 10 acres. The loans were given to buy seeds and sometimes cattle also. The break-up of loans between Land Improvement Loans and Agriculturists Loan is not available, but most probably the latter accounted for the entire amount, because the Collector of Cuttack pointed out that the zamindars did not do anything for the improvement of land except lending rice at a profitable rate. He also mentioned that the *raiyats* took *taccavi* or short-term loan to buy seeds for their lands.[32]

The reasons why the substantial *raiyats* and zamindars did not take any loans under Land Improvement Act are not far to seek. The Revision Settlement operation was going on during the period 1906-12,[33] so the zamindars were afraid that any improvement to the land would raise the revenue rates. Besides, most of the big zamindars were absentee landlords who stayed in Kolkata and were not interested in the improvement of the land. Most of the Oriya proprietors, on the other hand, had small estates: these petty proprietors were numerous in south Balasore and in the north Cuttack regions.[34] They too did not have the capacity to develop agriculture since they had limited capital. Besides, the procedure for giving loans to *raiyats* was very cumbersome. Under the Agriculturists Loans Act, for instance, the *raiyats* were to execute a joint liability bond whereby five or more *raiyats* were to be responsible for the loans. The *raiyats* were unwilling to do this as it involved paying for the defaulters. The government was unwilling to give loans to the individual *raiyat* because they thought that he did not have viable security.[35]

The amount given as loans under the Agriculturalists Loans Act was very little. Initially, the collector was willing to give Rs. 5 per acre, but the *raiyats* were unwilling to accept it, according to the collector, because they felt that they could get private credit to the extent of Rs. 20 per acre,[36] though he did not state whether the rate of interest would have been the same. Later on, the government gave altogether Rs. 2 per acre at the instance of the Commissioner.

Thus, one sees that the government did try to help the *raiyats* but in a very small measure. The *raiyats* not only needed seeds, but also cattle. The death rate and distress sale of cattle was very high during the famines as fodder and water were also scarce. Another problem was that sometimes the lands used to be covered with sand in the flooded area, and needed to be cleared after the floods. The special correspondent of *The Statesman* who visited the affected area pointed out that the *raiyats* were denied *taccavi* loans because their lands were covered with sand.[37] He also pointed out that the *taccavi* loans were not adequate and could not be used because there was neither work nor food. The collector of Cuttack stated that the farmers were not denied *taccavi* loans because of sand covered land,[38] but did not explicitly refute the charge that the *taccavi* loans were too little.

Most of all, the *raiyats* needed enough food to maintain themselves and their family to carry on cultivation efficiently. The Commissioner refuted this allegation saying that if the *raiyats* were so hard-pressed, they would have gone to the relief works started by the government.[39] This was not a convincing argument because some had to stay in the village to prepare and carry on the cultivation work for the next season. Besides, the wage paid for test relief work was barely enough for subsistence. According to the famine code, the test relief workers were to be given half a *seer* of rice just to maintain themselves. But in order to work in normal conditions, the labourers needed at least three-fourths of a *seer* of rice. Besides, just rice would not suffice to fulfil the entire requirements of a person. But the prevailing thinking regarding relief was still very restrictive and did not allow any notion of a nutritious diet.

In the famine of 1907-8, another practice was adopted that related to change of the composition of food grains. With regard to their daily dole in test relief work, the workers were given half in *mandia* (ragi) or *kulthi* (pulse) or *biri* (pulse) and the other half in rice. Presumably, it was decided at the instance of the Commissioner of the Orissa Division, because the P.A. to the Commissioner instructed that the substitution for rice should be gradual and it should not exceed half of the dole under any circumstance.[40] Had it been *kulthi* or *biri* with rice, then the victims would have been better off, but if they were given rice and *mandia* – both cereals – they would have been worse off, because *mandia* is nutritionally less than pulses in providing protein and is eaten as a last resort during famines. Thus, in addition to low nutritional value, *mandia* is also considered to be an inferior grain according to prevailing social preferences.

Many *raiyats* had to sell their cattle and land, the most important assets for their sustenance, and this had widespread, disruptive consequences for the area as a whole. Many migrated outside, which was not necessarily harmful as we shall see later. There are only a few references to sale of land and cattle. Just after the flood, in the month of August 1907, as mentioned earlier, Gopabandhu Das freedom fighter made an extensive tour of the affected area and gave a report to the government, which was also published in the *Utkal Dipika.* He noted that cattle were sold in the market to Muslims. Most cattle had been reduced to a skeleton for want of fodder for grazing. In response to this, the collector of Cuttack made a tour and wrote a diary starting from 13 November 1907.[41] He denied that there was lack of fodder for the cattle, and he also wrote that he saw several healthy cattle. The sale of cattle to the Muslims, the collector wrote, was an annual occurrence. But he did not state whether the number of cattle sold increased in the famine year or not, nor did he mention what price they fetched. There are no data on the number of cattle sold, but the prices certainly indicate that there was distress sale of cattle. For example, a correspondent of *Utkal Dipika* wrote that a number of cattle were coming to the weekly market of Ghanteswar in Bhadrak (Balasore); Muslim traders were buying them at the rate of Rs. 2-8 per cow against the normal price of Rs. 5 in Bhadrak subdivision of Balasore.[42] A letter in *Sambad Bahika,* another Oriya weekly, described the same phenomenon in some other places in Balasore. Muslims of some villages in Sadar subdivision of Balasore were reported to be killing cows every day for beef as it was much cheaper than rice. The letter writer also pointed out that the villagers were not accustomed to eating such flesh and this might have led to cholera.[43]

The distress sale of land had increased the workload of the Registry Office considerably. Since the revision settlement (1906-12) work was still going on in Orissa Division, the people may have taken advantage of this process and registered their lands. But the sudden spurt in registration of land in all categories in 1908 was an indication of distress sale of land by the *raiyats*. That the sale of land increased in 1908-9 was also noted in the Administration Report of 1908-9, and specially under the heads of sales, mortgages and bonds in Orissa Division. The report noted that this was due to the scarcity situation and the consequent dearness of food. According to the report in 1908, the registration of land under sales, mortgages, etc., increased by 74 per cent in Cuttack, 45 per cent in Balasore and 57 per cent in Puri, as compared to 1907;[44] among the three heads, the mortgages of land increased most. Incidentally, it is one of the safety nets which the peasant class adopt during famine periods. As a result, other transactions were not recorded in the Land Registration Office. We do not know what percentage of the transferred land came back to the original sellers but these figures do show that the *raiyats*, especially the smaller ones, were experiencing hardship during the famine period in spite of the *taccavi* loans and other limited support given by the government.

Weavers

There are only a few references to the condition of the artisans in general and weavers in particular, but our guess is that most artisans faced severe hardships barring a few blacksmiths and carpenters in towns who got work due to the boom in construction business, especially in Puri.[45] We do not know definitely why there was a construction boom in Puri, especially in a decade of a series of crop failures, but it was most probably because of coming of railways and industrial development in Bengal during 1901-11. Some wealthy Bengalis may also have decided to construct houses in Puri town since the district used to be a summer resort for them due to its proximity to the sea and the Jagannath Temple. It should be noted that the wage rate of the skilled workers had increased from 1901 onwards more than that of unskilled labourers. But those rural artisans who did not migrate and depended solely on their share of agricultural produce would have suffered in this condition. Generally, the practice was that the *raiyats* gave a share of their produce to the artisans to repair their agricultural tools, especially their harvesting instruments. But during the period of acute distress, they could have postponed the repair work for the next year. Hence, the share of the produce for the artisans would have declined even further, thereby leading to more suffering.

Weavers did not come to the regular relief centres as their caste prejudice was very strong. But that did not necessarily mean that they did not suffer. Some of them were given bundles of thread and were paid in cash for their product. Incidentally, the women of the Pana caste (a Dalit caste) were given advances to make baskets.[46] In Jagatsingpur subdivision, the Relief Committee had given thread worth Rs. 1,000 to the weavers, after which the cloth woven by them was to be distributed among the poor. In Kendrapara sub-division also, the sub-divisional officer had distributed 500 pairs of *dhotis* to the poor. [47] But whether it was woven by the local weavers or imported is not known. According to the *Utkal Dipika,* which gave a summary report on the work of the official Relief Committee, there was a mention that it had assigned money to the sub-divisional officer of Jajpur to distribute 100 pairs of *dhotis* woven by the local weavers.[48] Similarly, agricultural instruments like hoes and *kodalis* were ordered from the local blacksmiths in order to provide them a source of earning. The Bengal Nagpur Railways had started giving famine allowances to its permanent employees.[49] The primary schools in the famine-affected areas were, however, closed because parents could not pay the fees. As a result, the teachers were unable to get their salaries.[50]

The famine of 1907-8 was admittedly not as severe as that of the famine of 1866, but the agricultural labourers and the marginal *raiyats* and weavers did suffer. Here also the issues relating to women were not reported directly either in official documents or in the press, though they would have suffered the most. They were referred to in a casual way. For example, it was merely stated that the women of the fishing community depended either on selling fish or husking paddy. Still, piecing together evidences from various sources we find that during the distress period they preferred to sell fish rather than go for paddy husking, because paddy husking involved hard work and they were already emaciated due to lack of proper food. That Muslim women also suffered from the impact of the famine is evident from the collector's note. The collector mentioned that Muslim women were given thread to weave clothes which the government bought back from them. In their case it was reported that the *purdah* clad women refused to come to the relief centre. The government perhaps tried to help women but it was far from adequate. So women either migrated or died during the various epidemics. In fact, the mortality rates for both male and female increased considerably. Lack of food and outbreak of epidemics of malaria, cholera and dysentery caused serious consequences, which have been discussed in a subsequent chapter.

The Famine of 1918-19

The famine of 1918-19 was different from the earlier famines of Orissa Division, as there was an overarching context of the First World War. In that respect it was comparable to the later case of the Bengal famine of 1943. During this period, prices rose very high. Not only was rice dearer, but also the other necessities such as cloth, kerosene oil and salt were unavailable. The Census Superintendent of Bihar and Orissa noted that a pair of ordinary *dhotis* cost Rs. 1-10 *annas* and Rs. 1-12 *annas* in the Ranchi district of Bihar and Orissa Province before the war. In January 1918, the price increased between Rs. 4-12 *annas* and Rs. 7 (357 per cent), the average price being Rs. 5-8 *annas* or Rs. 6. The government then took action and purchased 16 million yards of cloth and sold them at controlled price. As a result, the cost of *dhotis* became less by the end of 1919. The shortage of cloth compelled people to wear shorter and narrower *dhotis*.[51] The government also arranged to sell oil, salt and rice at cheaper rates.

Unfortunately, data on sex differential mortality was not available for this period. But we have statements saying that more women died of influenza compared to men. It is also important to note that influenza became more virulent because of shortage of food as we will see in Chapter 7.

As noted above, another feature of this famine was that it was accompanied by the Great Influenza of 1918-19, known as 'war fever' and was not endemic to Orissa. This epidemic killed thousands all over India, but fortunately for Orissa, the coastal districts suffered relatively less in 1918.[52] On the other hand, Orissa suffered more from crop failures and other epidemics such as cholera, malaria and to some extent smallpox as well – all famine-related diseases.

Agricultural performance in Orissa Division was worse in the decade ending 1921 than in the previous decade. All three districts experienced repeated floods and droughts, which culminated in the famine, even though a famine was not declared officially. The agricultural year 1918-19 was declared as 'distress' year only. So the official information on prices, excess mortality and crop statistics was not available. Hence we will mostly depend on the Census Reports, Sanitary Commission Reports and local newspaper reports to construct the story of this famine.

Of the three districts, Balasore suffered the most in this decade due to continuous floods from 1911 to 1913. In all but two years, the grain output was below average. In 1918-19 also the crop had failed and the grain output was only 30 per cent of the normal. The drought of 1918 was followed by a flood in 1919 and hence famine conditions prevailed in Balasore. Puri also suffered from floods and droughts, except in the years from 1913 to 1916. From 1917 to 1920, Puri suffered from floods in 1917, 1919 and 1920 and drought and famine in 1918 and 1919.[53]

The worst victims of the famine of 1918-19 were the agricultural labourers, marginal *raiyats* and weavers, as in the case of the previous famines. It is worthwhile to look at their conditions in this specific context.

Agricultural Labourers

Rural labourers suffered from severe economic crisis during this famine. The retail price of rice rose from 3 *annas* per *seer* to 6 to 7 *annas* per *seer* in 1919, during this famine while the money wage rate remained constant.[54] Besides, jobs were scarce.[55] Normal employment opportunities had shrunk as there was a failure of rains in October 1918 and the harvest would have required fewer labourers. The *rabi* crop could not be grown on a large scale because of lack of moisture. Like previous experience, houses may not have been thatched because of the low quality of straw. In places such as Gope Police Station of Puri district, famished people were reduced to skeletons and nobody wanted to employ them.[56] The rainfall was also less than normal in September and October 1919. Fewer people would have been required for weeding.[57] The floods in November 1919 damaged the crops in Cuttack and Puri, which may have contributed to diminishing the employment opportunities further. Since the labourers had few assets, their economic conditions would have deteriorated first. They had to eat rice substitutes, as in earlier famines, as reported in the local newspapers. For example, the correspondent of *Sambalpur Hiteisini* wrote that the prices of rice and other necessities had increased to such an extent that poor people were eating forest produce, leaves, etc.[58] Similarly, the editor of *Utkal Sebaka* also reported that the children and women of the low castes in Puri ate different kinds of leaves (*sags*), snails, crabs and fish from nearby waterlogged lowlands.[59] The editor of the *Utkal Dipika* reiterated that Bauris and other poor people were eating *kendu* fruits and leaves.[60] The special correspondent of *Samaj* confirmed the same. He observed that even *sag* was not available after the floods.[61] These newspapers further reported that as a result of eating rice substitutes, people were suffering from cholera[62] and dysentery.[63]

The Raiyats

The *raiyats* were clearly better off than the landless labourers since they had land and other assets such as cattle, harvesting implements and some ornaments. During this period, there was a change in the range of rice substitutes available to them, because the area under *mandia* (ragi) and other food grains had declined, especially in Puri.[64] The potato crop had been introduced in Orissa Division by that time. But the extent of cultivation was probably small and the new crops may have taken a long time to be adopted.[65] Besides, potato, which had come to the market by 1908, was and (still is) used as a vegetable and not as a staple food. But during the famine period they would have eaten the same in large quantities to fill themselves up.

Unlike the earlier famines, the remission of land revenue was small during this famine, which reflected the wartime fiscal management. Here one recollects the remarks of Usta Patnaik, the Marxist economist to explain the causes of the Bengal Famine, 1943-4. We have referred to her work in the Introduction to this book. No remission of revenue was granted to the temporarily settled areas, or to the permanently settled areas within the district. But some portion of the government estate in Puri was granted a small amount of Rs. 3,808 as remission during the year July 1918 to June 1919. The government estates of Puri received Rs. 1,461 as remission the next year also.[66] On the other hand, a larger amount of loan under the Land Improvement Loans Act of 1883 and particularly under the Agriculturists' Loans Act of 1884 was advanced.[67] The *raiyats* of Puri received 2 to 3 Rupees per acre but those of Cuttack received 5 to 15 Rupees per acre.[68] The amount distributed as *taccavi* loan was not adequate as the distress sale of cattle, land and ornaments continued even after disbursement of the loans, especially in Puri. Besides, the *rabi* crop of 1918-19 which was cultivated by the help of the *taccavi* had been washed away.[69] The correspondent of the *Utkal Dipika* also noted that the terms and conditions of *taccavi* loan were not suitable for the *raiyats* and so not many people were accepting it.[70] There were many distress sales of cattle as the main fodder, namely, grass and husks of rice was not available. So people sold their cattle at a nominal price.[71] One local newspaper also reported that the people of the tributary states were selling cattle at a very cheap rate. Obviously the cattle were in famished condition as well. The skin dealers were getting good profits by selling the skin of the dead cattle.[72] Similarly, the *raiyats* disposed of their utensils and ornaments during the famine year.[73] As mentioned earlier, according to the investigation by the *Samaj*, out of 50 to 60 households in a village, at least 30 per cent had already disposed of their ornaments, utensils and also land. In one or two cases, however, families lived by selling inferior food grains, oilseeds and coconuts.[74] People in famine affected areas also mortgaged and sold land at throwaway prices.[75] The statistics of the Registration Department also showed that there was an increase in the number of registration deeds under sales and mortgages in 1919 and 1920 in Cuttack. Table 5.1 shows that in 1919 the highest number of sales and mortgages of land occurred in Balasore, followed by Puri and Cuttack.

Weavers

The weavers were also adversely affected during the famine years as the prices of the imported cotton thread had increased by the year 1916-17, because of war conditions.[76]

Simultaneously, the prices of imported cloth also increased.[77] In 1921, Census Superintendent Tallents reported that net imports of thread had decreased from 1915-16 onwards. But the decrease in imported cloth was even higher. He also pointed out that the local weavers of Bihar and Orissa were meeting the local demand to the extent of 1/7 in 1912-13 which had risen to 1/6 in 1921. From this he concluded that the hand-weaving industry had retained its 'vitality'. At the same time, however, Tallents noted that weaving was 'generally' combined with agriculture.[78] This was the story of normal times. It seemed that the competition between imported and homespun cloth had diminished because of war. In 1918-19 on the other hand, the effective demand for cloth would

TABLE 5.1 INDEX OF COMPULSORY REGISTRATION AFFECTING IMMOVABLE PROPERTY IN ORISSA, 1918-21

	Cuttack		*Balasore*		*Puri*	
	Mortgages	*Sales*	*Mortgages*	*Sales*	*Mortgages*	*Sales*
1918	100	100	100	100	100	100
1919	165	140	224	205	212	157
1920	179	160	187	161	197	173
1921	126	118	146	130	115	133

Source: Computed from the statistics given in the Report of Registration Department.

have fallen, and the subsidiary employment of weavers in the agricultural sector would thus have also fallen. Lastly, given the high price of imported thread, they would not have managed to buy thread to the extent of meeting the limited demand for cloth. As a result, some of the weavers migrated to Calcutta.[79] As usual not much attention was given to recording the conditions of women during this famine except a few reports in the local press mentioning that women and children were starving and collecting the rice substitutes to eat.

Overview

We have discussed the class composition of famine victims of three famines in Orissa after the 1866 famine to find out the emerging pattern of social impact and state response. It is noticed that the famine victims mainly came from among the agricultural labourers, small farmers and weavers. The agricultural labourers suffered because the *raiyats* sowed inferior crops or scaled down the demand for labour as soon as the prospect for the crop became bleak. The marginal *raiyats*, though better off than the agricultural labourers, also suffered. They did sow inferior food crops, but could not gain much because of the imbalanced weather conditions. For example, the *raiyats* sowed pulses after the floods of 1907, but did not get any crops because the soil was too moist and plants got insect-infested. The government distributed *taccavi* loans as a part of its response. But the terms and conditions were very cumbersome. Besides, the amount which they got through these loans was not adequate to manage the post-drought or post-flood agriculture. Thus the marginal farmers could not cope with the famines; they were so hard-pressed that they had to sell whatever assets they had, including their cattle.

The weavers became the victims of food shortages because they not only faced competition from imported cloth but they also depended on imported threads. Since their main occupation was not remunerative, they combined it with agriculture and thus shared the consequences of crop failures.

Thus one notices that in all three cases, the agricultural labourers, marginal farmers and weavers suffered considerably. We also note that the reports gave only a cursory view of the impact of famine on women. From the available sources we find that they suffered immensely in multiple ways. In all the cases, the production of the main crop suffered either because of floods or droughts. The *raiyats* switched over to cultivate inferior food grains but the condition of the soil was not suitable for these crops. So it yielded no results. The victims had to eat substitutes of their familiar food to sustain themselves, but in many cases it caused the outbreak of cholera, dysentery, etc. After the railways linked up the region with Calcutta, many men migrated there. We shall discuss this phenomenon in Chapter 10.

Notes

1. This famine had affected Khorda subdivision more, so more data is available on that.
2. *General Administration Report, 1888-9*, p. 10.
3. *Maddox Report 1890-1900,* vol. 1, para 193.
4. Rev/Agri/FP, June 1889, no. 770; From the Collector of Puri to the Commr, OD, dt. 17 June 1889.
5. *General Administration Report 1888-89*, p. 13.
6. *Maddox Report 1890-1900*, vol. 1, para 187.
7. Rev/Agri/FP, June 1889, no. 770. From the Collector, Puri to the Commr, OD, dt. 17 June 1889.
8. *General Administration Report, 1888-9*, p. 10.
9. The total number of castes who lived in Khorda was not given in subsequent censuses.
10. *General Administration Report, 1888-9*, p. 10. The first Forest Act was passed in 1865 and it was revised in 1878. The act banned the traditional communities from using the forest produce. But in 1888 and 1989 the Act was relaxed and the tribals could use the forest produce for their sustenance. https://en.wikipedia.org/wiki/Indian_Forest_Act,_1927
11. Ramachandra Guha 'Forestry in British and Post British India: A Historical Analysis', *Economic and Political Weekly,* vol. 18, issue no. 44, 29 October 1983, pp. 1882-95.
12. Rev/Agri/FP, June 1889, no. 770, From the Collector Puri to the Commr, OD, dt. 17 June 1889.

13. *General Administration Report 1888-89*, p. 11.
14. The Collector of Puri also wrote that the salt manufacturers supplemented their earnings by selling firewood and catching fish which also decreased in 1888.
15. *Maddox Report, 1890-1900*, vol. 1, para 189. Also see, the Collector of Puri wrote that the *raiyats* were given advances to cultivate more area under *mandia* and *kulthi*, in July 1888 as the rainfall was deficient for rice. REV/Agri./FP, June 1889, no. 770. From the Collector Puri to the Commr., OD, dt. 17 June, 1889.
16. *Maddox Report 1890-1900*, vol. 1, para 193.
17. Rev/Agri/FP, June 1889, no. 770, From the Collector Puri to the Commr, OD, dt. 17 June 1889.
18. Student groups sent by voluntary organizations reported that in some places the able-bodied labourers did not have any work to do and the Government officials also refused to register them for gratuitous relief as they appeared to be able-bodied, the *Utkal Dipika*, 11 April 1908.
19. Rev/Agri/FP, December 1907, no. 3972 from the Under Secretary, GOB to the Collector of Cuttack, dt. 10 December 1907.
20. At the same time, it should be noted that labourers did show preferences for particular types of jobs. For example, the Collector of Balasore suggested to the women who sold fish that they should switch over to paddy husking. But they refused to do paddy husking and wanted to stick to their occupation. *Source:* Rev/Agri/FP, November 1907, no. 3107; from the Collector of Balasore to the Commr, OD, dt. 7 November 1907.
21. The Engineer stated that instructions had been issued to supply water wherever it was possible for summer rice. PWD, December 1907, no. 11308, from the Superintending Engineer, OD to the Commr, OD, dt. 11 December 1907.
22.

The percentage of *rabi* harvest	*Cuttack*	*Balasore*	*Puri*
Total Harvest in 1903-4	11	3	10
The percentage of *rabi* harvest			
Total harvest in 1907-8	14	3	6

Source: GOI/Home/Public, June 1909, No. 67, T.R.: Final Resolution on the Relief Operations in Bengal during 1907-8, dt. 17 April 1909.

23. The area under *rabi* was very small and generated very little employment. Besides the soil was very damp in some parts of the affected area. So the pulses were affected by insects. *Source:* Rev/

Agri/FP, December 1907, no. 1893; from the Collector, Cuttack to the Commr, OD, dt. 4 December 1907.

In the Chilika tract, the places where salt manufacture had ceased and those had become perennial famine affected areas also suffered from flood and drought and then famine. In years when the rainfall was evenly distributed, the cultivators used to cultivate sugar cane, winter rice and *kulthi*. But in the year 1907-8, all three crops had withered away. Rev/Agri/FP, December 1907, no. 3768; from the Collector of Puri to the Commr, OD, dt. 4 December 1907.

24. Incidentally the tops of raw jutes taste very bitter. It is eaten when one suffers from having worms in the intestine. But it became the famine food since rice became scarcer.
25. Rev/Agri/FP, September 1907, no. 3078; From the Commr, OD to the Collector, Balasore, dt. 25 September 1907.
26. The *Utkal Dipika,* 11 April 1908.
27. The *Utkal Dipika,* 15 May 1908.
28. The *Statesman* 16 November 1907, 'Living on Tree Bark' had appeared along with other new items. Also, Maddox wrote that both *madaranga* and *moti* used to be eaten in times of scarcity. He also pointed out that Orissa contained a sufficient supply of *madaranga* and *muthi* to keep alive about 2 per cent or 40,000 persons for about 8 months from Kartick to Jaishtha (October to June), *Maddox Report 1890-1900*; vol. 1, p. 130.
29. Rev/Agri/FP, September 1908, no. 1106634-77; from the Collector of Cuttack to the Commr, OD, dt. 15 September 1908. Also the Sanitary Commissioner of Bengal wrote in 1908, that the poorer classes had to eke out their scanty food from unsuitable and unwholesome products. It seriously injured their resistance power. They became vulnerable to famine related diseases. *SCRB 1908*, p. 3.
30. Rev/Agri/FP, December 1907, no. F/2, file no. 1 Letter no. B, from the Collector of Cuttack to the Commr, OD, dt. 4 December 1907.
31. The government suspended the land revenue in the affected area amounting to Rs. 44,527 (1907-8) and Rs. 79,926 (1908-9) for Cuttack and Rs. 44,624 for Balasore. These were granted for two *kists* out of 4 *kists* (November 1907 and April 1908). Rev/Agri/FP, November 1907, no. 3565; from the Commr, OD, the Chief Secretary to GOB, dt. 9 November 1907.
32. Rev/Agri/FP, September 1908, no. 110665/34-77; from the Collector of Cuttack to the Commr, OD, dt. 15 September 1908. In Odisha

Rs. 1,58,649 was distributed just after the floods in August, 1907 and Rs. 45,69,119 was distributed for winter rice to be sown in 1908. It was done to enable small *raiyats* to procure seeds and to save lands from going out of cultivation. GOI/Rev/Agri/FP, June 1909, no. 67 T.R. Final Resolution on Relief Operation, dt. 17 April 1909.

33. It is interesting to note that the 1866 famine occurred when the settlement was about to expire. In 1908 too the settlement was in operation when the famine broke out. But the next settlement came after the famine of 1918-19.
34. *Final Report on the Revision Settlement Operation, Odisha 1906-12*, p. 38.
35. Rev/Agri/FP, December 1907, no. 20/07; from the Collector of Puri to the Commr, OD, dt. 20 December 1907.
36. Rev/Agri/FP, December, 1907, no. 3107; from the Collector of Balasore to the Commr, OD, dt. 17 December 1907.
37. GOI/Rev/Agri/FP, January 1908, no. 4141 Agri, from the Chief Secretary RD to GOB to the Secy. to Rev/Agri, GOI, dt. 9 December 1907.
38. Rev/Agri/FP, December 1907, no. 3679; from the Commr, OD to the Chief Secy, GOB, RD, dt. 14 December 1907.
39. Rev/Agri/FP, December, 1907, no. 4263; from the Commr, OD to the Collector of Puri, dt. 28 December 1907.
40. Rev/Agri/FP, January 1908, no. 356; from PA to the Commr, OD to Collector of Cuttack, dt. 30 January 1908. Also the SDO of Jajpur subdivision wanted to implement the suggestion of the PA to the Commr. by paying half *kulthi* or *biri* or *mandia* and half rice as gratuitous relief, Rev/Agri/FP, January 1908, from the Collector of Cuttack to the Commr of OD, dt. 12 January 1908.
41. Rev/Agri/FP, December 1907, no. 93; from the Collector of Cuttack to the Commr, OD, dt. 4 December 1907.
42. *Utkal Dipika*, 25 July 1908.
43. The Muslims, incidentally were semi-Hindus and used to observe rituals regarding ploughing and other processes like Hindus. *Sambad Bahika*, 6 February 1908.
44. *Bengal Administration Report 1908-09*, p. 42.
45. It was pointed out that the wage rate had increased after 1906 because of construction booms in Puri town (of both skilled and unskilled labourers). *Prices and Wages in India, 1910-11*.
46. Rev/Agri/FP/F/1, December 1907, no. 4104 RD; from the Collector of Puri to the Commr, OD, dt. 16 December 1907. Numbers of women and the amount spent were not given.

47. The *Utkal Dipika,* 28 March 1908.
48. The *Utkal Dipika* wrote that the Sub-divisional Officer of Jajpur, Cuttack was buying small towels (*gamcha*) and *dhotis* from the weavers of the flood affected area at a fair price and was distributing them among the famine victims, with money raised by public subscription. *Utkal Dipika,* 28 March 1908.
49. *Sambad Bahika,* 20 February 1908.
50. Rev/Agri/FP, F/1, March, 1908, no. 21; 'Allowance to school masters in famine affected areas'.
51. *Census of India, 1921*, vol. VII, pt. I, p. 19.
52. Ibid., p. 13.
53. *Census of India 1921*, vol. 8, pt. I.
54. *The Dipika* reported that the daily money wage rate amounted to 2 *annas* or 10 *pies*. So the daily wage labourers were unable to buy rice, because rice was selling at 7 *annas* per *seer*. *Utkal Dipika*, 19 April 1919. It was reported in Wage Census of Cuttack which was conducted in 1916 that the average daily wage rate of agricultural labourers was little more than 2 *annas*. *Prices and Wages in India, 1922-23*, pp. 188-9. Also see, *The Samaj*, 8 November 1919.
55. *The Samaj*, 4 October 1919.
56. *The Samaj,* 22 November 1919.
57. It was reported that in the lands which were flooded there was not a single blade of grass in some portions of Puri, *The Samaj*, 22 November 1919.
58. *Sambalpur Hiteisini*, 15 May 1919.

    It reported again that as a result of scarcity, a family ate the poisonous mushrooms and became unconscious after one hour, ibid., 28 June 1919.
59. *Utkal Sebaka*, Oriya Weekly, 5 June 1919.
60. *Utkal Dipika*, 28 June 1919.
61. *The Samaj*, 28 November 1919.
62. The *Utkal Dipika*, 28 June 1919.
63. *Utkal Sebaka*, 5 June 1919.
64. *Orissa Settlement Report*, *1922-32*, pp. 89 and 104.
65. The colonial rulers introduced potatoes, tomatoes and cauliflowers, these could not be served as offerings to Lord Jagannath. Even today, these vegetables are not offered in the temple. Since the Puri temple determines the pollution and purity of different food articles, it would have taken a long time for the Oriyas to accept these vegetables as food. However, some people did eat potatoes during the scarcity time.

66. *Land Revenues Administration in Bihar and Orissa, 1918-19*, p. 33.
67. Cuttack, Rs.156,976, Balasore, Rs. 86,000 and Puri Rs. 93,516, *Land Revenue Administration Report of Bihar and Orissa, 1919-20*, p. 33.
68. The *Utkal Dipika*, 16 August 1919.
69. *The Samaj*, 22 November 1919.
70. *Utkal Dipika*, 17 May 1919.
71. It was reported that the cattle of Banpur (Puri) did not have anything to eat. Husk was not available. There was nobody to cut grass for them. People were selling healthy cattle to the Muslims out of hunger. The *Utkal Dipika,* 8 November 1919.
72. *Sambalpur Hiteisini,* 22 March 1919.
73. The *Sebaka* expressed concern that there was no escape from the famine. Common people had already sold cattle and utensils and mortgaged ornaments to feed themselves, *Utkal Sebaka,* 29 May 1919.
74. *The Samaj*, 18 October 1919.
75. The *Utkal Dipika,* 3 May 1919. *The Samaj* reported that even if people wanted to sell their lands at a throw away price in the affected area, nobody wanted to buy them. Then it pointed out that the moneylenders were taking the possession of lands through mortgages by giving small paddy loans to the raiyats, *The Samaj*, 4 October 1919.
76. *General Administration Report of Bihar and Orissa, 1916-17*, p. 16.
77. Ibid. p. 57.
78. *Census of India 1921*, vol. 6, pt. 1, p. 259.
79. *Sambad Bahika,* 21 February 1918.

CHAPTER 6

Female Mortality in Famines, 1866-1974

Introduction

In this chapter we discuss the impact of famines on the sex ratio (SR) in the Indian subcontinent with a focus on Orissa and examine certain explanations.[1] As per the various census reports, the proportion of women vis-à-vis men in the population of India or SR (defined as the number of women per one thousand men) increased between 1872 and 1901, but began to steadily decline thereafter. It is important to note that famine and famine-related factors played a very important role in explaining both these trends. The explanations for these trends have a divergence of views among officials and scholars and present interesting insights into gender consequences of famines. We have used twentieth-century experiences in post-Independence India to examine if the later-day trends revealed significant changes regarding women's social condition.

First, it has been argued that frequent occurrences of famines up to 1901 explain the increase in SR, since the female death rate was supposedly lower than the male death rate during famines. Second, since famines occurred less frequently after 1901, these factors favouring women did not come into operation; the implicit assumption is that the epidemics were more frequent after 1901.[2] But this represents only one view. There are other views as well which will be discussed later. Before we discuss whether a general theory on famine and female mortality can be established or not, we will make some general observations regarding the SR and sex differential mortality between 1872 and 1921. For this we will take up the statements of the various Census authorities as well as those experts who have worked extensively on the issue.

SR and Sex Differential Mortality between 1881 and 1921: Some General Observations

Table 6.1 gives the SR of all India level as well as that of each zone. The table shows that the SR of India increased till 1901 and declined thereafter. At the zonal level, the SR of South Zone declined in 1891 but increased in 1901; thereafter it fluctuated. The SR of East Zone showed a continuous decline till 1921. But the rest of the zones followed the all-India pattern. Since we know that females were under-enumerated in early censuses, we do not know whether the increase in SR before 1901 was due to gradual improvement in enumeration or due to the fact that female death rates (fdr) was lower than the male death rate (mdr).

It has been observed that the statistical figures on birth and death registration were generally not reliable. But there was another source for a limited area and period, which was relatively more

TABLE 6.1: SEX RATIO (FEMALE PER THOUSAND MALES) FROM 1881-1921 FOR DIFFERENT ZONES

	Census years					
Zone	*1872*	*1881*	*1891*	*1901*	*1911*	*1921*
East	-	1,005	1,001	995	984	970
West	-	937	938	945	928	921
Central	-	962	959	981	979	972
North	-	897	903	907	884	881
South	-	1,022	1,015	1,018	1,021	1,015
India	940	954	958	963	954	945

Sources: Adapted from Visaria and Visaria, 1981 'Population' in Dharma Kumar (ed.), *Cambridge Economic History of India*, vol. 2, Cambridge: Cambridge University Press, p. 497.

Also, Ashok Mitra, 1978, *India's Population: Aspects of Quality and Control*, vol. 1, New Delhi: Abhinav Publications, p. 373.

reliable. For example, under the Act of 1870 for the prevention of female infanticide, the police had collected survival statistics of the population up to 12 years of the 'proclaimed clans' of North-Western Provinces for the years 1875 to 1879.[3] These statistics conclusively showed that female child mortality was higher than male child mortality rate. But this was in the areas where actual female infanticide was practiced.

Table 6.2 on the other hand, reveals that the SR at birth in the North-West Provinces was normal but the subsequent SR dropped sharply: thus the overall SR was reduced. That proved the point that female children were discriminated against. Table 6.3 also tells the other side of the story. It shows that the death ratio fluctuated dramatically and is above unity in most cases. We have also looked at the death rates in different parts of India in 1891, a year which was considered to be a normal year in the sense that there were no major famines in the decade 1881-91. All the provinces, except for Punjab had an excess of females over male children in the age group of 0-5. The baby girls of Punjab on the other hand, shared the fate of the baby girls of the proclaimed clans and sex ratio of children there was low.[4]

The decline in the sex ratio after 1901 was officially attributed

TABLE 6.2: RECORDED SEX RATIO (FEMALES PER THOUSAND MALES) OF PROCLAIMED CLANS POPULATION OF THE NORTH-WEST PROVINCES, 1875-9

Year	*At birth*	*Under 12*	*Over 12*	*Total*
1875-6	910	433	771	648
1876-7	960	430	749	636
1877-8	952	463	741	643
1878-9	943	504	731	652
1879-80	932	529	725	660
On the total population of the above years	939	469	744	648

Source: Table B, Actuarial Report of 1881, G.F. Hardy quoted in Mitra, *India's Population*, op. cit., vol. I, p. 6.

TABLE 6.3: FEMALE DEATHS PER 1000 MALE DEATHS OF THE PROCLAIMED CLANS (NORTH-WEST PROVINCES), 1876-82, BASED ON DEATHS OUT OF 10,000 OF LIVE BIRTHS AT RISK DURING THE FIRST TO TWELVE YEARS OF LIFE SEX RATIO OF DEATHS AT AGES (FEMALES PER THOUSAND MALES)

Year Ending 1st April	*0-1*	*1-2*	*2-3*	*3-4*	*4-5*	*5-6*	*6-7*	*7-8*	*8-9*	*9-10*	*10-11*	*11-12*
1876-7	937	1,110	1,198	1,423	1,371	1,247	1,404	1,529	1,391	676	1,109	1,240
1877-8	1,112	1,266	1,335	1,650	1,093	1,978	1,774	1,667	1,242	1,956	2,509	782
1878-9	1,039	1,117	1,333	1,445	1,143	1,220	1,163	1,458	1,421	1,155	1,147	1,120
1879-80	1,031	1,186	1,553	1,405	1,277	1,320	1,122	1,465	1,447	1,513	1,388	1,038
1880-1	985	1,023	1,269	1,523	1,453	1,045	1,333	1,533	1,437	807	1,466	3,372
1881-2	1,002	1,087	1,452	1,656	1,955	1,546	1,119	1,150	1,726	1,264	1,248	2,748
Mean	1,019	1,132	1,403	1,495	1,359	1,340	1,220	1,470	1,460	1,303	1,417	1,650

Sources: Table C of Actuarial Report of 1881 by G.F. Hardy.
Quoted from A. Mitra, *India's Population: Aspects of Quality and Control*, op. cit., vol. 1, p. 8.

to sex differential morality or the phenomenon of more female deaths (Table 6.3). For example, the Census Commissioner of 1921 observed that 'A marked feature of the statistics of the last twenty years has been the increase in proportion of female deaths since 1901'.[5] In order to support his contention, he had calculated the decennial death ratios for different parts of India for the decades ending 1901, 1911, and 1921. Table 6.4 shows that the death ratio was increasing in most parts of the country in the first twenty years of the twentieth century.

Since the absolute numbers of males and females differ, it is more useful to compare the death rates. Table 6.5 depicts the recorded average death rates of males and females in the decades ending 1901, 1911, and 1921. Even though the recorded death rate of females was lower than that of males in most of the provinces, in some the gap between the two narrowed down, including Bihar and Orissa. In Punjab the recorded female death rate was higher than that of males in 1911 as well as in 1921.

Using age-specific death figures from the official statistical reports as well as studies in villages of Punjab, Pravin Visaria has presented the ratios of sex-specific crude in death rates during

TABLE 6.4: PROPORTION OF FEMALE DEATHS PER THOUSAND MALE DEATHS IN THE DECADES ENDING 1901, 1911 AND 1921 FOR VARIOUS PARTS OF INDIA

Provinces	*Average for decade ending*		
	1901	*1911*	*1921*
Bengal	874	895	909
Bihar & Orissa	870	940	936
Bombay	901	936	957
Burma	817	849	901
Central Provinces & Berar	853	917	923
Madras	951	961	979
Punjab	918	983	928
United Provinces	881	957	918

Source: Census of India, 1921, vol. I, pt. I, p. 145.

TABLE 6.5: REPORTED AVERAGE DEATH RATES OF MALES AND FEMALES IN MAJOR PROVINCES OF INDIA IN THE DECADES ENDING 1901, 1911 AND 1921

	1901		*1911*		*1921*	
	Male	*Female*	*Male*	*Female*	*Male*	*Female*
Bengal	33.4	30.0	33.8	31.5	31.7	30.5
Bihar & Orissa	33.1	27.4	37.3	33.4	37.2	33.3
Bombay	35.9	34.8	34.7	34.5	36.2	37.6
Central Provinces & Berar	40.1	35.1	37.9	34.0	46.1	42.2
Madras	20.8	19.3	24.0	22.4	26.3	25.6
Punjab	32.6	25.6	41.3	47.1	34.6	39.0
United Provinces	33.5	31.7	38.9	39.7	40.1	40.3

Sources: Census of India 1911, vol. 1, pt. I, pp. 202, 232-3; *Census of India*, 1911, vol. 1, pt. II, p. 7; *Census of India*, 1921, vol. 1, pt. I, p. 60.

the period 1911 to 1947. He concluded that the registered female death rates were higher than those of males in 26 out of 36 years in places such as Punjab, Delhi, Bombay, Ajmer, Mewar and Coorg. Further he has also observed that in most parts of India, females experienced higher death rates in the age group of 15-39. But in Punjab, females had higher death rates in almost all the age groups. In other parts of India, the higher female mortality during the reproductive age groups was offset by a lower female death rate in the older age groups. But in Punjab higher female mortality continued till the age of 60.[6] Visaria has cited the findings of the study of 16 villages of Ludhiana, in the years between 1956 and 1960, known as the Khanna Study, which showed that in most of the age groups females died in larger numbers than males from a variety of causes.[7] Similarly, in another study by M.K. Jain, the author computed age-sex specific death rates from the life tables from 1921 to 1971 to show that the female death rate has been higher than the male death rate till the age of 50.[8] Let us compare these trends with situations much after Independence. For instance, if we take up two important studies on sex differential mortality conducted in India between 1960 and 1971,these two studies give conflicting results.

First we take up the all India case study Indian case by L.T. Ruzicka who has noted that the crude death rates have been declining between 1951-61 and 1961-71, the decennial decline of 17 per cent in India. This is based on official registration statistics. While the overall trend of rising life expectancy of Indians gives us a cheer there was bad news for women. According to the National Family Health Survey 2015-16 (NFHS-4) the life expectancy in India has increased by five years from 62.3 years for men and 63.9 years for women in 2001-5 to 67.3 years and 69.6 years respectively in 2011-15. But the death rate of the girl child still remains higher compared to that of male child. (Government of India, Ministry of Health and Family Welfare, National Family Health Survey (NFHS-4) 2015-16, p. 3.) One of the features of this 'mortality transition' is the difference between the life expectancy at birth of males and females. Ruzicka noted that the gap between two expectancies was 0.8 years in favour of males in the decade between 1941 and 1950. But it widened to about 1.3 years by 1961-71. According to Ruzicka, the reason for the widening of the gap is that there is a higher death rate among females at most ages under 50. He noted that India was the only country in Asia where the female death rate was higher than that of males even after the 'mortality transition'. Further, the author also observed that this was because women have a 'generally disadvantaged position in India'.[9]

N. Krishnaji who conducted similar tests has taken this discussion forward by bringing in differential experiences of social groups. Drawing attention to the class element and related migration, Krishnaji has significant points at the relatively balanced SR among agricultural labourer class and the households having small landholdings. This, he suggested, was due to narrower sex differential mortality. This important insight on lower death rates among women is worth further discussion.

Krishnaji took note of the fact that the SR of agricultural and rural labourers in 1971 was 980 and that of members of non-labour households was 940. Also the SR was 1,000 in the age groups of 15-49 among agricultural labourers, in 1974-5. In contrast, the rural population of India had an SR of 971 in the same age group.[10] Similarly, the SR among adult groups was actually high in the households with lower operational landholdings according to the 1961-2 National Sample Survey (NSS).

Since the SR was influenced by sex-selective outmigration, Krishnaji had analysed that factor also. He noted that in 1971, out of 438.8 million people in the rural areas, 23.7 million had migrated to urban areas. Even if one adds all these migrants to the rural labouring class, the SR of the labouring class (1/4th of all rural) would come down to 965 from 980, but it would still be much higher than the SR of the non-labouring class, which was 940. Besides, case studies done in various parts of the country showed that the migrants were drawn from all classes. Thus he ruled out the factor of outmigration in explaining the entire difference in the SR of agricultural labouring groups or land-poor households, compared to others.[11]

Krishnaji also tried to relate poverty (in terms of per capita income or expenditure) to high SR. The National Sample Survey of 1973-4 showed that the highest SR occurred in the groups with the lowest per capita expenditure. However, some individuals belonging to the high landholding group also got classified in lower per capita expenditure group, because of their large family size (NSS No. 140, 1956-7). But one fact clearly emerges from the analysis of per capita consumption normally that families with a high proportion of females and children are grouped in the categories of lower per capita income because of earning differentials between males and females.[12]

He then considered landholding size to show that land-poor families have high SRs. Krishnaji quoted Visaria and Visaria who had pointed out that households with small landholdings have a higher proportion of female heads than other rural families according to the 1961 census and that households with female heads tend to be small in size and have a higher proportion of females. Visaria and Visaria also speculated that females forming a higher proportion of households with small landholdings was perhaps because they are forced to sell part of their holding or get a small share after the death of their husband because of their low bargaining power. (The Visarias also observed that female heads are mainly widows.) Krishnaji speculated that the widowhood was the result of higher male mortalities in the various age groups. In other words, Krishnaji inferred that relatively balanced SR in the poorer agricultural classes is likely to be due to the fact that women of the labouring poor families had relatively less death rates than the rest.[13] We may note that while Ruzcika gave a generalized explanation for low the sex ratio, referring to women being disadvantaged, Krishnaji made a distinction between the experiences of women of labouring classes who had a higher sex ratio and that of the other sections of society who had a lower one.

After this we turn to the views of different Census authorities on sex differential mortality relating to famine, which were again not unanimous.

Census Views on Female and Famine Mortality

That the female death rates (fdr) was lower than the male death rates (mdr) during a famine and thus led to an increase in SR, has been propounded by different Census authorities since 1901 in a more systematic way.

The decade 1891-1901 suffered from two intense famines, one in 1896-7 and another 1899-1900, in the Central Provinces, Bombay Presidency, the United Provinces and Oudh, Punjab, Bengal Presidency, Rajputana and Madras Presidency. In 1901, Risley and Gait noticed that the SR had increased most in the Central Provinces, which suffered from both the famines; this was particularly true of the age group of 30 and over. They also quoted the Census Superintendents of the United Provinces and Rajputana who had observed that food shortage was the main cause of the 'relatively rapid growth of females' during the decade. The absence of famine and constancy of SR in Sind led Risley and Gait to infer that famine and SR were co-related. Moreover, they argued that epidemics such as kalazar harmed women less in Assam.[14] Thus they concluded,

It seems, therefore, clear that females are better than males to resist the ill effects of famine, and as the Census statistics show that the improvement in the ratio of women has occurred mainly at the age of 30 and upwards, it may be concluded that it is amongst adults that their constitutional superiority in this respect is most marked.[15]

Thus, according to them, women have stronger physical ability to cope with famine conditions.

The views of Risely & Gait were mainly based on the observations of the Census Superintendents of Central Provinces and that of the United Provinces and Oudh. The SR did increase in those places in 1901 compared to 1891. But there were some data problems. In particular there was a methodological problem as they have taken only one year (1891) as normal. There were also problems regarding the interpretation of data. For example, they assumed that the degree of under-enumeration of female deaths was constant in famine and non-famine years, but there was perhaps no reason to assume that, as the experience of United Provinces showed in 1911. The data relating to the female deaths was indeed under-enumerated. Second, the authors considered the actual calendar year of the famine only and noted that the female deaths and death rates were lower than those of males. But if they had considered the epidemic phase of the famine, they would have noticed that female deaths were the highest in the epidemic phase of the famine. Third, the Census Commissioners also assumed that the degree of under-enumeration of female population was constant both in 1891 and 1901. On the other hand, the Census Superintendents of Bombay and Rajputana observed that there was an improvement in the enumeration of females in the year 1901 compared to 1891. Finally, the sex selective out-migration or the phenomenon of more males going out in search of work, would have played some role in shaping the SR of 1901, as was the case in the United Provinces and Bombay Presidency.

Further, if the hypothesis of Risley and Gait was true that increase in fdr was lower than the increase in mdr, then other areas such as Madras Presidency and the Punjab which were also affected by the famine of 1896-7 and 1899-1900 respectively, should have shown the same trend, keeping other things constant. Indeed the

SR had increased in the post-famine year 1901, compared to 1891 both in Punjab and Madras.[16]

Further it was only a marginal increase in Punjab. The Famine Commissioner of Madras Presidency in 1896-7 stated that despite this, 'the increased rate of death of females in proportion to that of males, is of special significance. It is held in mind that the tendency on the part of the indifferent agency employed for registration is to *ignore occurrences affecting inferior sex.* The women undoubtedly exhibited more signs of deterioration than the men.'[17] (emphasis added).

While it is undoubtedly true that famines were on the whole much less severe after 1901, except for the Bengal Famine of 1943, some famines did occur, and it is particularly important to note that they were invariably accompanied by diseases, including malaria. And in many of these famines the female death rate increased more sharply than the male death rate. This was the case especially if one considers not merely the actual famine year but also the subsequent year for famine related epidemics. For instance, a famine was declared in 1907-8 in the United Provinces. Blunt, the then Census Superintendent of United Provinces, for example, observed that the age-specific death ratio of the famine year 1908 was lower than that of 1901. But a type of virulent malaria had prevailed in the later part of 1908 which had killed more women than men, especially in the reproductive age groups.[18] In order to show that the age-specific death ratio was higher because of virulent malaria and not because of the famine, Blunt had separated the death ratio of the famine period and that of the malarial period. According to him, the death ratio during the famine period, which lasted from January to August 1908, was 88. After August 1908 a malaria epidemic broke out from September 1908 to December 1908, and the ratio jumped to 106. Malaria accounted for 52 per cent of total deaths and famine accounted for 48 per cent of deaths. Thus Blunt observed that it was the epidemic and not the famine, which was responsible for raising the death ratio. Second, he also noticed that malaria was 'concomitant' and was not caused directly by the famine. However, as we shall discuss in Chapter 7, malaria was very much related to famine since people with lower level of nutrition in famine conditions were more prone to malaria. Superintendent Blunt further observed that malaria broke out during the famine of 1896-7 but he did not take the famine and the following epidemic years – as he regarded it as 'non-famine' year – together to calculate the female mortality rate.[19] He also noted that another feature of the famine of 1907-8 was that there was no 'aimless wandering'.[20] In other words, there was no great flow of out-migration.

However, it should be noted that even though the death ratio due to malaria did not rise in 1897 compared to non-famine years, but it rose considerably in the next year. This was because malaria had attacked malnourished people more virulently. A similar pattern was repeated in 1908. Blunt however, got a different result because he had a limited perspective on the impact of famine. Thus, it can be inferred that the higher death ratio of 1908 compared to 1901 was due to famine as well as famine related epidemics.

Again, in the decade of 1911-21, it was noticed that influenza epidemic followed crop failures in many parts of India in 1918-19 and had killed more adult women than men. It was most fatal to pregnant women according to J. Marten, the Census Commissioner of 1921, and also more dangerous to adult women than adult men because the women tended to the sick and did the household work.[21] To say that the higher death rate of female was not related to food shortage is incorrect as influenza epidemic and crop failure came together. This kind of problems relating to data had haunted not only the earlier analysts, they also dogged later thinking on this subject.

Biological and Sociological Factors behind Female Mortality: The Official Views

The Census commissioners and Census superintendents as well as famine relief administrators cited two sets of factors, namely, biological and sociological, which allegedly operated during the famine periods and helped in reducing death ratios of famine years compared to non-famine years.

(1) *Biological Factors:* According to Risley and Gait,[22] the biologi-

cal factors were: (a) females are less 'metabolic' so they require less food; (b) in a food crisis, the conception rate as well as birth rates fall, and so there are fewer deaths due to diseases related to pregnancy and childbirth; (c) after maturity, women are constitutionally stronger than men and (d) women have less bones and more muscles, so the wasting process is slower than that of men.

On close examination we find that the factors (a), (b), and (d) may be operative in the phase of direct impact of famine, but are not significant in the epidemic phase of the famine. Let us take the arguments on by one.

(a) Here women being less metabolic means that the rate of utilization of energy is lower for them than men. WHO/FAO experts have divided calorie requirements into three parts: 'maintenance', 'growth', and 'activity', all related to body weight. To maintain itself, the body requires one and a half times the 'basal metabolic rate'. This rate is not constant and it varies with the size of the body and is somewhat less for females than males.[23] We will see later that the notion of requirement cited in this context has been challenged. But assuming that females have a lesser metabolic rate, the rate of utilization of energy would not be lower if both sexes are subjected to similar tasks. The Famine Commissioner of Madras Presidency in the 1896-7 famine had observed that as women staying in the relief centres had lighter tasks, they would have required less food as compared to men.[24] But if women stayed at home and also worked at the relief centres along with men, they had a double workload, because they also had to look after their children as well as their household duties in addition to relief-related work. In this situation women would not require less food. In any case, as will be seen shortly, relief was given only to a small fraction of people.

(b) The second argument was that the conception rate and birth rate would have fallen during a severe food shortage period. It was indeed likely that the conception rate fell during past famines.[25] A study of the Bangladesh famine of 1974-5 showed that the fertility (conception and birth) rate had declined by 33 per cent.[26] The reasons were: aimless wandering, forced separation, stress and strain, and some biological changes during the period.[27] However, we should note that two contradictory factors would have been at work. First, it is likely that conception and birth rates fell. On the other hand, in an agrarian economy, a high proportion of women would already be pregnant or lactating, and they would be even more at risk during famines.[28] One cannot tell purely on a priori grounds what the net effect would be.

(c) The Census Commissioner did not elaborate on their contention that women are constitutionally stronger than men after maturity; perhaps they meant that women are constitutionally stronger to fight infection. It has, however, been shown in chapter 7 that this premise does not stand scrutiny and that the death rates of males and females due to different infections depended largely on the extent of exposure.

Thus the set of biological factors which allegedly favoured women in general need some qualifications. Since McAlpine has given some additional information on point (d) we will take up her arguments later in this chapter.

(2) *Sociological Factors:* According to the Census authorities, the sociological or non-biological factors favouring women were the following:

(a) Women received gratuitous relief more frequently than men and their work in relief centres was comparatively lighter.
(b) Women collected jungle produce, cooked food at home and had some precious ornaments, which they could sell in times of need.
(c) Women wandered less than men in search of food.
(d) There was a 'common feeling of tenderness' towards

women. Husbands usually offered to their wives whatever scanty food was available.

(e) Lastly, the authorities felt that the 'brunt of struggle' fell on men entirely and men were in constant tension of providing food to the family. Hence male death rate was higher than that of females.[29]

Let us see how far do these views stand scrutiny.

(i) First, as far as the available evidence is concerned, it is true that women did receive gratuitous relief in greater numbers than men. This was not important since only a small proportion of famine victims received relief in each famine during 1865-1900. The average number given relief daily ranged from 0.3 per cent of the total victims in 1865-6 to 8 per cent in 1896-7.[30] The majority of the famine-affected population were left to fend for themselves.

(ii) It is also true that women and children were assigned the task of collecting substitutes for staple food. They probably ate a larger share of those substitutes than men, in which case they would have suffered more from cholera and famine diarrhea. Famine literature is full of references to the consequences of eating rough substitutes, as was mentioned in Chapters 3 and 5.

There is no data available on asset disposal.[31] But two points are to be noted. First, a sizeable section of the famine victims were landless labourers and would not have had many ornaments or other assets. Small farmers would have had some assets, but it seems unlikely that their wives would dispose off their ornaments for their own needs. The noted expert on famine, Greenough observed that the *korta* (the husband) is the decision-maker regarding distribution of resources of the household and the welfare of the whole family in which the women have low priority.[32]

Points (c), (d) and (e) are somewhat related. Since men had more responsibility, they 'wandered aimlessly' in search of food during the famine years, and ate whatever food was available on the way. They also drank polluted water and the most important point to be stressed here is that as a result of 'aimless wandering' they were more exposed to infections. But the gap between male and female would have narrowed as famine advanced, and the women too had to leave home.

As regards the condition (d), i.e. 'tenderness towards women', both Russell and Burn have dismissed this.[33] Besides, this feeling looked like a mere assertion and similar opposite assertions could also be made. To sum up, of all the reasons said to favour women, only point (c), i.e. 'aimless wandering' by men seems somewhat significant.

Biological and Sociological Factors behind Female Mortality: Perspective of Scholars

Visaria examined the views of the Census commissioners that the absence of famines and the increased incidence of epidemics after 1900 had led to higher female than male mortality. However, he rejected the possibility of women taking advantage of their position in the household by selling their ornaments or eating more than their share while cooking. At the same time, he agreed with the Census commissioners of 1901 and 1911 regarding the 'aimless wandering' of males were possible factors influencing relatively less increase in female mortality during the famines. After 1900, the famines had become rare while the epidemics had prevailed. Hence, according to Visaria, the fact of female death rate being more than the male death rate was due to epidemics rather than famines.[34]

McAlpine also tried to test the hypothesis that female deaths was lower than that of males in the famine year in Bombay Presidency between 1872 and 1921. She used three types of arguments: biological, sociological and statistical, to prove her point. The biological and sociological arguments are more or less on the same lines as those of the Census Commissioner of 1911, though she observed that some of the sociological factors discriminate against females and some against males. So we will discuss only the points of departure.

First, McAlpine remarked that female infants had a lower

mortality rate than male infants. Second, females were biologically better able to fight infection. In other words, McAlpine assumed that number of female deaths in the age group of 0-5 would have been lower than that of excess male deaths in the corresponding age group. This goes against the findings of Risley and Gait, the Census commissioners of 1901. McAlpine also cites evidence from animal studies to point out that females adapted to protein deprivation more rapidly than males. Finally, she stated that some of the biological factors tended to get offset by the adverse sociological factors, but she pointed out that on balance the biological factors tended to favour women.[35]

We have discussed all the other allegedly favourable biological factors except the adaptation to protein deprivation. This seems unlikely to be important in India because females are more malnourished to begin with.

McAlpine used a test census of the famine of 1876-8 of Bombay conducted in the early months of 1878, which showed that the SR increased in the severely affected *talukas* between 1872 and 1878. She noted that women were under-reported in the Census of 1872, but argued that the increase in SR had a real element in it. In order to substantiate this point she quoted Dr. Cornish's evidence that the female death rate was lower than that of male in the relief camps of Salem district (Madras Presidency). Since Madras had shown similar kind of changes in SR as that of Bombay, McAlpine argued that the same kind of death pattern would have prevailed in the famine-affected area of Bombay Presidency as well.[36]

The above author also was of the opinion that a similar increase in the SR had occurred in the Divisions, which had suffered from severe famines since the middle of the nineteenth century. For example, the SRs of Karnataka and Deccan increased sharply in the decade 1872-81 and those of Gujarat and Deccan increased during 1891-1901. She then concluded that: 'Overall, periods of famine (i.e. periods when mortality is greatly increased due to food shortage) create a population which has a lower dependency ratio . . . than the pre-famine population and one with more females relative to males.'[37]

Similarly, Lardinois analysed the age and sex structures of the famine mortality of the Madras Presidency in the years of 1876 to 1878. He used the above test census results also. It was noticed that 'Totally, the decrease of those above 10 years is always stronger for male sex than for the female sex, between 1871 and 1878, the adult male population went down by 19.3 per cent as against only 13.3 per cent for the female sex.' The differential migration according to the sex takes into account to some extent the adult masculine and excess mortality during the famine. But in the juvenile and infant groups, the decrease was more in the case of female groups.[38]

However, McAlpine considered epidemics like plague and influenza as autonomous of famines.[39] Plague broke out in Bombay city and other cities in the early months of 1897 along with the famine in rural areas, leading to cross-currents of migration both to and from the village.[40] Migrant men might have caught plague fleas and died first. In that case excess female deaths would have been lower than that of males due to famine and famine-related epidemics.[41] But as we shall see in Chapter 7 plague and influenza may be related to famine, though indirectly.

Again, McAlpine did not consider the possibility that the increased SR in the Divisions may have been partly due to sex selective out-migration to Bombay city.[42] This possibility of larger number of male migrants is discussed in the Census Reports of 1891-1901.[43] Besides, Morris D. Morris pointed out that the majority of the textile workers in Bombay came from the districts of Konkan and Deccan.[44] After 1898, labourers did not leave the textile mills in spite of the outbreak of plague.[45] Male workers constituted not less than 69 per cent and women not more than 25 per cent of the total workforce.[46] Thus it was possible to suggest as pointed out by Landinois in the case of Madras Presidency, that the increased SR after the famine could be the result of sex-selective out-migration in Deccan. Presence of a large number of labourers in Bombay city and higher mortality due to the greater exposure to the infections could have led to increase in sex ratio and not due to the direct impact of famine.

Let us see what was the pattern of female and male deaths in the Bengal famine of 1943 and some other famines in the Indian subcontinent and what explanatory insights do the studies present.

The Bengal Famine of 1943

The views of the experts who studied the Bengal famine of 1943-4 varied greatly on the sex-differential mortality during the famine period. The Famine commissioners appointed at that time computed deaths due to famine of 1943-4 based their views on the deaths recorded in the Public Health Reports. The commissioners admitted that the figures were underestimates for two reasons. First, the village *chowkidars* who were the usual sources of information on births and deaths either deserted their duties or had died. Second, famine-affected people moved about from place to place making it difficult to collect exact data.[47] Admitting these factors, the commissioners upgraded the official mortality figures of the year 1943 by 40 per cent.[48]

The commissioners also noted that there was a possibility of under-enumeration of female deaths because of the carelessness of the reporting agency as many of the roadside dead bodies, consisting mainly of females and children, were not included in the death returns.[49] Further, it was observed that the percentage of excess female deaths compared to previous quinquennial deaths was much higher than that of males in Calcutta city.[50] But they still concluded that overall, 'If the average number of male and female deaths in the previous quinquennium is compared with the figures for 1943, it is found that the increase in male deaths was 62.5 per cent as compared with 53.2 per cent in case of female deaths.'[51] The Commissioners felt that it was difficult to conclusively assign reasons for the increase in excess male mortality but cited more or less the similar kind of biological and sociological factors as the earlier commissioners during 1901 such as 'higher food requirement by men', 'more stress borne by men' and 'more women and children seeking relief in the government kitchens'.[52]

They also quoted a sample survey conducted by one official named T. Das in different rural areas. The survey showed that of the 4,833 deaths investigated, the percentage of deaths among males was 56.7 and among females it was 42.3. The commissioners confirmed that the records of hospital deaths showed a similar phenomenon.[53]

Das also analysed 212 cases of deaths among the destitutes of Calcutta and found that the female deaths were 53.6 per cent of male deaths. Destitutes were asked about the number of deaths in each destitute family of the sample after they had left home and within six months of their departure.[54]

Further the commissioners cited a series of sample survey by the prominent statistician P.C. Mahalanobis in rural areas, which showed different results. The investigation, which covered 2,622 families living in villages of several sub-divisions, showed that, on the whole, the female mortality rate was higher than that of males. (The sample excluded infants below one year.)

The Commission criticized the findings of Mahalanobis on the ground that

> There was, however, considerable irregularity in the proportionate sex mortality in the various subdivisions, and in some sub-divisions the male mortality on a percentage basis exceeded the female. The aggregate figures are influenced by the data from one sub-division in which, for some reasons, female deaths greatly exceeded male deaths.[55]

However, the Census Superintendent of West Bengal of 1951 had a different story to tell. The Superintendent observed that the female death rate was higher than male death rate in the decade 1942-51. It was true of the famine year also, taking the entire province into account. But there were certain districts in which the reverse was true. This he attributed to underestimation of female deaths. Even though the rate was higher the absolute number of deaths of females was lower than that of the males. The Census Superintendent pointed out that it was due to two factors. The absolute number of male population was higher than that of the female population and there was constant migration of males to Bengal. Second, there was a steady decline in female population since 1901 through higher mortality.[56]

The Census authority of Bengal further observed that female deaths exceeded male deaths only in certain districts such as Burdwan, Calcutta, Nadia, and Jalpaiguri in the famine year of 1943. But all the other districts of West Bengal had joined this group in the year 1944.[57] It was due to underestimation of female deaths in 1943, he added.

With regard to the sex- and age-specific death rates, demographer Ashok Mitra more or less agreed with the earlier Census commissioners of 1901. For example, using the census data, he pointed out that the female death rate was higher than that of males in the age groups of 1-5, 5-10, 15-40 and 60 and over. In other age groups, namely, 0-1, 10-15 and 40-60, the male death rates were higher than that of females. The mortality pattern on the famine year reflected the normal pattern of mortality, but the differences had become more acute.[58] But he has not considered explicitly the impact of the famine on SR.

The reasons for higher female death rates in the above age groups were, the Census authority noted: comparative neglect of female children and females above 60 and greater risk involved in the reproductive age groups. The reasons for higher male death rates in the other age groups were sociological, namely, they happened to be the sole bread earners of the family and thus bore all the stress locally as well as while moving about.[59]

Amartya Sen's study of the Bengal famine of 1943 was a point of departure. He utilized the death registration data with suitable and uniform corrections of the death statistics.[60] Further he used a two-year average, taking 1941 and 1942, in contrast to the quinquennial average adopted by the Famine Commissioner, on the ground that the crude death rate was declining monotonically before the famine. His findings show that

> The ratios seem remarkably stable through the famine of (1943-6). While the proportion of men in excess mortality in 1943 is a bit higher than in the pre-famine average, the difference is small, and over the larger period of famine mortality the proportionate breakdown of the excess is just the same as for the pre-famine average.

The same pattern was true of old and young.[61]

Sen's way of treating famine is new in the sense that he extended the duration of the famine to the starvation and epidemic phase, since according to him the death rate which rose in 1943 did not come back to the pre-famine level till 1946. The starvation phase of the famine was limited from January 1943 to December 1943. The epidemic phase of the famine had started along with the arrival of a bumper crop in the market. He noticed that the sex differential mortality did not show much difference if we consider both starvation phase and that of epidemics.[62]

Unlike Sen, Paul R. Greenough has concentrated on the period between January 1943 to December 1943, the period of starvation.[63] Greenough depended on the ISI data as generated by P.C. Mahalanobis and his group through a series of sample surveys. Their notes were submitted to the Famine Commission but were not considered by them. But according to Greenough, these data were more reliable than those of the public registration system. He observed that these data were based on a sampling of 13,358 households distributed in 40 out of 86 sub-divisions of Bengal.[64] The samples were 'carefully stratified' according to the severity of the famine. Greenough noted three limitations of these data. First, the data related only to the calendar year of 1943 whereas the famine period extended beyond that. Second, words like 'household' and 'family' had been used interchangeably whereas families were often spread over different households. This however, did not create much of a problem since the investigators asked questions to the head of the family. Third, infant mortality figures were excluded. On this, Greenough has cited evidence that the proportion of infant deaths did not increase or decrease.[65]

Greenough also analysed the sex and age composition of those who had died in the sampled villages in the year 1943. The death rates were calculated from the population of those villages who were living in January 1943. Altogether there were 32,701 males and 30,202 females, out of which 2,093 males and 1,778 females had died within the year 1943. The average death rate has been taken from the Census of 1931, i.e. deaths which occurred between 1932 and 1941.[66] Greenough calculated the excess death rates for each age category. The results are very interesting. First, the mortality pattern or the famine year was different from that of the non-famine years. Second, excess female deaths were lower than that of male deaths. Third, excess death rates of the women of reproductive age group of 15-50 were lower than those of males of the corresponding age group. Fourth, children in the age group of 5-15 experienced the lowest mortality rate. [67] The lower excess death rate of females in the reproductive age group was due to decline in live births, which was reflected in both the years, 1943 and 1944, according to Greenough.[68] But it is to be pointed out that the above view contradicted the author's own *korta* model in which he showed that both children and women are neglected in general compared to men. The author has presumably taken the average death rate as given in the Census Report of 1931 for entire Bengal. But a more appropriate average would have been the average deaths of the pre-famine period of the villages.

Thus the Bengal famine of 1943 showed that the excess death rate of females was lower than that of males during the starvation phase. But if we consider both the starvation phase and epidemic phase together, we find no difference between the sex ratio of pre-famine period and famine deaths, as Sen has observed. This showed that the vulnerability of both women and men to the famine-related scarcity and disease persisted and certain age groups continued to bear the brunt of the impact. The story was not much different in case of the Bangladesh experience three decades later.

Bangladesh Famine of 1974

Two careful studies have been done on sex differential mortality during the famine of 1974 in Bangladesh, which is worth discussing here briefly. The proximate cause of the famine of 1974 was excessive rainfall causing severe floods. They occurred four times within span of four months, June to September, and damaged *aus* and *aman* rice crops in the flood-affected areas. The Government of Bangladesh, a newly independent country then, declared famine officially in September 1974.[69]

Alamgir, who studied the Bangladesh famine of 1974, has utilized the data collected by the Institute of Development Studies in Bangladesh from July 1973 to June 1974 and from July to October 1974 to show the excess deaths during the famine of 1974. The sample population consisted of 1974 households in eight villages and 788 inmates of eight *langar-khanas* (an eating place where everybody irrespective of caste or religion eat together). Four villages were selected from famine areas in three districts, and the others from non-famine areas. Of the eight *langar-khanas,* six were from famine areas, three rural and three urban areas, one in a non-famine affected area and one in Mirpur in Dacca, the capital, which was the main urban area of the country. The intensity of the famine was measured by using two criteria: (1) The flood level should have been six feet or more in a period of three months, (2) five per cent or more of the population should have sought relief.[70] Mortality data were collected during the months of August-October 1974; this period was officially declared as the peak period of the famine even though the crude death rate continued to increase till January 1975. The author has classified August-October 1974 as the starvation phase and November 1974-January 1975 as the epidemic phase.[71] According to the survey data, 136 deaths had occurred in 1,774 households of eight villages and 141 deaths had occurred in the households of 788 *langar-khana* inmates.[72]

Alamgir has broken up the mortality data into three broad categories: adult men (10 years and above), adult women and children below 10 years, and has calculated crude death rates of the respective age groups and compared them with the average crude death rate (1966-71). The 'excess death rate' (i.e. the difference between death rate in the famine year and the normal death rate) was higher for adult females than adult males in all the surveyed villages as well as the famine-affected villages. But in the case of the *langar-khanas* the results were different for adults only. The excess male death rate was significantly higher than that of the female death rate.[73] Thus the mortality pattern of relief centre households was different from that of the general population in the famine year. Even though the author has given no explanation for such phenomenon, it can be said that perhaps the directly affected people who came to the relief centres would have more casualties than the rest.

To further clarify the pattern of sex differential mortality, we now refer to another famous study in Bangladesh.

Deaths in the Famine of 1974 in Matlab Thana[74]

Just as the study of Salem district, Madras Presidency by Cornish has been used by different authorities to show the sex differential mortality in the past famines, the experience of Matlab Thana in Bangladesh has also been used in twentieth century to show the sex differential mortality in famine periods.[75] In Matlab Thana, systematic data were collected on every aspect of population from 1963 onwards and are taken as reliable and free from age misreporting bias and from under-reporting of vital events.

Stan D'Souza and L.C. Chen have taken demographic profiles of Matlab Thana on four years, out of which two (1974 and 1975) are famine years and the other two (1976 and 1977) are non-famine years. The results showed that the male crude death rate of 16.1 was marginally lower than that of females (16.7) over the entire period of four years. In one of the crisis years, 1974, the female crude death rate was higher than that of males but in 1975, the reverse was true. If we classify 1974 as the starvation phase and 1975 as the epidemic phase, as Alamgir had done, we will see that the female crude death rate was higher than the male crude death rate in the starvation phase and the opposite was true in the epidemic phase. These findings are different from the results of the famine of 1943 as shown by Sen and Greenough. The most novel part of the study is the analysis of differential mortality patterns of the neo-natal and post-neonatal age group. Even though the overall infant (under 1 year) mortality did not show much change, the changes in post-neonatal and neonatal mortality were quite significant. It is interesting to note that the male infants died at a higher rate than female infants in the neonatal phase. But in the post neonatal phase the reverse was true. This was the normal pattern. In famine years, the difference between the two rates increased sharply in the post-neonatal period. In other words, the excess death rate of female infants was higher than that of male infants in the post-neonatal phase.[76]

In the next age group, i.e. 1-4, the death rate of female children was higher than that of male children in all the four years. But the difference was more acute in the case of famine years compared to non-famine years.[77] The authors have analysed the mortality pattern of males and females in the age groups 5-14, 15-45 and 45 and over, for the famine and non-famine years. It is interesting to note that the excess female death rate was higher in the age group of 5-45 than the excess death rate of males of the corresponding age groups in the year 1974. But in 1975, the excess male death rate was higher than that of females in the age group 15-44. This was explained by the authors in terms of sex differential out-migration, which would have left the less healthy males behind.[78] The reasons for the changing pattern of mortality in infant groups, according to the authors, were that at the stage of neo-natal deaths the female child was biologically stronger, but thereafter sociological factors such as 'son preference in parental care', 'feeding patterns', 'intra-family distribution of food', 'medical treatment' and so forth were responsible for higher female deaths.[79]

Let us now refer to some other studies, which have presented important insights into the question of sex-differential mortality during famines.

Tim Dyson and Cormac O'Grada have studied the patterns of mortality in various famines all over the world. They observed that more females than males, died during the famine years in the past. But in the recent decades, the famines are more class specific and more males have died as compared to females.[80] That, however, does not necessarily support the argument highlighting the biological factors favouring women. In case of many past famines in Finland, they pointed out that the sex differential mortality was not significant at all. Thus the so-called favourable biological factors for women has little historical basis. Wherever it occurred, it was due to male migration in a larger scale. Taking Indian famines into consideration, Tim Dyson, on the other hand, pointed out that male death rates seemed to be more during the Berar famines of 1896-7 and 1899-1900. Hence the adult sex ratio increased. He also mentioned that the vital statistics of Berar were relatively accurate.[81] However, in another study, the author vouched that more males died compared to females because of the fat content. Most probably the consumption of fat slows down hunger, hence women have an advantage over men. During the famine period, fertility in women declined and hence women gained out of it. The author has analysed different types of population, different famines and different societies, including patriarchal ones and noticed that death rate among women in the age group of 20 to 45 coinciding with the reproductive span was lower.[82] However, one can say that perhaps the factor of the male bias in collecting death data has not been taken into account. Second, the nature of patriarchal society also matters a lot. For example, the social structures of USA and England are patriarchal but acute female bias in data collection is relatively absent. On the other hand, in a traditional society like India, which is a growing economy, the number of malnourished females was disproportionately high. Further, in case of India, the female deaths get underestimated and resistance to diseases is low. On top of it, the number of children per woman ratio is very high. So the gains reaped by the women in Western countries are absent in India.

Thus one notices that Western scholars were not uniform in their findings. Similarly, O'Grada, commenting on the views of Indian anthropologists, said that the latter had 'feminized the famines'. But on the contrary, ample evidence suggests a mixed picture, depending on the specific situation and in many instance men succumbed more than women. O'Grada analysed the historical evidence to conclude that more males than females died in the past famines. The explanation was that the women could store proportionately more fats in their body compared to men. Hence, according to him, the number of woman survivors are more. He was referring to the Potato Famine of Ireland, 1849, Leningrad blockade, and China's man-made famine in 1957-61.[83] He, however, rejected the views that biological factors helped women more.

In contrast, Vaughan commenting on African famines, felt that the sex differential mortality depended on several factors such as intra-family distribution of food, male migration, control over resources, particularly land, trade, and finally, government relief. She discussed the patterns of sex differential mortality in the famine of 1948-9 in Malawi, Africa. It was noticed that in situations where women had male support, they survived better. But if the men migrated and did not support the women, it was opposite.

Of course, if they received timely government relief then their death rates plummeted. Further, if they inherited land as they did in Malawi, they had a better bargaining power, but if the products were traded, then men had an upper hand. Hence it all depended on the specific conditions.[84]

On the question of sex differential mortality, we can say that as systematic data on this was not collected in India during the nineteenth- and early twentieth-century famines, we mainly rely on qualitative data. It showed that female mortality to be more in certain cases and male mortality more in others. But more old women remained in old age homes since they were all alone. Similarly, more women took to prostitution since it had an easy access.

As mentioned earlier, the acute famines always resulted in severe social disorder. Moreover, famines never come alone, but are often accompanied by epidemics. Of course, epidemics may have their own independent course as well. But in India it is noticed that famines and epidemics occurred simultaneously in the past and even now it is so in many cases. But no systematic data was collected during famines because the entire registration system of deaths and births used to collapse. The *chowkidars* who were in charge of collecting the data often themselves fled from the scene. If they did collect data, they would invariably ignore the female deaths completely. This was particularly the case in India. One reason behind this may be that the number of female deaths was often shown to be lower than that of males. But most Western scholars stuck to the view that women mortality was proportionately less compared to men. Verginia Zarulli et al. conducted a study recently by taking the population totals of high mortality area.[85] They have again resurrected the old argument of the Census commissioners of 1901. Even though the authors acknowledged that sociological factors did influence the mortality pattern, they concluded that the female life expectancy falls lower than that of males during severe famine periods because of the biological advantage of women over men. They have referred to the Bengal Famine Commission Report but have not taken note of Amartya

Sen's seminal work. Apart from citing just one study of India, they have taken up the experiences of the Western countries, which have a different kind of social setting.

Overview

In this chapter we have used evidence from various studies to examine the hypothesis that the increase in female death rate was lower than male death rate in general and in the age groups 30-60 in particular. And that this led to an increase in the sex ratio in the post-famine years, has been examined in the context of some of the major famines in the Indian subcontinent between 1876 and 1974. We can now argue that this hypothesis holds good for certain famines but does not hold good for other famines. Thus a general theory regarding the sex-selective impact of famine mortality cannot be constructed. First, the facts themselves are debatable. The quality of registration statistics of females and the records of temporary out-migration all over India were not good. More specifically, there was a strong possibility of under-enumeration of female deaths in famine years, partly because the *chawkidar* and also the head of the family ignored female deaths in the normal course. We saw this clearly in the United Provinces. Besides, the practice of taking just one year as a normal year is also debatable in the regime of fluctuating deaths and births. The endemic diseases of the region were becoming epidemics in the famine years.

Epidemics followed famines, and acted on the malnourished population, so the impact of the famines should include both the starvation and epidemic phases. If this is done, the apparent lower excess female deaths will not stand scrutiny and then it would be clear that more females deaths had indeed taken place in such cases.

The explanations of sex-selective mortality in the form of biological and sociological factors have also been critically examined. It is yet to be proved medically that women have a lower metabolic rate and hence require less food. Modern research has pointed out that there cannot be a fixed concept of 'requirement'. Similarly, it is yet to be proved that females are biologically better able to resist infection. It has also been shown that the so-called favourable sociological factors were not so favourable to women.

Notes

1. In India SR has been defined as females per thousand males, following the convention of the Census. In the West the SR is defined as males per thousand females.
2. Michelle B. McAlpine, *Subject to Famine: Food Crisis and Economic Change in Western India 1860-1920,* Princeton, Princeton University Press, 1983.
3. Ashok Mitra, *India's Population: Aspects of Quality and Control,* vol. I. New Delhi: Abhinav Publications, 1978. p. 6 Also Barbara Miller has pointed out that the juvenile sex ratio (males per 100 females) were highest in the districts of North-Western Provinces in 1872, where female infanticide was practised. Barbara Miller, *The Endangered Sex: The Neglect of Children in Rural North India,* pp. 61-2.
4. *Census of India, 1891*, vol.19, pt. I, pp. 215-17.
   Ibid., vol. 3, pt. I. p. 177.
   Ibid., vol. 11, pt. I, p. 85
   Ibid., vol. 7, pt. I, p. 73.
5. Ibid., 1921, Vol. 1, pt. 1, p. 145.
   Asok Mitra also pointed out that the female death rate which was lower than that of males till 1901, officially overtook the male death rate after that.
   Mitra, *India's Population*, pp. 378-80.
6. Pravin Visaria, 'The Sex Ratio of Population of India', *Census of India* Census monograph no. 10, New Delhi: Office of the Registrar General, 1961, pp. 356-7.
7. J.B Wyan and J.E. Gordon, *The Khanna Study: Population Problems in Rural Punjab,* Cambridge, Harvard University Press, 1971.
8. M.K. Jain, 'Growing Imbalance in the Sex Composition of India', *Demography India*, vol. 4(2), no. 2, December 1975, pp. 310-11.
9. L.T. Ruzicka, 'Mortality in India: Past Trends and Future Prospects', in Tim Dyson and Nigel Crook (ed.) *India's Demography: Essays on the Contemporary Population*, New Delhi, South Asia Publishers, 1984, p. 14.

10. N. Krishnaji, 'Poverty and Sex Ratio: Some Data and Some Speculations', *Economic and Political Weekly*, 22 (23), 6 June 1987, p. 893.
11. Ibid., p. 895.
12. Krishnaji, 'Poverty and Sex Ratio', p. 896.
13. Ibid.
14. *Census of India 1901*, vol. I, pt. 1, pp. 109-10.
15. Ibid., pp. 119-21.
16. In Punjab the SR had increased from 851 to 854 from 1891 to 1901. In Madras Presidency SR rose from 1,023 to 1,029 between 2 years. *Census of India 1901*, vol. XV, pt. 1. 64.
17. The Census Commissioner of 1911 (Gait), however noted that the famine of 1896-7 in the Madras Presidency was not very severe and the excess mortality was not very high. *Source:* Extracts from the *Report on the Famine in the Madras Presidency During 1896-97*, pp. 165 and 166 quoted in *Census of India, 1911*, vol. 1, pt. 1, p. 221.
18. *Census of India 1911*, vol. 15, pt. 1, pp. 195-6.
19. Ibid., pp. 196-7.
20. Ibid., p. 197.
21. Influenza had killed 8½, million people in two years according to Marten and he felt that it was an underestimate. It was the highest killer of the decade. *Census of India, 1921*, vol.1, pt. 1, p. 13.

    Also see, I.D. Mills, 'The 1918-19 Influenza Pandemic: The Indian Experience', *The Indian Economic and Social History Review*, 23(1), 1 March 1986, p. 34.
22. *Census of India, 1901*, vol. 1, pt. 1, p. 118.
    Also *Census of India 1911*, vol. 1, pt. 1, p. 212, Appendix, pp. 220-2. Incidentally Risley and Gait (1901) pointed out that 'When scarcity begins to be felt, conception takes place less freely, and this means fewer deaths from diseases of pregnancy and parturition'. *Census of India 1901*, vol.1, pt. 1, p. 118.

    But according to them the most important factor was the biological resistance to diseases. Ibid.

    In 1911, it seemed that Gait emphasized more on decline in connection. He pointed out that there was 'a great diminution of their fecundity with the result that there are fewer deaths than usual from childbirth.' He gave less emphasis to resistance factor. *Source: Census of India 1911*, vol. 1, pt. 1, p. 212.
23. WHO, 'Energy and protein requirement'. Report of a joint FAO/WHO ad hoc expert Committee. Technical Report Series no. 522

(Geneva, 1973), Annex 1, quoted in R.H. Cassen, *India's Population,* pp. 96-7. *Source:* Reginald Passmore has observed that women, children and persons of small built need lower intake of food than others to survive. But if they are subjected to hard labour, the deterioration of health will be more rapid and 'equilibrium' cannot be established. Reginald Passmore, 'Famine', *Encyclopedia Britannica,* vol. 9, 1969, p. 59.

24. 'Extract from the Report on the Famine in the Madras Presidency during 1896-97', pp. 165-6 quoted in *Census of India 1911*, vol. 1, pt. 1, p. 222.
25. Emmanuel E.L. Roy Ladurie, for example has documented evidence from the First World War and the Second World War and from the experience of animal population as well as evidence from the doctors to show that there occurred symptoms of 'Amenorrhea' caused by food crisis. This led to a fall in the conception rate. E.L. Roy Ladurie, 'Amenorrhea Due to Famine (17th to 20th centuries)', *Annales: Economics, Societies, Civilization*, and vol. 24, no. 6, and Nov.-Dec. 1969, pp. 1589-1601.
 'Amenorrhea' has been defined as temporary menopause resulting from severe food crisis.
26. Quoted in Susan Cotts, Watkins, Jane Menken, 'Famines in Historical Perspective', *Population and Development Review* 11(4), 1985, p. 656.
27. Ibid.
28. Another study conducted in Bangladesh has revealed that 75 per cent of women in the reproductive age groups were either pregnant or lactating at any point of time.
 Quoted in Paul Greenough, *The Prosperity and Misery of Modern Bengal: The Famine of 1943-44*, New York: Oxford University Press, 1982, p. 243, fn. 10.
29. *Census of India 1911*, vol. 1, pt. 1, p. 120.
30. Calculated from Klein, 'When The Rains Failed', Table 2, p. 190.
31. It is interesting to compare at this point the control of assets by the African women and their suffering during the famine. Vaughan, for example, has pointed out that in Southern Malawi women suffered less from the famine of 1949, because they had access to food and had independent sources of income. But the women of a particular area of Zimbabwe were evicted from their husbands' villages in the famine of 1890. Megan Vaughan, *The Story of an African Famine: Gender and Famine in Twentieth Century,* Cambridge, Cambridge

University Press, 1987, p. 147. At the same time it should be pointed out the women of India face different set of problems namely, they don't inherit any property.

32. Paul R. Greenough, *Prosperity and Misery in Modern Bengal: The Famine of 1943-1944*, New York, Oxford University Press, 1982, pp. 217 and pp. 235.

    Ian Stone points out in the case of United Provinces that women offered their ornaments for the irrigation facilities of *rabi* crops in the famine of 1907-8. Ian Stone, *Canal Irrigation in British India*. Cambridge: Cambridge University Press, 1984, p. 257.
33. *Census of India 1901*, vol. II, pt. 1, p. 116. Also see, *Census of India 1901*, vol. 16, part 1, p. 111.
34. P. M. Visaria, 'The Sex Ratio of the Population', p. 61.
35. Michelle B. McAlpine, op. cit., pp. 57-8.
36. Ibid., p. 64.
37. Michelle McAlpine, op. cit., p. 67.
38. Roland Lardinois, 'Famine, Epidemics and Mortality in South India: A Reappraisal of the Demographic Crises of 1876 = 78', *Economic and Political Weekly*, 20(11), 16 March 1985, noted that more males had migrated (63 per cent) than females (23 per cent) during the crisis period, ibid., p. 458.

    Lardinois has also pointed out that the birth rate fell during the famine of 1876-8 due to biological causes such as 'amenorrhea' and sociological reason namely, separation of the couples due to outmigration and stay at the relief camps. Hence the excess female deaths was lower than that of males, ibid., p. 462.
39. In fact, the Census Superintendent of Bombay Presidency of 1901 had analysed the proportion of widows to widowers in some districts which were active in migration. For example, the Census Superintendent found that the proportion of widows to widowers per thousand is the following. Ratnagiri 5,862, Satara 4,005, Kanara 3,924, Kolaba 3,794. Then he pointed out that Ratnagiri, Satara and Kolaba were well-known centres of emigrants to Bombay city. Thus the high proportion of widows to widowers suggested that the widowhood was perhaps the result of plague epidemics. Then he pointed out that 'the famine districts do not disclose nearly so high a ratio of widows to widowers possibly because the famine had in these cases equal incidence on both sexes. . .' *Census of India 1901*, vol. 9, pt. I, p. 92.
40. Morris D. Morris, *The Emergence of an Industrial Labour Force in*

India: A Study of the Bombay Cotton Mills 1854-1947, California, University of California, 1965, pp. 55-6. Also see, I.J. Catanach, 'Plague and the Indian Village, 1896-1914', in Peter Robb (ed.), *Rural India, Land, Power and Society under British Rule*, London, Curzon Press, 1983, p. 220.

41. The Census Superintendent of Bombay 1921 remarked that the increase in SR since 1872 till 1901 was due to the impact of famines. After 1901, the extent of crop failures was either 'equal' to or even 'greater' than those of the 'great famines of the past'. 'But, as is well known, deaths due directly to famine have ceased to occur'. *Census of India, 1921*, vol. 9, pt. I, p. 109. But the Census Superintendent has not elaborated on this. Perhaps he had in mind that famine was responsible indirectly for accelerated deaths through plague, malaria and influenza.
42. William Digby had reproduced the loss of population through migration in some of the most severely famine affected *talukas*. For example, the migration rate was calculated as Madh 134.10, Badami 106.76, Bagalkot 117.09, Khatau 93.46, William Digby, *Famine Campaign in Southern India: Madras and Bombay Presidencies and Province of Mysore,* vol. II, London, Longmans, Green and Co., 1878, p. 387. Also see, Ira Klein, 'When the Rains Failed', especially fn. 141 of p. 210.
43. *Census of India 1891*, vol. 8, pt. 1, p. 67. Also see, *Census of India 1901*, vol. XIA, pt. 6, p. 88.

    In percentage terms; 8 percent of total population of Satara and 3 per cent of total population of Surat were found in Bombay city in the year 1901. Also see, *Census of India 1901*, vol. XI, pt. 1, p. 44.
44. Morris, *The Emergence of Labour Force*, p. 63.
45. In fact, the mills were closed because of lack of market demand and wages were cut and unemployment also rose according to the author. The author has speculated regarding the non-withdrawal of the laboures from the city of Bombay, because of famine conditions in various parts of the hinterland.

    Ibid., p. 58, and fn. 60.
46. Ibid., 10.65.
47. *Famine Inquiry commission Report on Bengal,* Delhi, Manager Publications, 1945, p. 109.
48. Ibid.
49. Ibid., pp. 110-11.
50. *FCRB 1943*, p. 111.

51. Ibid., p. 110.
52. Ibid., p. 112.
53. Ibid.
54. Tarak Chandra Das, *Bengal Famine 1943: As Revealed in a Survey of the Destitute in Calcutta,* Calcutta, University of Calcutta Press, 1949, p. 91.
55. *FCRB 1943,* p. 111.
56. *Census of India 1951,* 'Vital Statistics of West Bengal', vol. 6, pt. IB, p. 5.
57. Ibid.
58. *Census of India 1951,* vol. 6, Part IB, p. 6.
59. Ibid., p. 5.
60. Amrtya K. Sen., *Poverty and Famine: An Essay on Entitlement and Deprivation*, Oxford, Oxford University Press, 1982, p. 199.
    Sen has, however, not considered the fact that females' deaths were particularly underestimated in the famine year of 1943.
61. Sen, op. cit., pp. 211-13.
62. Ibid., p. 203.
63. Paul R. Greenough, *Prosperity and Misery in Modern Bengal: The Famine of 1943-44,* New Delhi, Oxford University Press, 1983, p. 306.
64. Incidentally the Famine commission had reported that Mahalanobis presented a sample survey of 2,622 families (13,652 individuals) living in villages of 7 sub-divisions *FCRB 1943*, p. 111. Greenough perhaps, has used a different series which was more comprehensive. But Greenough has not mentioned the other series, which incidentally showed that fdr was significantly higher than mdr at least in one sub-division. We have already referred to this while discussing the views of the Famine Commissioner of 1943.
65. Greenough, *Prosperity and Misery*, pp. 305-6.
66. Ibid., p. 311.
67. Ibid., p. 313.
68. Ibid.
69. Sen, *Poverty and Famines*, p. 131.
70. Mohiuddin Alamgir, *Famine in South Asia: Political Economy O Mass Starvation in Bangladesh,* Cambridge, Mass, Oalgeschlager, Gunn and Hain, 1980, pp. 102-4.
71. Ibid., pp. 140-1.
72. Ibid., pp. 144-5.
73. Alamgir, *Famine in South Asia,* pp. 144-5.

74. Matlab thana is in Comilla district of Bangladesh. There has been a demographic surveillance system since 1963 conducted by International Centre for Diarrheal Diseases Research. It consists of 228 villages with a population 263,000 in 1974. The population of the study area is 88 per cent Muslim and 12 per cent Hindu. Stan D'Souza and L.C. Chen, 'Sex Differentials in Mortality in Rural Bangladesh', *Population and Development Review*, 16(2), June 1980, p. 258.
75. Ray Langsten, 'Determinates of Higher female Mortality', p. 23. Also see Watkins and Menken , 'Famine in Historical Perspective', p. 656. It is interesting to note that even though D'Souza and Chen have mentioned that the food crisis of 1974 had duration of two years: 1974-5, both the authors Ray Langsten and Watkins and Menken have taken the year 1975 as the famine year.
76. Neo-natal babies are in the age group up to one month; post-neonatal babies are up to 1-12 months. Tan D'Souza and L.C. Chen, 'Sex Differentials in Mortality', pp. 259-60.
77. D'Souza and Chen, 'Sex Differentials in Mortality', p. 260.
78. Ibid., p. 262.
79. Ibid., p. 268.
80. Tim Dyson and Carmac O. Grada (eds.), *Famine Demography: Perspective from Past and Present,* New York, Oxford University Press, 1999, p. 1.
81. Ibid., p. 4.
82. Ibid., p. 7.
83. Ograda, op. cit. (Chapter 3), pp. 98-102.
84. Megan Vaughan, *The Story of an African Famine: Gender and Famine in Twentieth Century, Malawi,* Cambridge, Cambridge University Press, 1987, pp. 119-47.

85 Verginia Zarulli, A. Julia, Barthold Jones, Anna Oksuzyan, Rune Lindahl Jacobson, Kaare Christensen and Jarnes W. Vaupel, 'Women Live Longer than Men even during Extreme Famines and Epidemics', *Physical Sciences and Social Sciences*, 115(4), 23 January 2018, pp. 832-40.

CHAPTER 7

Gender and Class Incidence of Infectious Diseases

Introduction

Since we take famine not as an event but as a process which includes both the starvation phase as well as that of epidemics, it is important to see who suffered and why in the context of the famines. In this chapter we will take up the impact of infectious diseases, which very often accompanied famines, on people in terms of gender, caste and class.

In studying the impact of epidemics and infectious diseases on vulnerable groups in a society, gender is very often ignored. However, it is a well-known fact that the poorer sections of society are the first ones to fall victims, though later on the infectious diseases catch up with the other sections as well. We have seen in the earlier chapters that endemic diseases like dysentery, cholera, malaria, smallpox, plague and influenza became epidemics in the wake of famines and scarcities. In this chapter we first take up the impact of these diseases, in both epidemic and endemic phases, on both the sexes, to test the hypothesis that females in general, and females after the reproductive age in particular, are more resistant to infection than men.[1] We shall then discuss the age and class composition of the victims of different epidemics. Before that let us have a broad view of the main endemic diseases of Orissa Division.

Diseases and Deaths in Orissa Division, 1866-1921

It is a well-known fact that endemic diseases like cholera, dysentery, malaria and plague used to become epidemics during Indian famines in the nineteenth century. These epidemics took a heavy toll in the famine years because of many reasons, especially inadequate nutrition and the breakdown of public health system. This was accentuated also because of increased mobility of people in search of food. But the epidemics also had autonomous cycles and so used to erupt even in non-famine years.[2] Further, the incidence of the diseases led to heavy mortality also, because the local people didn't believe in the efficacy of Western medicine.[3] They preferred traditional medicine, which had been a 'way of life and learned component of human behavior such as indigenous knowledge, language, religion, custom and convention'.[4] The entire focus in traditional medicine is on the preventive side. In contrast, Western medicine believes more on curative method. Hence it was difficult for Indians to accept the Western system of treatment. India has a long tradition of using various traditional methods to treat diseases including Ayurveda and Unani as well as a slightly modified Homeopathy suitable to Indian conditions. Regarding the introduction of Western medicine by the colonial rulers, there are many theories. One group of experts argued that it was for the benefit of the British subjects living in India since the damp weather did not suit them. Another group observed that the welfare state wanted to take care of their Indian subjects. In fact, evidence does not support the view that colonial rulers were interested per se in putting in place welfare policies for Indian people. Clearly, they did not want their own people serving in India to die due to the contagious diseases prevalent in India. Hence they introduced Western system of medicine. But in the process these measures had long-term consequences including seriously affecting people's mobility as well as livelihood.[5]

Next we take up the indigenous diseases of Orissa Division between 1866 and 1921.

First, it should be noted that the main diseases of Orissa Division were cholera, dysentery, malaria and smallpox. Plague never visited the Division. The incidence of smallpox also declined after 1900. Even influenza that played havoc in Europe in 1918-19 was not very virulent in Orissa. The main diseases were cholera and dysentery and malaria (Ironically, even now these diseases are still prevalent in Orissa except perhaps cholera in acute form). These diseases killed a large number of people both during famine and non-famine years, though the incidence used to rise in the famine years. It was also observed that cholera used to erupt in Orissa even in the non-famine years supposedly because of the vast stream of pilgrims going to Puri. People used to congregate in large numbers on the occasion of the chariot festival that always falls during the rainy season. The available food items sold in the markets were unhygenic. The water too was not purified. Hence the pilgrims used to get cholera that spread *en route*.

As for the data on diseases, since it was the *chowkidar* who had to do the diagnosis of the causes of death, the experts are hesitant to use this data.[6] However, it is a well-known fact that the data on cholera and smallpox were more reliable than the data on fever.

Sex Composition of the Victims of Different Diseases

Whether women had some biological advantage to overcome serious epidemics has been a point of debate. We shall enter this debate by examining evidence from different studies done by various medical doctors.

Study of the impact of every disease involves two components – medical and sociological. This chapter and the next deal with these components.

Medical Component

William Burrows has pointed out that available reports showed differences of impact of certain diseases on men and women. For example, pneumonia and epidemic meningitis affected men more than women. But diseases like scarlet fever and typhoid fever occur more frequently among women than men. Tuberculosis and influenza in 1918-19 were more fatal to young women. The thesis has been advanced in medical literature that these differences in incidence could be sex-linked. More specifically, since the differences in incidence had been more pronounced during as well as after puberty, it could be due to 'maturation immunity'. However, Burrows concluded that there was no 'sound evidence' that incidence of diseases can be associated to sex-linked biological attributes. He used two examples based on animal studies. In the first example it was found that female rabbits are more susceptible to 'skin permeability' than male rabbits. In the second example it was noticed that female chicks are significantly more susceptible to malarial parasites than male chicks. It cannot be deduced however, that female chicks are more susceptible to malaria because they lack the male hormone. Finally, Burrows concluded that 'Any explanation of the observed sex differences must, of course, take into consideration other factors such as occupation, risk of exposure and the like.'[7]

Rodney J. Anderson and Dean A. Sobieski have also stated that there are examples of 'sex-related innate immunity to infectious diseases but the differences are small'. However, the most important point is that nobody yet knows the mechanism through which the immunity works. The authors speculated that 'probably' the death rate from infectious diseases among males is higher than that of females, based on evidence from rates of death of mice.[8] However, it can be argued that the experiments done on animals may not be fully true of human beings.

Samuel H. Preston has analysed data on the causes of death for all the major countries (165 groups of population figures in 43 nations from 1861 to 1964) of the world for which reliable data are available.[9] According to Preston, the female death rate due to infectious diseases is 'consistently' higher than that of males between 1 and 30 years, in a population with 'lowest life expectancy'. But 'the magnitude of the differential tends to be minor except for respiratory tuberculosis'.[10] After the age of 40, the female death rate due to infectious diseases becomes lower than that of males in high mortality populations. Preston has given two explanations – sociological and biological. He observes that the 'cross over' of the death curves at 40 could be due to the fact that social status of females rises after the age of 40 and hence their 'health environment improves'.[11] An alternative explanation is that some changes take place in 'the process of maturation and senescence'.[12] This latter explanation seems more appropriate to Preston's proposition. It is so because of the additional evidence, which has been cited, namely, women in the age group of 60 and above, are perceived with less value in society. Yet their death rates are lower than that of men in the same age group.[13] Preston however, has not included India, where discrimination against women is very acute in terms of dietary and health-care matters.

Ingrid Waldron, who tried to explain the pattern of sex differential mortality for the American population after 1900, thinks that females are more resistant to infections than men because of biological reasons. First of all, the 'x' chromosome helps to produce immunoglobulin 'm' at a higher level compared to the 'y' chromosome. Second, other elements of female hormones stimulate 'phagocytosis' to fight infections. But she also admits that the effects of sex hormones on antibody response or resistance to infection are variable, 'depending on experimental conditions'.

However, it is to be noted that the characteristics of American population is quite different from that of India. So the findings of Waldron may not be quite appropriate in this case. Still, many analysts cite this evidence to show that males were more vulnerable to infectious diseases compared to females. This brief review of evidence from medical studies on the impact of biological factors on men and women, questions the belief in some quarters that women in general are biologically more resistant to infection. However, there is some evidence to suggest that after their reproductive age, women develop some immunity to certain types of infectious diseases.

Evidence from the Case Studies of Different Epidemics

Great epidemics such as plague, typhus, smallpox, cholera and malaria have occurred from time to time all over the world. But the impact of these epidemics on different sexes has not been uniform. In some places and at some times these epidemics have killed more males and at other times or places more females.

Let us now discuss the impact of epidemics of plague, cholera, malaria and influenza and also diarrheal diseases on different sexes because some of them occurred during or on the aftermath of the famines. These diseases, except plague, were typical of nineteenth century and early twentieth century India/Odisha.

PLAGUE[14]

Even though Odisha did not experience plague, still we would like to discuss it because it was an infectious disease and accompanied famine in many cases, though it may not be directly related to food crisis. We get some important insights from looking at this experience elsewhere. In the late nineteenth century and the early part of the twentieth century, one finds that plague killed more women proportionately than men in the reproductive age groups 15-45, both in the United Provinces and in Punjab.[15] In 1904 plague became an epidemic in the Punjab. The ratio of male death rate from plague to female death rate was 1:1.3 in the epidemic phase of plague in 1904.

C.A. Gill, who did a lot of research on plague, malaria and influenza, observed that the female death rate was higher than that of males in cases of plague deaths throughout India in the early part of the nineteenth century. According to Gill, the disparity between male and female deaths was 'variable' but always 'appreciable'. The ratio of male to female death rates due to plague in the Punjab and the United Provinces in 1904 were 1:1.3 but for 1907-16 those were 1:1.2. Thus it seemed that the incidence of plague was declining.

In the Punjab, it was observed that the female death rate was 'invariably relatively high' in the years of major epidemics. For example, the total deaths due to plague mortality was 2,51,261 in 1924. The female death rate was 3.23 per thousand in excess of the males. But in 1925, the total plague mortality was 37,630 and the excess of the female deaths over the male death rate was only 0.47 per thousand.[16]

Gill has done an analysis of age- and sex-specific incidence of plague mortality in the Punjab, which indicated that plague was more fatal to the women of child bearing age of 15-45,[17] but he did not provide any explanation for this phenomenon.

The reasons according to the Census Commissioner of India, 1911 were the 'social habits' of women. Interestingly one of these habits is similar to those given by Hollingsworth and Hollingworth for seventeenth-century England, namely, that women stayed at home. Yet Indian women died in greater numbers than men due to plague, unlike in England. One difference was that Indian women walked barefoot, tended to the sick, surrounded the dead relatives for mourning, and thus became more susceptible to plague.[18] This experience showed that some social customs in India made women more vulnerable to certain infectious diseases.

CHOLERA

The sex incidence of cholera victims both abroad and in India also depended on the exposure to the germ. John Snow, a London doctor, worked extensively to find out the mode of communication of cholera based on the experience of the first local cholera outbreak and epidemic in London which occurred in 1830s to 1850s. He collected data on the sex composition of cholera victims from Dr. Far who worked at the Registrar-General's office during this period. Overall, Dr. Far observed that in the beginning of the epidemic, i.e. in the months of October, November and December, 1848, the deaths due to cholera occurred in the proportion of 100 males to 80 females, the absolute number being 612 males and 493 females. But when the mortality from cholera attained a very high rate, the number of female deaths exceeded male deaths.[19]

Since Snow was the first to analyse the causes of cholera deaths, it is worthwhile to discuss it briefly. For example, Snow pointed out that men were more mobile and ate and drank more frequently outside their home than women and so men were more exposed to the infection than women at the start of the epidemic. But when the cholera was more diffused it spread to homes as well. Since women stayed at home and tended to the sick, they had become more exposed to cholera germs.[20]

The reason for this higher female death rate, Snow surmised, was that women in England usually drank less beer than men and hence drank soiled water more frequently than men.[21] This explanation may seem unconvincing to some, but cannot be dismissed altogether.

John Macpherson, the Inspector General of Hospitals in the Bengal Army, who examined the different types of cholera in the West and in Asia, held the view that cholera attacked both the sexes equally. He noted that such 'diseases have, on the whole, been supposed to attack adults most; but neither age nor sex, nor race has afforded any real immunity.'[22] This important observation was based on his general understanding rather than any statistical, social or biological evidence in support.

MALARIA

Malaria is still a leading cause of death in Asia and Africa. But it is difficult to estimate the exact number of deaths even today because many people do not go to the hospitals for treatment. It is even more true of the past. With regard to the sex incidence of malaria, the World Health Organization observed in 2005 that it is important to have a gender approach to prevent as well as to combat the outbreak of malaria. In a highly patriarchal society, women are neither in the decision-making process nor play a role in resource allocation to a significant degree. So in order to have complete prevention of diseases like malaria it is important to have the gender dimension built into the policy and practice at every stage. WHO also observed that pregnant women had lower immunity and were particularly vulnerable.[23] The sex incidence of malaria also depended on the exposure to mosquitoes and social habits. This is pointed out very well by Paul Russell who has observed that gender by itself does not determine vulnerability, but habits and practices may. He showed how different habits or types of clothing worn by men and women may result in different levels of incidence. To quote him: 'This is true for instance, in communities where men fish at night on a malarious marshy lake, while their wives remain in a non-malarial region.... In hot countries girls are apt to be better with clothing than are their brothers at night.'[24] This may explain less parasites in the spleen of the girls in Madras.

The degree of exposure is important as is seen in the case of United Provinces earlier. More women than men in the United Provinces were infected with the malaria parasite and consequently their death rate was higher than that of men in 1908 because they were more exposed to malaria,[25] which has been corroborated further by Hehir. He notes that with equal exposure, men and women will be infected equally. He cited an example of a large canal work constructed on the Ravi and Beas rivers in Punjab where 1,700 men and 2,800 women were employed. Out of them 32.5 per cent of the women (910) and 32.41 per cent of the men (551) had malaria were detected with parasites in their blood. He also quoted the example of Manipur, a highly malaria-prone region, where men and women were equally affected by the infection.[26]

INFLUENZA (1918-19)

Like malaria, influenza continues to be a very serious disease in the world even today. As in the case of malaria, treatment for influenza too requires a gender perspective. Like malaria it also kills more pregnant women because of their lower immunity.[27] In this case too, the virulence of the attack rate of the disease depends on social habits, perhaps more, than biological factors, though the latter are extremely important as well.

THE GENDER DIMENSION IN THE OFFICIAL REPORTS

The Census Commissioner of India in 1921 J. Marten, had observed that influenza was particularly fatal to women in the reproductive age group of 20-40, and more so in young married women. The reasons were the familiar one such as tending to the sick, walking barefoot, mourning around dead bodies and thus getting exposed to the virus of flu.[28] The sex incidence of influenza varied from province to province even though the Census Commissioner, 1921, had observed that overall it had hit women of the reproductive age group more.

Interestingly, in 1921, the Census Superintendent of United Provinces E.H.H. Edye disagreed with the views of his senior official, the Census Commissioner. Edye did not even agree with the view of the Sanitary Commissioner of United Provinces in 1918, that the death rates of both men and women, from influenza were equal. He argued that the recorded death ratios given by the Sanitary Commissioner were not reliable. The recorded death ratios (female per thousand male deaths) were 921 for the entire period of 1918, and 960 for the influenza period of early winter (2 months). Edye argued that the vital statistics were probably under-reported especially during the influenza epidemics because the *chowkidars* might not have been able to keep track of deaths occurring in tens and twenties, or he might have gone elsewhere to report other events. Besides, the *chowkidar* might himself be sick. After discussing the viewpoint of the Sanitary Commissioner of 1918, Edye concluded that 'As a matter of a priori reasoning the influenza should have hit men much harder than women.'[29] The reasons according to Edye were: men were more exposed to the flu virus than women and because the flu came at the harvest time and men had to attend to the harvest in spite of being ill.[30] Edye also noted that if the observation made by the Sanitary Commissioner of 1918 regarding the severity of influenza in the western part of the province were true, then the number of women would have declined relatively to men in the West and the opposite would have been true in the East in 1921. But in fact in 1921 women's population increased more than that of men in the western part of United Provinces and it was the opposite in the east.

The views of Edye need to be seriously qualified. First, we agree with Edye that the vital statistics were not reliable, but Edye did not throw any light on the direction of unreliability. Presumably he had in mind that male recorded deaths were under-reported to a greater degree than female deaths since according to him there were reasons for which men would have died in greater numbers. But from the past history of the same province, Blunt, the Census Superintendent of 1911, had concluded that female deaths were under-recorded to a greater degree than male deaths, especially in times of famines and epidemics. If this is correct, it follows that if the recorded death ratio showed that more females died in the epidemic period compared to the non-epidemic period, then the actual female death rate due to influenza would have been even higher than the male death rate. Second, it is true that a section of men would have been more exposed to the flu virus because they were compelled to attend to the harvest even if they were ill. But at the same time another section of women were also more exposed than men to flu virus because of social factors such as nursing the sick. Lastly, with regard to increase in relative number of women to men in the severely affected areas, Edye did not eliminate the role of sex-selective out-migration which could also have led to the same result.

In contrast to Edye, Tallents, the Census Superintendent of Bihar and Orissa, 1921, argued that the female death rate due to influenza was actually higher than that of males in 1918 but it was not reflected in the vital statistics because of their unreliability. He observed that the recorded death rate of females due to fever was lower than that of males in 1918, the difference being 3.6 per thousand. But Tallents observed that 'the number of female deaths from all causes in proportion to the number of male deaths was markedly higher than in any other year of the decade'.[31] This ratio was also higher in 1918 than in other provinces according to him. From this Tallents inferred that since the *chowkidar* was unable to diagnose different diseases properly he would have attributed deaths due to influenza to some other cause. Tallents also noted that the *chowkidar* had missed out many female deaths occurring in 1918. In support of this he cited two pieces of evidence, namely, (a) the actual data collected in other provinces showed that female death rate due to influenza was higher than that of males, and (b) the medical doctors who were associated with the treatment of influenza certified that female death rate was higher than that of males due to influenza.[32]

Even though we broadly agree with Tallents, we have one reservation. It is true that the *chowkidar* mixed up the causes of deaths, but they generally attributed an unknown cause to fever. In this case it is possible that influenza showed different symptoms from malaria and often led to pneumonia and was attributed to other causes. But one cannot be certain about this explanation.

The Census Superintendents of Punjab and Bombay, on the other hand, agreed with the Census Commissioner of 1921 that the female death rate was higher than that of males in 1918 due to influenza[33] but neither discussed the factors responsible for higher female mortality.

The Census Superintendent of the Central Provinces noted, 'Famine and influenza are held to be more unfavourable to females than to males, and in 1918, the figure which is the highest during the last 30 years.' He also noticed that the loss of women was particularly heavy in the child-bearing age group.[34] Thus most of the Census Superintendents agreed with Marten, the Census Commissioner of 1921, that influenza killed more women than men.

Dr. I.D. Mills has also noted that in the influenza epidemic of 1918-19 in India, the female death rate was 12 per cent higher than the male death rate in the age group 20-40. He also observed that the disease was particularly virulent to pregnant women, which was also evidenced by the increase of premature birth-linked deaths among mothers, and also by the increased number of still-births in September and October 1919, the peak months of influenza mortality in Bombay city.[35] The explanation he has given tallies with that given by Marten in 1921, i.e. women ran the additional risk of tending the sick. Besides, he also argued that women were biologically 'more susceptible to the disease', though he was unable to substantiate this due to lack of data on general morbidity.[36]

DIARRHEAL DISEASES

Just like malaria and influenza, diarrhea continues to pose serious challenges even today. Diarrhea is the second leading cause of death in the world. The diseases attacks about 5,25,000 children every year.[37] One should remember that these diseases are the end product of many other diseases, so it is difficult to quantify their incidence. But two studies, one conducted in India and another in Bangladesh show that the sex-incidence depended very much on exposure to the germ.

In a seminal study, Mitra has analysed the sex composition of diarrheal diseases for the entire population of India. The data have been taken from selected primary healthcare centres for the years 1966, 1967 and 1971. He has observed that girls died at a higher rate in the age group 1-4 but the boys' death rate was higher in the age group 5-14. Females in the age group 55 and above had a higher death rate than that of men due to diarrhea.[38]

This has to be reconciled with another study in which Chen et al. have observed that 'The lack of strong sex differential in infection rates is consistent with the interpretation that disease exposure is similar between sexes.'[39] They have analyzed the number of episodes (morbidity) of various infectious diseases like diarrhea among male and female children in the age group of 0-4 separately, in Matlab Thana of Bangladesh, for July 1978 to June 1979. The authors have noted that there were no strong differences between the two rates because though the attack rate of female children has been consistently lower than that of male children, the difference is not statistically significant.

Tables on reported death rates due to important diseases are available from the 1901 Census onwards and the data for the two decades 1901-10 and 1911-20 have been collated in Table 7.1 for fever, cholera and plague in India. The authorities calculated the death rates by taking the population of 1901 and that of 1911 into account respectively. It is striking that the recorded average annual death rates of males and females due to different diseases *do not show any consistent pattern* either across the provinces or across the decades. In some provinces the female death rate due to fever was higher than that of males or equal to even in the decade 1901-10, when there was no influenza. In the decade 1911-20, the results were no different. With regard to cholera, in most cases the rates were equal. In the plague-ridden places such as Bombay, Punjab and United Provinces the female death rates due to plague were higher than that of males. Only in Madras, which was not affected by plague much, had a female death rate lower than that of male death rate.

Thus any mechanical generalization on the sex-differential vulnerability to epidemics including famine-related epidemics needs to be seriously qualified, as the data shows a complex picture where both sexes were vulnerable in specific contexts and some like pregnant women were more susceptible to infection.

Vulnerability by Age Groups

It is important to note that children had special vulnerability to epidemics. On the basis of some studies, William Burrows has observed that children were susceptible to certain diseases such as measles, mumps and chickenpox because adults generally acquired immunity in childhood. To quote Burrows: 'Man appears to be highly susceptible to diseases such as measles, mumps and

TABLE 7.1 AVERAGE ANNUAL RECORDED DEATH RATE PER THOUSAND OF MALES AND FEMALES DUE TO CERTAIN DISEASES IN MAIN PROVINCES OF INDIA BETWEEN 1901-11 AND 1911-21.*

		Cholera		*Fever*		*Plague*	
		1901-11	*1911-21*	*1901-11*	*1911-21*	*1901-11*	*1911-21*
Bengal	M	3.0	2.0	24.0	23.0	-	-
	F	3.0	2.0	23.0	23.0	-	-
Bihar & Orissa	M	3.0	3.0	23.0	24.0	-	1.0
	F	3.0	3.0	20.0	22.0	-	1.0
Berar	M	1.0	1.0	18.0	26.0	-	1.0
	F	1.0	1.0	16.0	24.0	-	1.0
Bombay	M	1.0	1.0	14.0	18.0	6.0	3.0
	F	1.0	1.0	14.0	19.0	6.0	3.0
Punjab	M	0.2	0.2	21.0	22.0	9.0	3.0
	F	0.2	0.2	24.0	25.0	11.0	4.0
Madras	M	2.0	2.0	8.0	9.0	-	-
	F	2.0	1.0	8.0	9.0	-	-
United Provinces	M	1.0	1.0	28.0	30.0	-	2.0
	F	1.0	1.0	28.0	30.0	-	3.0

Notes: *The rates have been computed from the population of 1901 and 1911 respectively.
M = male, F = female

Sources: Census of India 1911, vol. I, pt. 1, p. 204; *Census of India 1921*, vol. I, pt. 1, p. 61.

chickenpox, but the infectious agents are sufficiently prevalent in the human population that the probability of encountering them early in life is great.'[40]

In case of newborn infants, however, even though they have an underdeveloped immune system, the mother's antibodies protect them from various kinds of infections temporarily, but Burrows observes that this kind of protection is not always sufficient.[41]

At the same time, the older people are more susceptible to infectious diseases than the other age groups because of 'an accumulation of degenerative changes'.[42]

In India, scholars like Gill have observed that bubonic plague in the Punjab in 1924 attacked adolescents (aged 10-15) more and infants and old less.[43] He compared recorded death rate due to all causes in 1924 when plague was most prevalent, with the normal recorded death rate. He also compared the percentage difference between the mean recorded death rate of 1924 and that of 1901-11 (see Table 7.2), Gill gave another instance of plague, which occurred in a Punjab town, Bhera, with a population of 17,027. Bhera was free of plague from the seventeenth century onwards, but in 1904, 964 deaths occurred which were recorded as due to plague. He compared the age distribution of such recorded death rates with the normal death rates and this also confirmed his earlier finding, that plague was more fatal to adolescents.[44] In neither case, however, did Gill specify the normal year or 'normal death rate'.

A case study of pneumonic plague in two villages in India in 1919 revealed that children up to age 5 were immune but the death rate increased in the age group of 20-30.[45] In other words, pneumonic plague was most fatal to adolescents, according to Gill.

MALARIA

In this case too, children were more vulnerable. Ronald Ross who has done extensive research on malaria in India noticed that children were more affected by malaria than adults.[46]

Analysing the mortality data of malaria between 1891 and 1907 for India as a whole, Hehir noticed that malaria attacked children under 10 more than infants and old people.[47] As referred to before, Gill had analysed the age distribution of malaria mortality of Punjab and using Ronald Ross's observation on the age incidence of malaria mortality of Amritsar city in 1908 and his own findings on the age distribution of malaria victims of Behra town in 1921, he concluded that malaria attacked the young (between ages 0-10) more virulently. Gill also pointed out that even in mild epidemics of malaria, the death rate would increase more than the normal death rate in the age group 0-5. But in severe epidemics, the death rate of the age group of 0-10 increased considerably. Based on the experience of Behra town in 1921, Gill pointed out that in the initial phase of the epidemic, children in the age group of 0-10 were attacked more than the other age groups. But towards the termination of the epidemic, the older age groups were attacked in a greater number.[48]

TABLE 7.2 AGE INCIDENCE OF MORTALITY IN THE PUNJAB DUE TO ALL CAUSES, 1924

Age Group	*Mean death rate (1924)*	*Normal death rate*	*% departure in (1901-11)*
0-1	308.0	195.5	+ 57.0
1-5	68.5	51.6	+ 32.0
5-10	21.0	10.6	+ 98.0
10-15	21.0	9.8	+ 114.0
15-20	21.5	12.3	+ 74.0
20-30	22.5	13.8	+ 63.0
30-40	26.5	16.5	+ 60.0
40-50	34.5	21.2	+ 62.0
50-60	48.0	30.4	+ 58.0
60 and up	100.0	74.0	+ 35.0

Note: Plague was more prevalent in 1924 than in other years.

Source: C.A. Gill, 1928, *The Genesis of Epidemics*, London: Baillere, Tindall and Cox, p. 339.

INFLUENZA

The story was somewhat different in case of influenza. Examining the experience during the outbreak of the influenza of 1918-19, the Census Commissioner of 1921 observed that the disease had killed adults in the 20-40 age groups more than the young age group 0-10. He compared the proportion of children (0-10) per 100 of adults in the age group of 15-40 and also to married women of the same group of 1921 with that of 1911 and 1901. It is interesting to note that the proportion of children had increased in the decade ending in 1921. It is important to note that this was not due to increase in fertility, but due to the depletion in adults in the age group of 15-30, especially among married women, since ratio between women to children increased. The increase in the proportion of children was highest in the tracts where the virulence of influenza was the greatest.[49]

This phenomenon has been confirmed by I.D. Mills who has taken the age-specific death rates of 1913-17 as the average and has calculated the excess deaths due to influenza in the year 1918. The highest percentage (42 per cent) occurred in the age group of 20-30. Another feature of this particular influenza of 1918-19 was that infants (0-1 age group) had escaped lightly as it was noticed that the excess mortality was lower than that of the age group of 1-4.[50] It was because newborn babies have more resistance than the other age group though children as a whole had less immunity.

Mills has speculated on the plausible causes of the age pattern of the mortality due to the influenza of 1918-19. He actually rejected the immunity theory as the disease attacked the adults who were supposed to have acquired immunity. He has also considered the 'huddling theory' or people crowded together and suffered more. This view took into account the fact that the youth and adults worked together in ammunition factories during the First World War. But he observed that this huddling together would have been a partial explanation because the age incidence of influenza mortality was the same even in places where there were no such factories.[51]

Mills has finally put forward a biological explanation for the age pattern of influenza mortality. The influenza of 1918-19 was a different kind of epidemic from other influenza epidemics and was more virulent. There was no general resistance to that type of virus, which was brought by the 1918 influenza. So the defence mechanism of the body in general worked unaided by 'acquired immunity.' Since the defence mechanism of children is more efficient and healthy, the children survived better.[52]

Through his analysis, Mills raised several interesting questions. First, he points out that the biological factor, namely healthier resistance system of the children, prevented them from getting the virus. But Mills should have considered the greater exposure of adults to the virus compared to children, because of greater mobility. This may be more important than the cited biological factor because a famine had also occurred in the epidemic year 1918-19. It is possible too, as Greenough has shown for Bengal in 1943, that the intra-family distribution of food discriminated more against children in famine years.

Malnourishment and Sex Incidence of Diseases

Unfortunately, the earlier data did not classify the extent of malnourishment and incidence of various diseases on the basis of sex, even though it was noted that malnourished people died in a larger number. Recent data on the incidence of malnourishment showed that women are more malnourished. For example, Ren Mu and Xiao Zhang have discussed the gender differential impact of the great famine of 1958-61 in China. They noticed that the nutritional deficiency among women survivors of the famine led to significant negative impacts on their health. It was in turn attributed to the differential allocation of food in the family in the normal period.[53] In other words, women were more malnourished than men. In case of India, more girl children are malnourished than boys in the same age groups. It is due to the low social status of the girls, the UNICEF reported recently. The same source also observed that one-third of Indian adult women are under-nourished.[54] The undernourishment led to stunted growth of children.

Of course, the recent data or interpretation cannot be transported to the remote past. But there has been one common thread, namely, the preference for sons and neglect of girls still continued. So it can be safely presumed that a similar discrimination would have prevailed during the nineteenth century. In that sense, the epidemics and endemic diseases would be striking more severely to women, though one does not have any quantitative data to prove this. Recently also authors like Shrikant Kuntla, Srinivas Goli and Kshipra Jain have discussed the sex differentials of male and female babies and factors responsible for that.[55] The authors have used data from national Family Health Surveys at two points of time namely, 1992 and that of 2006. They pointed out that though inequality on major indicators between the two sexes has declined it still persists substantially. They have also discussed the factors and noticed that breast-feeding turned to be most important factor, which contributed around 40 per cent of the differentials. On the other hand, the birth order contributed less than that of breast-feeding. Interestingly, mother's education could explain only 9 per cent of the differentials.

Having seen that women and certain age groups were more vulnerable to infectious diseases, let us now turn to the economic condition of the affected groups.

Class Composition of Victims of Diseases

Mortality data are rarely classified in terms of economic characteristics or class. However, some observations on the class incidence of epidemics are in order. Obviously, poor victims far exceeded the rich in total numbers. It is no doubt obvious that the death rate was higher amongst the poor. This can be argued on a priori grounds: the poor had less resistance, lived in unsanitary conditions and could hardly afford adequate medical treatment. But some direct evidence from different countries, and different diseases gives us some insights.[56]

Among the scholars, Ronald Ross was more cautious regarding the class composition of malaria mortality. First, he observed that malaria not only killed directly but also killed indirectly by creating conditions for the entry of other diseases such as dysentery and pneumonia. So it is difficult to point out whether the death was due to malaria or due to other diseases.[57] Second, Ross observed that the death statistics kept in tropics in general and in India in particular were faulty because the doctor never certified death. The *chowkidar* often registered a death due to malaria, if he failed to diagnose its cause.[58] Ross concluded that 'probably the great majority of malaria deaths occurred among the children of the poor, and in the tropics these are seldom brought to hospital or even attended by medical men.' Ross verified the malarial death rate among European troops, Indian troops and prisoners in India in 1907. He noticed that even though the prisoners stayed in healthy environments, their death rate was higher than the other groups. From this he concluded that the higher death rate from malaria must have some relationship with the conditions of their growing up as poor children.[59] The same conclusion is valid for recent times also. For example N.S. Narang in 1984 wrote: 'The poor and underprivileged with insufficient nutrition are more vulnerable to the disease.'[60]

Dealing with this question, Ira Klein has pointed out that deaths due to different diseases were class oriented even though different communities had similar 'sanitary practices' and 'similar exposure'.[61] But still the poor got more of cholera, dysentery, and diarrhea because these diseases flourished most under the conditions of 'crowding, poverty and malnutrition'.[62] In the same way, Gangarosa and Mosley have observed that cholera is a disease of the poor because malnutrition predisposes them to the disease. At the same time they admit that the scientific evidence to prove this link is yet to be found.[63]

Going back to I.D. Mills, we find that in case of influenza of 1918-19, the death rate of low caste Hindus was 7.5 times higher than that of Europeans, while the death rate due to all other causes was 5.5 times higher. Influenza became the disease of the poor because it often led to pneumonic complications and there are links between malnutrition and pneumonia. Hence the death rate of the poor from influenza was higher than that of other groups.[64]

Thus it is noticed that most of the diseases, including plague, have been class-oriented because of malnutrition, insanitary practices, crowding and poverty as well as finally due to lack of medical care.

Sufferings of Women, Children and the Poor

In this chapter, the hypothesis that females in general and in the age group of 30 and above in particular are more resistant biologically to infectious diseases than men in the corresponding age groups has been considered in addition to the age and class incidence of diseases. Even though the evidence shows that women do not seem to be more fit than men in so far as infectious diseases are concerned, we find that in certain age groups and class situation they are more vulnerable than men. Perhaps age of the women, particularly after the reproductive age, is a more decisive factor to determine the incidence of the infectious diseases. In other words, it cannot be conclusively asserted that they are more or less prone to infectious diseases. However, it is true that in addition to the biological factor, it is the social practices which act as barrier to availing good health care services, which explains high death rates.

The sex incidence of different diseases such as plague, cholera, malaria and influenza, which had become epidemics both in Europe and the United States and also in Asia and India at different times, revealed that sometimes more females died in relation to males and at other times it was the reverse. The pattern of mortality mostly depended on the social habits of males and females. Sometimes males died in greater numbers in plague because they were more exposed due to their social habits. At some other times, women died in greater numbers from plague because their social habits brought them nearer to the rat fleas. Same was true for other diseases. The medical literature also notes that the extent of exposure to the infection determines the pattern of morbidity and mortality.

With regard to age incidence, plague did not attack infants and old people, but attacked the children and adolescents most. We also saw that the age incidence of malaria and cholera varied. Finally, we referred to the extent malnourishment determined the sex incidence of diseases, using some of the recent data as such data was not available for the past decades. All the diseases particularly attacked the poor and undernourished.[65]

Notes

1. Risley and Gait, the Census Commissioners of India were of the opinion that the death rates of females were less than that of males during the famine period because of certain biological and social factors. The sociological factors have been discussed in the next chapter. *Census of India 1901*, vol. 1, pt. 1, p. 118. Also, *Census of India 1911*, vol. 1, pt. 1 p. 212, Appendix pp. 220-2. In this chapter we have discussed regarding the constitutional strength of women due to different epidemics that accompany the famines.
2. Benjamin M. Althouse and Laurent Hebert-Dufresne, 'Epidemic Cycles, Driven by Host Behavior', *Journal of the Royal Society Interface*. October, 2014. https://royalsocietypublishing.org/doi/full/10.1098/rsif.2014.0575
3. Chandi Prasad Nanda, 'Disciplining a "Pathological" Province? Epidemic Disease and Health Interventions in Colonial Odisha', *Indian History Congress,* vol. 76 (2015), pp. 305-17.
4. Madhulika Banerjee, *Power, Knowledge, Medicine: Ayurvedic Pharmaceuticals at Home and in the World,* New Delhi, Orient BlackSwan, 2009, p. 6.
5. Jasriya Yoosof U.V., 'Epidemics and the City: A Study of Colonial Calicut', *Proceedings of Indian History Congress*, 78 Session, New Delhi, *Indian History Congress*, 2018, pp. 549-58.
6. The percentage share of recorded deaths to 'other cause' was very high. It fluctuated 20 to 35 per cent between 1881 and 1921 in Cuttack. In other two districts the share was still higher in some years. But it is to be pointed out that the percentage share of deaths due to other causes fell in famine years in all the three districts.
7. William Burrows, *Textbook of Microbiology*, Philadelphia W.B. Saunders Company, 1908, rpt. 1963, pp. 332-3.
8. Dean A. Anderson and Rodney J. Sobieski, *Introduction to Microbiology,* St. Louis, The C.V. Mosby Company; 1980, 2nd edn., p. 358.
9. India was not included, but Ceylon was included.
10. Samuel H. Preston, *Mortality Patterns in National Populations with Special Reference to Recorded Causes of Death,* New York, Academic Press, 1976, pp. 121-2.

11. Ibid., p. 122.
12. Idem.
13. Social discrimination in terms of nutritional deprivation of women is reflected in the higher death rate of females due to diarrheal diseases. But Preston adds that this source is unlikely to influence the cross over after 40. Preston, *Mortality Pattern*, p. 123.
14. The impact of plague on sex was not uniform among European Communities. In 1603 and 1625 the proportion of female deaths to male deaths due to plague was higher than the pre-plague period in St. Botolph's parish without Bishops Gate, London. The explanations were the social habits of women who stayed back home and did not come into contact of rat fleas, M.F. Hollingsworth and T.H. Hollingsworth, 'Plague Mortality Rates by Age and Sex in the Parish of St. Botolph's without Bishop's Gate London 1603', *Population Studies*, vol. 25, March 1971, pp. 145 and 152. Paul Slack points out that the impact of plague was not uniform. Plague killed more women proportionately than men in some other parishes of London both in 1603 and 1625. In other plague epidemics sometimes it was lower. Slack speculates that the plausible explanation could be the peculiar social habits and more exposure to the rat fleas. Paul Slack, *The Impact of Plague in Tudor and Stuart England*, London, Routledge and Kegan Paul, 1985, pp. 179-81.
15. They (plague and malaria) both affected women more than men, 'Plague affected them chiefly in the prime of life, malaria directly and indirectly all through life', *Census of India 1911*, vol. 13, pt. 1, p. 77. *Census of India 1911*, vol. 1, pt. 1, p. 212.
16. C.A. Gill, *The Genesis of Epidemics and the Natural History of Diseases: An Introduction to the Science of Epidemiology based upon the Study of Epidemics of Malaria, Influenza and Plague*, London, Bailliere Tindall and Cox, 1928, p. 343.
17. Ibid.
18. *Census of India, 1911*, vol. 1, pt. 1, p. 212.
19. Dr. Farr had given the monthly distribution of cholera deaths, which showed more males died than females in the beginning of the epidemics. But later on more females died than males. For example in four weeks of October 1848 there occurred 86 deaths among males and only 42 deaths among females in London. But in the week when the mortality was the highest (in July 1849) there were 1131 female deaths and 895 male deaths due to cholera.

    John Snow, *Mode of Communication of Cholera*. London, John Churchill, 1854, 2nd edn., p. 119.

20. John Snow, *Mode of Communication of Cholera*, pp. 119-20.
21. Ibid., p. 120. Smillie pointed out that the ratio of male to female deaths due to mild cholera epidemic was 3:2 in USA in 1873. William Smillie, *Public Health, Its Promises for the Future: A Chronicle of the Development of Public Health in the United States 1807-1914,* New York, Macmillan, 1955, p. 132. Also see, S.A. Meegama, who pointed out that cholera was equally fatal to male and female among the poor Tamilians during the epidemic phase on 1878 in Ceylon. S.A. Meegama, 'Cholera Epidemics and their control in Ceylon', *Population Studies,* 33(1), March 1979, p. 150.
22. John Macpherson, *Annals of Cholera: from the Earliest Periods to the Year 1817,* London, Ranken and Co., 1872, p. 213.
23. https://www.who.int/gender/documents/gender_health_malaria.pdf
24. Russell also notes that throughout the world, agricultural practices have bearing on the incidence of malaria. For example, men sleep outside to watch crops, and irrigate at night. Thus the menfolk are more exposed to infections. Paul F. Russell, *Malaria: Basic Principles Briefly Stated,* Oxford: Blackwell Scientific Publication, 1952, pp. 98-9. S.P. James has shown than an interesting change did take place in England since 1880 Till 1880, the death rates due to malaria were equal for both the sexes, but after 1880 deaths due to malaria fell rapidly but only young men died of the disease. S.P. James, *Malaria: At Home and Abroad,* London, John Bales Sons and Daniels Son Ltd., 1920, pp. 147-8. Palestine experience shows that female and male are equally affected by malaria. If the spleen rate is higher for some boys in some villages, it was due to greater exposure. I.J. Kligler, *The Epidemiology and the Control of Malaria in Palestine,* Chicago, Universityof Chicago Press, 1980, p. 101.
25. *Census of India, 1911*, vol. 1, pt. 1, p. 212. Ira Klein has pointed out that malaria was most virulent to the pregnant women. Ira Klein, 'Malaria and Mortality in Bengal 1840-1921', *Indian Economic and Social History Review,* 12(2), June 1972, p. 125.
26. P. Hehir, *Prophylaxis of Malaria,* Allahabad: Pioneer Press, 1901, p. 28. The data of the canal construction is not given. C.A Gill, however did not elaborate on the sex incidence of malaria.
27. https://apps.who.int/iris/bitstream/handle/10665/44401/9789241500111_eng.pdf?sequence=1
28. *Census of India, 1921*, vol. 1, pt. 1, pp. 13, 130 and 146.
29. *Census of India, 1921*, vol. XVI, pt. 1, pp. 87-8.

30. Ibid., p. 88.
31. *Census of India, 1921*, vol. 7, pt. 1, p. 168.
32. Ibid., vol. 7, pt. 1 p. 168.
33. Ibid., vol. 15, pt. 1 p. 226. Also see *Census of India, 1921*, vol. 8, pt. 1, p. 111.
34. Ibid., vol. 11, pt. 1, p. 90. We have not analysed the remarks of the Census Superintendent of Bengal and Madras since influenza was mild in those provinces.
35. I.D. Mills, 'The 1918-1919 Influenza Pandemic: The Indian Experience', *Indian Economic and Social History Review*, 23(1), 1986, pp. 23-4.
36. Ibid., p. 23.
37. https://www.who.int/news-room/fact-sheets/detail/diarrhoeal-disease
38. Mitra, *India's Population*, vol. 1, pp. 168-9.
39. L.C. Chen, Hoq and S. D'Souza, 'Sex-Biased Behaviour of Food and use of Health Care Services in Rural Bangladesh'. *Population and Development Review*, 7(1), March 1981, p. 64.
40. William Burrows, *Textbook of Microbiology*, p. 321. Also Anderson and Sobieski have observed that resistance or/and susceptibility fluctuates significantly with age. But certain diseases attack populations of all ages. They have also written that certain diseases such as mumps, chickenpox, etc., attack children more, because of their lack of 'acquired immunity'. Anderson and Sobieski, *Introduction to Microbiology*, p. 356.
41. William Burrows, *Textbook of Microbiology*, Philadelphia, W.B. Saunders Co., 1979, p. 321.
42. Ibid., p. 322.
43. C.A. Gill, *The Genesis of Epidemics and the Natural History of Diseases: An Introduction to the Science of Epidemiology based on the Study of Malaria, Influenza and Plague*, London, Bailliere, Tindall and Cox., 1928, p. 341.
44. Ibid., pp. 340-1. In England, plague attacked adolescents more and infants and old people less. Paul Slack, *Impact of Plague in Tudor and Stuart England*, New York, Oxford University Press, 1990, pp. 181-2. Hollingsworth and Hollingsworth, 'Plague Mortality', p. 1135.
45. C.A. Gill, *The Genesis of Epidemics*, pp. 342-3.
46. Ronald Ross, *Prevention of Malaria*, London, John Murray, 1910, p. 235. Also Ira Klein has found that the death rate of children due

to malaria was higher than the other age groups of the population in Bengal, 1840-1920. Ira Klein, 'Malaria and Mortality in Bengal 1840-1921', p. 135. For similar kind of observations see, Bernard Notch and Martin Mayer, *Malaria: A Handbook of Treatment – Parasitology and Prevention,* London, John Bales Medical Publications, 1937, pp. 18 and 174. Also, L.W. Hackett, *Malaria in Europe: An Ecological Study*, London, Oxford University Press, 1937. Also see, I.J. Kligler, 'The Epidemiology of Malaria in Palestine: A Contribution to the Epidemiology of Malaria', *American Journal of Epidemiology*, 6(3), pp. 431-49.

47. P. Hehir, *Prophylaxis of Malaria*, p. 28.
48. C.A. Gill, *The Genesis of Epidemics*, pp. 72-7.
49. *Census of India, 1921*, vol. 1, pt. 1, p. 130. Also see, John Eyles and K.J. Woods, *The Social Geography of Medicine and Health,* London, Croom Helm, 1983, p. 71.
50. I.D. Mills, 'The 1918-1919 Influenza Pandemic', p. 22.
51. Ibid.
52. Ibid., pp. 20-2.
53. Ren Mu and Xiao Zhang, 'Gender Differences in the Long Term Impact of Famine' Iffri Discussion paper 00760 (March 2008). Cite: www.iffri.org/sites/default /files/publications/iffri p00760. pdf
54. UNICEF (n.d.) 'Nutrition' Cite: www.unicef.org/india/children_2356.htm
55. Shrikant Kuntla, Srinivas Goli and Kshipra Jain, 'Explaining Sex Differentials in Child Mortality in India: Trends and Determinants', *International Journal of Population Research,* 2014. http://dx .doi.org/10.1155/2014/649741, pp. 1-8.
56. Geddes Smith noted that the plague of 1348 attacked the poor more because '...; poor of London, living as Bell says in "Low over-hanging houses, ill kept, dark and congested" that "covered the ground in seemingly impenetrable rookeries of filthy courts and blind allies". The rich could usually keep infection at arm's length, if not by cleanliness...; at least by flight.' Geddes Smith, *Plague on US,* New York, The Commonwealth Fund, 1943, pp. 8-9. Wilson Smillie observed the same pattern of class composition of deaths in case of cholera deaths in 1873 of USA. W.S. Millie, *The Public Health,* pp. 131-2.The medical officer of Colombo had observed in 1875 that cholera disease had claimed lives from the poorest class of native races, Sinhalese, Tamils, Moors and Malays. S.A. Meegama, 'Cholera Epidemics and their Control in Ceylon', p. 150. In 1933,

J.W.H. Chun also observed that cholera was a disease of the poor, though some deaths had occurred amongst the rich. J.W.H. Chun, 'Clinical Aspects', in D.Wu Lien Tech, J.W.H. Chun, R. Pollitzer and C.Y. Wu, *Cholera: A Manual for the Medical Profession in China*, Shanghai, National Quarantine Service, 1934, p. 103. Similar views are also expressed by some experts on malaria. For example, Kligler has noted that the attack rate of malaria was higher among the lower classes. In fact he has classed malaria as a 'social disease' which gets eradicated as society improves economically. I.J. Kligler, *The Epidemiology and Control of Malaria in Palestine*, p. 12. Robin Barlow who has done research on the economic cost of malaria control in Sri Lanka during the 1930s has pointed out that it was a disease of the poor. Robin Barlow, 'The Economic Effects of Malaria Eradication', *The American Economic Review*, 50(2), May 1967, p. 134.

57. Ronald Ross, *Prevention of Malaria*, p. 246.
58. Ibid., p. 248.
59. Ibid. Also Ira Klein has pointed out that 'An abundance of evidence shows that the prevalence of malaria was related to economic, geological and ecological conditions all of which interacted on each other.' He was discussing the malaria mortality in Bengal for 1840-1921. The death rate due to malaria was highest where the economic condition was worst. Ira Klein, 'Malaria and Mortality in Bengal, 1840-1921', pp. 143-4.
60. N.S. Narang also has pointed out that the poor not only suffer from malaria at a higher rate but also are reservoirs of malarial parasite because they live in insanitary conditions and cannot afford to have proper treatment. N.S. Narang, 'Malaria Strikes Back', *Science Today*, October 1984, p. 37.
61. Ira Klein, 'Death in India', p. 643.
62. Ibid., pp. 648-9.
63. E. J. Gangarosa and W.H. Mosley, 'Epidemiology and Surveillance of Cholera', in D. Barua and W. Burrows (eds.), *Cholera*, Philadelphia, W.B. Saunders, 1974, p. 385.
64. I.D. Mills, 'The 1918-19 Influenza Pandemic', p. 34.
65. *Census of India*, 1911, op. cit.

CHAPTER 8

Gender Discrimination in Food and Health Care

Introduction

As we have seen in Chapter 7, biological factors are relatively less important than social factors in explaining changes in sex ratio. It was so because given similar kind of exposure, male and female death rates in epidemics tended to be more or less similar. But the impact of social factors is a very complex issue and many questions arise in this context. Are there special social factors 'favouring women' in famines, as some Census commissioners and superintendents had asserted? Are females generally discriminated against in India? Has the degree of discrimination changed over time? Are there regional variations? Historically, social issues have not been carefully analyzed, but we present some relevant findings here.

General Bias against Women

Various Census commissioners have discussed at length special social factors favourable to women during famines.[1] We will examine this issue before taking up the phenomenon of social discrimination against women in normal periods. It is important because the same kind of discriminations continue or rather accentuate when the resources are scarce. The Census commissioners kept on citing those social factors to explain the increasing sex ratios particularly during the famine period.

Social Factors Affecting Women during the Famine Period

The Census commissioners narrated a set of biological and social factors which allegedly operated during the famine period and helped in reducing the death ratios during famine years compared to non-famine years.

We have discussed the set of biological factors in the previous chapter. In this chapter we briefly discuss the social factors to find out if those really helped women.

Here are the main sociological arguments given by the Census Commissioners:

1. Women received gratuitous relief more frequently than men and their work in the relief centre was relatively light compared to them.
2. Women collected jungle produce and cooked food and had precious metal ornaments, which they could dispose off for obtaining food for themselves. Since they had access to food items they would be eating those alone without sharing with the family members.
3. Women wandered less than men in search for food.
4. The authorities felt that the 'brunt of struggle' fell on men entirely and they were in constant tension to provide food for the family.

Let us examine these explanations.

It is true that women did get food in the relief centres and their work was relatively lighter. But only a small portion of population got relief in the relief centres any way.[2] The average number of population who got relief daily between 1865 and 1900 was only 0.3 per cent of the total victims on an average, though in 1896-7 and 1899-1900 the percentage increased to 24 per cent, according to Dyson. As has been mentioned before, women did not go to the relief centres during the famine of 1866 for fear of losing caste. Further, the relief centres maintained at a distance from the villages to test people's fitness to get relief. It became a deterrent for women to travel long distance. In addition, the able-bodied men did try to corner the food easing out the weak women and relatively less able men. Further, as we have seen in Chapter 4, the food distributed in the relief centres was not at all nutritious nor was the centre hygienic. Thus the suggestion that women availed more food in the relief centre is not at all true.

Women indeed collected forest produce and other famine substitutes when crops failed. Hence they might have had more food to eat while men starved. But food substitutes often did not suit their stomach and they suffered from dysentery, as we have seen during the famine of 1866 as well as in the later famines. Further as we will discuss later, women are so brainwashed with traditional values that even if food is available they would be reluctant to eat alone. Of course, the pangs of hunger would definitely erode moral values, further those sources of food declined during the famine period.

There are no data available on the disposal of ornaments since most of the famine victims came from families of labourers and small farmers. The latter may have possessed some ornaments but it was unlikely that the women would have disposed off their ornaments for their self-interest, if Greenough's *Korta* model is to be believed. He pointed out that the *Korta* was the decision maker of the household and he decided how to distribute the resources of the households.[3] Even if they had some ornaments, the value of those would decline during the food crisis. But what the colonial administrators did not discuss was that women had some advantage phyically. We have noticed that during the famine of 1866, the agents sold women as prostitutes in Calcutta. Famine literature on the European famines and that of Bengal Famine of 1943 are full of those references.[4] There is however, some element of truth in the arguments that women wandered less and men being the procurers of food were more stressed. As we will see later, Chapter 10 during the wandering period men were more exposed to epidemics and the fatality rate was higher. Even in this case it would be true of the initial stage of the famine, but when it becomes acute both male and female wander aimlessly.

Social Discrimination During Normal Period

Social practices in many countries discriminate against women, and therefore led to differential mortality.[5] In India, women in general and female children in particular, are less valued than males. Factors responsible for the discriminations are economic as well as social reasons. It is believed that a son would support the parents whereas daughters are married off. They go away taking a part of the property. Socially, the son would carry the family name and offer annual rituals after the death of the parents. Thus for both the reasons women in general and girl children in particular have low value in the family setup. Moreover, women's household work is also not recognized as work. Of course, it varies from caste to caste. For example, women of the peasant caste as well as the service castes – barbers, washerman, etc., and labouring castes are involved in the process of rice cultivation. In those castes, women and girl children are generally less discriminated. It is true that when they climb in the ladder of economic prosperity, these households withdraw their women from doing work in the fields and start adopting the practices of the upper castes such as giving dowry. At that point, women's work, become less valued. During the nineteenth century as well as early twentieth century, women would have been relatively more valued because at that time the various stages of agricultural production were not mechanized.

Paul G. Greenough has depicted in his study of Bengal Famine, why females are discriminated against. His model relates to Bengal, but since Bengali culture shares a great deal with the cultural practices of other parts of India, this model is applicable in certain respects to other parts of India also. In the Korta model, the family is a moral unity, with codes regarding duties and rights. In order to enforce such duties and rights, a figure of authority in the family or Korta is needed who is generally a married male who is morally and physically fit. The Korta has the right to manage the family resources. In the family, adults are given preferred treatment over children and males over females. The reason for such preference is that the main objective of the Korta is to maintain the *kul* or patrilineage.[6] In other words, males in general and married males in the age group of 20-4 in particular are the most valued persons because they are the most fit to ensure the continuity of the family tree along with their spouses.

Since the males of this age group needed their spouses to maintain family continuity, the spouses were also in the preferred group, i.e. they were given preference over the old and the young of both sexes. This model also states that male children are more valuable than female children. This was the picture of a normal situation. The exercise of preference became more acute when resources were scarce, as during famines.[7]

Measuring Discrimination

The male preference manifested in various forms of discrimination, of which the most extreme form was female infanticide.[8] The neglect of female children in general, and giving less food and medical attention to girls, in fact to women of all ages, were the other manifestations. If we stretch it further to the recent times, one will notice that female infanticide has taken yet another form, namely, elimination of the female fetus. It is important to note that such discrimination may result in higher female mortality.

(a) Access to Food: The factor, access to food, is very much dependent on the class/caste of the family. For example, as we will see below, women from those castes which provided traditional services in rural society were relatively less discriminated than the men in their castes since their labour was recognized by their family as well as by the user of their services. This has been the case in the past as well as now. But none the less, ironic as it may appear to be, it is also true, particularly in high caste groups, that adult women and girls get a smaller proportion of their nutritional requirements than men and boys in the developing countries has been noticed in a number of studies though many lack a firm quantitative basis.[9] For India and Bangladesh some works have been done on the intra-family distribution of food but these studies are neither consistent in their findings nor in their methodology.

A pioneering, systematic study on the intra-family distribution of food was conducted by the Institute of Nutrition and Food Science of Dacca University in 1975-6 of 60 households each from 12 locations in rural Bangladesh.[10]

According to this study, females over the age of ten had calorie intakes which were more than those of males when compared with their requirements; this was particularly true of females in the age group 20 to 69.[11] But among the female children in the age group of 0-10, the nutritional deficiency was very acute compared to their requirements.[12]

Ray Langsten has come to the same conclusion on the basis of another study, which was conducted also in Bangladesh by R.H. Chaudhury in 1983. This was a more detailed study conducted among 572 members of 108 households. For this, data were collected once a month for a whole year by actual weighing of food, tracking conversation and memory recall. The study also applied a set of requirements according to metabolic needs.

The level of physical activities was determined by talking to the members of the household. The author concluded that women were 'more likely' to consume calories according to their requirements than men.[13]

Langsten arrived at the conclusion that intra-family distribution of food did not discriminate against women while taking the 'requirement' adjustments into account.[14] He believed that on an average, men were larger in size and did more hard work compared to women, so their food requirements were higher. Thus he observed that comparison of the ratio of intake to requirements could be an imprecise exercise.[15] However, this view can be qualified on the ground that if the resource was scarce, then it was the woman who got less in the distribution of food. In a traditional family generally, it was the woman who ate last after distributing food to all. Hence in the process she may not get enough food to eat as per her requirement.

In 1978, L. Chen, E. Hoq and S. D'Souza conducted dietary surveys among 130 families in Matlab thana of Bangladesh.[16] Based on the surveys, Chen et al. noticed that without making any adjustments for 'requirements', the per capita food intake of males exceeded that of females on an average by 16 per cent in the age group of 0-5. The largest shortfall occurs in the age group of persons 45 and above. In this age group the per capita consumption of males exceeded that of females by 61 per cent. Similar age-specific differences also occurred in protein consumption.[17] After this, various adjustments in terms of 'requirements' were done and calorie intakes were compared while adjusting for metabolic need which depends on body mass. (For example, it was found that in general, Bangladesh males weighed more than the females.) The calorie intake ratio does not change at all in the age group of 0-5 and the sharp disparity in the age group of 45+ gets reduced. After this an extra amount of calorie intake of 288 was added to women's requirements for child bearing and breast-feeding children. In this case the calorie intake ratio became worse in the reproductive age group only, as is expected.

Now after these two adjustments, Chen et al. tried to make another adjustment based on differences in physical activities. In order to find out that the incremental calorie requirement for different physical activities, they checked the labour participation data from the Census of Bangladesh in 1974 and WHO/FAO guidelines. Since males contributed more to agricultural work, especially during the peak period, an extra 500 calorie on an average were added to the requirement of adult men. But for adult women only 100 calories extra on an average was added following FAO/WHO guidelines. Thus the calorie intake ratio becomes equal to requirement ratio in all age groups except the young in the age group of 0-5.[18] However, the authors have taken only the harvesting time as the peak period in paddy cultivation. It is true that during ploughing and harvesting men work more, but during transplantation and weeding it is the woman who becomes busier. Similarly, in a poor family, if a man cuts the paddy it is the woman who carries the load which is equally labour intensive. Therefore, their finding has to be interpreted with caution.

However, the above authors were aware of the crudeness of the guidelines given by FAO/WHO. So they noted that these adjustments were 'illustrative' rather than 'precise'.[19] Even though the above study relates to Bangladesh, it can be applied to India as well. Because as Chen et al. have pointed out, the food distribution system in a family favours males and male children.[20] Second, 'in-depth studies in rural Maharashtra and the Punjab have documented similar phenomena with regard to gender-biased nutrition and health practices'.[21] Since the culture of Orissa Division was a combination of pan Indian and local one, the above kind of intra-family distribution of food may be applicable to the Orissa Division.

Joycelyn Kynch and Amartya Sen have observed that discrimination against access to food may not operate directly through differential distribution of food in the family, though that possibility is always where. If a mother of a baby son gets preferential treatment in the family, then ultimately the male children will emerge as better fed without any observed discrimination in the family.[22]

We get some insights into gender discrimination also from a few studies of south India.

In 1978, Leela Gulati published a profile of a woman who is an agricultural labourer in Kerala. Her husband was also an agricultural labourer. Both husband and wife used to eat out on working days. Gulati interviewed the family for an extended period. Based on her interviews, she compared the food intake of the wife and the husband. The ICMR standard of calorie requirement had been adopted to measure the calorie shortfalls. However, Gulati had not described the method of measuring the food value of the intake of the male and female separately. According to her, on a working day the wife had a shortfall in requirement by 19.7 per cent while the husband's shortfall was 10.8 per cent. On non-working days, the wife's shortfall was 49.1 per cent but the husband's was 26.4 per cent short.[23]

Two important features of the study are to be noted. First, eating out when on work is accepted as normal practice in Kerala. Gulati treated this as an indicator of 'possibly a major source of imbalance in food intake within the household'.[24] Because at that time the wife of the agricultural labourer earned Rs. 7, on a working day spent Rs. 2 on her food and the rest on household expenditure. The husband earned Rs. 10 but spent Rs. 4 to 5 on his food and the remaining amount went for household expenses. So proportionately the husband spent more on his own food than the wife. Second, when asked as to why her husband spent twice the amount she spent on food, the wife said that her husband did hard work and should eat more than the wife.[25] Even though the study was based on the experience of just one family, it is possible to take it as a representative case. It is significant to notice that the intra-family distribution of food favoured the man in spite of the fact that both husband and wife were working.

We can mention yet another case suggesting the same phenomenon. In a study, S. Batliwala has calculated the actual calorie intake based on oral answers by the rural women of households in six villages in Karnataka. On the basis of basal metabolic rate needs (the rate at which the body uses energy while at rest to maintain vital functions such as breathing and keeping warm) and activity level, the calorie requirements were set at 2,473 calories for men, 2,505 calories for women and 1,598 calories for children. She found that balls made up of the cereal *ragi* are distributed with 2 balls for each man, 1.5 for the woman while a child got 1 ball. From this the author came to the conclusion that 'the relative food intake per man, woman and child would then be 3270 calories, 2410 calories and 1640 calories per day respectively.' This meant an intake deficit of nearly 100 calories per day per woman whereas a man had an intake surplus of nearly 800 calories.[26]

All these studies have adopted the norms of 'requirements' as given by FAO/WHO or ICMR. It is, however, to be noted that the concept itself is suspect as Sen and Chen have pointed out.

Amartya Sen has criticized the concept of 'requirement' recommended by the WHO and FAO and adopted by the Institute of Nutrition and Food Science, Dhaka for the above study. He noted that, nutritionists like Sukhatme and Scrimshaw feel that there is no 'normal' requirement for men or women. There is not only 'interpersonal variability' but also 'intrapersonal variation' of 'requirements'. The same individual would require different amounts of food at different times. Besides, experts who calculate the 'requirement' of women tend to assume that the work of a woman is 'sedentary', but it is not always so. Sen also observes that the extra nutrition needed during pregnancy and lactation is not taken into account in a proper way. It should have been weighted at a higher rate of energy utilization.[27] Finally, Sen concludes that the reasoning is 'circular' because the 'energy requirements' are calculated by multiplying the body weight while at the same time the body weight and activity level basically depend on the 'energy intake of the person'.[28]

(b) *Health Care*: Accessing health care is a complex issue. It not only depends on the providers' behaviour, but also severity of disease, the cost of the care, facilities and finally physical accessibility.[29] These factors have always been relevant. For example, during the colonial period, all doctors were perhaps males. That would often deter women and female children going to him.[30] Second, the health-care facilities were few and far between. Discrimination of females (adults and children) is also reflected in the type and relative frequency of health care. Finally, women believed relatively more on the efficacy of traditional medicine. Coupled with that they also felt shy to confide with a male doctor who was neither conversant with their culture nor language. Further, the medical officials were more worried about the health condition of the British subjects. So they took very strict measures such as isolating the patients to treat them. They also compelled people to evict from their own houses. It led to riots in Bombay presidency. In addition, it also fuelled the sentiments of the nationalists to take anti-plague steps.[31] The data show that males received better medical treatment than females in all age groups but this is more prominent in case of children.

Miller, for example, has quoted the sex ratios of children (age not mentioned) of hospital admissions from some parts of India. But the samples varied widely from 30 to 1,846 cases of observations. The hospitals covered included two from Punjab, one from New Delhi, two from U.P., one from M.P., two from Bombay and two from Vellore. The samples were collected between 1959 and 1978 and the results are consistent with earlier results. In north India the proportion of boys to girls taken to the hospital is 2.2:1. In Vellore and Bombay also more boys were taken to hospitals but the ratios are 1.3:1 and 1.5:1 respectively.[32] None the less the gap between the males and females existed everywhere.

Kumudini Dandekar has also confirmed that females (including babies) are discriminated against in getting medical treatment in western India. This she has shown by conducting a health survey in six rural communities of six districts in Bombay State in 1957, covering a total population of 37,000.[33] The percentage of people getting some kind of treatment is much higher among adult males than females.[34] Again, in her data, the percentage of the 'ailing' who were not getting any kind of treatment was in this case higher for both non-adult and adult females. In Dhanare area, the percentage of girls below 15 years who did not receive any treatment was 8 per cent as against 19 per cent among boys.[35] But only 16 per cent of Dhanare adult males did not receive any kind of treatment in contrast to 34 per cent of adult females.[36] The percentage of adult males going to doctors was much higher than that of females. For example, in Mudalgi the percentage of adult males going to doctors was 69 per cent in contrast to only 24 per cent of females, with 66 per cent of the females not getting any kind of treatment.[37] Dandekar observes that '. . . the male female differences were more striking in the backward villages which enjoyed less communication with the outside world.'[38]

We are giving more evidence to not only substantiate the point about gender discrimination in health matters, but also to stress that discrimination in famine period would be far more intense than that in normal times. But cultural practices and social preferences did intervene in both circumstances presenting a nuanced picture in some cases.

Let us continue the discussion.

Kynch and Sen have used hospital admission and death data of major hospitals of Bombay city for 1958-78 to show that medical facilities are availed of by males more than females in all age groups; this differential is 'particularly large' in case of children. They have taken data relating to 'non-gynaecological and non-obstructing cases'. In order to show the seriousness of the illness they have constructed two ratios: (1) ratio of in-patient hospital treatment to death; (2) in-patient plus out-patient hospital treatments to deaths in the city. In both the cases it is shown that over the years the excess male preferential treatment has declined, but still the utilization of health facilities was higher for males. Kynch and Sen have underlined this particular finding because though

Bombay was the most organized city in India, it still manifested cultural prejudices against female children regarding medical treatment.[39] In a worker's family if a son is ill he is rushed to the hospital. But if a girl is ill, the parent wait till it is serious or she is taken to a traditional doctor.

The authors of the famous Khanna Study also concluded that perhaps the parents give their boys 'higher quality of medical care and good supplementary food' in case they are ill. Otherwise, the authors could not explain the fact that girls in the same age groups die at higher rates from the same set of diseases which attack both boys and girls.[40]

Sen used Calcutta Metropolitan Development Authority data in 1981, to show that more women were ill and in indifferent health compared to men in all the age groups; but the difference being most striking in case of 26-45 age group.[41]

Sen has said that there is 'an element of perception-bias' among women about what is 'well-being'. They perhaps accepted the prevailing condition of destitution out of helplessness. He has quoted a study conducted in Singur near Calcutta in 1944, just after the famine, among a group of destitutes consisting of widows and widowers. When they were asked about 'being ill' or in 'indifferent health', as many as 48.5 per cent of the widowers answered that they were ill but only 2.5 per cent of widows said that they were ill, regards 'being in indifferent health', 45.6 per cent of the widowers felt that they were so but none of the widows felt that way.[42]

Sen has also used Calcutta morbidity statistics to conclude that 'As is to be expected, the incidence of illness typically goes down with rise in household per capita expenditure – a rough index of economic prosperity – but females have consistently greater morbidity in each expenditure group.'[43]

Similar discrimination was also noticed in Bangladesh. It is striking that even though both medical treatment and transport are given free to the inhabitants of Matlab thana, more boys were brought for diarrheal treatment than girls in spite of the fact that the attack rate due to diarrhea was almost similar in both the cases. But in the age group of 15-44 years more females had availed themselves of the treatment. The authors felt this was because the attack rate of diarrhea would have been higher in their case, since females handled sick children more.[44]

The surveys reviewed above refer to different regions and have adopted different methods. Yet all show that female children in the age group of 0-5 were nutritionally disadvantaged compared to male children.

For older age groups the evidence is conflicting.

In Bangladesh, which has a cultural affinity with India, the recent surveys show that women over 45 are eating 61 per cent less than the males of that age group. But when adjustments are made based on 'requirements', one study shows that females in the age group of 20-69 are eating more than their requirements, or as Chen et al. have shown, the ratio of food intake to requirements is equal for males and females in the above age groups. As is shown above, Sen and Chen et al. have criticized the concept of 'requirement' because they think that women's activities are wrongly termed as 'sedentary', and hence the above requirements as recommended are not defined properly. Even now women are more under-nourished as compared to men.[45] Recent data shows that 40 per cent of Indian women are reported to be anaemic compared to 12 per cent among men. Similarly, 67 per cent of the above women complained of at least one problem in accessing health care facilities.[46]

Anthropometric Measures

Discrimination with regard to food and health care, especially in the age group of 0-5, get reflected at least partly in anthropometric measures.

Nowadays, it has been recognized that the anthropometric measures do not reveal the nutritional status alone, because height and weight will be stunted if the subject is repeatedly attacked by disease.[47]

The 'Harvard Standard' measure – that took a certain standard height, weight and age as the reference point – is used to see to what extent the children are under-nourished in a particular locality. There is no single anthropometric study covering the whole of India but there are some regional studies, which reveal that in every age group females are more malnourished than males. For example, the Punjab Nutrition Development Project (PNDP) had conducted an anthropometric survey, according to which virtually in all the classifications of malnutrition, the number of females exceeded males; among the 'severely malnourished' infants the female percentage was eight times that of the males; among toddlers (in the age group of 12-36 months old) almost 100 per cent more and over 50 per cent more in the pre-school age group.[48] The method used by the PNDP incidentally was in a way superior to other studies because they did not employ the 'Harvard Standard' for measures and instead took the standards of a group of well-nourished children from the study area itself.[49] In 1979, a random sample was conducted among children of various groups in the relief centres in West Bengal after the floods of 1978. The sample included 1001 male babies and 922 female babies ranging from 0-12 months to 61-72 months. The results showed that except in the age group of 61-72 months (5-6 years), the female child was more undernourished than the male child.[50] This, however, was taken during a crisis period. In contrast, Sen has quoted another small sample taken from all parts of Bengal in the early part of 1978, which was a normal year. It showed that female children were less undernourished than male children in the age group of 0-5.[51] This study, which is small, has exceptional results.

Sen and Sengupta have done anthropometric studies taking 236 children below 5 in two villages of West Bengal as a sample, in the year 1983. In both the villages (Sahajpur and Kuchli), they found girls were more malnourished than boys. The gap between boys and girls in Sahajpur (which also has a midday meal scheme, more people worked in urban areas, and had acute landlessness compared to Kuchli) was less than in Kuchli, which has benefited by land reforms, but not otherwise.[52]

But most of these studies were conducted at a point of time. As Cassen has pointed out, these anthropometric studies did not follow up by surveying the consequences of malnourishment over a period of time; though a number of studies have shown the consequences of being extremely malnourished at an early age.[53]

Cassen refers to a unique study conducted on 9,000 children

in Bangladesh in the 1970s, which was followed up for two years, to observe the consequences of being malnourished in a certain range. The study showed that children in the severest form of malnourishment had much 'higher risk of mortality than others.'[54]

Chen has referred to another anthropometric study conducted on 882 children in six selected villages of Matlab thana between 1977 and 1979, to show that 14.4 per cent of female children could be classified as severely malnourished in contrast to 5.1 per cent of male children. It was also found that 59.6 per cent of girls in contrast to 54.8 per cent of boys were moderately malnourished.[55]

To find out the interaction between malnutrition and infection, an experiment was conducted in ten villages of Narangwal of Ludhiana district of Punjab from April 1968 to May 1973. The target population was 2,900 children ranging from birth to 36 months. Simultaneously, the authors wanted to find out the impact of intervention of outside variables such as nutrition care and medical care on the growth and mortality patterns of male and female children. Their findings showed that in spite of the fact that there were outside interventions, 'Low caste female children in control villages were about 2.5 kg lower in weight and 6 cm less in height at 36 months of age than high caste boys in nutrition study village.'[56] It is because the female children of lower castes lived in more crowded places and got less medical care when ill.[57] So the authors concluded that social factors other than diseases determined the nutritional status of females. Today in the twenty-first century it is no different. At least 51.4 per cent of the females are undernourished in India.[58]

These studies show that the nutritional status of the female child is worse than the male child in Bangladesh where intensive studies have been done. We can safely say that since it is true of Indian population, it would be true of Orissa also. Further, as per the National Family Health Survey 2015-16, as many as half of the pregnant women in Scheduled Caste population of Orissa were below body mass index (BMI) and 43 per cent of them were anaemic.[59] It is noticed that certain types of discrimination against women in general and girl child in particular has relatively declined over the years in terms of access to health care and that of food.[60] Mortality rates due to those factors have also declined and the gap between two rates has also declined. But now there is another trend. The girl fetus is eliminated before even she is born. The sum total still is the decline in child sex ratio over the years. Thus, while one set of discriminations has declined due to many public initiatives and social change, some new factors have emerged, which are perhaps even more acute and worrisome, that continue the same situation of discrimination.[61] It is not only due to persisting cultural phenomenon of 'son preference' but also due to availability of cheap machines which facilitate the elimination of female fetus among many other factors.

Economic Causes of Discrimination

One reason for social discrimination may be what is perceived as the 'low economic value of women'. For example, Pranab Bardhan has pointed out that perhaps in the areas where rice is cultivated, such as Bengal, Orissa and Tamil Nadu, the economic role of women and the economic value of the women are higher than in wheat growing regions; this is partly because there are stages of rice cultivation, like transplantation and weeding that require a kind of 'delicate care' which only women can give.[62] This is particularly true if stages of cultivation are not mechanized. This is reflected in many cultural practices including worship of female goddesses like Lakshmi.[63]

In an econometric study using the data of a sample of 1,331 rural households in 1971 in India, Rosenzwig and Schultz have concluded: 'children who are expected to be more economically productive adults, receive a larger share of family resources and have a greater prospect to survive'.[64] The authors also noticed a significant positive correlation between normal rainfall at the district level and the probability of women's employment. In other words, their finding is consistent with the hypothesis that wet agriculture (rice cultivation) employs more women.[65]

But the evidence is not consistent. In order to test the hypothesis that the nature of crops determines the extent of female participation, Leela Gulati has categorized different states of India in terms of the areas devoted to different crops, taking 1971-2 estimates of the area and production. She has classified seven states, which grow rice, namely, Kerala, Assam, West Bengal, Orissa, Bihar, Tamil Nadu and Andhra Pradesh in which the major portion of the cultivated area is devoted to rice. She has tried to match the female participation rate calculated from the 1971 Census with the percentage of area devoted to rice. She finds that even though West Bengal and Orissa devoted 91 per cent of total area to rice, the female participation rate turned out to be only 5.4 per cent and 7.62 per cent respectively. In Andhra Pradesh and Tamil Nadu, however, the participation rate of women was 28.59 per cent and 19.88 per cent respectively even though the percentage of area devoted to rice was 44 per cent in Andhra and 57 per cent in Tamil Nadu.[66] She also calculates the participation rate of three major wheat growing regions – Punjab, Haryana and Himachal Pradesh. The former two showed very low participation rates of 1.26 per cent and 3.01 per cent respectively, while in Himachal Pradesh the rate was as high as 22.37 per cent which was higher than in the rice growing areas of Orissa and Bengal. The other states which grow both wheat and rice also showed similar results. Thus she concludes, 'The nature of the crop grown in terms of rice or wheat does not seem to influence female participation rates noticeable.'[67]

Gita Sen also analyses paddy cultivation and the female participation rate in agriculture in 1961 and confirms Gulati's finding that there is no correlation between the two. Though paddy cultivation does require a large number of women workers, which the Census does not capture, partly because the Census is taken in March which is a lean month agriculturally. Also women labourers are migrant tribal labourers in many regions, especially in the north-eastern region. Gita Sen feels that there is a tendency in the Census to undercount tribal women.[68]

In this respect, Barbara Miller has taken north India as a test case but has added three other variables, namely, culture, distribution of wealth and cost of marriage. She found that except for Orissa, West Bengal and Kerala, where female participation rate was relatively high, the pattern was broadly compatible with Bardhan's hypothesis.

Miller further found that the female participation rate in agricultural work was low among the propertied groups of north India. She noted that in those areas the marriage cost was high. Most importantly she found that sex ratio was low there. In the south too the female participation rate was high, but the marriage cost was low and sex ratio was high among the people having no property at all.

Miller concluded that '..., where FLP (female labour participation) is high there will always be high preservation of female life, but where female labour participation is low, female children may or may not be preserved'.[69]

Sen and Sengupta have also used economic indicators in West Bengal to explain the lower sex bias in Sahajpur compared to Kuchli. They compiled data on (a) 'support in old age' from son, and from son's side (namely daughter-in-law or son's son); (b) 'work support' from adult co-inhabitants on son's side or daughter's side when the head is below 60 and also 'economically active'; (c) 'earning' power of boys and girls before they become adults.[70]

They noticed that with regard to the first criterion, the son's side provided more security in old age. But with regard to the second and third criteria, females had an edge over the males in Sahajpur. So it can be inferred that the work support and gainful activities of women in Sahajpur along with the integration of urban values would have reduced the sex bias in Sahajpur.[71]

In case of Orissa Division one did not come across systematic data on the economic benefits accruing to women due to their direct work participation, except for the proportion of women workers in certain occupations. This point has been discussed briefly in Chapter 2. It was also observed that the sex ratio of certain caste groups continued to increase till 1931. For example, the Census Commissioner J.H. Hutton reported that the sex ratio of Hari caste (manual scavenger) was 1,009 per 1,000 males and that of Brahmin was 964 in 1931. He also mentioned that the provinces such as Bihar and Orissa, Central Provinces and Madras in which females exceeded males. In all the other provinces the sex ratios were not in favour of women.[72]

Discrimination Persisted

Taking all these evidences into consideration we can say that discrimination against women and girls in India persisted throughout our period of study, especially in regard to access to food and health care. The discrimination is sharpest in the north and north-west regions of India and relatively less in the south. The degree of discrimination has become more acute in recent years. We also notice that the sex ratio in the eastern region was consistently above the all-India average for many decades, but has deteriorated over time. There is some evidence that the discrimination is partly determined by economic factors such as the female work participation rate, and partly by sociological factors and are probably shaped by the availability of resources. The above analysis no doubt took the case studies done in the twentieth century but they provided much insight to understand the situation in the nineteenth century. The Census commissioners described the situation of nineteenth and early twentieth century within their frameworks comparing the famine situations with normal conditions. Our studies point out factors whose impact is likely to aggravate during the famine periods. Studying the two periods together is important because the basic factors of discrimination such as son preference and economic security would be even more acute during the scarcity periods. In other words, it may be pointed out that women of India did not get any favourable social conditions to reduce their mortality during the famine periods.

Notes

1. *Census of India 1901*, vol. 1, pt. 1, p. 118 and *Census of India, 1911,* vol. 1, pt. 1, p. 212.
2. Ira Klein, 'When the Rains Failed: Famine Relief and Mortality in British India', *The Indian Economic and Social History Review*, 21(2), 1984, p. 190, Tim Dyson, *The Population Dynamics from the First Modern People to the Present Day.* New Delhi, Oxford University Press. 2018. Dyson writes that during the famines of 1896-7 and that of 1899-1900, out of 17 millions affected people only 4 millions got relief, p. 138.

3. Paul Greenough, *Prosperity and Misery in Modern Bengal: The Famine of 1943-44,* New York, Oxford University Press, 1982, pp. 217 and 235.
4. Janam Mukerjee 'Hungry Bengal: War, Famines, Riots and the End of Empire 1939-1946', a dissertation submitted for partial fulfilment of PhD in Michigan University, 2011, Introduction, p. 1.
5. In Orissa one comes across many social practices saying that women should not eat while cooking since it would pollute the food. Or for that matter if they eat without feeding the family members they are termed as symbol of bad luck or devoid of Goddess Lakshmi. Further the girls are taught to eat last after distributing food equally to the members of the family. Several mythological stories are available in Odia to give sanction to these practices.
6. Paul G. Greenough, 1982, op. cit., pp. 215-17.
7. Ibid., p. 246.
8. Barbara Miller has used extensive official reports and the views of the census officials from 1871 to 1901 to show that female infanticide was practiced in north and north-western region from Gujarat in the west to the eastern border of present day Uttar Pradesh. *Source:* Barbara Miller, *The Endangered Sex: Neglect of Female Children in Rural North India*, New York, Cornell University Press, 1981, pp. 48-67.
9. Amartya Sen, 'Family and Food: Sex Bias in Poverty' in Amartya Sen, *Resources, Values and Development.* Oxford, Basil Blackwell, 1984, p. 347.
10. Institute of Nutrition and Food Science, *Nutrition Survey of Rural Bangladesh, 1975-76,* Dacca, University of Dacca, 1977, quoted in A.K. Sen, 'Family and Food: Sex Bias in Poverty', p. 348. Ray Langsten, however has pointed out the existence of another nutritional study conducted in Tamil Nadu in the early 1970s. But he has not revealed the source, size of sample, method of collection. Ray Langsten, 'Determinants of High Female Mortality in South Asia: Are Data consistent with Theory?' A paper presented in a seminar of Regional Conference for Asia on 'Women and Household', New Delhi, 27-31 January 1985, pp. 13 and 44. Another systematic study on intra-family distribution of food was done in Matlab thana, Bangladesh in 1978. Lincoln Chen, 1982, 'Where Have the Women Gone?: Insights from Bangladesh on Low Sex Ratio of India's population'. *Economic and Political Weekly*, 17(10), 6 March 1982, pp. 364-72.

11. Ray Langsten, 'Determinants of High Female Mortality', p. 14. Also see, Sen, 'Family and Food', pp. 349-50.
12. Sen, p. 349.
13. R.H. Chaudhury, 'Determinants of Intra-Familial Distribution of Food and Nutrient Intake in a Rural Area of Bangladesh'. 'An Introduction to some tables', quoted in Langsten, 'Determinants of High Female Mortality', p. 14.
14. Ibid., p. 13.
15. Ibid. Also Maclachlan observes: 'an average man of Yaavahalli substantially better suited to do heavy manual labour than the average woman'. Morgan D. Maclachlan, *Why They Did Not Starve, Biocultural Adaptation in a South Indian Village*, Philadelphia, Institute for the Study of Human Issues, 1983, p. 89
16. Chen et al. have pointed out that the method of data collection in Bangladesh in general '. . . involved a standard 24 hour measurement of all pre-cooked for in household, associated concurrently with an assessment of individual food intake through volumetric measurement of post-cooked food distribution'. Chen has criticized the method on the following grounds. According to him, the containers may not be standardized. People are not literate. Besides, people sometimes eat in the bazaar and get food as payment in the employers' house, etc. Chen, 'Where Have Women', fn. 7, p. 372. Villagers also take part in community feasts where the distribution and consumption pattern would have changed. On the whole, the 24 hours measurement of food is not very suitable for observing the intra-family distribution of food in developing countries, he added. Similarly Chen observes that more than one twenty-four hour observation is necessary. While conducting the surveys the authors have done that but have not eliminated the other errors namely standardization of utensils, etc. Second, the presence of outsiders might 'change the food distribution'. But this need not be serious depending on how familiar the surveyor is with the family. Incidentally, Chen et.al. have chosen families purposefully in the sense that families should have one or more children below 5 years, and accessible to observation while eating. The families are grouped according to land distribution as well.
17. Chen, 'Where Have the Women Gone?', p. 367. Chen incidentally has used the results collected by three authors. Chen, Hoq and D'Souza, 1981. to trace the implications for India.
18. Chen, 'Where Have the Women Gone?', pp. 367-8.

19. Ibid., p. 368.
20. Ibid., p. 369.
21. Chen, 'Where Have the Women Gone?', p. 370.
22. Jocelyn Kynch and A.K. Sen, 'Indian Women: Well-being and Survival', *Cambridge Journal of Economics*, 7(3-4), 1983, p. 370.
23. Leela Gulati, 'Profile of a Female Agricultural Labaourer', *Economic and Political Weekly, Review of Agriculture*, 13(12), 25 March 1978, p. A-34.
24. Ibid., p. A-33.
25. Ibid.
26. S. Batliwala, 'Women in Poverty: Energy,Health and Nutrition Syndrome', in Devaki Jain and Nirmala Banerjee (ed.), *Tyranny of the Household: Investigative Essays on Women's Work*, New Delhi, Vikas Publishing House, 1985, pp. 44-5.
27. Sen, 'Family and Food', p. 35. Also see, R.H. Cassen, *India: Population, Economy, Society* London, Macmillan, 1978. pp. 103-4. Also see, L.C. Chen E. Hoq, S. D'Souza, 'Sex Bias in the Family Allocation of Food and Health Care in Rural Bangladesh', *Population and Development Review*, 7(1), March 1981, p. 63. Also L.C. Chen, points out '. . . absolute requirements may be an ill-defined concept, that geographic, climatic and historical variables may alter requirements. . . .' Chen also recognizes the adaptability of human beings. L.C. Chen, 'Where Have the Women Gone?: Insight from Bangladesh on Low Sex Ratio of India's Population', *Economic and Political Weekly*, 17(10), 6 March 1982, fn. 15, p. 372.
28. Sen, 'Family and Food', p. 351. Further Chen, Hoq and D'Souza, point out that adjustment done on the basis of body weight ignores the fact that females weigh less because of 'stringent adaptation to chronic calorie deficiency', Chen et al., 'Sex Bias', p. 63.
29. Narayan Chandra Nayak, Sharmita Dhar, and Pratap Kumar Mahakur, 'Education, Health and Poverty', in Pulin Nayak, Santosh K. Panda and Prasanta K. Pattnaik (eds.), *The Economy of Odisha: A Profile*, New Delhi, Oxford University Press, 2018, p. 350.
30. I remember during my childhood the nearest hospital was situated in the subdivisional head quarters. The mode of transportation was only foot or bullock cart. One person carried me all the way through to the doctor for my severe eye infection. But never again I visited him though, he was an Indian male, and my eyes were cured by using the traditional medicine but with a cost of swollen eyelids. In the nineteenth century same set of factors would be more acute.

31. Tim Dyson, *A Population History of India*, op. cit., chapter 3, pp. 142-3.
32. Miller, *The Endangered Sex*, p. 100.
33. Kumudini Dandekar, 'Why has the Proportion of Women in India's Population been Declining?', *Economic and Political Weekly*, 10(4), 18 October 1975, p. 1664.
34. Ibid.
35. Dandekar, 'Why the Proportion', pp. 1664-5.
36. Ibid., p. 1666.
37. Ibid.
38. Ibid.
39. Kynch and Sen, 'Indian Women: Well Being and Survival', p. 371.
40. J.B.Wyan and J.E. Gordon, *The Khanna Study: Population Problems in Rural Punjab*, Cambridge, Harvard University Press, 1971. This study on higher female mortality and other problems of population was based on an area of rural Punjab from the years of 1957 to 1959. The sample size of the population was 12,000. Monica Das Gupta who has studied the villages of the Khanna study also points out that the mechanism of sex discrimination is very strong through medi-care. Monica Das Gupta 'Selective Discrimination Against Female Children in Rural Punjab, India', *Population and Development Review*, 13(1), March 1987, pp. 77-96.
41. Kynch and Sen, 'Indian Women', p. 376.
42. Amartya K. Sen, 'Conflicts in Access to Food', *Mainstream*, 21(8), 1983, p. 13.
43. This survey on morbidity was conducted both for greater Calcutta and for slum areas of Calcutta for the years 1976-8. The sample consisted of 4,728 households out of 2.19 million households. Sen, 'Family and Food'. p. 360.
44. Chen et al., 'Sex Bias', pp. 64-5.
45. https://onlinelibrary.wiley.com/doi/pdf/10.1111/j.2040-0209.2013.00430.x retrieved on 13 June 2019.
46. http://rchiips.org/NFHS/NFHS-4Reports/India.pdf (retrieved on 1 August 2019).
47. Watkins and Walle have quoted C.E. Taylor, J.E. Gordon, *Interactions of Nutrition and Infection*, Geneva, 1968. On this Watkins and Walle, 'Nutrition, Mortality and Population', pp. 223. Also, Chen et al., 'Sex Bias', pp. 58-9.
48. 'The common 'Harvard Standard' is a set of weight, height and age tables derived from an American population in that they tried to

use healthy children from the study area as a reference', Cassen, *India: Population*, p. 93.

49. Ibid.
50. Sen, 'Family and Food', pp. 352-3. The UNICEF had conducted the random sample. Following the conventional standard adopted by the Indian Academy of Pediatrics, children are classified as 'normal', 'moderate', substantial' and 'severe', ibid., p. 353.
51. Ibid., p. 354.
52. A. Sen and S. Sengupta, 'Malnutrition of Rural Children and the Sex Bias', in Jain and Banerjee (ed.), *Tyranny of the Household*, p. 9.
53. Cassen, *India: Population*, pp. 93-4.
54. A. Sommer and M.S. Lowenstein, 'Nutritional Status and Mortality: A Perspective Validation of the QMAC Stick', *American Journal of Clinical Nutrition*; vol. 28, March 1975, quoted in Cassen, *India: Population*, p. 94.
55. Chen, 'Where Have Women Gone?', p. 367. Incidentally Chen along with other authors namely A.K.M.A. Chowdhury, S.L. Haffman have taken up studies which have followed up the consequences of being malnourished in the sense of higher mortality rate. Chen, Ibid., fn. 5, p. 371.
56. E. Taylor et al., 'The Narangwal Experiment and Infections-I Project Design and Effects upon Growth', *Indian Journal of Medical Research*, vol. 68 (Supplement), December 1978, pp. 1-2.
57. Ibid., pt. 11, p. 39.
58. *State of Food Security and Nutrition in the World, 2017* reported in livemint.com
59. *International Institute of Population Studies (IIPS)*, National Family Health Survey, Orissa, 2015-16
60. https://www.indiaspend.com/indias-under-5-mortality-now-matches-global-average-but-bangladesh-nepal-do-better/
61. Stephan Klasen and Claudia Wink 'Missing Women', in Bina Agarwal, Jane Humphries and Ingrid Robeyns (eds.), *Capabilities, Freedom, and Equality: Amartya Sen's Work from a Gender Perspective,* New Delhi, Oxford University Press, 2006.
62. P.K. Bardhan, 'On Life and Death Questions', *Economic & Political Weekly*, Special Number, August 1974, p. 1304.
63. Bidyut Mohanty, *Lakshmi the Rebel: Culture, Economy and Women's Agency*, New Delhi: Shakti Books-Har Anand Publications, 2019.
64. Mark R. Rosenzweig and T. Paul Schultz, 'Market Opportunities, Genetic Endowment and Intra-family Resource Distribution: Child

Survival in Rural India', *American Economic Review,* LXXII(11), September 1982, p. 814.

65. Ibid.
66. Leela Gulati, 'Female Work Participation: A Study of Inter-State Differences', *Economic and Political Weekly*, 10(1-2), 11 January 1975.
67. Ibid., p. 39.
68. Gita Sen, 'Women Agricultural Labourers in Indian Census', in K. Saradamoni (ed.), *Women Work and Society,* Calcutta, ISI, 1985, pp. 382-3.
69. Miller, *The Endangered Sex*, pp. 114-15. Bardhan also is of the same opinion as that of Miller on the low economic valuation of females and cost of marriage and points out that dowry is 'a possible compensation for the lower economic value of women not working in agriculture'. The higher amount of dowry from the propertied class may be due to the fact that women of this class participate outside work less than that of property less people. Pranab Bardhan 'Little Girls and Death in India'. He expressed this view while reviewing the book written by Barbara Miller. *Economic and Political Weekly*, 17(36), 4 September 1982, p. 1449. *Source:* Further Indira Rajaraman has observed that the replacement of the system of bride price to the system of dowry can be due to the decline in the participation of women in economic activities. She was looking at the findings of the Report of the Status of Women Committee and National Sample Surveys for this. Indira Rajaraman, 'Economics of Bride Price and Dowry', *Economic and Political Weekly*, 18(8), 19 February 1982, p. 278.
70. Amartya Sen and S. Sengupta, 'Malnutrition of Rural Children and the Sex Bias', *Economic and Political Weekly*, 18(19, 20), 21 May 1983, p. 861.
71. Ibid., p. 863.
72. http://indpaedia.com/ind/index.php/Census_India_1931:_Sex_Ratio (retrieved on 1 August 2019).

CHAPTER 9

Rise and Fall of Sex Ratio

Introduction

One notable aspect of the demographic picture of Orissa during the past century and a half needs to be highlighted. In contrast to the all India scenario, the sex ratio (SR, i.e. females per thousand males) of the Orissa Division was above unity (i.e. more females per one hundred males) and continued to increase between 1872 and 1921 (Table 9.1). The population of the Orissa Division grew at a faster rate than the rest of India in the decades 1872-81. After that the growth rate declined a bit. However, since the population totals were severely underestimated till 1881, we have focused on 1891 and the next few censuses. It was clear that the population was still recovering from the devastating impact of the famine of 1866. In the next decade (1901-11), the population of the Division grew at a low rate (Table 9.2). During this decade Orissa saw the famine of 1907-8 and high death rates for a number of years caused by droughts and floods. As a result, in the decade, 1911-21, the population of Orissa decreased by 4.6 per cent; while the population of India as a whole increased by 1.2 per cent. This decade was also marked with the famine of 1918-19 as well as high mortality years (Table 9.2). Even though, the decade 1911-21 had shown more deaths, both in India as well as Orissa Division, the forces in operation were not the same. In the case of India as a whole, the influenza epidemic had become more important and in many parts of the country famine accentuated the intensity and spread of influenza. In Orissa Division however, food shortages

TABLE 9.1: SEX RATIO OF ACTUAL POPULATION OF ORISSA DIVISION, 1891-1921

	1891	*1901*	*1911*	*1921*
Orissa	1,044	1,055	1,081	1,133
Cuttack	1,060	1,072	1,107	1,168
Balasore	1,065	1,070	1,092	1,104
Puri	991	1,007	1,020	1,089

Sources: Census of India, 1901, vol. VI, pt. 1, p. 242; *Census of India 1921*, vol. VII, pt. 1, p. 175.

TABLE 9.2: PERCENTAGE VARIATION OF POPULATION OF ORISSA DIVISION AND THAT OF INDIA BETWEEN 1872 AND 1921

	1872-81	*1881-91*	*1891-1901*	*1901-11*	*1911-21*
India	+23.1	+13.1	+2.4	+7.1	+1.2
Orissa Division	+17.6	+6.8	+7.06	+0.9	-4.6
Cuttack	+13.0	+7.9	+6.5	+2.4	-2.1
Balasore	+22.02	+5.2	+7.7	-1.7	-7.1
Puri	+15.4	+6.3	+7.6	+0.6	-7.0

Sources: For 1881-1901 (1 and 2). For 1901-21 (3 and 4); *Census of India,* 1901, vol. 1, pt. 1, p. 96; *Census of India,* 1901, vol. 6, pt. 1, p. 124; *Census of India,* 1921, vol. 1, pt. 1, p. 58; *Census of India,* 1931, vol. 1, VII, pt. 1, p. 76.

and epidemics such as cholera, malaria and dysentery and to some extent influenza as well, continued to occur for many years.

The variation of population is evident in Tables 9.1 and 9.2. The SR of Orissa Division and all the three districts separately increased during this period[1] (Table 9.2). Interestingly, the sex ratio of Orissa continued to increase with mild fluctuations till 1931 after which it continued to decline but remained above unity till 1961. It became a matter of concern when it slided below unity and continued to decline till 2001 after which there was a marginal increase (see Appendix 9-1A.). Since Orissa remained drought and flood prone even in the succeeding decades and a high rate of migration continued that explained the trend of the rise in sex ratio. The causes of decline in sex ratio after 1961 could be due to, among other things, the withdrawal of women labour from agriculture and some other production processes, strong son preference and the easy availability of ultrasound machines leading to sex-selective abortions. The marginal increase in 2011 could be explained in terms of the decline in female death rates compared to male ones. A fuller discussion of the contemporary trends cannot be undertaken here except to stress that the historical explanations still throw light on this question.

Now let us analyse the mortality trends. Keeping the factor of volatility, we tested the hypothesis that the increase in the female death rate (fdr) was lower than the increase in the male death rate (mdr) in high mortality years, including famine years, thus leading to increase in SR after the high mortality years. In order to do this we have applied two tests: (1) an indirect test based on the ratio of widows to widowers, and (2) a direct test based on measuring the statistical significance of differences of means of two death rates (male and female) in high mortality and low mortality years. In addition, we have also discussed the sex ratio of different castes to find out if the sex ratios of low castes rose higher than that of high castes since the low caste groups were affected more as we noticed before. We have first analysed the behavior of age-specific SRs before discussing the results of the tests.

Age-Specific SRs in High Mortality and Low Mortality Decades

It has been argued by different authorities that females in the adult age group 15-60 were least affected by the famines and epidemics.[2] If this were true, the age-specific SR (hereafter ASR) of this group at the end of the high mortality decade should be higher than that of the low morality decade.

We have ASRs of the census years of 1881, 1891, 1901, 1911 and 1921, but have excluded the census year of 1881, because

Orissa Division was still recovering from the terrible famine of 1866-7, and 1901 because age data in intervals of 10 years or less are not available at the divisional level.[3] Thus, we are left with one census year namely 1891 representing the end of the low mortality decade and two high mortality census years 1911 and 1921 representing the end of two high mortality decades.

Results[4]

Table 9.3 (A), (B) and (C) shows the following results: (1) ASRs in the age groups 0-1 and 60+ were lower at the end of the high mortality decade than at the end of the low mortality decade in all the three districts. (2) The ASR in the age group of 60+ fluctuated at the end of two high mortality decades except in Balasore,

TABLE 9.3 (A): CUTTACK AGE-SPECIFIC SEX RATIO 1881-1921

Age groups	*SRs by Census years*		
	1891	*1911*	*1921*
0-1	1,042	1,001	996
1-5	1,064	1,061	1,067
5-10	974	988	1,015
10-15	891	936	977
15-20	973	1,065	1,088
20-30	1,065	1,214	1,310
30-40	1,098	1,081	1,294
40-50	1,083	1,197	1,256
50-60	1,199	1,276	1,241
60+	1,675	1,539	1,597
Overall	1,060	1,107	1,168
15-40	1,055	1,117	1,167

Source: Computed from Appendix 7.1 A, B, and C. From the unpublished thesis, Bidyut Mohanty, 'Famines and Demographic Structure of Orissa Division between 1860-1921', submitted to Delhi School of Economics, University of Delhi, 1988.

TABLE 9.3 (B): BALASORE AGE-SPECIFIC SEX RATIO 1891-1921

Age groups	*SRs by Census years*				
	1881	*1891*	*1901*	*1911*	*1921*
0-1	-	1,020	-	993	980
1-5	-	1,080	-	1,053	1,057
5-10	-	972	-	995	979
10-15	-	878		913	915
15-20	-	1,008	-	1,079	1,098
20-30	-	1,054	-	1,190	1,194
30-40	-	1,095	-	1,060	1,179
40-50	-	1,145	-	1,160	1,156
50-60	-	1,197	-	1,236	1,166
60+	-	1,754	-	1,605	1,528
Overall	1,048	1,065	1,070	1,092	1,104
15-40	-	1,055	1,072	1,117	1,167

Source: Census Report of India 1921, part I, vol. 6, p. 259.

TABLE 9.3 (C): PURI AGE-SPECIFIC SEX RATIO 1891-1921

Age groups	*SRs by Census years*			
	1891	*1901*	*1911*	*1921*
0-1	1,017		1,017	991
1-5	1,082		1,079	1,094
5-10	995		1,009	1,045
10-15	889		902	951
15-20	917		1,001	1,018
20-30	991		1,073	1,221
30-40	967		955	1,153
40-50	974		1,013	1,063
50-60	999		1,080	1,061
60+	1,415		1,254	1,324
Overall	991	1,007	1,020	1,089
15-40	965	987	1,013	1,150

Source: Same as Table 9.3(B).

which showed a decline. (3) The ASR from 5-10 onwards showed an increase between the end of the low mortality decades and high mortality ones. At the end of two high mortality decades, the ASRs of 40-50 and 50-60 decreased in Balasore. Cuttack and Puri joined Balasore in the latter age group. (4) The most salient feature of the above tables is that the values of ASRs of 15-60 were higher than the ASRs of younger age groups in all the three districts in all the decades. (5) Again, the ASRs of 15-40 increased monotonically between 1891 and 1921. (In this case, we have included the results of 1901 also because of availability of data. These results support the hypothesis that the famines and epidemics did affect women in the age group of 15-60 least and as a result the ASRs of 15-60 were higher at the end of the high mortality decade (Identification of high mortality and low mortality decades have been taken up in Appendix 9.3). However, one qualification is to be made, namely, during that period the male migration also increased as discussed in Chapter 10. In spite of the possible age-specific errors, the indices clearly showed that children suffered more during the famine period. While stating this we may note that the weaknesses of age statistics have been referred to by almost all the leading demographers who have worked on vital statistics.[5]

Relative Ratio of Widows to Widowers

Given the fact that nearly all males above the age of 15-20 and all females above 13 were married,[6] the ratio of widows to widowers should throw light on the relative death rates, other things being equal. Thus, if the increase in fdr (female death rate) is lower than the increase in the mdr (male death rate) during a high mortality year, the proportion of widows to widowers should rise, keeping other things equal. But other things were not.

(a) One complication is remarriage. If many men were unmarried before the high mortality year and large numbers of widows remarried after that year then sex-selective mortality need not lead to a rise in the ratio of widows to widowers. It is true that in many of the lower castes (and these were the most affected by the forces of high morality), widow remarriage was permitted but there was not such a stock of bachelors (note that in Orissa the SR was above unity and went on increasing. In other words, there was no scarcity of women). Hence we can ignore this factor.

(b) Another major factor was that the male outmigration from Orissa rose sharply during years of high mortality. Many of these men died in the place to which they migrated, which would be an additional factor leading to the rise in the ratio of widows to widowers (unless no widowers migrated). Unfortunately, the effects of these two factors cannot be separated, but some idea of their relative strength is given by the fact that 18 per cent of the total male population were enumerated outside Cuttack in 1921. The recorded death rate rose to 62 per thousand in 1919 in Cuttack. Thus, if high mortality years were marked by both a lower death rate for women and outmigration by men, we would expect to find a marked rise in the proportion of widows to widowers. But if the former is not true, the net effect would depend on the relative strength of these two factors.

We have calculated the ratio of widows to widowers in each of the three districts in different age groups (Table 9.4). However, no clear picture emerges. In the age groups above 20, there are both rises and falls, but generally not of a large order. The only change is in the age group 15-20, where there is a sharp rise in the ratio between 1891 and 1921, in Cuttack and Balasore. There are at least two possible explanations for this. First, a larger proportion of girls in this group were married, since women married younger. Second, larger numbers of men in this group out-migrated. Finally, the age-specific death rate of female was higher than that of males in the age group of 15-20, though it would have become bit lower in a high mortality year.[7]

Given the fact that there was out-migration in the older age groups too, the high fluctuation in the ratio in the age group of 15-20 could perhaps be explained in terms of sex differential mortality, though the decreased ratio of Puri poses some problems.

TABLE 9.4: RATIO OF WIDOWS TO WIDOWERS IN HIGH MORALITY DECADES AND LOW MORTALITY DECADES IN CUTTACK, BALASORE AND PURI

Census years/ Districts	*Age Groups*				
	15-20	*20-40*	*40-60*	*60 & above*	*Total*
Cuttack					
1881	6.1	5.6	8.8	6.9	7.3
1891	11.0	6.6	6.6	6.0	6.5
1901	15.3	7.0	6.5	5.5	6.4
1911	19.4	7.5	6.6	4.7	6.1
1921	24.0	7.8	6.7	4.8	6.4
Balasore					
1881	6.2	6.5	8.5	6.6	7.3
1891	10.4	7.5	6.6	6.1	6.7
1901	14.7	8.1	6.9	5.3	6.8
1911	13.5	7.0	6.1	4.6	6.0
1921	18.0	6.9	5.6	4.2	5.8
Puri					
1881	5.7	3.6	6.2	5.5	5.3
1891	9.8	4.1	4.9	4.8	4.7
1901	11.9	5.0	5.2	4.3	4.9
1911	16.5	4.9	5.2	3.8	4.7
1921	9.0	5.5	5.0	3.6	4.8

Sources: Census of India 1881, vol. II, pp. 70-1; *Census of India 1891*, vol. IV, pt. A; *Census of India 1901*, vol. VIA, pt. II, pp. 47-8; *Census of India 1911*, vol. V, pt. III, pp. 34-5; *Census of India 1921*, vol. VII, pt. II, pp. 36-8.

T Tests

In Appendix 9.3 (A, B, C) tables give numbers of the male death rate and female death rate of high mortality years and low mortality years. In Appendix 9.2 we have discussed the criteria for choosing high and low mortality years. It is remarkable that, in spite of the under-enumeration of the female deaths, both mdr and fdr moved in the same direction in high mortality and low mortality years (see Appendix 9.1 of this chapter).

To find out whether the means of the difference of mdr and fdr in high and low mortality years were different from each other in a statistically significant way or not we applied 't' tests, since our study period of 40 years came under the category of small sample.[8] The theoretical value of 't' is 1.68; if the calculated 't' value exceeds this value then the differences will be statistically significant. Strictly speaking, the 't' test is applied to data taken from a random sample. If it is applied to time series data the 't' test is likely to overstate the statistical significance of the tested difference.

In order to conduct the 't' test, we have formulated the hypotheses for three districts separately, taking the recorded death rate into account (Appendix 9. 3A, B, C):

H_0: mdr 1m - fdr 1m = mdr hm - fdr hm

H_1: mdr hm - fdr hm > mdr 1m - fdr 1m

In other words, we are assuming that the differences between two recorded death rates (males and females) were equal in low mortality and high mortality years. If the calculated 't' values of means of differences becomes higher than the theoretical values of 't' then we accept the alternative hypothesis based on observations that the differences between the rates increased in high mortality years compared to low mortality years

where mdr = male death rate
fdr = female death rate
lm = low mortality years
hm = high mortality years.

When we conducted the 't' tests for three districts separately it is noticed that the 't' values are statistically significant in all the three districts. For Cuttack, the value was 2.56, for Balasore 4.23 and for Puri it was 3.005. Thus on the face of it, it seems that the difference between two rates increased in high mortality years compared to low morality years.

Before we speculate on plausible explanations for the observed differences we would like to repeat a comment on the weakness of the registration data especially in high morality years. It is a well-known fact that female deaths were more under-enumerated than male deaths even in non-famine years. If we further assume (and it was plausible) that the female deaths were under-enumerated in a much greater degree than make deaths in high mortality years, this will vitiate our results in that the excess of mdr over fdr will be exaggerated. It is not possible to estimate the importance of this factor at this point of time.

The Census Commissioners Risley and Gait had enumerated the biological and sociological factors to explain the lower death rates for the females compared to male death rates in the context of India. We have already seen in Chapters 7 and 8 that females were not more resistant to infection due to epidemics than males, nor were they favoured sociologically during the famine periods. Here we will discuss other biological factors such as the fall in conception rate. It is based on recorded birth statistics of Cuttack, Balasore and Puri.

Conception Rate

This rate can be defined as the number of women at the stage of conception per thousand of married women in child-bearing age groups. As mentioned above, the conception rate fell during the high mortality years. Hence, increase in fdr was lower than the increase in mdr. An attempt has been made here to test this proposition using imperfect data on annual number of births. Up to 1892, the birth statistics were incomplete, as shown by the very low figures. After that year the coverage improved. However, throughout the period, death statistics were better than birth statistics. Even though birth statistics were defective they may have reflected short-run fluctuations. We have used estimated population totals to calculate the recorded birth rates annually for three districts separately from 1894 to 1921 (Tables 9.5 A, B, C).

We have two types of situations. In the last decade of the nineteenth century we have two high mortality years, one in 1896-7 and another in 1900. In the early years of twentieth century, we have several high mortality years with the highest number of such years in the decade 1911-21.

Table 9.5 A: Cuttack – Total Birth Rates in Low Mortality and High Mortality Years between 1894 and 1921

Year	*Total Population*	*Total Births*	*Birth Rates*
1894	1,974,360	60,660	30.7
1895	1,986,744	58.350	29.4
1896	1,999,208	84,052	42.0
1897	2,011,750	83,740	41.6
1898	2,024,371	71,230	35.2
1899	2,037,071	96,269	47.3
1900	2,049,853	83,440	40.7*
1901	2,062,758	77,097	37.4*
1902	2,067,526	77,638	37.6
1903	2,072,310	90,067	43.5
1904	2,077,109	89,283	43.0
1905	2,081,924	97,899	47.0
1906	2,086,755	90,607	43.4
1907	2,091,602	87,939	42.0*
1908	2,096,464	74,786	35.7*
1909	2,101,342	66,746	31.8
1910	2,106,237	94,265	44.8
1911	2,109,139	91,170	43.2
1912	–	–	–
1913	2,100,054	92,509	44.1
1914	2,095,544	96,669	46.1
1915	2,091,069	82,784	39.6*
1916	2,086,613	75,642	36.3
1917	2,082,180	84,841	40.7
1918	2,077,773	75,419	36.3*
1919	2,073,390	69,684	33.6*
1920	2,069,031	66,709	32.2*
1921	2,064,678	69,025	33.4

Note: * High mortality years.

Source: Sanitary Commission Reports for respective years.

TABLE 9.5 B: BALASORE – TOTAL BIRTH RATES IN LOW MORTALITY AND HIGH MORTALITY YEARS BETWEEN 1894 AND 1921

Year	*Total Population*	*Total Births*	*Birth Rates*
1894	1,017,012	32.458	31.9
1895	1,024,585	37.103	36.2
1896	1,032,216	34,856	33.8
1897	1,039,903	43,420	41.8
1898	1,047,648	36,267	34.6
1899	1,055,450	45,783	43.4
1900	1,063,309	40,175	37.8
1901	1,071,197	41,119	38.4
1902	1,069,618	41,604	38.9
1903	1,068,042	43,101	40.4
1904	1,066,470	40,314	37.8
1905	1,064,901	42,771	40.2
1906	1,063,335	41,907	38.5*
1907	1,061,773	42,037	39.6*
1908	1,060,215	36,080	34.0*
1909	1,058,659	34,634	32.7
1910	1,057,108	44,209	41.8
1911	1,055,568	40,570	38.4
1912	–	–	–
1913	1,039,906	40,628	39.1
1914	1,038,460	42,467	41.1
1915	1,024,871	39,312	38.4*
1916	1,017,337	28,937	28.4*
1917	1,009,860	35,769	35.4
1918	1,002,438	34,986	34.9*
1919	995,071	32,919	33.1*
1920	987,758	30,045	30.4*
1921	980,504	28,804	29.4*

Note: * High mortality years.

Source: Sanitary Commission Reports for respective years.

Table 9.5 C: Puri – Total Birth Rates in Low Mortality and High Mortality Years between 1894 and 1921

Year	*Total Population*	*Total Births*	*Birth Rates*
1894	966,124	28,655	29.7
1895	973,273	31,401	32.3
1896	990,474	34,378	35.1
1897	987,729	35,908	36.4*
1898	995,045	30,911	31.1
1899	1,002,402	40,816	40.7
1900	1,009,822	37,642	37.3
1901	1,017,284	30,085	29.6*
1902	1,017,892	32,144	31.6
1903	1,018,500	39,243	38.5
1904	1,019,109	39,559	38.8
1905	1,019,720	41,054	40.3
1906	1,020,330	41,176	40.4
1907	1,020,941	37,605	36.8*
1908	1,021,554	36,160	35.3*
1909	1,022,167	33,354	32.6
1910	1,022,781	41,025	40.1
1911	1,023,402	41,033	40.1
1912	–	–	–
1913	1,013,844	40,198	39.6
1914	1,005,760	43,802	43.6
1915	9,998,447	39,462	39.5
1916	991,198	36,190	36.5
1917	984,012	34,747	35.3*
1918	976,890	26,178	26.8*
1919	969,828	33,729	34.8*
1920	962,828	26,495	27.5*
1921	951,651	30,444	32.0

Source: Sanitary Commission Reports for respective years.

The above tables show the following:

(i) The recorded birth rate fell in all high morality years except in one year 1897, when a famine was declared in Puri. In 1897, it rose slightly.

(ii) In some cases the birth rate fell more sharply a year after the famine as in the case of Puri in 1898. The fall in recorded birth rate was also higher in 1909 than that of 1908 in all the three districts. A similar pattern was also noticed in the years 1915 and 1916 in Cuttack district. The year 1915 was a high mortality year.

(iii) The birth rate continued to remain depressed throughout the high mortality years in the decade 1911-21. The fall in recorded birth rate, however, could not be equivalent to a fall in the conception rate in the same year for two reasons. First, the impact of low nutrition would increase the number of still-births.[9] It might also have led to abortions. Second, the impact of low nutrition on conception will be visible through births only after 9 months or more.

(iv) The percentage of fever deaths to total deaths was sometimes higher just after the famine year. This was true of Puri in 1898 and was also true of all the other three districts in 1909 (Appendix 9.3A at the end of the chapter). Since fever, generally malaria, was particularly fatal to young and pregnant women, the proportion of female deaths to male deaths due to fever increased in those years, thus reducing birth rate at least partially. However, in years where the fall in the birth rate was very high or continued to be depressed there probably was a real fall in the conception rate as well.

Caste and Sex Ratio

Comparison of changes of SRs of different castes can be made to test the hypothesis that the increase in fdr was lower than the mdr in high mortality years, which may be related to caste behaviour. Since we do not have the death figures for different castes, we have adopted an indirect method to establish the above hypothesis. If the hypothesis: that increase in female death rate was lower than male death rate was valid, then the increase in SRs of lower castes would be higher than the increase in SRs of higher castes in the high mortality decades compared to low mortality decades. In other words, the decrease in SR of lower castes would be lower than that of high castes, keeping other things constant.

This is based on two assumptions: (i) Famine hits hard the lower castes (belonging to the lower classes) compared to higher castes (belonging to higher classes). In other words, both fdr and mdr increased for lower castes to a greater extent in famine years than that of the higher castes. (ii) There were no differences in the degree of discrimination against females between castes.

The first assumption is realistic. Not much research has been done on the second assumption except in reference to the Ramdasia girls and Sahajpur Scheduled Caste girls.[10] There was no data on agricultural labourers, marginal *raiyats* and landholding class. So we have used caste data as proxy for class. Altogether we have considered eight castes. Out of these, three dalit castes, Bauri, Kandara and Pan – have been categorized as agricultural labouring class. Tanti is the caste of weavers. Along with the other labouring castes, Tantis also suffered a lot. Chasa caste has been taken as marginal *raiyats*; Karans, Brahmins and Khandayats could be classified under landholding castes.

We have two types of rates of change of SRs. One represents a low mortality decade. Another represents the high mortality decades. Our objective is to see whether the SRs of Bauri, Pan, Kandara, Tanti and Chasa grew faster than that of the other castes in high mortality decades compared to low mortality decades.

Tables 9.6 (A, B, C) show that the SRs of the lower castes did rise faster than the SRs of the higher castes in Cuttack. The SRs of Tanti and Chasa also rose fast like that of the other lower castes, at least for one high mortality decade. The SR of Khandayats increased most in the high mortality decade 1911-21. In Puri again, it was true of the high mortality decade 1901-11 for the lower castes and marginal *raiyats* but not for Tantis. In the next decade, the SR of one of the lower castes did not rise faster than that of some of the landholding castes. The SRs of Tanti and Chasa castes did behave predictably. Thus the hypothesis that the increase in fdr was lower than the increase in mdr is not established in all cases, but some. Migration also played a role in the increase of sex ratio since members of high castes did migrate to Calcutta as we will see in the Chapter 10.

TABLE 9.6 (A): CUTTACK – CASTE AND SEX RATIO 1891-1921

	1891	*1901*	*1911*	*1921*
Bauri	1,036	1,059 (1.9)	1,102 (3.8)	1,202 (9.1)
Kandara	1,007	1,041 (3.0)	1,096 (5.8)	1,171 (6.4)
Pan	1,029	1,032 (–)	1,078 (4.9)	1,145 (6.5)
Tanti	985	1,039 (5.1)	1,047 (1.0)	1,154 (9.5)
Chasa	1,035	1,025 (-1.0)	1,055 (2.9)	1,109 (4.7)
Khandayats	1,077	1,083 (–)	1,121 (3.7)	1,176 (5.4)
Karan	1,222	1,239 (1.6)	1,252 (0.8)	1,326 (6.4)
Brahmin	1,054	1,065 (1.9)	1,089 (1.9)	111 (2.8)

Note: Figures in parenthesis are percentage rates of change over from the previous SR.

Sources: Census of India 1891 vol. 5, pp. 94-7; *Census of India 1901,* vol. 6A, pt. II, pp. 192-266; *Census of India 1911*, vol. 5, pt. III, pp. 95-129; *Census of India 1921*, vol. 7, pt. II, pp. 94-104.

TABLE 9.6 (B): BALASORE – CASTE AND SEX RATIO 1891-1921

	1891	*1901*	*1911*	*1921*
Kandara	1,026	1,055 (2.9)	1,072 (0.9)	1,064 (-0.9)
Pan	1,092	1,090 (–)	1,129 (3.7)	1,151 (1.8)

Tanti	1,053	1,042 (-1.0)	1,092 (4.8)	1,116 (2.8)
Chasa	1,077	1,027 (-4.6)	1,084 (4.9)	1,118 (3.7)
Khandayats	1,095	1,113 (0.9)	1,139 (2.7)	1,177 (3.5)
Karan	1,003	1,036 (4.0)	1,059 (1.9)	1,070 (0.9)
Brahmin	1,048	1,046 (–)	1,076 (2.9)	1,057 (-1.9)

Note: We have left out of the labouring caste Bauris of Balasore because the number was small – only 400 or so.

Source: As above.

TABLE 9.6 (C): PURI – CASTE AND SEX RATIO 1891-1921

	1891	*1901*	*1911*	*1921*
Bauri	985	979 (-1.0)	1,032 (5.1)	1,086 (5.8)
Kandara	931	925 (--)	958 (3.2)	1,016 (6.3)
Pan	967	960 (-1.03)	1,003 (4.2)	1,010 (1.0)
Tanti	990	1,121 (13.0)	994 (-11.6)	1,110 (12.0)
Chasa	996	1,010 (1.0)	1,033 (2.0)	1,114 (7.8)
Khandayats	909	969 (6.6)	970 (–)	1,054 (8.2)
Karan	1,012	1,035 (3.0)	1,022 (1.9)	1,076 (5.9)
Brahmin	1042	1049 (1.0)	1039 (-1.0)	1078 (3.8)

Source: As above.

Social Factors

In Chapter 8 we have discussed the social factors having a pan-Indian character. But in this chapter we are taking up those aspects which are perhaps peculiar to Orissa. The social factors may provide some meaning to the demographic data.

Orissa's value system has been a combination of pan-Indian values, which discriminate against women and indigenous values that are relatively less anti-women, partly because of the Bhakti tradition.[11] Case of female infanticide did occur in Orissa Division but only among a few communities such as the Kandha tribe,[12] which constituted a small fraction of the total population of Orissa Division. There were occurrences of 'Sati' occasionally in different parts of Orissa among high castes and chieftains[13] but chieftains were relatively few. The high castes did not allow their widows to remarry, but widow remarriage was prevalent among the lower castes. The female children were neglected no doubt but they got better treatment than their sisters in north India. Yet on the whole, the strong preference for sons was reflected in intra-family distribution of food and better medical treatment of boys in normal years. Though widows were not treated like sisters as in Bengal because of reform movements, they were not treated well. For example they were not invited to auspicious occasions such as weddings. Widows were considered as ill omen if a calamity occurred in the family. They were also blamed if their husbands died before them.[14]

Differential Access to Food

Precise data are not available for intra-family distribution of food, but some light is thrown on this problem in the literary writings. For example, the freedom fighter and poet Godabarish Misra (1866-1956) wrote in his autobiography that women were discriminated against in food distribution.

When our cow is milching I drink that milk; only father and I eat rice, whereas my mother and grandmother satisfy their hunger by drinking *peja* (the hot liquid separated from boiled rice) and *mandia jau* (cooked ground *ragi*). Only on festive occasions do they have a taste of rice. Poor households cannot afford to keep servants. The members of the family share the household work among themselves and likewise who is to eat what automatically gets decided. It is difficult to comprehend how the family tradition is maintained through this kind of management.[15]

This would be true of the higher castes.

There is no evidence on intra-family distribution of food among the lower castes. Since the son is considered to be a support in old age, one might infer that girls would be discriminated against in terms of intra-family distribution of food.

We do not have any data regarding food crises, but there were three incidents relating to three different famines, the famines of 1866, 1918 and 1920, which reveal strong son preference. The grandmother of the poet Mansingh, who was newly married during the famine of 1866, narrated the first incident.[16] We have discussed this in the earlier chapters. Here we recall from that account that the men and not the women sold their assets. (In contrast, in discussing social factors, Risley and Gait were of the opinion that women could sell the household assets to buy food for their own use).[17]

In another incident of intra-family distribution of food, in 1918, Puri faced famine, and Upendra Tripathy (a twentieth-century writer) used to stay with his grandmother. His grandmother fed him first and she used to eat later. Sometimes she used to drink only water in which the cooked rice was soaked.[18]

In the third incident relating to the famine of 1920 in Puri, it was revealed that women and girls were deprived of food. In this case there were no family assets to fall back upon. Gopabandhu Das (an eminent freedom fighter of Orissa) narrated an account in which he says that a Brahmin had received some relief rice which was not adequate for his family of four; father, mother, son and daughter. So he cooked the rice in his client's place, and both father and son ate. The rest of the family had nothing to eat. So they ate wild substitutes which proved toxic and they died after a few days.[19]

Differential Access to Medical Treatment

Here too information is not available except on the numbers of out-patients treated in various charitable hospitals in three districts for two years, 1912 and 1913 in Public Health Reports of Bihar and Orissa. Data for other years are not available. Table 9.7 shows that ratios of females per thousand male were consistently low in all the districts, though the ratios for children were somewhat better in 1913. Even though the sample is very small, and only for two years and based on urban areas, it is suggestive. The SR of outdoor patients is higher for children in all the districts and for all the years than that of the adult groups.[20] This finding is in line with the findings of Sen and Chen that more men and boys went to hospitals than women and girls. But the sex ratio of children is higher than the sex ratio of adults; this is different from the Bombay hospital admission pattern observed by Sen and cited in Chapter 8.

Thus, taking two indicators, namely, access to food and medical treatment, it is observed that girl children are discriminated against but the level of discrimination is perhaps lower than that

TABLE 9.7: TOTAL OUTDOOR PATIENTS AND SR TREATED IN CHARITABLE DISPENSARIES IN 1912-13

	1912			*1913*		
	Cuttack	*Balasore*	*Puri*	*Cuttack*	*Balasore*	*Puri*
Men	97,049	63,300	93,539	90,062	72,591	1,00,287
Women	20,141	14,038	18,205	19,625	15,094	17,618
Females per 1,000 males	208	222	195	218	208	176
Male child	18,556	10,263	17,556	18,724	12,292	15,172
Female child	10,817	5,795	9,552	11,279	7,152	9,569
Females per 1,000 males	583	565	544	636	582	631

Source: Monthly Proceedings of Municipal Department of Bihar and Orissa, September 1914.

against north Indian women, though females were discriminated against in crisis situations.

Economic Role and Discriminations against Women

As shown earlier in Chapter 8, Leela Gulati has tried to test Bardhan's hypothesis that paddy cultivation requires more female labour so female children are less discriminated against in Eastern India. Leela Gulati noticed that the participation rate of women in agriculture was one of the lowest in West Bengal and Orissa, even though paddy constituted a significant percentage of area under cultivation in 1971. However, not only the cropping pattern, but also related activities like grain trade, husking and selling of grain products (participation rate in food industry), etc. should also be included. The participation rates along castes lines (to show traditional occupations) should also be considered. For instance, a woman of the Gaur caste (pastoral caste) may not work as an agricultural labourer, but she is economically active because she manufactures and sells milk products to the villagers. She must be engaged in feeding the cow and looking after the small calves. Similarly, for women from fishing castes who not only collected fish but also sold the same. They were also engaged in curating the fish. Again, a woman from the cultivating caste with a few acres of land, may not be able to work in the field openly but she would participate in grain trade[21] and in paddy husking as well. If the farmer was from the poorer class, then she would also participate in the other cultivating activities. Percentages of women to total workers in particular occupational categories have been computed for 1911 and 1921 in cases of Orissa Division and Madras Presidency, where the female participation rate was high, and was also the case for all India.

Table 9.8 gives the proportion of workers to total workers in the categories of the total workers in field and farm workers, food industries, trade in other foodstuff and trade in fuel. While the percentage share of the females to males for all workers field and farm servants in Orissa Division was less than for all-India and the

TABLE 9.8: PROPORTION OF FEMALE WORKERS TO TOTAL WORKERS IN CERTAIN OCCUPATIONAL CATEGORIES IN 1911 AND 1921 IN ORISSA DIVISION, MADRAS PRESIDENCY AND INDIA, BRITISH TERRITORY

	India		*Madras*		*Orissa*	
	1911	*1921*	*1911*	*1921*	*1911*	*1921*
Field and Farm Servants	49.0	46.0	54.0	55.0	33.0	37.0
Food Industry	62.0	56.0	47.0	33.0	87.0	85.0
Other Trade in Food Stuff	37.0	35.0	41.0	38.0	60.0	58.0
Trade in Fuel	64.0	57.0	57.0	51.0	96.0	87.0

Sources: Census of India 1911, vol. I, pt. II, pp. 260-2; *Census of India 1911*, vol. I, pt. II, pp. 200-209; *Census of India 1911*, vol. 12, pt. II, pp. 126-37; *Census of India 1911*, vol. 13, pt. II, pp. 140-236; *Census of India 1911*, vol. 5, pt. III, pp. 150-201; *Census of India 1921*, vol. 2, pt. II, pp. 130-86.

Madras Presidency, but for the other categories the proportion is much higher in Orissa. And in paddy husking (included in food industries) almost all the workers were females in Orissa Division.

Thus the economic value of female in the Orissa Division was relatively higher than shown by the work participation rate in farm labour alone along the Census line. The 'willingness' of females to participate in such economic activities was determined by the level of poverty which drove Oriya males to seek jobs in Calcutta and Assam. In 1891 the Bengal Census Superintendent wrote that the women of Orissa were not considered as burdens since they were economically active.[22] Similarly, in 1911 also, the Census Superintendent of Bengal wrote that in Bengal as a whole there were 36 workers to 64 dependents, but in Bihar and Orissa the ratio was 48 : 62. Again, he observed that there was one female worker to every two male workers in Orissa. The causes for the disparities between Bengal on the one hand and Bihar and Orissa on the other according to him were: (a) Bengal was a richer province than Bihar or Orissa, (b) the proportion of Muslims is higher in Bengal than in Bihar and Orissa, and (c) the proportion of low castes and tribals is much higher in Bihar and Orissa.[23] The women of low castes were more willing to work than the women of higher castes because they did not have cultural taboos against work. However, it should be noted that the women of low castes of Orissa did not come to public works during the famine of 1907-8, so the Bengal famine code of 1905 was amended to allow gratuitous relief to dependents in later famines, while men were engaged in test relief work.[24] In India, the deficit of females, especially after 1901 was very probably due to sex differential mortality and this in truth reflected discrimination in access to food and medical treatment, etc.

Orissa partly shared the all-India culture and the preference for sons was probably reflected in the intra-family distribution of food and medical treatment. Yet the economic value of the women of Orissa was not as low as that of north Indian women. The women of Orissa participated in gainful activities like activities allied to rice cultivation because of poor economic conditions and also because of out-migration of the menfolk. There may also have been cultural reasons for the relatively less inferior position of women in Orissa as compared to north India, and these factors must be borne in mind in considering trends in the SR in Orissa. As we have mentioned above the sex ratio continued to increase till 1961 after which it started to decline (see Appendix 9.2).

Rise in Sex Ratio Explained

In conclusion, the various direct and indirect tests set out above, support the hypothesis that the increase in the SR at the end of the high mortality decade was partly due to a lower increase in the female death rate compared to the increase in male death rate. But it is important to note that the increase in male death rate is not due to infectious diseases given the equal exposure to the diseases by females and males. The increase in death rate of males could be due to greater exposure to the epidemics because of their economic role which made them wandering aimlessly during the famine period (see Tables and Graphs 9.2 to 9.6 in Appendix to this chapter).

Notes

1. It was argued by Risley and Gait in 1901 that because of biological and social factors women died less than the men. It was already discussed in the Chapters 7 and 8. Both Sen and Greenough have differed from them. We have discussed at length at the relevant places.
2. Greenough, op. cit., 1982, Chapter 8.
3. Those groups were available for Bengal Presidency as a whole, but we cannot use the population of Bengal Presidency to get the age-specific population of Orissa Division at small intervals because Orissa Division was more migration prone than Bengal Presidency as a whole. We also lack age data in 10 years or less in 1911. But we have derived such data from the provincial population because both Bihar Divisions and Orissa Division were migration prone.
4. In this chapter we have discussed each district separately.
5. K. Davis, *Population of India and Pakistan,* New York, Russell, 1969. pp. 26-7. Also Asok Mitra, *India's Population: Aspects of Quality Control,* vols. 1 and 2, Delhi, Abhinav Publications, 1978. p 371. These demographers as well as others have discussed age-specific errors of the census data on deaths and births.
6. *Census of India 1891*, vol. 3, pp. 181 and 185.
7. We have data on age-specific recorded deaths and population for 1921, which was a high mortality year (famine year) in Balasore. The ratio of age-specific death rates in the age group of 15-20 was above unity 1.050. It was of course a bit lower than the ratio of the corresponding age group (1.136) in another census year 1911, which was not a high mortality year.
8. We could not conduct 't' tests on death ratios of high mortality and low mortality years because female population was greater than male population and high mortality years generated considerable sex selective mobility.
9. Zena Stein, Mervyn Susser Gerhart Saenger and Francis Marolla, *Famine and Human Development: The Dutch Hunger, Winter of 1944-45,* New York, Oxford University Press, 1975, p. 224. Also see, Michelle B. McAlpine, *Subject to Famine : Food Crisis and Economic Change in Western India 1860-1920,* Princeton, N.J. Princeton University Press, 1983 p. 72.
10. Discussed in Chapter 8.

11. Another indigenous institution probably of limited relevance in this context is the institution of *devadasis* in the Puri temple. See, F.A. Marglin, *Wives of the God-King: The Rituals of the Devadasis of Puri*, Delhi, Oxford University Press, 1985. pp. 1-349.
12. *Census of India 1911,* vol. 5, pt. 1, p. 548.
13. Instances of *sati* in Orissa and India:

Years	*Cases in British India*	*Cases in Orissa*
1815	378	8
1816	442	9
1817	707	14
1818	832	14

P. Mukerjee has quoted these figures from G. Toynbee, *A Sketch of History of Orissa 1803-1828*, pt. III, p. 70. P. Mukherjee, *History of Orissa in the Nineteenth Century,* Cuttack, Utkal University Press, 1964. pp. 499-511.

14. Fakir Mohan Senapati had described how a newly married bride was held responsible for destruction of a house by fire by the villagers. Senapati, *Chhaman Athaguntha, in Fakir Mohan Granthabali* (Oriya) pt. 1 and 2, Cuttack, Cuttack Student Store, 1963, p. 109.
15. Godbarish Mishra, *Godabarish Granthabnali*, vol. 1, Cuttack, Students Store, 1961, rpt. 1975, p. 17; Oriya writings are translated by us. He also wrote that 'even though the society needs both boys and girls, especially boys get better treatment than girls', ibid., p. 19. Since he was a reformer, he had written many short stories depicting various social evils such as widowhood, infant marriage and dowry in which women were affected.
16. Mayadhar Mansingh, *Durbhikshya* (Oriya), Cuttack, Cuttack Student Store, 1955, p. 1.
17. Please refer to Chapters 7 and 8 in relevant places.
18. Upendra Tripathy, *Pundit Upendra Granthabali: An Autobiography 1903-1969,* Cuttack, J. Mohapatra & Co., 1969, p. 19.
19. Gopabandhu Das, *Gopbandhu Rachnabali: Orissare Banya O' Durbhiksya*, pt. II, Cuttack, Gopabandhu Bhavan, 1977, pp. 14-15.
20. In order to know whether the urban area of Orissa Division contained disproportionately more males, the sex ratios of Cuttack, Balasore and Puri town have been calculated based on the population of 1911. The sex ratios were 843 for Cuttack; 903 for Balasore and 733 for Puri. *Census of India 1911*, vol. 5, pt. III, p. 14.

21. Tallents, the Census Superintendent of Bihar and Orissa Census Report 1921 – wrote extensively on the grain trade in Bihar and Orissa and how women were actively participating in the grain trade '. . . and in Orissa, where there is a superstitious dread of selling crops from the threshing floor, they are sold either at the market or at the golas described below. In Sambalpur the first hands through which the crops pass after leaving the cultivators are those of a class of women called *kochnis*, whose profession is to collect and clean the grain before bringing it to small dealers.' *Census of India, 1921*, vol. 7, pt. I, p. 266. Also see *District Gazetteer of Balasore, 1907*, p. 141. Also see, *Banking Enquiry Committee Report 1929-30*, Bihar and Orissa, vol. 3, p. 90.
22. *Census of Bengal, 1891*, vol. 3, p. 319.
23. *Census of India 1911*, vol. 5, pt. 1, p. 548.
24. GOI/Rev/Agri/FP, July 1911, no. 1899 T-R; From the Secy. To the Government of Bengal to the Secy. To the Government of India, Rev/Agri, dt. 4 October 1910.

APPENDIX 9.1

A Note on the Method of Identification of High Mortality Years

To identify high mortality years, we have taken those years when the recorded male death rate was 40 per thousand. The rate of 40 per thousand was chosen by scrutinizing the recorded death rates of the famines of 1896-7, 1899-1900 and 1907-8. In 1896-7, in three cases, namely Bombay, Madras and United Provinces, the male death rates were 41, 28 and 45 per thousand respectively. All of the major provinces, which suffered from the famine of 1899-1900 had recorded death rates above 42 per thousand. The reported male death rate of United Provinces in 1908 when the famine was declared officially, was only 26 per thousand; but this is not typical. Generally, the death rates exceed 40 per thousand in famine years, so we have adopted the rate of 40 per thousand to identify our high mortality years.

In order to identify high mortality years in census period for Orissa Division first we identified calendar years in which male death rate touched 40 according to registration statistics. The rate has been calculated by assuming a steady compound rate of growth of population. This assumption is superior to the stationary population total which did not capture any change of population inter-census period at all. The steady compound rate of growth on the other hand does not capture yearly fluctuations. In order to gauge the extent of such bias we tried to estimate annual death rate from annual population totals based on defective registration statistics (births and deaths ignoring migration). It is encouraging to find that there is no significant difference between the death rate calculated through the former method as well as the latter method. In other words, the years which had recorded death rate as 40 through the former method remained so in the latter method also.

The rationale for considering only male recorded deaths is that female deaths were under-enumerated.

Under this criterion we found the following years in which male death rate had touched 40 (see Appendix Table 9.3 A, B, C).

(1) Cuttack : 1889, 1892, 1900, 1901, 1907, 1908, 1915, 1918, 1919 and 1920.

(2) Balasore : 1889, 1892,1906, 1907, 1908, 1915, 1916, 1918, 1919, 1920, 1921.

(3) Puri : 1889, 1892, 1897, 1901, 1907, 1908, 1917, 1918, 1919, 1920.

Then we checked the Administration Reports, Settlement Reports, Famine Proceedings, Census Reports, Sanitary Commission Reports and Land Revenue Administration Reports to find out whether any mention has been made regarding the above years as high mortality years due to food shortage or otherwise. There we found that the following agricultural years: 1888-9, 1891-2, 1896-7, 1900-1, 1907-8 and 1918-19 have been mentioned as having crop failures in all the three districts except Balasore in 1900-1901. For the period of 1891-2 to 1900, we also checked the Agricultural Statistics of India.[1] The area under rice was given district-wise and condition factors were given in the General Administration Reports. But there are some problems regarding the data. The area under different rice (early, winter and spring) was not given separately. The standard yield of different kinds of rice was also not given.[2] But the standard yield in terms of irrigated and non-irrigated land was given, though the area under rice was not given in that manner as we have referred to earlier. Of course, the area under canal irrigation was given in the Annual Administration Reports but not from other sources. The standard yield was also given in terms of broadcast and transplant yield though area of classification was not done likewise. In this case, however, Maddox pointed out that there was not much difference between two types of yields.[3] Beset with all these problems we decided not to depend on the agricultural statistics but on the above sources to find out whether the crops had failed or not. After 1901 things were a little better. The annual Season and Crop Reports of Bengal and Bihar and Orissa gave the total yield of rice in tons except from 1905-6 to 1910-11. One of the flaws of this series is that the area under spring rice was not given except for one or two years. But the area under spring rice was not significant, as we have seen in Chapter 2. Second, both autumn rice and spring rice are varieties of coarse rice. Those varieties were considered to be indigestible. Moreover, new rice was considered to be impure. So the people of high castes did not use it. Besides, both the varieties of rice produced diarrhea.[4]

Since output series has been constructed for 1901-2 to 1920-1, by taking the Season and Crop Reports, we have used that series and have measured the shortfall by taking the quinquennial annual average of output taking 1901-2 to 1905-6 to be normal. We matched this series with the earlier series of death rates. It is noticed that in most years the output fell. But in some it did not. For example, in the agricultural year of 1906-7 and 1916-17 in Puri, the crop outputs did not fall. Similarly, in case of Cuttack, the crop output fell by only 5 per cent in 1914-15. Balasore, on the other hand, did face a number of years with high mortality rate and in all the years except the year of 1919-20, the crop output fell.

Since some years such as 1888-9, 1896-7, 1906-7, 1914-15, 1916-17 and 1919-20 presented anomalies we tried to explain those years as to why we have included those years. For example, the recorded male death rate did not touch 40 in 1889 for Cuttack or in 1897 for Puri. Yet we have included those years as high mortality years because the government had declared scarcity/famine in those years.

The agricultural year 1906-7 experienced bumper crop in Puri, yet the recorded male death rate touched 40. We have included this year as high mortality year because cholera had become epidemic in the year 1907. The years 1916-17 and 1917-18 were also included as high mortality years in Puri because even though there was bumper crop in those years, epidemics of cholera and influenza had spread and recorded male death rate touched 40.

Finally, the year 1918-19 was chosen as the high mortality year because not only crop output fell but also epidemics like influenza, malaria and cholera took a heavy toll. Last, the year 1919-20 was chosen in Balasore as high mortality year because the crop had failed for the last few years. In that year even though the crop did not fail, the epidemic continued. Thus we have justified for the inclusion. Thus, we define high mortality years as those years in which recorded male death rate touched 40 per thousand and in many cases the crop output fell in the previous year.

Characterization of the High Mortality Decades and Low Mortality Decades

After we identified the years of high mortality it is noticed that the numbers of high mortality years were more numerous (more than 3) in the latter two decades than the former two decades. So we have characterized the former two decades of our study as the low mortality decades and the latter two decades as the high mortality decades. Not only that high mortality years were more numerous in the latter two decades of our study, the rate of growth of population was also very low. For the decade 1901-11, the population grew by 0.9 per cent. In the next decade it fell by 4.6 per cent. Balasore was identified as the most mortality-prone district in the decade of 1911-21 because the number of high mortality years were more numerous and population loss was the highest.

Thus, we define high mortality decades as those decades in which the number of high mortality years was three or more and population grew less rapidly than during the low mortality decades.

Notes

1. Collection of data on area under different crops started from 1891-2 onwards in Bengal Presidency.
2. According to Maddox, the standard yields of early rice and spring rice were lower than that of winter rice. *Maddox Report 1890-1900,* vol. I, para 187.
3. Ibid.
4. Hunter, *Statistical Account of Bengal,* vol. XVIII, pp. 99-100.

APPENDIX 9.2

Trends in the Sex Ratio from 1901 to 2011

Years	*Sex Ratio*
1901	1,037
1911	1,056
1921	1,086
1931	1,067
1941	1,053
1951	1,022
1961	1,001
1971	988
1981	982
1991	971
2001	972
2011	979

Source: http://medind.nic.in/jah/t03/i1/jaht03i1p43g.pdf (retrieved on 5 August 2019)

APPENDIX 9.3A

Population Totals and Sex Ratios in Different Age Groups from 1891 to 1921

A: Cuttack

Age Groups	*1872*		*1891*		*1911*		*1921*	
	Male	*Female*	*Male*	*Female*	*Male*	*Female*	*Male*	*Female*
0-1	-	-	25,527	26,604	32,045	32,075	24,877	24,785
1-5	-	-	95,634	1,01,756	96,975	1,02,920	81,408	86,832
5-10	-	-	1,38,300	1,34,659	1,48,385	1,46,603	1,46,671	1,48,799
10-15	-	-	1,30,007	1,15,885	1,33,229	1,24,717	1,35,686	1,32,573
15-20	-	-	97,527	94,925	88,182	93,874	90,389	98,365
20-30	-	-	1,39,956	1,49,051	1,58,311	1,92,147	1,44,503	1,89,361
30-40	-	-	1,20,845	1,32,524	1,45,272	1,57,009	1,27,963	1,65,632
40-50	-	-	94,428	1,02,285	95,222	1,14,000	1,00,268	1,25,944
50-60	-	-	53,128	63,698	55,937	71,353	59,193	73,429
60 & above	-	-	45,205	75,727	47,617	73,266	41,585	66,415
Total	7,25,330	7,69,454	9,40,557	9,97,114	10,01,175	11,07,964	9,52,543	11,12,135

B: Balasore

Age Groups	*1872*		*1891*		*1911*		*1921*	
	Male	*Female*	*Male*	*Female*	*Male*	*Female*	*Male*	*Female*
0-1	-	-	14,196	14,481	15,093	14,991	10,836	10,615
1-5	-	-	45,580	49,227	45,675	48,102	33,751	35,688
5-10	-	-	67,458	65,558	71,531	71,181	66,081	64,713
10-15	-	-	66,180	58,116	68,849	62,853	64,743	59,211
15-20	-	-	52,178	52,570	47,512	51,280	45,397	49,864
20-30	-	-	76,077	80,217	83,386	99,260	82,537	98,551
30-40	-	-	63,843	69,897	76,519	81,108	68,149	80,349
40-50	-	-	49,546	56,713	48,355	56,099	51,768	59,850
50-60	-	-	27,836	33,327	28,406	35,113	27,480	32,039
60 & above	-	-	18,744	32,881	19,289	30,967	15,380	23,502
Total	3,79,077	3,91,155	4,81,638	5,12,987	5,04,615	5,50,954	4,66,122	5,14,382

(contd.)

APPENDIX 9.3A (contd.)

C: Puri

Age Groups	*1872*		*1891*		*1911*		*1921*	
	Male	*Female*	*Male*	*Female*	*Male*	*Female*	*Male*	*Female*
0-1	-	-	12,421	12,629	15,430	15,698	9,891	9,802
1-5	-	-	42,988	46,502	46,696	50,372	36,360	39,772
5-10	-	-	67,090	66,763	69,376	69,997	68,757	71,863
10-15	-	-	63,628	56,577	62,857	56,680	66,418	63,188
15-20	-	-	43,752	40,140	40,592	40,619	39,496	40,193
20-30	-	-	74,741	74,088	85,356	91,547	70,044	85,553
30-40	-	-	67,615	65,378	78,326	74,805	65,295	75,285
40-50	-	-	50,060	47,413	53,100	53,804	50,747	54,210
50-60	-	-	31,057	31,013	31,193	33,676	30,464	32,320
60 & above	-	-	21,178	29,965	23,644	29,654	18,071	23,922
Total	-	-	4,74,530	4,70,468	5,06,570	5,16,832	4,55,543	4,96,108

Note: The Appendix 2 identification of high and low mortality years is given separately.

Sources: Census of India 1891, vol. 1, pt. I, pp. 52-5; *Census of India 1901*, vol. 6, pt. II, pp. 1047-8; *Census of India 1891*, vol. V, pt. 3, pp. 34-5; *Census of India 1891*, vol. 7, pt. II, pp. 37-8.

APPENDIX 9.3B

Calculated Annual Population Figures, Total Deaths, Revised Crude Death Rates and Rates due to Different Diseases for Male and Female between 1881 and 1921

A. Cuttack: 1881-90

Year	Population		Total Deaths		Cholera Deaths		*Dysentery Deaths		Fever Deaths	
	Male	Female	Male	Female	Male	Female	Male	Female	Male	Female
1881	849,254	888,911	21,064	19,694	2,550	2,451	2,355	1,447	8,375	8,505
			(24.80)	(22.16)	(3.00)	(2.77)	(2.77)	(1.63)	(9.86)	(9.57)
1882	857,967	899,178	17,796	15,786	3,690	2,032	2,032	1,158	6,486	5,985
			(20.74)	(17.66)	(4.30)	(2.37)	(2.37)	(1.29)	(7.56)	(6.66)
1883	866,770	909,563	15,757	13,887	1,725	2,009	2,009	1,172	6,566	6,240
			(18.18)	(15.27)	(2.07)	(2,32)	(2.32)	(1.29)	(7.58)	(6.86)
1884	875,663	920,069	20,007	18,639	3,641	2,464	2,464	1,581	8,103	7,861
			(22,85)	(20.26)	(4.16)	(2.81)	(2.81)	(1.17)	(9.25)	(8.54)
1885	884,647	930,696	21,067	20,550	5,034	2,520	2,520	1,688	7,593	7,927
			(23.81)	(22.08)	(5.69)	(2..85)	(2.85)	(1.81)	(8.58)	(8.52)
1886	893,714	941,445	18,145	17,031	3,550	2,077	2,077	1,361	7,898	7,734
			(20.30)	(18.09)	(3.97)	(2.32)	(2.32)	(1.45)	(8.84)	(8.22)

(contd.)

APPENDIX 9.3B (contd.)

Year	*Population*		*Total Deaths*		*Cholera Deaths*		**Dysentery Deaths*		*Fever Deaths*	
	Male	*Female*	*Male*	*Female*	*Male*	*Female*	*Male*	*Female*	*Male*	*Female*
1887	902,893	952,319	17,212	16,718	2,305	2,269	2,269	1,605	7,571	7,865
			(19.06)	(17.56)	(2.55)	(2.51)	(2.51)	(1.69)	(8.39)	(8.26)
1888	912,157	963,318	19,008	17,884	1,929	2,596	2,596	1,815	8,203	8,323
			(20.84)	(18.50)	(2.11)	(2.85)	(2.85)	(1.88)	(8.99)	(8.64)
1889	921,516	974,444	27,988	26,425	7,602	7,285	2,966	1,931	10,084	10,577
			(30.37)	(27.12)	(8.25)	(7.48)	(3.22)	(1.98)	(10.94)	(10.85)
1890	930,971	985,699	21,41	20,073	2,202	2,092	2,304	1,560	10,462	10,639
			(23.00)	(20.36)	(2.37)	(2.12)	(2.47)	(1.58)	(11.24)	(10.79)

Notes: *Dysentery included diarrhea and other bowel complaints also.
Figures in parenthesis are rates per thousand population.
Annual growth rate of male population = 1.01026 and
Annual growth rate of female population = 1.01155.

B. Cuttack: 1891-1900

Year	*Population*		*Total Deaths*		*Cholera Deaths*		**Dysentery Deaths*		*Fever Deaths*	
	Male	*Female*	*Male*	*Female*	*Male*	*Female*	*Male*	*Female*	*Male*	*Female*
1891	940	997,114	23,632 (25.12)	22,660 (22.73)	1,662 (1.77)	1,685 (1.69)	2,316 (2.46)	1,,570 (1.57)	10,877 (11.96)	11,314 (11.35)
1892	945,899	1,003,924	37,900 (40.7)	36,389 (36.25)	10,794 (11.410	10,495 (10.45)	2,833 (3.00)	1,841 (1.83)	14,315 (15.13)	14,445 (14.39)
1893	951,272	1,010,781	24,365 (25.61)	22,757 (22.51)	1,607 (1.69)	1,364 (1.35)	2,122 (3.37)	1,979 (1.96)	11,921 (12.53)	13,989 (13.84)
1894	956,675	1,017,685	34,765 (36.34)	33,315 (32.74)	3,377 (3.53)	3,335 (3.28)	3,221 (3.37)	2,009 (1.97)	18,323 (19.15)	19,051 (18.72)
1895	962,109	1,024,635	26,489 (27.53)	24,009 (23.43)	2,114 (2.20)	2,010 (1.96)	2,624 (2.73)	1,555 (1.52)	13,752 (14.29)	13,425 (13.10)
1896	967,574	1,031,634	27,951 (28.89)	24,682 (23.93)	2,737 (2.83)	2,558 (2.48)	2,301 (2,38)	1,406 (1.36)	12,724 (13.15)	11,986 (11.62)
1897	973,070	1,038,680	33,456 (34.38)	31,255 (30.09)	5,563 (5.72)	5,805 (5.59)	3,037 (3.12)	1,881 (1.81)	13,518 (13.89)	13,235 (12.74)
1898	978,597	1,045,774	24,123 (24.65)	21,900 (20.94)	943 (0.96)	912 (0.87)	2,241 (2.29)	1,503 (1.44)	11,652 (11.91)	11,491 (10.99)

(contd.)

APPENDIX 9.3B (contd.)

Year	*Population*		*Total Deaths*		*Cholera Deaths*		**Dysentery Deaths*		*Fever Deaths*	
	Male	*Female*	*Male*	*Female*	*Male*	*Female*	*Male*	*Female*	*Male*	*Female*
1899	984,155	1,052,916	32,359	29,831	3,200	3,182	2,854	2,050	12,474	12,385
			(32.88)	(28.33)	(3.25)	(3.02)	(2.90)	(1.95)	(12.67)	(11.76)
1900	989,745	1,060,108	40,642	38,548	8,075	8,375	3,607	2,565	14,363	14,391
			(41.06)	(36.36)	(8.16)	(7.90)	(3.64)	(2.42)	(14.51)	(13.58)

Notes: Annual growth rate of male population = 1.00562.
Annual growth rate of female population = 1.00683.
Source: Sanitary Commission Reports for corresponding years.

C. Cuttack: 1901-10

Year	*Population*		*Total Deaths*		*Cholera Deaths*		*Dysentery Deaths**		*Fever Deaths*	
	Male	*Female*	*Male*	*Female*	*Male*	*Female*	*Male*	*Female*	*Male*	*Female*
1901	995,409	1,067,349	41,877	39,333	5,982	6,101	4,286	3,004	16,356	16,654
			(42.07)	(36.85)	(6.01)	(5.72)	(4.31)	(2.81)	(16.43)	(15.00)
1902	996,185	1,071,341	35,387	32,116	2,224	2,214	4,722	3,262	15,567	15,502
			(35.52)	(29.98)	(2.23)	(2.07	(4.74)	(3.04)	(15.62)	(14.47)
1903	996,962	1,075,348	39,231	36,988	5,327	5,262	4,881	3,545	15,581	16,352
			(39.35)	(34.40)	(5.34)	(4.89)	(4.90)	(3.30)	(15.63)	(15.29)

1904	997,740	1,079,369	30,422	27,974	359	410	3,816	2,727	13,952	14,001
			(30.49)	(25.92)	(0.36)	(0.38)	(3.82)	(2,53)	(13.88)	(12.97)
1905	998,518	1,083,406	34,118	31,843	3,845	4,189	3,788	2,865	13,046	12,960
			(34.12)	(29.39)	(3.85)	(3.87)	(3.79)	(2.64)	(13.07)	(11.96)
1906	999,297	1,087,458	35,372	34,105	5,172	5,617	4,241	3,334	13,267	14,600
			(35.40)	(31.36)	(5.18)	(5.17)	(4.24)	(3.07	(13.28)	(13.43)
1907	10,00,077	1,091,525	47,428	48,640	14,904	16,901	5,057	4,156	14,184	15,584
			(47.42)	(44.56)	(14.90)	(15.48)	(5.06)	(3.81)	(14.18	(14.28)
1908	10,00,857	1,095,607	58,197	59,067	8,783	9,300	8,931	7,711	23,476	26,669
			(58.15)	(53.91)	(8.78)	(8.49)	(8,92)	(7,04)	(23.63)	(24.34)
1909	10,01,637	10,99,705	25,828	26,072	316	344	3,52	2,804	12.476	14,092
			(25.79)	(23.71)	(0.32)	(10.31)	(3.52)	(2.58)	(12.46)	(12.81)
1910	10,02,419	11,03,818	33,312	32,407	1,045	1,190	5,098	4,283	14,047	14,848
			(33.23)	(29.36)	(1.04)	(1.08)	(5.09)	(3.86)	(14.01)	(13.45)

Notes: *Annual growth rate of male population = 1.00078
Annual growth rate of female population = 1.00374.

(contd.)

APPENDIX 9.3B (contd.)

Cuttack: 1911-21

Year	*Population**		*Total Deaths*		*Cholera Deaths*		*Dysentery Deaths**		*Fever Deaths*	
	Male	*Female*	*Male*	*Female*	*Male*	*Female*	*Male*	*Female*	*Male*	*Female*
1911	10,01,175	11,07,964	29,332 (29.30)	27,456 (24.78)	2,242 (2.24)	2,305 (2,08)	3,692 (36.9)	2,769 (25.0)	11,707 (11.69)	11,833 (10.68)
1912	N.A.	N.A.	N.A.	N.A.	N.A.	N.A.	N.A.	N.A.	N.A.	N.A.
1913	99,10,248	11,08,806	30,716 (30.99)	27,824 (25.09)	2,614 (2.64)	2,762 (2.49)	4,378 (4.42)	3,076 (2.77)	11,979 (12.08)	11,573 (10.44)
1914	9,86,322	11,09,227	32,992 (33.45)	31,626 (28.50)	3,132 (3.20)	3,334 (3.01)	4,687 (4.75)	3,791 (3.42	12,373 (12.54	12,934 (11.66)
1915	9,81,420	11,09,649	40,870 (41.64)	40,475 (36.48)	5,122 (5.22)	5,479 (4.94)	6,197 (6.31)	5,225 (4.71)	15,292 (15.38)	16,421 (14.80)
1916	9,76,542	11,10,071	36,605 (37.48)	35,867 (32.21)	2,914 (2.98)	3,022 (2.72)	5,423 (5.55)	4,427 (3.99)	15,315 (15.68)	16,726 (15.07)
1917	9,71,688	11,10,492	35,464 (36.49)	34,018 (30.63)	1,713 (1.76)	1,776 (1.60)	5,065 (5.21)	3,817 (3.44)	15,361 (15.81)	16,113 (14.51)
1918	9,66,859	11,10,914	48,076 (49.72)	47,173 (42.46)	2,362 (2.44)	2,421 (2.18)	5,834 (6.03)	4,459 (4.01)	25,405 (26.28)	27,056 (24.35)

1919	9,62.054	11,11,336	59,193	57,174	9,332	9,390	7,526	6,088	27,152	27,776
			(63.53)	(51.45)	(9.70)	(8,45)	(7.82)	(5.48)	(28.22)	(24.99)
1920	9,57,272	11,11,759	41,864	41,257	3,739	3,847	6,113	5,014	20,214	21,278
			(43.73)	(37.20)	(3.91)	(3.46)	(6.39)	(4.51)	(21.12)	(19.14)
1921	9,52,543	11,12,135	36,189	33,459	1,183	1,285	6,029	4,292	18,199	18,196
			(37.99)	(30.09)	(1.24)	(1.16)	(6.33)	(3.86)	(19.11)	(16.36)

Notes: Annual growth rate of male population = 0.99503.
Annual growth rate of female population = 1.00038.
*Population figures are calculated from Appendix Table 7.1 A, B, C.

APPENDIX 9.3C

Calculated Annual Population Figures, Total Deaths, Revised Crude Death Rates and Rates due to Different Diseases for Male and Female between 1881 and 1921

A. Balasore: 1881-90

Years	*Population*		*Total Deaths*		*Cholera Deaths*		*Dysentery Deaths*		*Fever Deaths*	
	Male	*Female*	*Male*	*Female*	*Male*	*Female*	*Male*	*Female*	*Male*	*Female*
1881	4,61,461	4,83,819	10,922	9,857	1,981	1,819	2,517	1,985	3,262	3,052
			(23.67	(20.37)	(4.29)	(3.76)	(5.45)	(4.10)	(7.07)	(6.31)
1882	4,63,441	4,86,659	13,627	12,158	3,146	2,731	3,325	2,601	3,826	3,651
			(29.40)	(24.98)	(6.79)	(5.61)	(7.17)	(5.34)	(8.26)	(7.50)
1883	4,65,429	4,89,516	10,888	9,750	1,089	918	2,843	2,156	3,810	3,613
			(23.39)	(19.92)	(2.34)	(1.88)	(6.11)	(4.40)	(8.19)	(7.38)
1884	4,67,426	4,92,389	13,602	12,743	3,830	3,543	2,760	2,172	3,983	3,964
			(29.53)	(25.88)	(8.19)	(7.20)	(5.90)	(4.41)	(8.52)	(8.05)
1885	4,69,431	4,95,279	10,916	10,181	1,837	1,677	2,658	2,134	3,408	3,473
			(23.25)	(20.56)	(3.91)	(3.39)	(5.66)	(4.31)	(7.26)	(7.01)
1886	4,71,445	4,98,187	12,540	12,115	2,169	2,053	2,386	2,046	5,035	5,164
			(26.60)	(24.32)	(4.60)	(4.12)	(5.06)	(4.11)	(10.68)	(10.37)

1887	4,73,467	5,01,111	11,672)	11,100	2,226	2,087	2,387	2,006	4,024	4,091
			(24.65)	(22.15)	(4.79)	(4.16)	(5.04)	(4.00)	(8.50)	(8.16)
1888	4,75,498	5,04,053	10,689	10,062	1,042	824	2,525	2,055	3,877	3,991
			(22.48)	(19.96)	(2.19)	(1.63)	(5.31)	(4.08)	(8.15)	(7.92)
1889	4,77,538	507,011	19,012	17,592	6,801	6,192	3,327	2,552	5,177	5,331
			(39.81)	(34.70)	(14.24)	(12.21)	(6.97)	(5.03)	(10.84)	(10.51)
1890	4,79,587	509,988	12,726	11,804	777	641	2,536	1,907	5,537	5,648
			(26.62)	(23.15)	(1.62)	(1.26)	(5.29)	(3.74	(11.55)	(11.07)

Note: Annual growth rate of male population = 1,00,429
Annual growth rate of female population = 1.00,587.

B. Balasore: 1891-1900

Years	*Population*		*Total Deaths*		*Cholera Deaths*		*Dysentery Deaths*		*Fever Deaths*	
	Male	*Female*	*Male*	*Female*	*Male*	*Female*	*Male*	*Female*	*Male*	*Female*
1891	4,81,638	5,12,987	13,528	12,521	1,056	1,000	2,211	1,592	5,836	5,857
			(28.09)	(24.41)	(2.19)	(1.95)	(4.59)	(3.10)	(12.12)	(11.42)
1892	4,85,115	5,16,916	22,068	21,305	7,480	7,446	2,631	2,041	6,955	7,185
			(45.49)	(41.22)	(15.45)	(14.40)	(5.42)	(3.95)	(14.34)	(13.90)
1893	4,88,618	5,20,876	13,283	12,442	933	892	1,802	1,453	5,694	5,596
			(27.18)	(23.89)	(1.91)	(1.71)	(3.69)	(2.79)	(11.65)	(10.74)

(contd.)

APPENDIX 9.3C (contd.)

Years	*Population*		*Total Deaths*		*Cholera Deaths*		*Dysentery Deaths*		*Fever Deaths*	
	Male	*Female*	*Male*	*Female*	*Male*	*Female*	*Male*	*Female*	*Male*	*Female*
1894	4,92,146	5,24,866	16,842	15,915	2,562	2,343	2,136	1,644	7,383	7,476
			(34.22)	(30.32)	(5.21)	(4.46)	(4.34)	(3.13)	(15.00)	(14.24)
1895	4,95,699	5,28,886	15,295	14,184	1,160	1,101	1,884	1,315	6,767	6,833
			(30.86)	(26.82)	(2.34)	(2.08)	(3.80)	(2.49)	(13.65)	(12.92)
1896	4,99,278	5,28,938	18,554	16,946	4,079	3,600	1,817	1,416	6,967	6,646
			(37.16)	(31.80)	(8.17)	(6.76)	(3.64)	(2.66)	(13.95)	(12.47)
1897	5,02,883	5,37,020	16,051	14,305	1,796	1,408	1,632	1,260	6,672	6,175
			(31.92)	(26.64)	(3.57)	(2.62)	(3.25)	(2.35)	(13.27)	(11.50)
1898	5,06,514	5,41,134	14,410	13,247	1,663	1,474	1,400	1,026	6,133	5,910
			(28.45)	(24.48)	(3.28)	(2.72)	(27.76)	(1.90)	(12.11)	(10.92)
1899	5,10,171	5,45,279	14,381	13,571	1,073	1,113	1,204	881	5,786	5,530
			(28.19)	(24.89)	(2.10)	(2.04)	(2.36)	(1.62)	(11.34)	(10.14)
1900	5,13,854	5,49,455	17,407	16,061	2,306	2,146	1,263	997	7,025	6,712
			(33.88)	(29.23)	(4.49)	(3.91)	(2.46)	(1.81)	(12.67)	(12.22)

Note: Annual growth rate of male population = 1.00,722
Annual growth rate of female population = 1.00,766.

C. Balasore: 1901-10

Years	*Population*		*Total Deaths*		*Cholera Deaths*		*Dysentery Deaths*		*Fever Deaths*	
	Male	*Female*	*Male*	*Female*	*Male*	*Female*	*Male*	*Female*	*Male*	*Female*
1901	5,17,543	5,53,654	20,170	18,482	3,224	2,955	1,519	1,032	7,681	7,674
			(38.97)	(33.38)	(6.23)	(5.54)	(2.94)	(1.86)	(14.84)	(13.86)
1902	5,16,235	5,53,383	17,649	16,169	1,341	1,259	1,115	760	7,019	6,647
			(34.19)	(29.22)	(2.60)	(2.28)	(2.16)	(1.37)	(13.60)	(12.01)
1903	5,14,930	5,53,112	20,180	19,455	2,524	2,335	1,189	883	7,735	7,631
			(39.19)	(35.17)	(4.90)	(4.22)	(2.31)	(1.60)	(15.02)	(13.80)
1904	5,13,629	5,52,841	17,365	16,554	2,001	2,014	998	823	6,605	6,570
			(33.81)	(29.94)	(4.09)	(3.64)	(1.94)	(1.49)	(12.86)	(11.88)
1905	5,12,331	5,52,570	19,508	19,259	1,913	1,837	1,015	851	7,646	7,799
			(38.08)	(34.85)	(3.73)	(3.32)	(1,98)	(1.54)	(14.92)	(14.12)
1906	5,11,036	5,52,299	21,445	21,016	2,871	2,756	1,201	1,051	7,940	8,077
			(41.96)	(38.05)	(5.62)	(4.99)	(2.35)	(1.90)	(15.54)	(14.12)
1907	5,09,745	5,52,028	22,835	23,186	5,263	5,767	1,133	902	6,893	7,112
			(44.80)	(42.00)	(10.32)	(10.45)	(2.22)	(1.63)	(13.52)	(12.88)
1908	5,08,457	5,51,758	35,516	36,726	13,723	14,347	1,569	1,276	8,180	8,744
			(69.85)	(66.56)	(26.99)	(26.00)	(3.09)	(2.31)	(16.09)	(15.85)
1909	5,07,172	5,51,487	13,688	13,917	173	198	664	678	5,251	5,641
			(26.99)	(25.24)	(0.34)	(0.36)	(1.31)	(1.23)	(10.35)	(10.23)

(contd.)

APPENDIX 9.3C (contd.)

Years	*Population*		*Total Deaths*		*Cholera Deaths*		*Dysentery Deaths*		*Fever Deaths*	
	Male	*Female*	*Male*	*Female*	*Male*	*Female*	*Male*	*Female*	*Male*	*Female*
1910	5,05,891	5,51,217	16,059	15,545	723	665	774	631	5,291	5,537
			(31.74)	(28.20)	(1.43)	(1.21)	(1.53)	(1.14)	(10.46)	(9.72)

Note: Annual growth rate of male population = 0.99,747.
Annual growth rate of female population = 1.99.951

D. Balasore: 1911-21

Years	*Population*		*Total Deaths*		*Cholera Deaths*		*Dysentery Deaths*		*Fever Deaths*	
	Male	*Female*	*Male*	*Female*	*Male*	*Female*	*Male*	*Female*	*Male*	*Female*
1911	504,615	550,953	15,138	14,815	659	650	803	690	5,322	5,304
			(30.00)	(26.39)	(1.31)	(1.18)	(1.59)	(1.25)	(10.55)	(9.63)
1912	NA	NA	NA	NA	NA	NA	NA	NA	NA	NA
1913	4,96,464	5,43,442	16,971	16,410	2,002	2,053	886	681	6,282	5,959
			(34.34)	(30.20)	(4.03)	(3.78)	(1.78)	(1.25)	(12.65)	(10.97)
1914	4,92,735	5,39,725	15,964	15,139	524	482	709	518	5,949	5,659
			(32.32)	(28.05)	(1.1)	(0.09)	(1.44)	(0.10)	(12.07)	(10.48)
1915	4,88,838	5,36,033	23.206	23,498	2,689	2,910	1,083	826	7,911	8,366
			(47.47)	(43.84)	(5.50)	(5.43)	(2.22)	(1.15)	(16.18)	(15.61)

1916	4,84,971	5,32,366	20,927	21,582	1,888	1,969	1,009	737	8,975	9,510
			(43.15)	(40.54)	(3.89)	(3.70)	(2.08)	(1.38)	(18.51)	(17.86)
1917	5,81,135	5,28,725	17,453	17,362	1,299	1,257	747	570	7,583	7,469
			(36.27)	(32.84)	(2.70)	(2.38)	(1.55)	(1.08)	(15.76)	(14.13)
1918	4,77,329	5,25,109	24,090	23,384	1,962	1,806	682	576	12,493	12,214
			(50.47)	(44.53)	(4.11)	(3.44)	(1.43)	(1.10)	(26.17)	(23.26)
1919	4,73,554	5,21,517	27,062	26,187	3,161	2,812	737	507	13,494	13,178
			(57.25)	(50.21)	(6.68)	(5.39)	(1.56)	(1.00)	(28.50)	(25.27)
1920	4,69,808	5,17,950	21,872	21,863	1,078	989	540	431	11,438	11,812
			(46.56)	(42.21)	(2.29)	(1.91)	(1.15)	(0.08)	(24.35)	(22.81)
1921	4,66,122	5,14,382	20,070	20,093	526	506	618	427	11,697	11,979
			(43.00)	(39.06)	(1.13)	(1.00)	(1.33)	(0.08)	(25.09)	(23.29)

Note: Annual growth rate of male population = 0.99209.
Annual growth rate of female population = 0.99316.

APPENDIX 9.3D

Calculated Annual Population Figures Total Deaths Revised Crude Death Rates and Rates due to Different Diseases for Male and Female between 1881-1921

A. Puri: 1881-90

Years	*Population*		*Total Deaths*		*Cholera Deaths*		*Dysentery Deaths*		*Fever Deaths*	
	Male	*Female*	*Male*	*Female*	*Male*	*Female*	*Male*	*Female*	*Male*	*Female*
1881	4,46,609	4,41,878	10,305	9,217	1,177	985	1,205	849	2,567	2,519
			(23.07)	(20.86)	(2.64)	(2.23)	(2.70)	(1.19)	(5.74)	(5.70)
1882	4,49,324	4,44,657	10,143	9,054	2,028	1,755	1,293	948	2,514	2,568
			(22.57)	(20.36)	(4.51)	(3.95)	(2.88)	(2.13)	(5.60)	(5.78)
1883	4,52,056	4,47,454	9,609	8,410	630	492	1,369	926	2,319	2,124
			(21.26)	(18.80)	(1,39)	(1.1)	(3.03)	(2.07)	(5.13)	(4.75)
1884	4,54,805	4,50,268	10,512	10,005	1,642	1,486	1,519	1,173	1,275	1,337
			(23.11)	(22.22)	(3.61)	(3.30)	(3.34)	(2.61)	(2.80)	(3.00)
1885	4,57,570	4,53,101	10,774	9,867	2,790	2,529	1,474	1,135	1,011	982
			(23.55)	(21.78)	(6.10)	(5.58)	(3.22)	(2.50)	(2.21)	(2.17)
1886	4,60,352	4,55,951	10,566	10,121	2,024	1,789	1,295	1,067	1,539	1,756
			(22.95)	(22.20)	(4.40)	(3.92)	(2.81)	(2.34)	(3.34)	(3.85)

1887	4,63,151	4,58,819	14,973 (32.33)	14,685 (32.01)	4,516 (9.75)	4,152 (9.05)	1,809 (3.91)	1,522 (3.32)	1,829 (3.95)	2,114 (4.61)
1888	4,65,967	4,61,705	10,057 (21.58)	9,319 (20.18)	1,151 (2.47)	978 (2.12)	1,241 (2.66)	947 (2.05)	1,336 (2.87)	1,335 (2.89)
1889	4,68,800	4,64,609	21,307 (45.45)	18,874 (40.62)	10,001 (21.33)	8,668 (18.66)	1,547 (3.30)	1,072 (2.29)	1,780 (3.00)	1,663 (3.58)
1890	4,71,650	4,67,531	12,268 (26.01)	11,452 (24.49)	1,755 (3.72)	1,582 (3.38)	1,177 (2.25)	1,072 (2.29)	2,367 (5.02)	2,387 (5.11)

Note: Annual growth rate of male population = 1.00608.
Annual growth rate of female population = 1.00629.

B. Puri: 1891-1900

Years	*Population*		*Total Deaths*		*Cholera Deaths*		*Dysentery Deaths*		*Fever Deaths*	
	Male	*Female*	*Male*	*Female*	*Male*	*Female*	*Male*	*Female*	*Male*	*Female*
1891	4,74,530	4,70,468	11,437 (24.10)	10,451 (22.50)	586 (1.23)	449 (1.0)	1,376 (2.90)	1,101 (2.34)	2,321 (4.90)	2,390 (5.08)
1892	4,77,667	4,74,321	19,207 (40.21)	17,359 (36.60)	5,685 (11.90)	5,001 (10.54)	1,898 (3.97)	1,470 (3.10)	3,121 (6.53)	3,224 (6.80)
1893	4,80,824	4,78,206	14,109 (29.34)	13,320 (27.85)	1,056 (2.20)	697 (1.46)	1,501 (3.12)	1,142 (2.39)	5,694 (11.84)	5,596 (11.70)

(contd.)

APPENDIX 9.3D (contd.)

Years	*Population*		*Total Deaths*		*Cholera Deaths*		*Dysentery Deaths*		*Fever Deaths*	
	Male	*Female*	*Male*	*Female*	*Male*	*Female*	*Male*	*Female*	*Male*	*Female*
1894	4,84,002	4,82,122	14.751	14,316	1,020	973	1,976	1,587	3,903	4,399
			(30.48)	(29.69)	(2.11)	(2.02)	(4.08)	(3.29)	(8.06)	(9.12)
1895	4,87,202	4,86,071	13,192	12,768	1,181	1,147	1,653	1,373	3,160	3,381
			(27.08)	(26.27)	(2.42)	(2.36)	(3.40)	(2.82)	(6.49)	(6.96)
1896	4,90,422	4,90,052	12,604	10,908	1,814	1,491	1,410	1,021	2,580	2,439
			(25.70)	(22.26)	(3.70)	(3.04)	(2.88)	(2.08)	(5.26)	(4.98)
1897	4,93,664	4,94,065	19,456	17,464	4,795	4,255	2,142	1,723	3,238	3,267
			(39.41)	(35.35)	(9.71)	(8.61)	(4.34)	(3.49)	(6.56)	(6.61)
1898	4,96,927	4,98,118	12,440	11,652	228	204	1,137	932	2,600	2,632
			(25.03)	(23.39)	(0.46)	(8.61)	(2.29)	(1.87)	(5.23)	(5.20)
1899	5,00,211	5,02,191	15,868	14,988	2,171	2,171	1,519	1,222	2,835	2,966
			(32.72)	(29.85)	(4.34)	(4.32)	(3.04)	92.43)	(5.67)	(5.91)
1900	5,03,518	5,06,304	17,682	16,825	1,769	1,654	2,518	2,066	4,077	4,567
			(35.12)	(33.23)	(3.51)	(3.27)	(5.00)	(4.08)	(8.10)	(9.02)

Note: Annual growth rate of male population = 1.00661.
Annual growth rate of female population = 1.00819.

C. Puri: 1901-10

Years	*Population*		*Total Deaths*		*Cholera Deaths*		*Dysentery Deaths*		*Fever Deaths*	
	Male	*Female*	*Male*	*Female*	*Male*	*Female*	*Male*	*Female*	*Male*	*Female*
1901	5,06,839	5,10,445	21,433	20,606	4,668	4,695	3,157	2,509	4,875	5,283
			(42.29)	(40.37)	(9.21)	(9.20)	(6.23)	(4.92)	(9.62)	(10.35)
1902	5,06,614	5,11,078	16,775	15,832	1,839	1,926	2,730	2,103	4,222	4,510
			(33.10)	(30.96)	(3.63)	(3.77)	(5.39)	(4.11)	(8.33)	(8.82)
1903	5,06,780	5,11,712	18,038	16,718	3,342	3,086	2,211	1,835	4,280	4,379
			(35.39)	(32.67)	(6.59)	(6.03)	(4.36)	(3.59)	(8.45)	(8.56)
1904	5,06,763	5,12,346	14,302	13,079	505	503	1,766	1,466	4,750	4,206
			(28.22)	(25.53)	(0.10)	(0.10)	(3.48)	(2.86)	(8.39)	(8.21)
1905	5,06,738	5,12,982	16,449	15,103	2,136	1,907	2,016	1,619	3,831	3,900
			(32.46)	(29.44)	(4.22)	(3.72)	(3.98)	(3.16)	(7.56)	(7.60)
1906	5,06,712	5,13,618	16,830	15,804	1,251	1,198	2,064	1,623	5,533	3,869
			(33.21)	(30.77)	(2.47)	(2.33)	(4.07)	(3,16)	(6.97)	(7.53)
1907	5,06,687	5,14,254	2,663	20,215	4,635	4,562	2,634	2,288	3,786	4,407
			(40.78)	(39.31)	(9.15)	(8.87)	(5.20)	(4.45)	(7.47)	(13.68)
1908	5,06,662	5,14,892	30,624	29,510	7,555	7,111	5,121	4,459	6,274	7,044
			(60.44)	(57.31)	(14.91)	(13.81)	(10.11)	(8.67)	(12.38)	(13.68)
1909	5,06,636	5,15,531	13,497	13,307	1,105	1,223	2,285	2,083	3,378	3,877
			(26.64)	(25.81)	(2.18)	(2.37)	(4.51)	(4.04)	(6.67)	(7.52)

(contd.)

APPENDIX 9.3D (contd.)

Years	*Population*		*Total Deaths*		*Cholera Deaths*		*Dysentery Deaths*		*Fever Deaths*	
	Male	*Female*	*Male*	*Female*	*Male*	*Female*	*Male*	*Female*	*Male*	*Female*
1910	5,06,611	5,16,170	16,437	16,224	688	726	3,123	2,701	4,553	5,307
			(32.45)	(31.43)	(1.36)	(1.41)	(6.16)	(5.23)	(8.99)	(10.20)

Note: Annual growth rate of male population = 0.99995.
Annual growth rate of female population = 1.00124.

D. Puri: 1911-21

Years	*Population*		*Total Deaths*		*Cholera Deaths*		*Dysentery Deaths*		*Fever Deaths*	
	Male	*Female*	*Male*	*Female*	*Male*	*Female*	*Male*	*Female*	*Male*	*Female*
1911	5,06,839	5,16,832	15,430	14,508	2,036	1,894	2,184	1,930	3,757	3,964
			(30.46)	(28.07)	(4.00)	(3.66)	(4.31)	(3.73)	(7.45)	(7.67)
1912	NA	NA	NA	NA	NA	NA	NA	NA	NA	NA
1913	5,01,221	5,12,623	14,154	13,149	1,064	1,002	2,408	2,058	3,600	3,635
			(28.24)	(25.65)	(2.12)	(1.95)	(4.80)	(4.01)	(7.12)	(7.09)
1914	4,95,228	5,10,532	15,252	14,619	1,258	1,267	2,630	2,344	3,493	3,873
			(30.80)	(28.63)	(2.54)	(2.48)	(5.31)	(4.59)	(7.05)	(7.59)
1915	4,89,998	5,08,449	16,291	15,302	1,979	1,889	2,896	2,440	3,471	3,924
			(33.25)	(30.10)	(4.04)	(3.72)	(5.91)	(4.80)	(7.08)	(7.72)

1916	4,84,824	5,06,374	15,623 (32.22)	15,582 (30.77)	781 (1.61)	769 (1.52)	2,726 (5.62)	2,374 (4.69)	4,487 (9.25)	5,166 (10.20)
1917	4,79,704	5,04,308	19,956 (41.60)	20,187 (40.03)	1,224 (2.55)	1,322 (2.62)	3,262 (6.80)	2,965 (5.88)	6,753 (14.08)	7,029 (13.94)
1918	4,74,639	5,02,251	24,096 (50.77)	24,514 (48.81)	1,115 (2.35)	1,115 (2.22)	3,580 (7.54)	3,290 (6.55)	10,259 (21.61)	11,490 (22.88)
1919	4,69,626	5,00,202	36,799 (78.36)	35,166 (70.30)	6,577 (14.00)	6,526 (13.05)	6,203 (13.21)	5,284 (10.56)	11,734 (24.99)	12,068 (24.13)
1920	4,64,667	4,98,161	23,978 (51.60)	23,594 (47.36)	2,481 (5.34)	2,509 (5.04)	4,410 (9.49)	3,972 (7.97)	8,247 (17.75)	8,807 (17.68)
1921	4,55,543	4,96,108	16,462 (34.14)	15,158 (30.55)	1,163 (2.55)	1,15 (2.33)	2,951 (6.48)	2,283 (4.60)	5,651 (12.40)	5,977 (12.05)

Note: Annual growth rate of male population = 0.98944.
Annual growth rate of female population = 0.99592.

Sources: Annual Sanitary Commission Report on Bengal 1881-1912; Annual Sanitary Commission Report on Bihar and Orissa 1913-18; Annual Public Head Commission Report on Bihar and Orissa 1918-1921.

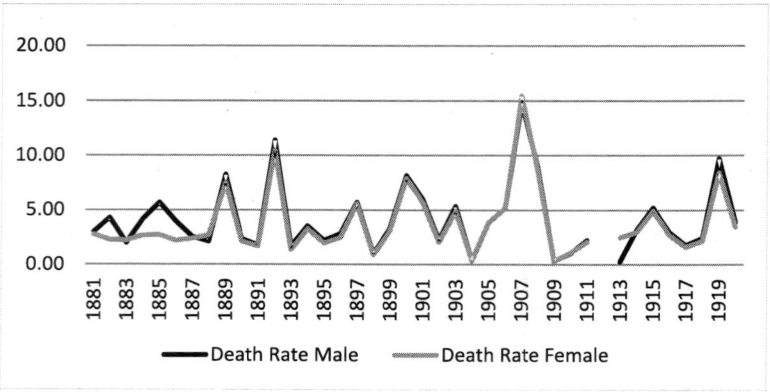

Source: Sanitary Commission Reports of Bengal, Orissa and Bihar for respective years.

GRAPH 9.1: CHOLERA DEATH RATES IN CUTTACK, 1881-1920.

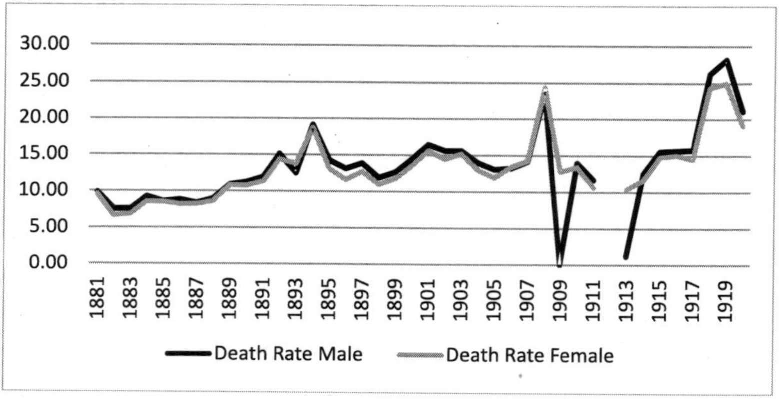

Source: Sanitary Commission Reports of Bengal, Orissa and Bihar for respective years.

GRAPH 9.2: FEVER DEATH RATES IN CUTTACK, 1881-1920.

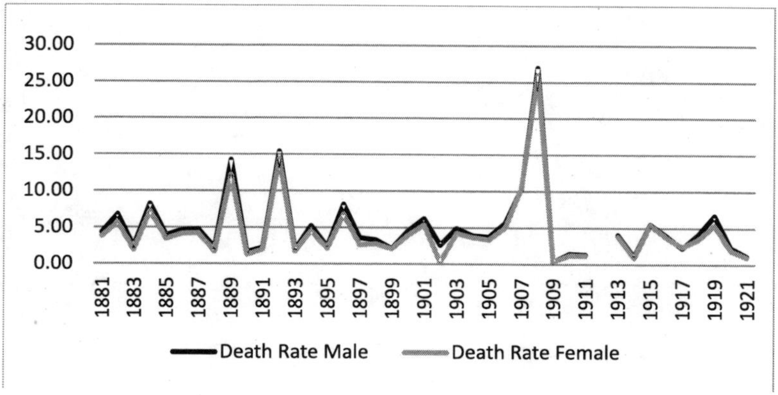

Source: Sanitary Commission Reports for the respective years.

GRAPH 9.3: CHOLERA DEATH RATES IN BALASORE, 1881-1921.

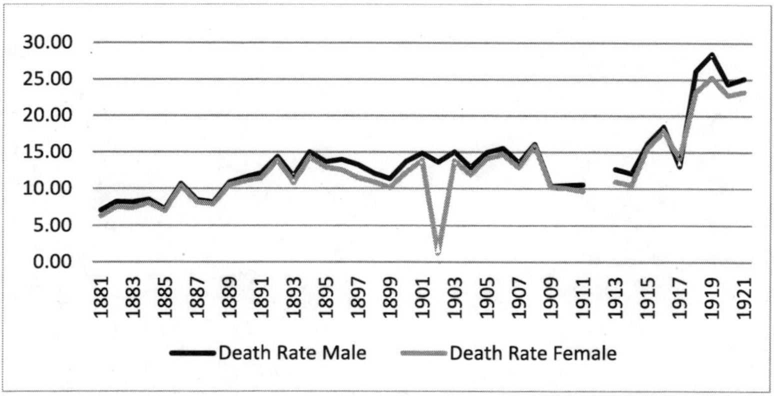

Source: Sanitary Commission Reports for the respective years.

GRAPH 9.4: FEVER DEATH RATES IN BALASORE, 1881-1921.

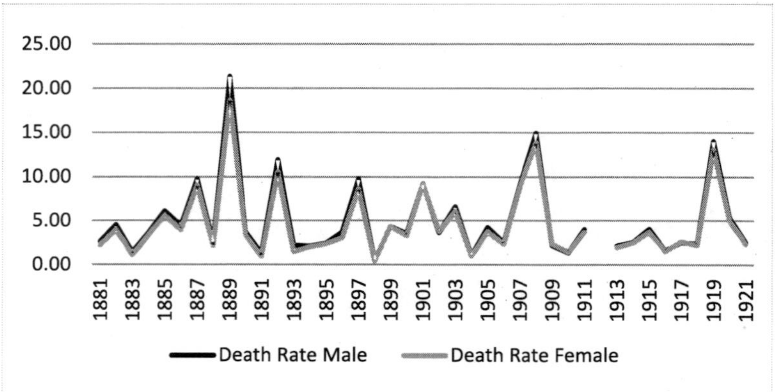

Source: Sanitary Commission Reports for the respective years.

GRAPH 9.5: CHOLERA DEATH RATES IN PURI, 1881-1921.

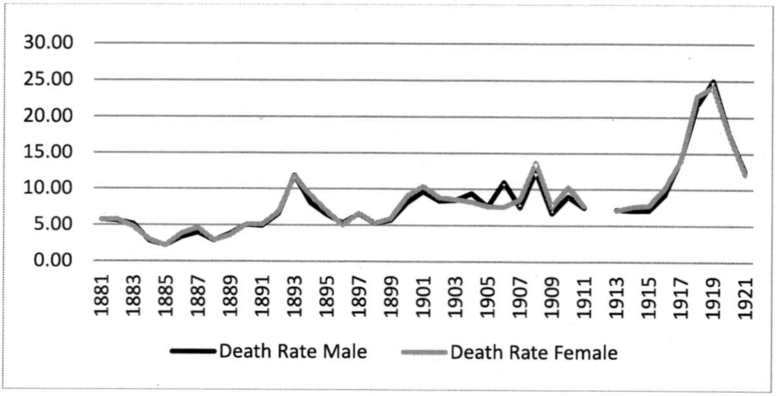

Source: Sanitary Commission Reports for the respective years.

GRAPH 9.6: FEVER DEATH RATES IN PURI, 1881-1921.

CHAPTER 10

Migration in the Famine Era
Gender, Caste and Class

In this chapter we shall assess the impact of sex-selective out-migration on the sex ratio (SR) in the three districts of Cuttack, Balasore and Puri between 1881 and 1921.[1] Incidentally, here we are dealing with historical migration. The process is very different from that of modern age and is much more complex. For example, nowadays many single and young women are migrating in search of job unlike in the past. Some of them are going for economic reasons but many are victims of trafficking.[2] The main hypothesis of this chapter is that part of the increased sex ratio is due to sex differential migration contrary to the views of the Census commissioners 1901 and many other famine scholars. This discussion is important to understand the prevailing social conditions and impact of various policies introduced during the colonial period, in a region that had frequently experienced famines. This can also throw some light on why this pattern of migration, actually distress migration, continued till the present time in regions such as Orissa.

The chapter has been divided into two parts. In the first part, we will assess the magnitude of migration, and analyse certain characteristics of migration as revealed through Census reports, literary sources, administration reports, Oriya newspapers, etc. In the second part, we will present the statistical results and then reflect upon it.

Before that, let us record a methodological caution.

Accuracy of Birth Place Statistics

Strictly speaking, in the initial years, the Census reports did not record migration but only birthplace statistics, i.e. the number of people born in a particular district. The Census also noted the names of those who were born in a particular district, but recorded elsewhere by the Census workers. From this the Census authorities inferred the extent of gross emigration in different Census years. Similar set of problems existed for immigration. While explaining the growth of population within a decade, they used to take net migration (immigration-emigration) into account, along with imperfect birth and death statistics.

The problem with this procedure is that short-term migrants, such as pilgrims or those who happened to be out of the district on that particular day when the Census was taken, would also be included. Second, the decennial figures on migration would underestimate the volume of migration, especially if famine or other disrupting forces caused such migration within that period. To give one example, the famine of 1907-8 did generate a lot of emigration but this would not have been reflected fully in the figures recorded in 1911, because the years 1910 and 1911 were non-famine years. The extent of famine emigration could also be temporary. Permanent or semi-permanent emigration during the famine period would, of course, be reflected in the decennial figures. Keeping these limitations in mind, we still use the birthplace data as it gives rough estimates of migration within India, especially if one only takes figures for non-contiguous districts.[3]

Classification of Out-migration[4] from Orissa Division

The Census categorizes migration streams according to the places such as: (a) contiguous parts of Orissa Division; (b) non-contiguous parts of Orissa; (c) contiguous parts of other provinces; (d) non-contiguous parts of other provinces; and (e) outside India.[5] Females dominated (a) and (c), i.e. out-migration to contiguous parts inside the division and to contiguous parts outside the division. In these kinds of emigration the females outnumbered males.

These types of emigration of females were considered to be marriage migration.[6] The other two categories of emigration, (b) and (d), reflect economic pressures, so we have considered only the latter two categories. In these categories males predominated.

Tables 10.1 and 10.2 show the proportion of emigrants to total population going to contiguous and non-contiguous parts of Cuttack, Balasore and Puri separately. It is evident from the Tables that the proportion of emigrants going to contiguous parts of the districts remained more or less constant but migration to non-contiguous parts inside and outside Orissa went on increasing.[7] Table 10.3 shows emigrants going to Bengal, Burma and Assam. As many as 70 per cent of the total emigrants of Cuttack went to Bengal in 1891; the proportion came down to 57 per cent in 1921. But the proportion of emigrants to Assam increased to 26 per cent. Balasore and Puri showed similar trends.

TABLE 10.1: EMIGRANTS FROM CUTTACK, BALASORE AND PURI, 1891-1921: TO CONTIGUOUS DISTRICTS

Contiguous Districts	*1891*	*1901*	*1911*	*1921*
Cuttack				
M	29,223	22,925	26,000	23,000
	(3.0)	(2.0)	(3.0)	(2.0)
F	36,479	27,762	33,000	33,000
	(4.0)	(3.0)	(3.0)	(3.0)
Balasore				
M	13,107	10,,953	9,000	8,000
	(3.0)	(2.0)	(2.0)	(2.0)
F	22,762	19,729	19,000	20,000
	(4.0)	(4.0)	(3.0)	(4.0)
Puri				
M	6,873	7,503	7,030	8,000
	(1.0)	(1.0)	(1.0)	(2.0)
F	16,185	16,911	17,010	20,000
	(3.0)	(3.0)	(3.0)	(4.0)

Note: The figures in parenthesis are percentages to total population.

Sources: Census of India 1891, vol. 8, pp. 120-1; *Census of India 1901*, vol. 6, pt. 1, p. 141; *Census of India 1911*, vol. 5, pt. 1, p. 189; *Census of India 1921*, vol. 7, pt. 1, p. 116.

TABLE 10.2: EMIGRANTS FROM CUTTACK, BALASORE AND PURI (1891-1921) TO NON-CONTIGUOUS DISTRICTS

Non-Contiguous Districts	*1891*	*1901*	*1911*	*1921*
Cuttack				
M	25,048	58,358	92,000	1,51,000
	(3.0)	(6.0)	(9.000)	(16.0)
F	11,508	7,714	21,000	49,000
	(1.0)	(1.0)	(2.0)	(4.0)
Balasore				
M	11,566	18,071	31,000	42,000
	(2.0)	(4.0)	(6.0)	(9.0)
F	2,205	3,010	4,000	6,000
	(0.4)	(1.0)	(1.0)	(1.0)
Puri				
M	1,614	3,899	8,800	24,100
	(0.3)	(1.0)	(2.0)	(5.0)
F	1,000	575	2,200	4,300
	(0.2)	(0.4)	(0.4)	(1.0)

Source: Same as in Table 10.1.

Table 10.1 depicts the absolute numbers as well as percentages of the emigrants going to the contiguous districts. More women than men migrated to contiguous districts. The Census commissioners observed that women migrated only for marriage purpose. It was termed as associational migration. Interestingly, however, clubbing women's migration only as marriage migration reflected the patriarchal mindset of the colonial officials. Recent research shows that women also traditionally migrated for economic purposes as well, though not the long distance. For example, T.A. Hema Kumari has done extensive research on the women migrants of coastal Andhra Pradesh. She observed that women were the best tobacco graders. In addition, they also got engaged in chilli plucking, sugar cane cutting, etc., though all these tasks were done seasonally.[8] Similar views are expressed by Jan Breman based on his research on Gujarat.[9] These streams of migration have become more prominent in the recent period. For example, women migrant workers joined in large numbers the apparel manufacturing industry both in Kerala and Bangalore after getting training in Bhubaneswar. They are mostly recruited from among those in the age group of 25-35.[10] Further, the findings of a research project of the Centre for Women's Development Studies also showed that women from SC and ST categories predominated in the 'circular migration'. In this case they migrate during the agriculturally lean season and come back home during the harvesting season. They were engaged in brick-kiln making and cutting of sugar canes in Hyderabad and other places.[11]

In the past however, most of the Oriya emigrants to Bengal were found in Calcutta. Hence more data on the characteristics of emigrants to the city are available. Interestingly, Oriya emigrants went alone unlike the migrants from Bihar.[12] The same trend continues even now. That is because the Oriya migrants generally belonged to the marginal peasant caste. They usually had a piece of land back home. Besides, the migrant worker may have had old parents to look after. So the family was always left behind in the village.

Age Distribution of Emigrants: Migration of Men in Prime of Life

The age distribution of Oriya emigrants who went outside Orissa, was important since the sex ratio in the age group of 15 to 60 was above unity and was increasing from 1891 to 1921. But unfortunately, the age distribution of emigrants from the Orissa Division was available only for Calcutta city in 1911 and 1921 censuses. In 1911, as Table 10.4 shows, 73 per cent of the total emigrants going to Calcutta from Cuttack were in the age group of 15-40. In case of Balasore, which is closer to Calcutta, the proportion was even higher, 75 per cent. In 1921 again, 68 per cent of the total emigrants from Cuttack to Calcutta belonged to the age group of 15-40. In Balasore, the proportion was 72 per cent (Table 10.4). Even though the numbers of crop failure were numerous, the percentage of migrants going from Cuttack to Calcutta had slightly declined. Perhaps Oriya migrants went to Assam in large num-

Table 10.3: Emigrants to Non-Contiguous Parts of Other Districts of India

	Bengal	*Assam*	*Burma*
Cuttack			
1891	25,619 (70%)	694	–
1901	49,103 (74%)	6,388 (10%)	–
1911	–	27,000 (24%)	–
1921	1,14,390 (57%)*	67,183 (26%)	1,240 (1%)
Balasore			
1891	12,904 (64%)	–	–
1901	17,159 (81%)	991 (5%)	–
1911	30,414 (87%)	2,000 (6%)	–
1921	39,287 (82%)	5,553 (12%)	740 (2%)
Puri			
1891	1,545 (59%)	–	–
1901	2,671 (60%)	381 (9%)	–
1911	–	–	–
1921	16,338 (58%)	5,653 (19%)	4,031 (14%)

Note: * These represent the percentage of emigrants going to non-contiguous parts of India.

Sources: Census of India 1891, vol. 3, pp. 120-1; *Census of India 1891*, vol. 3, pt. II, p. liii. The data on Assam was given at the divisional level *Census of India 1901*, vol. 6, pt. II, pp. 140-1; *Census of India, 1911*, vol. 5, pt. II; *Census of India 1921,* vol. 7, pt. 1, p. 112.

ber as the statistics showed (Table. 10.3). Again, Thompson, the Census Superintendent of Calcutta city in 1921 observed: 'seven out of every ten persons from Orissa were workers in the prime of their life'.[13] It is important to note that during these decades, a vast number of the working age male population continued to migrate to Calcutta or elsewhere as making a living in their village or even the region itself was difficult.

Thus, it is seen that nearly 3/4 of the Oriya emigrants belonged to the age group of 15-40, and nearly all the rest were in the age group of 40 and above (Table 10.4). It is likely that the age distribution of emigrants to other areas was similar, since the male population in this cohort was the most active. Of course, in the case of family migration, the children accompanied their parents and the SR of emigrants would be nearly one.[14]

Hence, there was strong possibility that the above unity SR in the age group 15-60 could be explained, at least partly, by increasing sex selective migration.

TABLE 10.4: EMIGRANTS FROM ORISSA TO CALCUTTA BY AGE GROUPS IN 1911 AND 1921

		Cuttack		*Balasore*	
		1911	*1921*	*1911*	*1921*
0-15	Male	999	3068	406	1240
	Female	189	445	71	113
15-40	Male	14,533 (72.60)	28,611 (68.7)	6,114 (74.1)	11,595 (72.7)
	Female	781	1,653	209	455
40 & above	Male	4,459	9,932	1,713	3,097
	Female	409	714	161	217
Total*	Male	19,991	41,611	8,233	15,932
	Female	1,379	2,812	441	785

Note: * Total included dependents also.

Sources: Census of India 1911, vol. 6, pt. II, p. 32; *Census of India 1921*, vol. 6, pt. II, p. 90.

Caste and Occupational Structure of Oriya Emigrants in Calcutta City

The caste composition and the occupational structure of Oriya emigrants were not available for all the census years. Data are available for three different periods but they are not comparable. However, a few points can be discerned from this data. First, it seemed that people from practically all caste groups migrated to Calcutta for work. Second, it was also evident that most of the Oriya emigrants were unskilled labourers. In 1895 a small sample of 465 workers of Cuttack and Balasore working in Durbar Cotton Mill, Shamya Nagar, Calcutta were interviewed for their caste identification. It was revealed that they belonged to various castes, including Khandayat, Brahmin, Karan, Gaur and Dhobi.[15] The sample was small. Still we can see that poverty and distress cut across castes, forcing them to go out in search of a living.

In 1911, the caste distribution of all Oriya emigrants (only for two districts) to Calcutta city and its suburbs was recorded. Table 10.5 shows that people from all castes went to Calcutta. But Khandayats, Karanas and Brahmins predominated. This was partly due to the fact that these higher castes had more access to resources and information, but also due to their higher percentage among the total population (particularly Khandayats).[16] Also noticeable is the absence of Bauris and Kandaras (both of these were untouchables and agricultural labouring castes) among the emigrants. This could be partly due to the fact that the emigrants from these castes did not reveal their caste identity. We do find occasional references regarding the Bauris as emigrants.[17] Another explanation may be that they found some unskilled work in the region or nearby. Or they lacked necessary capital to migrate to distant places. In 1921 again the caste composition of emigrants to Calcutta city and its suburbs was available, but separate figures for Oriyas were not given. But mention is made of the Khandayats (a typical Oriya cultivating caste) who were present among the emigrants to Calcutta city.[18] Various settlement reports, gazetteers and administration reports also pointed out that emigrants

TABLE 10.5: CASTE COMPOSITION OF EMIGRANTS FROM CUTTACK AND BALASORE TO CALCUTTA AND HER SUBURBS IN 1911 (PERCENTAGES IN THE PARENTHESIS)

Caste Name	*Cuttack*		*Balasore*	
	Total Number	*Suburbs*	*Total Number*	*Suburbs*
Vaishnava[19]	281 (1.3)		–	–
Brahmin	3,709 (17.49)		1,620 (18.68)	
Chasikaibarta	441 (2.06)		306 (3.53)	
Dhobis	821 (3.84)	222 (7.55)	245 (2.82)	
Goala	4,316 (20.20)	333 (11.33)	1,408 (16.23)	
Kayastha	2,286 (10.70)	329 (11.19)	1,261 (14.54)	
Khandayat	5,802 (27.15)	1,283 (43.64)	2,225 (26.23)	248 (34.40)
Napit	668 (3.13)		–	
Rajput	856 (4.10)		–	
Tanti	355 (1.61)		423 (4.88)	
Teli	620 (2.90)		298 (3.44)	
Pathan	458 (2.14)		–	
Others	757 (3.54)	773 (26.29)	8.38 (9.66)	473 (65.60)
Total	21,370	2,940	8,674	721

Note: Figures in parenthesis is the percentage.

Source: Census of India 1911, vol. 6, pt. II.

were drawn from almost all the castes. The literary sources also presented similar impressions. It is also possible to suggest that a larger number of migrants to Calcutta came from the Dalit castes. For example, Fakir Mohan Senapati wrote in his autobiography that people of very low castes used to go to Calcutta for odd jobs even in the early nineteenth century, usually in groups of 25 or 30 and some times, just as they crossed the border into Bengal, robbers used to pounce upon them.[20]

Hunter also noted that a large number of Gaur, Chasa and Telis – who would be called OBCs in the present-day parlance – migrated to Calcutta in search of employment. The former two castes supplied the servants and palanquin bearers whereas the Telis supplied porters and goods-carriers. He reported that all of them went back home after saving a little money.[21] N.N. Banerjee, Assistant to the Director of the Department of Land Revenue and Agriculture, presented a picture of Oriya migrants in Calcutta as to who did what. Brahmins were employed as cooks in *maths* and also in the homes of upper middle class Bengalis and Hindustanis; Goalas (Gaurs) served as palanquin bearers and domestic servants; Khandayats worked as *darwans;* Gurias (the sweet-maker caste who parched rice and paddy to prepare snacks) worked as vendors/shopkeepers of edibles as *murrimurki, chura* and *masala.*[22] Bhandaris (barbers) worked in the gas companies.[23] The caste order and the ascribed occupation were almost directly reflected even in the urban setting far away from their birth places, with minor variations.

The Commissioner of Orissa Division wrote in 1883-4 that there were 4,93,950 (17 per cent of the natural population of Cuttack and Balasore) 'lower class' people who were settled in Bengal according to the Census of 1881.[24] Various census reports of Bengal and Bihar and Orissa made references to the caste composition of Oriya migrants.[25] In 1908, the editor of *Utkal Barta* – published from Ganjam (Orissa) – quoting the Census report of 1901, commented that most Oriya emigrants had gone to Bengal either for daily wage labour or for jobs in the mills.[26] O'Malley, the author of *Cuttack Gazetteer 1933*, wrote in 1911 that Oriyas contributed to the rank of operatives in cotton mills and worked as carriers in jute mills.[27] Let us now look at the kind of work that they did a little more closely.

Occupational Structure of Migrants

Quantitative data on the occupational structure of the Oriya emigrants to Bengal are not available except for 1911 for Calcutta, and in 1921 for Bengal industrial workers. There are scattered references though, to some of the activities done by them. These data suggest that most of the Oriya migrants worked in the unorganized sector. Even in the organized sector they worked as unskilled labourers. For example, the census reports of 1911 as well as that of 1921 revealed that 29 per cent of Cuttack's migrants and 22 per cent of Balasore's migrants to Calcutta were in domestic service. The other large category was daily wage labour with 27 per cent of Cuttack's emigrants and 32 per cent of Balasore's emigrants working as daily labourers. Other miscellaneous occupations such as that of gardeners, absorbed 20 per cent of Cuttack's emigrants and 15 per cent of Balasore's emigrants in 1911. In 1921 this broad picture was maintained. But one noticed that more people had been absorbed in mills and factories and in miscellaneous jobs. In 1921, 71 per cent of the total Oriya emigrants who were working in industries were unskilled labourers.[28] Of the different industries, the jute industry employed the largest number of Oriya emigrants, both as skilled and unskilled workers. Incidentally, a few educated Oriyas like Madhusudan Das, studied law and was appointed as the resident tutor of Sir Ashutosh Mukherjee who became Vice-Chancellor of University of Calcutta. Similarly, Radhanath Rai studied in Calcutta but he did not like the food of the local people and thus decided to come back to Orissa. Further, Sachi Routray who later became a most famous poet of Orissa, even occupied managerial positions in jute mills. Skilled Oriya labourers constituted 7 per cent of the total workforce and unskilled 15 per cent of the total work force[29] in the jute industries. Among these migrants, one section from the Khandayat caste group developed skills as plumbers in Calcutta. Gradually this group spread to other cities of India. Interestingly, even now plumbers migrate to different parts of India from certain villages of one district of Orissa.[30]

Other Features of Migrants to Calcutta

The Census Report of 1921 for Calcutta city shows that the Sirdars (labour contractors) were employed by factory owners to recruit the labourers from different regions. Generally, the Sirdars belonged to the villages from where they recruited gangs of men to work as labourers, and as operatives in Calcutta. Quite often they accompanied them to Calcutta, kept them together and maintained some sort of discipline and control over them until they returned to their homes.[31] In 1907 the District Gazetteer of Balasore also described this phenomenon, of Oriyas would leave home so long as they could go with someone in whom they had confidence.[32] Again, the Bengal Census Report for 1921 reported that the migrants generally came from a closely circumscribed area, often a few adjoining villages, because of the Sirdari system.[33] The Sirdars generally brought their poorer co-villagers with them.[34] It was reported that Oriya migrants visited their native villages once every two or three years. Migrants generally returned in the peak of the agricultural season according to the various census report. On the other hand, the commissioners of the Royal Commission of Labour noted that the labourers left the jute mills in the slack season in agriculture.[35] It is quite possible that this was the case as the Great Depression was beginning to emerge. Perhaps the demand for jute products had declined. It is also interesting to note the Sirdari system still continues even now, particularly in western Orissa. Labourers migrate to various small-scale industries in the neighbouring states during the slack season of the agriculture or in the wake of a drought situation. The labourers are recruited by Sirdars, who pay an advance to them and keep them as bonded labourers. Of course, the kind of torture which the migrants face nowadays becomes viral because of the presence of the press and the social media. Earlier however, such type of news was absent, though that does not mean that the Sirdars were lenient then.

Characteristics of Migrants to Other Places

Admittedly, the characteristics of the emigrants to other places were different. For example, migrants also went to the Tributary States where vast fallow lands were available. According to O'Malley, the nearly equal number of male and female migrants from Cuttack indicated that they were permanent. These migrants were attracted towards the arable land of the Tributary States.[36] Table 10.6 shows that females predominated in the migration streams from Balasore and Puri to the Tributary States, and that the volume of out-migration did not increase between 1901 and 1921, so it did not influence the increased SR. In the case of Cuttack, the SR of migrants was unity and it did not influence the increased SR. But in the case of Balasore and Puri, the SRs of the migrants were above one, in which case, if the volume of migration increased it would lead to an increase in SR. However, the volume

TABLE 10.6: EMIGRANTS FROM CUTTACK, BALASORE AND PURI TO TRIBUTARY STATES, 1901, 1911 AND 1921

		1901	*1911*	*1921*
Cuttack				
	Male	11,488	14,456	12,859
	Female	9,606*	13,575	14,516
		(836)	(939)	(1,126)
Balasore				
	Male	7,306	7,977	7,032
	Female	13,376	14,606	14,961
		(1,830)	(1,831)	(2,128)
Puri				
	Male	4,635	4,346	4,018
	Female	8,525	8,769	9,204
		(1,839)	(2,018)	(2,291)

Note: *Figures in parenthesis is sex ratio females per thousand males.

Sources: Census of India 1901, vol. 6, pt. 1, Appendix 1, p. viii; *Census of India 1911*, vol. 5, pt. III, Imperial Table XI, pt. A; *Census of India, 1921*, vol. 7, pt. II, Imperial Table XI, pt. A.

did not increase. From this it can be inferred that migration to the Tributary States did not influence the increased SR.

The caste composition and occupational structure of these migrants are not known, except that according to Senapati's autobiography, some of the emigrants belonged to the writers' caste (Karan) and they went to the Tributary States to maintain the court records.[37] At the same time it can be inferred from the nature of the occupation – agriculture in what was fallow land – a large number of the migrants were likely to be from the farmer's caste. Sometimes the kings of the princely states also needed Brahmins from the coastal areas. So some of them would be from that caste as well.

The Oriya emigrants also went to Assam and Burma and the volume of migration was becoming significant – 34 per cent of the total emigrants went to Assam from Cuttack in 1921. Recently we have not come across any serious study on the pattern of migration from Orissa to Assam, though it had steadily increased over many decades. But studies from other parts of India, namely, Jharkhand, shed very interesting light on the system. Migrants from Tributary States also used to go to Assam for working in tea plantations. It was happening in other parts of India also. Tribal people's migration to Assam took place in an environment of tribal revolt against the colonial rulers in the early part of the nineteenth century. At that time, the practice of slavery was abolished in Britain and the planters were afraid of losing cheap labour. So to continue their trade and production activities and at the same time in order to tame the rebelling tribals, the colonial administration took them to Assam in the form of indentured labour.[38] This happened throughout the British empire with relocation of labouring population in many regions overseas. As mentioned earlier, in Orissa also the tribals had rebelled against the colonial rulers. So the rulers recruited them for the Assam tea plantations. But the most important point to note is that earlier the labourers were recruited under the Sirdari system or labour-contractor system. But later it took the form of worker-agent system. In this case the relationship acquired some new features, which has been described by some as a transition from the Sirdari sytem to Ristedari system.[39] In practice, however, the agent's control over the labourer remained in tact. Even though Ristedari system suggested some element of patronage and personal support to the person and the family, the system under its many modern forms continued to carry the stamp of the grip of the powerful middleman despite many regulations. The 'dadan labour' migration out of Kalahandi, Bolangir, Ganjam and Mayurbhanj in contemporary Orissa bore witness to this phenomenon.[40]

The emigration to Burma from Puri – 12 per cent by 1921 (Table 10.3) – had also assumed some significance. Unfortunately, little data are available on migrants to Assam in 1901, which showed that the SR of emigrants was higher than those going to Calcutta, at least in one Census year (Table 10.7). According to Tallents, the Census Superintendent of 1921, most migrants going to Assam were from the Tributary States, though they were registered in Cuttack and Balasore.[41] In fact, the migrants from Tributary States comprised tribal population and generally the entire family migrated out of this region. Further, the number of migrants going to these places was much smaller than to Calcutta.

TABLE 10.7: TOTAL EMIGRANTS TO ASSAM FROM CUTTACK, BALASORE AND PURI BETWEEN 1901 AND 1921

		1901	*1911*	*1921*
Cuttack				
	Male	4,156	27,000 (3%)	67183 (7%)
	Female	2,232	--	
Balasore				
	Male	814	2,000	5,553
	Female	991		
Puri				
	Male	199	N.A.	5,653
	Female	182		

Sources: Census of India 1901, vol. 3, pt. II, Table 11; *Census of India 1911*, vol. 5, pt. 1, p. 182; *Census of India, 1921*, vol. 7, pt. I, p. 112.

So our general conclusion regarding the characteristics of migrants will hold good even if we have less information on the characteristics of migrants going to places other than Calcutta.

Quantitative Evidence of Famine Migration between 1866 and 1921 in Orissa Division

Famine generated a lot of migration and many died on the way. As Maharanta observed, it generated 'mapless migration'.[42] For example, during the Irish famine of 1845-9, nearly 10,000 famine victims sailed to Canada out of whom one-sixth died on the way.[43]

Cormac O' Grada et al. also rang a similar note. The authors observed that the Irish Famine generated mass migration, which had significant impact on society, economy and even culture. After the famine, Ireland developed the capitalist pattern of agricultural growth.[44] Besides, the authors have mentioned various streams of migration during the historical era. According to them, men migrated to long distance places and women went to nearby cities. Another international experience was the famine of 1921-2 in Russia, when large number of people became nomadics and left for the city. In this case in large number, women and children became the victims and died while searching for food.[45]

In case of India, the subsistence crisis in 1876-8 which also known as 'Madras Famine' or 'Temple Famine', not only killed many people but led to large-scale migration to Ceylon. Between 1891 and 1900 and a series of famines generated migration in the range of 1,40,000 to 1,60,000 on an average.[46] Similarly, Maharatna also observed that Bombay Presidency experienced famines in 1905-6 and 1911-12, which led to migration of adult males to more prosperous areas. In fact, Bipin Shah argues that the Indian diaspora was formed due to excessive famines during the colonial period.[47]

Famines did generate a lot of purposeful as well as aimless wandering in Orissa Division as in famines elsewhere. The emigration statistics for the 1866 famine were collected in June and July 1867, along with the statistics of mortality. The zamindars had been given forms to note the statistics on emigration along with that of death. It should be pointed out that the data on emigration related to the number of emigrants who had left at the beginning of the famine, so they did not include distress migration during the peak period of the famine of 1866.[48] Therefore, it would be a gross under-reporting of emigration. According to Table 10.8, only 4 per cent of the total population had emigrated. During the famine of 1866, the Collector of Balasore was so concerned about the lack of rice that he wanted the people of Balasore to migrate to Calcutta.[49] In the present global context, perhaps famines do not kill a lot of people, but besides the health and other socio-economic effects, migration, both permanent and temporary has emerged as a major safety net.[50] The march of a stream of people of Honduras across Mexico to cross the border into the US is one modern example of this phenomenon. Besides waves of refugees from Africa and West Asia are going to Europe by sea.[51]

Those who reached Calcutta in 1866 were not allowed to stay there. The authorities raised some money and sent the paupers back in September 1866 when the famine was at its height.[52] The authorities in Calcutta felt threatened that the paupers would spread diseases. Further, they did not want to show the ugly side of the administration.

Since the salt tracts of Puri were most affected by the famine,

TABLE 10.8: MIGRATION FROM ORISSA DIVISION IN THE INITIAL STAGE OF THE FAMINE AT 1866*

	Cuttack	*Balasore*	*Puri*
Estimated Population in 1865	1,503,829	732,269	779,718
Emigrants	53,357	29,558	32,113
Percentage of emigration to population of 1865	3.5	4.01	4.1

Note: * The Collectors did not give any specific time period as the initial stage of the famine. But presumably it started from January 1866 because estimate of mortality covered the period beginning at that time.

Sources: GOI/Home/Public, January 1868, nos. 21-2, pt. A.
Also see, the *Utkal Dipika,* 18 August 1868.

the people migrated to other parts of the district besides going outside the region during the famine of 1866.[53] It was reported in the General Administration Report for 1867-8, that the destitute of the salt tract could not live in their original places after the famine and so were brought to other parts of the Khorda government estate to be settled.[54] It was also reported by the Famine Commissioner of 1866 that only women and children had come to the relief centres because able-bodied men had left for the districts which were relatively less affected by the famine. They usually left their families behind.[55] As we have discussed earlier in Chapter 4, one of the reasons the Oriya migrants went to far off places searching for food and work was that they had a sense of shame if not guilt, in eating in the relief centres. Even in present-day India, the number of migrants swells up as and when the food crisis becomes imminent. In recent times, the press has reported large-scale migration in the wake of drought situation both in the economically developed states of Tamil Nadu and Maharashtra.[56]

The Bengal records show that a large number of migrants from Cuttack and Balasore had gone to Hugli and Howrah.[57] The Collectors of Hugli and Howrah had set up relief centres and hospitals for them. In 24-Parganas also, deaths had occurred on a considerable scale among the migrants from Midnapur and the districts of Orissa from where people had come in search of employment during the famine of 1866.[58] As we have noted in the Chapter 4 many families left for British colonies by ship and died on the way because of hazardous environment. In 1888-9 there was a partial famine in Orissa Division. In that year many people had left earlier than usual for Calcutta in search of employment and the number of emigrants was also greater than usual.[59] Similarly, in the famine year of 1908, the Sanitary Commissioner of Bengal Presidency had noted that the birth rate had fallen following the famine, partly because the poorer people had left in search of employment elsewhere.[60]

The Collectors' reports on the famine of 1908 were full of references to famine migration. Even though they did not give the total number of emigrants from Orissa during that particular famine year, it was evident from their remarks that the number of emigrants had increased significantly compared to non-famine years. The Collector of Puri described the famine situation of Puri in a detailed manner. He wrote that the Chilika tract that was affected most had depended on one crop only and when this crop failed, men migrated to Rangoon, Calcutta and other places. Women, children and old persons were left behind in the villages.[61] But in the other parts of the district (Puri), which were equally affected people did not migrate to Calcutta, instead they went to Puri city to look for jobs,[62] because the temple in Puri had various activities such as supplying vegetables, flowers, basil leaves, firewood and clay pots round the year. Besides, pilgrims come to the temple throughout the year. For each of the activities people were required. Hence most of the migrants were absorbed in the city itself.

In Balasore the Collector informed the Commissioner that a 'large exodus' of labourers was going on from all parts of Bhadrakh subdivision to Calcutta. Every week at least 1,000 people were leaving for Calcutta via the Bengal-Nagpur railway.[63] During the famine of 1907-8, the SDO of Jajpur thana in Cuttack had estimated that roughly 50,000 people or 9 per cent of the total population of 1901 of that thana had emigrated in search of jobs.[64]

The Census Superintendent of Bengal of 1911 noted that the pressure of hard times had induced the labourers and small cultivators to migrate to different places for supplementing their earnings.[65]

In the decade 1911-21, even though Orissa suffered from a series of crop failures, famine was never declared, but the Annual Administration reports continued to report distress migration from Orissa and Bihar.[66] In the years 1918-19 and also 1919-20, out-migration had increased considerably following the famine in Orissa.[67] In the year 1919-20 it was reported that 99 per cent of the coolies to Assam were recruited from Chhota Nagpur and Orissa who had gone there because of scarcity conditions.[68] It should be emphasized that in the conditions of distress migration the labourers do not have any bargaining power to influence the wage rate. Thus the nature of distress in the famine context does not secure even minimum level of human rights. Further as mentioned in this chapter below, the local people always looked down upon the coolies.

That the famine of 1919 also induced a lot of migration to Calcutta and Assam is also evident from the Oriya newspapers. During this year the *Utkal Dipika* published a series of news items and letters about the increased outmigration. In March 1919, for example, a letter was published from Puri that people who had migrated due to famine were sending two to four rupees per head to their families.[69] On 15 March 1919, the same weekly reported that cholera was spreading in Cuttack and people were migrating to Assam as coolies, a large number from the princely states, due to shortage of food.[70] The census report also wrote that for every 100 males enumerated in Cuttack, 18.2 males born in the district were enumerated outside; for Balasore it was 11.4 and for Puri it was 7.0.[71] In 1928 it was stated in the report of the Royal Commission on Agriculture that emigration from North Bihar had decreased but that from the Orissa Division had increased considerably in 1921, compared to 1911, reflecting scarcity conditions in Puri.[72]

Other Indicators of Famine Emigration

More statistical evidence is available for the famines of 1907-8 and 1918-19, especially on emigrants to Assam tea plantations, the amount of money orders received and related aspects. Gopabandhu Das of Orissa conducted a sample survey. The result of the survey presented valuable information. All these indicated that emigration did increase following the famine of 1918-19. Again a question was raised in the Legislative Council of Bihar and Orissa, regarding the increase in emigration to Assam, following the famine in Orissa in 1918-19. Table 10.9 gives the data supplied on a number of emigrants to Assam. It shows a considerable increase in the number of emigrants in January and February of 1919, which was the beginning period of the famine. It also gave data on the period just after the harvest of the winter paddy with

TABLE 10.9: ABSOLUTE NUMBER OF ORIYA EMIGRANTS TO ASSAM TEA PLANTATIONS ON MONTHLY BASIS FROM 1914-15 TO 1918-19

Districts/Years	*Months*						
	August	*September*	*October*	*November*	*December*	*January*	*February*
Cuttack							
1914-15	11	4	5	3	15	85	70
1915-16	80	38	41	18	40	113	129
1916-17	4	Nil	1	3	10	15	41
1917-18	Nil	Nil	3	9	5	28	39
1918-19	5	3	3	13	65	329	315
Balasore							
1916-17	181	70	48	51	49	142	384
1917-18	19	17	28	10	13	35	59
1918-19	17	11	14	17	175	482	621
Puri							
1918-19	15	12	93	119	194	584	611

Sources: Proceedings of Bihar and Orissa Legislative Council, 4 March 1919, p. 66. For Cuttack, ibid., 1 April 1919, p. 269.

TABLE 10.10: THE NUMBER OF EMIGRANTS FROM ORISSA (MOSTLY FROM CUTTACK AND BALASORE)

Year	*No. of emigrants*	*Index number*
1915-16	32,000	640
1916-17	5,000	100
1917-18	2,000	40
1918-19	51,000	1,020
1919-20	12,000	240

Source: Census of India 1921, vol. VII, pt. 1.

comparisons with corresponding months of the previous years. However, the authorities did not provide much systematic data on the nature and extent of migration.

Tallents noted in 1921 that the volume of emigrants had increased in the last quinquennium of the decade 1911-21. Table 10.11 shows that the index number of emigration increased by more than 10 times within a year if we take 1916-17 as the base year. The volume of emigration was also large in the year 1915-16, indicating the fact that famine conditions had prevailed in that year as well. Tallents also commented, 'The great development of emigration is an indication of the hard times that Orissa has passed through since 1918 and also shows how it was that a repetition of the tragedy of 1866 was avoided.[73] Dyson also mentioned about the emigration of tea estate workers from Orissa and about their bad living conditions and the shabby treatment they got from the local people and that they did not protest despite all that.[74] This showed the miserable condition, which lay behind their emigration.

Money order data also throw some light on migration but have to be used with care. For instance, an increase in money orders was perhaps a sign that migration had increased. It is, of course, possible that migrants did not obtain employment or they sent money by other means, in both of which cases the money order data would have under-estimated emigration. However, these factors are unlikely to have increased during the famines. Further, we only have data on the number of money orders and the total amounts.

TABLE 10.11: THE AMOUNT RECEIVED BY POSTAL MONEY ORDER IN VARIOUS UNIONS OF SUBDIVISIONS OF JAJPUR AND KENDRAPARA; CUTTACK DISTRICT DURING THE PERIOD OF THE FLOOD OF 1907, COMPARED THE CORRESPONDING PERIOD OF 1906

Name of Post Office	*Amount received during August-November 1906*	*Amount received during August-November 1907*	*Index number taking first column as base*
Patamundai	28,000	34,000	121
Albha	8,000	13,000	163
Dharamsala	25,268	35,001	139
Jenapur	6,738	7,276	108
Jajpur	33,079	41,520	126
Kabirpur	20,914	31,317	150
Rambag	22,045	23,017	104
Aul	22,000	31,000	141
Total	1,67,046	2,16,132	129

Sources: GOI/Rev/Agri/FP, January 1908, no. 4141 Agri; From the Chief Secy., RD to GOB to the Secy; to Rev/Agri. GOI, 9 December 1907, Statement no. 8.

The amounts and number of money orders sent, differed from migrant to migrant; so one should not make mechanical inferences regarding the number of migrants. With these qualifications in mind, we can turn to the actual data.

The available data on money orders related only to certain affected areas and for two famines: 1907-8 and 1918-19. For earlier famines such data are not available. The amount of money sent by each of the Oriya emigrants was perhaps small.[75] According to Tallents, the average value of each of the money order was between Rs. 10 and 11.[76]

Table 10.11 shows the amounts received by some of the post offices of the flood affected area of Cuttack in October-November, 1906 which was a normal year and in the corresponding months of 1907, which was visited by floods, famine and cholera epidemic. There was a significant increase in the latter period. In case of the famine of 1918-19 again, data on money orders are available for

Bihar and Orissa taken together from 1915-20. The data was also available for Orissa Division separately for the year 1918-19 only.

When we calculated the index number of money orders received, taking 1915 as base, it is noticed that the amount received in 1919 had increased by 44 per cent. Next year, it went up still further (Table 10.12). It shows that the amount of money that came through money orders was quite substantial in Cuttack amounting to Rs. 33.9 million. Next in order of importance were Puri and Balasore. Thus, money order transfers contributed some relief to some families in the devastated economy. But it was too meagre, if we take the population of the Orissa Division and the Princely States as a whole.

On 29 March 1919 the *Dipika* reported that many persons belonging to *bhadralok* (gentry) families had emigrated to Calcutta because of the famine. After a few days, they used to send Rs. 1 to 1.50 each to their families through money orders.[77]

Even though it is hazardous to infer the volume of outmigration during the famine period from the increase in the extent of money order, the remarks of Tallents and the news-report in the *Dipika* did indicate that perhaps the volume of out-migration during famine increased. A second point to note is that the receiving families in the famine affected areas would have tided over the economic crisis with some ease than the non-receiving families.

TABLE 10.12: TOTAL SUMS REMITTED BY MONEY ORDER TO BIHAR AND ORISSA BETWEEN 1915 AND 1920 (RS. IN MILLION)

Years	*Amount*	*Percentage increase taking 1915 as base 100*
1915	42.1	100
1916	48.7	116
1917	45.0	107
1918	54.1	129
1919	60.8	144
1920	66.6	158

Source: Census of India 1921, vol. VII, pt. 1, p. 109.

Table 10.13: Sums by Money Order sent by Emigrants of Orissa between 1915 and 1920 from Outside Orissa

Name of the district	*Number of money orders*	*Total sums remitted in Rupees million*
Cuttack (including Angul)	3,101	33.9
Balasore	1,081	11.2
Puri	869	12.0

Source: Census of India, 1921, vol. VII, pt. 1, p. 108.

The editor of *The Samaj*, Gopabandhu Das, conducted a sample survey of some villages in Puri in order to ascertain the extent of mortality and of emigration from each village. The object of this sample survey was to show that even though people were dying of starvation, the government did not declare famine in Orissa. This data collected by a prominent social worker at that time may have a different perspective from that underlying government statistics. Keeping that in mind, we can analyse these statistics, which relate to 6 months from June to November 1919.

From Gopabandhu's survey we have prepared Table 10.14, which shows that emigration took place in a majority of villages. But in most cases it was well below 5 per cent, assuming 5 people per family (the ratio generally assumed). Only in one village Kubajanga did it amount to as much as 10 per cent. Total deaths were 257 or 4 per cent of the total population and the total migration was 53 or 1 per cent of the total population.

From other sources we find that the decennial migration figures also showed that the outmigration had increased considerably during the decade ending 1921 compared to other decades, which we will discuss later. This decade experienced the maximum number of years of crop failures, so much so that the relief work continued till 1920 in all the three districts, because of floods that followed the drought of 1919.[78] Even Puri which was so far a receiving district, started sending male and female emigrants out to the extent of 6.48 per cent males and 4.8 per cent females.

One may argue that the migration from Orissa Division

TABLE 10.14: STATISTICS OF MORTALITY AND EMIGRATION COLLECTED BY GOPABANDHU DAS'S SAMPLE SURVEY IN PURI DISTRICT – JUNE TO NOVEMBER 1919

Names	*No.of families**	*Deaths during last 6 months (persons)*	*Emigrants*	*% of emigration to total persons*
Bhuaun	12	11	1	2
Babarada	30	1	1	1
Chhaitana	200	60	–	–
Sahadapada	120	14	2	0.3
Nuapara	35	13	2	1.1
Kabirajpur	40	3	–	–
Bagha	20	8	–	–
Chotolo	30	12	5	3
Paikpara	40	4	2	2
Odo Sahi	20	3	5	5
Sunder	50	1	–	–
Dalaisahi	10	1	–	–
Balibasant	30	20	–	–
Kubajanga	4	3	2	10
Enchol	100	12	–	–
Torkar	150	25	14	2
Enchra	220	4	3	0.3
Padmapara	35	4	3	2
Chashiri	50	4	3	1
Behereda	22	43	4	4
Chundhra	40	3	3	2
Nand geroda	25	–	1	1
Podtata	35	2	2	1
Sannapur	60	5	–	–
Aaima	8	–	–	–
Gunia	90	1	–	–
Total	7050	257	53	

Note: *Let us assume that each family was comprised five members.

Source: The Samaj, 25 October and 1 November 1919.

increased during the decade ending 1921 because of the industrial expansion in Calcutta and its suburbs, the boom in the tea industry of Assam, and the introduction of the labour contract system in the tea industry. Undoubtedly, the pull factors also helped to increase out-migration in general. But there is no reason to assume that during this particular year 1921, the demand for labour was so unusually high as to attract such a large number of emigrants. The fact that the out-migration from Orissa, particularly in the decade ending 1921, was more due to distress than to industrial expansion is evident from two factors.

First, the decade ending 1911 had a series of crop failures and excess deaths culminating in the famine years of 1907 and 1908, whereas 1910 agriculturally was a good year. The decade ending 1921 also had a series of crop failures and excess deaths culminating in the famine years of 1918 and 1919. The end year 1920 was also a year with floods, crop failures and excess deaths. Hence, emigration from Orissa had increased more than in the previous decade.

Second, that the extent of out-migration from Orissa had increased due to distress rather than industrial expansion was evident from the narratives of the Census Superintendent of Assam and recent researches. There was stagnation both in tea plantations (and jute industry), which were the major employers of Oriya emigrants.[79] Scholars like Jagabandhu Acharya and Pradipta Chaudhuri have attributed the migration of Oriyas to Calcutta and Assam to the serious nature of the credit relations. Acharya considers the period from 1866 to 1921, while Chaudhuri concentrates on 1901-31. Acharya is of the view that the majority of *raiyats* were indebted to moneylenders and zamindars. The *raiyats* sold their holdings to the moneylenders and the zamindars in order to clear their debts. The class composition of the buyers of the *raiyati* lands as given in the Maddox Report has been cited as evidence. In addition, Acharya observes that there was a decline in the productivity in agriculture in the early part of the twentieth century, as shown in the lower utilization of irrigation water and the decline in the total number of cattle, ploughs and carts. There was a decline in the standard yield per acre of land also. So Acharya concluded that employment opportunities shrunk in Orissa forcing Oriyas to migrate to Calcutta.[80]

In a similar light, Pradipta Chaudhuri points out that the majority of the small *raiyats* were indebted to moneylenders and the zamindars. In order to clear their debts they had to first dispose of their produce at harvest price and later when they needed rice for their own consumption they had to buy at pre-harvest price. If they could not meet their debt obligations out of their current output, they mortgaged their land to the zamindars. If this process continued for a long time they had to sell the land to the zamindars. In order to show that the *raiyats* were selling or mortgaging their lands in distress, the author has matched the annual series of output and the total registration of mortgaged holdings and sales and noticed that the series were related inversely sometimes with a lag. According to Chaudhuri, the average value of sales as well as that of mortgage 'generally declined' in the years of heavy sales and mortgages. From this he inferred that small *raiyats* were selling off their lands under distress. He also concluded that a large stratum of agricultural labourers was created out of small *raiyats*. He showed that the average size of the holding also decreased between 1890 and 1931. A large percentage of such lands were actually cultivated by hired labour. Hence the employment opportunity of small peasants declined. Put it together with the fact that the real wage in the jute industry and tea plantation had declined. Despite that, the volume of the Oriya migrants increased in the decade ending in 1921. Chaudhuri concluded that the Oriya migrants, especially the small *raiyats*, were migrating under distress.[81]

Both the authors confirm the hypothesis that outmigration took place because of distress though the pull factors were also in operation. While agreeing with them we put more emphasis on food shortage and epidemics.

Outmigration and Increasing Sex Ratio: The Statistical Indicators

Finally, we wanted to check whether there was an association between the increasing sex ratio during 1891-1921 and out-migration from Orissa Division. For this we have adopted two indicators:

1. Comparison of SR of currently married at the end of low mortality and high mortality decades, and
2. Comparison of the percentages of emigrants to total population at the end of low mortality and high mortality decades.

Comparison of SR of Currently Married in Low Mortality and High Mortality Decades

The Census gives data on the currently married for the relevant census years. The logic of using this ratio to indicate the sex selective outmigration is as follows:

The SR of the currently married will be unity unless: (a) there is polyandry or polygamy. There was no polyandry, but there was some polygamy: some men had more than one wife;[82] but this was probably not very widespread. (b) There were some currently married wives outside the district at the time of the Census. (c) There were some currently married men outside the district. (Note that if monogamy is the rule whether or not mortality is sex-differential is irrelevant; dead women and their widowers both drop out of the calculation.) In fact, both men and women migrated. The major part of female migration (currently married) was for delivery. Men migrated mostly for economic reasons. We are interested particularly in comparing the SRs of currently married at the end of the decades. Table 10.15 gives such ratios. Note that the SR of currently

TABLE 10.15: SEX RATIO OF THE CURRENTLY MARRIED IN CUTTACK, BALASORE AND PURI – 1891-1921

District	*1891*	*1901*	*1911*	*1921*
Cuttack	1,079	1,091	1,138	1,187
Balasore	1,068	1,075	1,117	1,107
Puri	998	1,009	1,017	1,080

Sources: Census of India 1891, vol. 4, pp. 113-259; *Census of India 1901*, vol. 6 A, pt. II, pp. 47-8; *Census of India 1911*, vol. 5, pt. III, pp. 34-5; *Census of India 1921*, vol. 7, pt. II, pp. 37-8

married (along with the SR of general population) increased over time in the previous decade and particularly sharply over 1911-21. This could be due to three reasons:

(a) Polygamy went up after famines, so there were more wives than husbands. This may have happened because fathers may have allowed their daughters to become second or third wives for economic reasons. But there was no reason to believe that this occurred on a wide scale.[83]
(b) The net out-migration of married women for first deliveries fell. This was likely, since fewer conceptions may have taken place.[84] We also have data on in-migration of females and males and out-migration of males and females to contiguous parts. Note that the currently married ratio increased over time in all the three districts taking 1891 as base. But the ratio slightly declined in Balasore in the year 1921 and the rate of change was almost the same as that of the previous census year in the case of Cuttack. Nonetheless the ratio increased over the decades.

It could have been due to three factors. First, polygamy was on the increase. This was perhaps not widespread because various social reform movements were taking place all over India including Orissa. Second, the net migration of females may have fallen. The data show that the percentage of the female immigrants was constant in Cuttack and Puri and had slightly declined in Balasore (Table 10.16). Similarly, the percentage of the female emigrants to contiguous districts increased over the previous decade (Table 10.1). In other words, the immigration of females did not affect the sex ratio of currently married. On the other hand, the increased female emigrants to contiguous districts would have reduced the number of females in Orissa Division. Third, male outmigration may have increased over the decades, thus leading to increased SR of currently married. This in fact seems the most likely (Table 10.15). Table 10.15 shows that the SR of currently married had slightly declined in Balasore in 1921. Perhaps more unmarried and widowers than currently married persons were migrating.

TABLE 10.16: PROPORTION OF IMMIGRANTS TO TOTAL ACTUAL POPULATION, 1891-1921*

Districts/Years	*Actual Population*		*Immigration (female per 1,000 males)*	
	Male	*Female*	*Male*	*Female*
Cuttack				
1891	9,40,557	9,97,114	8,817 (1.0)	21,117 (2.0)
1901	9,95,409	10,67,349	11,696 (1.0)	21,338 (2.0)
1911	10,01,175	11,07,964	10,349 (1.0)	22,905 (2.0)
1921	9,52,543	11,12,135	10,051 (1.0)	23,224 (2.0)
Balasore				
1891	4,81,638	5,12,987	15,006 (3.0)	19,917 (4.0)
1901	5,17,543	5,53,654	13,235 (3.0)	16,232 (3.0)
1911	5,04,615	5,50,953	12,257 (2.0)	20,172 (4.0)
1921	4,66,122	5,14,382	10,869 (2.0)	17,302 (3.0)
Puri				
1891	4,74,530	4,70,468	15,797 (3.0)	24,132 (5.0)
1901	5,06,839	5,10,445	20,919 (4.0)	32,114 (6.0)
1911	5,06,570	5,16,832	17,667 (3.0)	25,773 (5.0)
1921	4,55,543	4,96,108	13,519 (3.0)	23,291 (5.0)

Note: *Figures in parenthesis are percentages to total actual population.

Sources: Census of India 1891, vol. 8, pp. 120-1; *Census of India 1901,* vol. 6, pt. I, pp. 98-100 and 141; *Census of India 1911*, vol. 6, pt. I, p. 189; *Census of India 1921*, vol. 7, pt. 1, pp. 44-7 and 116.

Pattern of Emigration through Birthplace Data

Table 10.17 shows the volume of emigration (taking contiguous and non-contiguous together) from 1891 to 1921. The percentage of male emigrants to actual population increased from 6 per cent to 18 per cent between 1891 and 1921, but the percentage of female emigrants fluctuated between ¯ and 7 in Cuttack. Next we take emigrants contiguous and non-contiguous parts separately. The percentage of male emigrants to non-contiguous parts of other parts of the Division and to other provinces, to actual population increased from 3 to 16 and that of females from 1 to 4, in Cuttack. Similar trends are also noticed in Balasore and Puri. Tables 10.16 and 10.17 are calculated without correcting the mortality effect on migrants. The Census authorities did not include the mortality effect. They took the increase of emigration over the previous decade assuming the fact that immigration was more or less stationary.

A study by Zachariah on the other hand, has included the mortality effect as well.[85] Since he has computed the survival ratio as well, it will not be out of place to discuss the procedure briefly since we are using his estimated survival ratio. Zachariah, for example, first wanted to estimate the all-India mortality level for the general population of 1901. So he chose the expectation of life at 10, because the mortality level of the expectation of life at zero was not reliable. He then scrutinized the set of Model Life Tables in the United Nations Manual III and chose the one with same expectation of life at 10, i.e. the expectation of life at zero was 25.5. From this table he computed 10 years survival ratio for each of the five years. The survival ratio of the all-India population was not applicable to the migrants because of two reasons. First, migrants have a different mortality schedule; second, migrants have different age distribution. He noted that on both the counts there was no information; except for the fact that the age distribution of the communities, which contained a large percentage of migrants was known. He had cited the example of Bombay city where 77.4 per cent of the male population and 70.5 per cent of the female population were born outside Bombay in 1931. A similar percent-

TABLE 10.17: PROPORTION OF TOTAL EMIGRANTS TO ACTUAL POPULATION – 1891-1921*

	Actual population		*Emigrants*	
	Male	*Female*	*Male*	*Female*
Cuttack				
1891	9,40,557	9,97,114	54,271 (6.0)`	47,987 (5.0)
1901	9,95,409	10,67,349	81,283 (8.0)	35,476 (3.0)
1911	1,10,01,175	11,07,964	118,277 (12.0)	54,397 (5.10)
1921	9,52,543	11,12,135	173,557 (18.0)	82,264 (7.0)
Balasore				
1891	4,81,638	5,12,987	24,673 (5.0)	24,967 (5.0)
1901	5,17,543	5,53,654	29,024 (5.0)	22,739 (4.0)
1911	5,04,615	5,50,953	43,319 (9.0)	29,157 (5.0)
1921	4,66,122	5,14,382	53,251 (11.0)	30,206 (6.0)
Puri				
1891	4,74,530	4,70,468	8,487 (2.0)	17,185 (4.0)
1901	5,06,839	5,10,445	11,487 (2.0)	17,504 (3.0)
1911	5,06,570	5,16,832	16,123 (3.0)	19,397 (4.0)
1921	4,55,543	4,96,108	31,552 (7.0)	25,035 (5.0)

Note: * Figures in parenthesis are percentages to total actual population.

Source: As per Table 10.16.

age of immigrants were also noticed in 1951. By using the overall survival ratio to the age distribution of the population of Bombay in 1951 (where age distribution of the migrants were given), he calculated the overall survival of the Bombay city. He found that it was 2 to 3 per cent higher than the overall ratio for all India. Based on the experience of Bombay city having 72 per cent of immigrants, Zachariah observed that the survival ratio will be slightly above the overall Indian survival ratio, i.e. 75.[86] The estimation of survival ratio has certain limitations since it assumed that all the migrants have similar age distributions in all the communities. Second, it also assumed that the difference between the age distributions was entirely due to proportion of emigrants. This might not be so, because differential birth rate might play some role in this difference.[87] After computing the net emigration through the census method we tried to assess the relative contribution of out-migration in different decades.

Before we interpret the results, it should be borne in mind that these were more illustrative because the registration statistics and that of migration were underestimates. In the decade 1891-1901 for example, half of the gain in the actual population in all the three districts of Orissa Division could be explained by the net addition to emigration by the census method. In this decade, incidentally the birth statistics were more imperfect than the later decades. So we have not computed the natural increase or decrease (births and deaths) but from the figures of the net addition to emigration. From this it can be inferred that natural increase played a more dominant role than out-migration. During this period, 1891-1901, as referred to earlier, population grew by 7.06 per cent.

The extent of emigration did increase as is evident from Table 10.18. In the decade 1901-11, for instance, the loss of female population could be explained in terms of the net addition to net emigration to a great extent. But for male population, the loss in actual population could be explained to an extent by natural increase and emigration.

When we analysed the district level data, the performance of the decade followed the Divisional pattern in all the three districts. But for the next decade the actual loss of population could be

TABLE 10.18: RELATIVE CONTRIBUTION OF BIRTHS, DEATHS AND NET MIGRATION TO EXPLAIN GAIN OR LOSS IN ACTUAL POPULATION OF ORISSA DIVISION, 1901-21

Districts/Years	*Gain/Loss in Actual Population*		*Natural increase/decrease*		*Census method Net emigration over previous decade*		*Zachariah's method* $(I_2\text{-}O_2)\text{-}S(I_1\text{-}O_1)2$	
	M	F	M	F	M	F	M	F
Cuttack								
1891-1901	+54852	+70235	–	–	–27,012	+12,511	–	–
1901-11	+5,766 (+7,009)*	+40,615 (41,817)	+53,346	+43,264	–36,994	–18,921	–52,594	–10,464
1911-21	–48,632	+4,171	+23,033	+14,412	–55,280	–27,867	–82,560	–35,736
Balasore								
1891-1901	+35,905	+40,667	–	–	–4,351	+2,228	–	–
1901-11	–1,29,281 (–14,171)*	–2,701 (–3,903)	+4,217	–2,155	–14,295	–6,418	–18,589	–3,910
1911-21	–38,493	–36,571	–12,000	–19,000	–9,932	–869	–19,086	–6,075
Puri								
1891-1901	+32,309	+39,977	–	–	–3,000	–319	–	–
1901-11	–269	+6,387	+4,636	+5,445	–4,636	–1,893	–5,907	–5,020
1911-21	–51,027	–20,724	–13,238	–15,408	–15,429	–5,638	–19,191	–6,462

(contd.)

TABLE 10.18 (contd.)

Districts/Years	*Gain/Loss in Actual Population*		*Natural increase/decrease*		*Census method Net emigration over previous decade*		*Zachariah's method* $(I_2\text{-}O_2)\text{-}S(I_1\text{-}O_1)2$	
	M	F	M	F	M	F	M	F
Orissa								
1891-1901	+1,23,066	+1,50,879	–	–	–	–		
1901-11	–7,431	+44,301	+62,227	+46,549	–55,925	–27,232	–77,450	–29,394
1911-21	–1,38,152	–53,124	+13,500	–3,500	–86,000	–39,000	–120,837	–48,273

Notes: * The bracketed figures were given in the Census Report.

1. The district level births and deaths figures are from the Sanitary Commission Reports for the individual year. All the other figures are from the respective census year.
2. Since district level figures on births and deaths excluded (except Balasore) the figure for the year 1912, the divisional and the district level data didn't tally for 1911-21.

   I = Immigration, O = Out-migration

Sources: Census of India 1901, vol. 6, pt. 1, p. 141; *Census of India 1911,* vol. 5, pt. 1, p. 312; *Census of India 1921,* vol. 7, pt. 1, p. 116; *Sanitary Commission Report 1901-1921* (on Bengal and Bihar and Orissa); Zachariah, *Internal Migration*, p. 88.

explained by net addition to Cuttack. In the other two districts it did not. When the mortality effect was applied, the volume of net emigration increased, but still it could not explain the entire loss in actual population.

Thus it is noticed that the volume and the proportion of emigration to the total actual population increased and reached the highest value in 1921 in all the three districts. Second, the emigration was sex selective – far more males emigrated than females. The proportion of emigration to population was increasing for both males and females, but the proportion of male emigration was increasing at a faster rate that that of females'. This was most noticeable in Cuttack, next to that was Balasore and then Puri (see Table 10.18) We have also taken the individual example of Balasore which became most mortality-prone in the decade of 1911-21. In fact, the Census Superintendent (Tallents), 1921, noted that the places where mortality was heavier, the sex ratio was either equal or below unity. But the places where outmigration took place, the sex ratio became above unity.

Recent Trends in Migration

Interestingly, the pattern of migration has not changed till the present time. Like in the past, able-bodied youths still flock to the important industrial places showing several important points. Orissa's economy is still dominated by agriculture and mining. Not many manufacturing industries have come up in the state as yet. The employment opportunities in industries are still meagre. Investors who show interest mostly want to utilize the mineral resources. These companies do not show interest in setting up industries to manufacture mineral-based products. Of course, setting up industries involves capital as well as land, water, and power and demands much more effort than had been taken so far. The kind of integrated development that promotes agriculture and a multi-faceted rural and forest economy along with light and heavy industries with the aim of giving gainful employment to the state's working force is still awaited in Orissa. Therefore, migration, even distress migration, continues to be a major trend.

Unlike the past, Calcutta does not any longer attract migrants from Orissa. Instead they go to Surat, Kerala, Bangalore and Andhra Pradesh. Migrants mostly from western and southern Orissa going for brick kiln units often go with their families and all of them, women and children included, are engaged in such work. It is mostly seasonal. The system of Sirdari still persists and families take advance and that is how they become bonded or *dadan* labour. Exploitation of men, women and children is inbuilt in this system. At the same time, like in the past years, the migrants also send remittances to the family to help them in subsistence, even come out of the poverty and improve their standard of living. The yearly remittances amount to one billion rupees as per some sources.[88] Yet another source noted that the annual remittances amounted to 14.25 billion rupees. It is the sixth largest receiver in the country.[89]

On the other hand, the story of '*dadan* labour' has many unfortunate aspects. The migrants from the poorer areas go to brick kiln factories and construction sites in the neighbouring states. Of course, the wages they get are higher than that prevailing in Orissa, but they are still less than minimum wages under the law. The labour laws are not implemented in those places; as a result, they suffer from various difficulties including payment of wages on time. The living conditions are extremely bad. On the top of it, they suffer from various occupation-related diseases such as AIDS, TB, etc.[90] It is also interesting to note that even now the *sirdars* or labour contractors are the main channels of recruitment, particularly in western Orissa. They give money in advance and take the family to various brick kiln factories. The labourers are treated as bonded labour and are subjected to various tortures. As mentioned before, the harsh treatment meted out to the migrant worker by the labour contractors is a common practice. The case of hands chopped off by a contractor of two workers who had tried to escape, drew national an attention in 2009.[91]

Migration and its Relationship with Sex Ratio

In this chapter, we tried to establish an association between the increasing SR and sex selective out-migration for 1891-1921.

Before showing this association, we discussed the principal characteristics of the migrants. The most important stream of migration was to Bengal and especially to Calcutta; Assam being the second, followed by Burma (Myanmar).

The migrants were mostly males and belonged to the age group of 15-40. In this age group and above, the population of the birth place had higher SR than the earlier age group. The caste composition of the migrants revealed that people from all caste groups migrated. But an important point to note was that a large number of migrants came from the cultivating caste, namely, Khandayats. This was, first, because the percentage share of that caste was significant in the total population, and second, because it reflected the fact that Orissa Division faced a series of crop failures, especially in the decade ending 1921.The occupational break-up of the Oriya migrants revealed that most of the migrants worked in unorganized sectors and domestic services, or as day labourers. Some of them also worked in jute mills. Most of them worked as unskilled workers.

After that we discussed the relationship between famine and emigration. It was noticed that famine generated a considerable amount of out-migration through the period studied. In spite of the fact that there were no metalled roads and other forms of communication were poor between Orissa and Calcutta, Orissa migrants flocked there. Famine literature are also full of references to famine migration. Migration, both famine induced as well as that of pull factor, had a multidimensional impact on the economy, society and polity, some of which we have analysed in the other chapters. But there are questions which require a separate exercise. For instance, it is a well-known fact that migration induced capitalistic pattern of growth in agriculture in Ireland. That, however, did not happen in Orissa. Similarly, in many instances, the remittances sent by the migrants helped the rest of the family members to improve their standard of living. But it had only marginal effects in Orissa. Socially, the family bond is broken when migration takes place. But it was hardly so in this case. In case of young couples, migration brings intense agony in the minds of both. Sometimes it leads to problems relating to mental health. Long separation just after marriage sometimes leads to attraction towards other women which in turn creates tension in the relationship between the couple.

Sometimes the migrants carried urban values and introduced relatively more modern attitudes and behaviour to their villages, which in turn encouraged other young people to migrate to the same destination or elsewhere. The migrants also bring new products which are not available in their weekly market. At the same time, the villages get depleted of the youth population, leaving just the children, women and old people. Women's workload gets compounded with so many tasks. They not only have to look after their children but also old people. Earlier the presumption was that migrants would go from joint families. Generally, the youngest son migrated leaving other brothers to look after the family agriculture, in addition to looking after the other family members. But it is not generally true. In that case, young women had to look after the cultivation activities as well. In such situations the young woman may acquire a say in family matters since her husband was not only earning money but also sending a part of it to the family. That happens only when the husband stands by her, which is not always the case.

We also tried to measure the sex selectiveness of the out-migration by calculating the SR of the currently married and percentage of emigrants to total population. Besides this, the relative contribution of different variables, namely, births, deaths and out-migration, especially in the decades of 1901-11 and 1911-21, was assessed. All these measures showed that the sex selectiveness of the emigration increased. It also showed that the sex selective emigration – more male migrating out – perhaps explains a major part of the increased sex ratio, especially in the decade ending 1921. But this result only proved the conditions of distress and poverty, rather than any special strength of the female gender in Orissa.

Notes

1. SR fell to 1,117 in Cuttack; 1,062 in Balasore and 1,069 in Puri by 1931 in relation to 1921. The volume of emigration had fallen consid-

erably. Orissa Division was not free from a high mortality rate. The male death rate touched 40 per thousand in three years in the decade 1921-31. Proportion of female deaths to male deaths had increased. Population grew but mostly due to return migration. *Census of India 1931,* vol. 7, pt. 1, pp. 139 and 147.

2. Bandana Pattanaik and Leah Sullivan 'India's Anti-Trafficking Bill Ignores Socio-Economic Realities of the Trafficked Persons', https://www.epw.in/engage/article/trafficking-persons-prevention-protection-rehabilitation-bill-2018-ignores-socio-economic-realities-gaatw.
3. Davis, *Population of India and Pakistan,* p. 107.
   Also see, K.C. Zachariah, *Historical Study of Internal Migration in the Indian Subcontinent, 1901-1931,* Bombay, Demographic Training and Research Centre, 1963. p. 80.
4. According to the Census Commissioner of India 1911, there were five types of migration based on objectives:
   a. *Minor movement:* This type of migration takes place within very short distance, so it is not considered migration if it occurs within two villages of the same district. But if it takes place between two villages on opposite sides of the district boundary, then it is accepted as migration.
   b. *Temporary migration:* As a type of migration in which coolies move to construct railways, canals, and people go for pilgrimage as well as marriage ceremonies. The Census generally excludes such auspicious events when people congregate in such places. Famine according to the Census Commissioner was a 'potent cause of periodic migration'.
   c. *Periodic:* In this kind of migration, the labourers go annually to cultivate rice in Sundarbans, Burma and the wheat districts of Upper India, etc.
   d. *Semi-permanent:* In this category people of one place earn their livelihood in another but keep their connection with their families.
   e. *Permanent:* It is in the nature of colonization. It takes place if one place becomes more fertile due to improved irrigation, or changed political situation. A minor form of this kind of migration is the old widows migration to sacred places.
   Census of India 1911, vol. 1, pt. 1, pp. 89-90.

   We do not have data on all these types of migration. We have some data on the 4th category, namely on people going to Calcutta.

5. *Census of India 1911,* vol. 5, pt. 1, p. 188.
   Incidentally outmigration to places outside India was not very significant.
6 Davis, *Population of India and Pakistan*, p. 107. But recent experts like Hema Kumari, Priya Desingkar don't agree with Davis. Of course, it may be argued that Davis was talking about the historical migration and the other two are referring to the modern trend. However, it can also argued that if women could migrate to Calcutta in the wake of the great famine of 1866 of Orissa it would not be a surprise to find that women were indeed migrating for economic causes in the past as well. Only point is that no research has been done to find out that. Both of the authors noted above note that women migrants outnumber men for economic reason also. For example T.A. Hema Kumari and U. Tataji argued a large number of women migrants keep on going to grade tobacco every year seasonally. Similarly women migrants go to cultivate sugarcane from one part of Gujarat to another part. T.A. Hema Kumari and U.Tataji 'Seasonal Migration of Women Workers: Process, Pattern and Consequences' http://www.shram.org/uploadFiles/20170718125904.pdf
   Similarly, Priya Deshingkar et al. have documented female domestic workers who migrate to improve their economic conditions. The authors have taken up Madhya Pradesh as a test case. Priya Deshingkar, Pramod Sharma, Sushil Kumar, Shaheen Akhater and John Farrington 'Circular Migration in Madhya Pradesh: Changing Patterns and Protection Needs', *The European Journal of Development Research*, 20(4), December 2008, pp. 612-28. Retrieved on 14 January 2014 https://link.springer.com/10.1057/ejdr.2008.38
7. Non-contiguous parts of Orissa Division inside Orissa mainly consisted of Tributary States. As will be evident later the proportion of emigrants going to be Tributary States also remained more or less constant.
8. T. A. Hema Kumari and U. Tataji, po. cit.
9. https://books.google.co.in/books?hl=en&lr=&id=vDV7Y1cn-QawC&oi=fnd&pg=PP11&dq=jan+breman+footloose+labour&ots=DLlSHNcGBF&sig=DaPIv1tOGx3EAVnR-03Z9H7iYrm4#v=onepage&q=jan%20breman%20footloose%20labour&f=false
10. Manasi Mohanty 'Skills for Employment Programme in Apparel Industries and Trends in Female Migration: A Study of SEAM', in Asha Hans, Amrita Patel, Swarnamayee Tripathy and Bidyut

Mohanty (eds.), *Women Reinventing Development*, New Delhi, Aakar, 2020.

11. http://www.cwds.ac.in/wp-content/uploads/2016/09/SummaryKeyFindings.pdf
12. The sex composition of Oriya migrants to Bengal is not available for all the Census years. In 1911, the statistics were not available for Cuttack and Puri. But see, the comments of the Census Superintendent of Calcutta in 1921 '. . . the man who most readily separates himself from his family'. *Census of India 1921*, vol. 6, pt. I, p. 25. Interestingly there are many folk songs sung by the women whose husbands migrate for a long time. These songs are more prevalent in Bihar region.
13. *Census of India 1921*, vol. 6, pt. 1, p. 25
14. In Orissa this type of outmigration did take place to Tributary States from the coastal districts because land was available on payment of easy installments. The Chief of the Tributary States also encouraged such outmigration. But as will be seen later, this stream was neither large nor did it increase over time.
15. *The Report of the Labour Enquiry Commission, 1895 Bengal*, Calcutta, Government Press, 1896, Appendix, p. 1.
16. In 1911, Khandayats constituted 20 per cent, Karans 2 per cent, Brahmins 11 per cent, Gaur 7 per cent and Kandara 3 per cent of the total population of Balasore. The caste Bauri, however, formed 1 per cent of the population. Similar features were also noticed in case of Cuttack and Puri.
17. According to Ranjit Das Gupta the lowest caste such as Bauri, Doms, Hari, etc. formed a very high proportion of labour force in jute mills of Calcutta. Ranjit Das Gupta, 'Factory Labour in Eastern India', *Indian Economic and Social History Review,* 13(3), 1976, p. 315.
18. *Census of India 1921,* vol. 5, Table 22. Deshingkar et al., pointed out that migrants from high caste are migrating in large number in recent years.
19. Vaishnava caste consisted of people from multiple castes.
20. Senapati gave a vivid description of such journeys. 'The road was muddy during the rainy season and dusty during the summer. The boatmen, the shopkeepers and the petty robbers harassed the migrants on the way. Sometimes the shopkeepers used to add a kind of poison to the turmeric powder and after taking the turmeric powder, the migrants used to become unconscious'. F.M. Senapati, *Atma Charita*, p. 19.

21. Hunter, *Statistical Account of Bengal*, vol. 18, p. 71.
22. Both these articles are edibles made from paddy. The caste Guria (grain parcher) does specialize in the occupation but the association of goldsmith with this kind of occupation is surprising.
23. N.N. Banerjee, *Report on the Agriculture of the District Cuttack.* Calcutta, Secretariat Press, 1898. p. 10.
24. *Annual Administration Report*, 1883-4, p. 7.
25. 'The emigrants from Orissa are mostly Brahmins who are nearly always cooks, Goalas who act as bearers in European household and also as door keepers and various castes who work in the mills and as labourers in metropolitan districts'. *Census of India, 1901,* vol. 6, pt. 1, p. 144.
26. *Utkal Barta,* 1 August 1908.
27. *Census of India, 1911*, vol. 5, pt. 1, p. 530.
28. Haraprasad Chattopadhyaya who has done an extensive study on internal migration of Bengal Presidency 1872-1931 has also noted that Oriya migrants worked as skilled and unskilled labourers. Haraprasad Chattopadhaya, *Internal Migration in India: A Case Study of Bengal,* Calcutta, K.P. Bagchi and Company, 1987, p. 473.
29. *Census of India 1921,* vol. 5, pt. 2, Table 22, pts. 4 and 5. Also see, *Census of India, 1921*, vol. 6, pt. 2, pp. 143 and 151.
30. Bibek Debroy 'Kendrapara Model', *Indian Express*, 16 May 2019, Delhi edition.
31. *Census of India, 1921,* vol. 6, pt. 1, p. 22.
32. *Balasore District Gazetteer,* 1907, p. 122.
33. Similarly the diamond cutters to Gujarat are from Ganjam district. There is a special train going from Ganjam to Surat almost everyday. This train carries Oriya migrants every day.
34. *Census of India 1921,* vol. 5, pt. 1, p. 143.
    A.K. Bagchi, *Private Investment in India 1900-1939*, Cambridge, Cambridge University Press, 1972, pp. 133-5.
35. *Report of the Royal Commission on Labour in India,* Calcutta, Government Press, 1931, p. 14.
36. *Cuttack District Gazetteer,* 1933, p. 45.
37. Senapati, *Atma Charita,* p. 3.
38. Jayaseelan Ru and Richard Axelby 'From Labour contractors to worker agents: Transformations in the recruitment of migrant labourers in India', *Contribution to Indian Sociology*, 53(2), June 2019, pp. 272-98.
39. Ibid.

40. https://economictimes.indiatimes.com/news/politics-and-nation/labour-migrants-in-a-fix-post-demonetisation/articleshow/55608105.cms?from=mdr
41. *Census of India 1921,* vol. 7, pt. 1, p. 113.
    The Census Superintendent, however, did treat those emigrants as going from Cuttack and Balasore. So we have done likewise.
42. Arup Maharanta 'Food Scarcity and Migration: An Overview', *Social Research*, 81(2), 2014, pp. 277-98.
43. V. Suganya and B. Padmanabhan, 'The Famine Eviction, Destitution and Survival Migrants', in V. Sangitha, B.J. Geetha, K. Sindhu, S. Bhupathi and S. Snekha (eds.), http://www.languageinindia.com/2019 retrieved from Academia Edu.
44. Cormac O'Grada, and Kevin H.R. Rourke 'Migration as Disaster Relief: Lessons from the Great Irish Famine', *European History of Economic Review,* 1(1), 1997, pp. 1-35.
45. Cormac O'Grada, *Famine,* Princeton, Princeton University Press, 2009, pp. 81-9.
46. Maharanta, op. cit.
47. Bipin Shah, 'The Famines of India and Formation of Indian Diaspora'. https://www.academia.edu/8753763/The_Famines_of_India_and_the_formation_of_Indian_Diaspora?auto=download. Retrieved on 3 September 2019.
48. The Collector of Puri reported that roadside deaths among the 'aimless wanderers' were not included. GOI/Home/Public, January 1868, nos. 21-2; pt. A: From the Collector of Puri to the Commr,, OD, 15 June, 1867.
49. Indeed many starving people did migrate to Calcutta. *FCRO 1866,* pt. I, para 234.
50. Maharantna, op. cit.
51. https://www.theguardian.com/news/2018/jun/05/five-myths-about-the-refugee-crisis
52. *FCRO 1866,* pt. 1, para 234.
    In the month of September 1866, the *Dipika* wrote that famine emigrants who were receiving relief in Calcutta wanted to come back (even though the famine had not ended). So they were sent back by sea. *The Utkal Dipika*, 29 September 1866.
53. GOI/Home/Public, June 1867, General Narrative of the Week ending Monday, 15 April 1867, by the Collector of Puri.
54. *Bengal Administration Report 1867-68*, p. 216.
55. *FCRO 1866,* pt. 1, para 241.

56. https://www.theguardian.com/global-development/2016/apr/27/india-drought-migrants-head-to-cities-in-desperate-search-for-water retrieved on 26 June 2019Contribution.
57. Hunter, *Statistical Account of Bengal,* vol. 3, Delhi, D.K. Publishing House, 1876, rpt. 1973, p. 365.
58. Ibid., 1875, vol. 1, p. 162.
59. *General Administration Report, 1888-89,* p. 12.
60. *SCRB 1908*, p. 3.
61. GOI/Rev/Agri/FP, December 1907, no. 3768; from the Collector of Puri to the Commr, OD, 7 December 1907.
62. Ibid.
63. Rev/Agri/FP, December 1907, No. 3565; From the Commr, OD, to the Secy., RD, 9 December 1907.
64. *Census of India 1911,* vol. 5, pt. 1, pp. 133-4.
65. 'The pressure of hard times in Cuttack and Balasore has led to a large number of labourers and small cultivators leaving their homes for a time in order to obtain employment elsewhere and so supplement the resources of their families'.
    Census of India 1911, vol. 5, pt. 1, p. 182.
66. *Annual Administration Report of Bihar and Orissa*, 1914-15, p. 107. In the year 1915-16, it was reported that more people migrated from Bihar and Orissa partly because of bad harvests and partly because of abolition of the system of recruitment by contractors. Ibid., 1915-16, p. 88. In 1916-17 on the other hand, it was noticed that there was a decline in emigration. The reason given by the authorities was that there was heavy recruitment by the Civil and Military Department. But it was also true that crops were good in that year.
    Annual Administration Report, 1916-17, pp. 99-100. Similar decrease in number was also noticed in the year 1917-18, p. 96.
67. Ibid., 1918-19, p. 97.
68. Ibid., 1919-20, p. 85.
69. As a result, the workload had increased considerably in the nearby post offices. So a letter writer to the editor pleaded for the employment of more post peons, *The Utkal Dipika,* 8 March 1919.
70. *The Utkal Dipika,* 15 March 1919.
71. *Census of India 1921*, vol. 7, pt. 1, p. 112.
72. *Royal Commission on Agriculture in India: Evidence Taken in Bihar and Orissa, 1928*, vol. 13, p. 28.
73. *Census of India 1921,* vol. 7, pt. 1, p. 113.
74. Dyson referred to in the chapters 3 and 6, p. 154.

75. Maddox noted that in 1897, 72,000 Oriyas were staying outside. They were sending Rs.40 per head through money orders. *Maddox Report 1890-1900*, vol. 1, para 185. It was likely to be exaggerated.
76. 'It may be added that the average of the money order remittances to Cuttack and Balasore, the most important recruiting districts in Orissa, is small, being between Rs. 10 and 11. A certain type of Oriya emigrants notably bearers from Balasore, has been known to make fortunes but the great majority of the emigrants work in less exalted capacity and are not in a position to make heavy remittances to their homes'.
    Census of India 1921, vol. 7, pt. 1, p. 113.
77. *The Utkal Dipika,* 29 March 1919.
78. *Census of* India 1921, vol. 7, pt. 1, pp. 43 and 47.
    Royal Commission on Agriculture, 1929, vol. 13, p. 28.
79. In 1921, G.T. Lloyd the Census Superintendent of Assam wrote. 'The tea industry continued to flourish up to 1919, but in 1920 dislocation of trade and especially closure of the Russian market caused a serious depression and accumulation of stocks. Many companies which had paid away high profits of previous years in large dividends and had kept no reserve came near to financial crisis. The number of labourers was reduced, considerable areas were allowed to go out of cultivation and riots and other disturbances occurred among the coolies in several districts'. *Census of India 1921*, vol. 3, pt. 1, p. 5. Again Lloyd observed that 'The number of labourers on tea gardens rose to above a million in 1918-19 when no less than 324,000 new coolies were imported in two years.' Ibid., p. 37. Also, *Prices and Wages in India 1922-23*, p. 228. Also see, D.R. Gadgil, *The Industrial Evolution of India in Recent Times 1860-1939*, Delhi, Oxford University Press, 1973, rpt. 1979, p. 270. Bagchi also pointed out that the real wages declined in jute mills during the war period and after 1921 it remained stagnant. A.K. Bagchi, *Private Investment in India, 1900-1939*, p. 172. Regarding on decline in average employment after 1911, Ranjit Das Gupta, 'Factory Labour', p. 281.
80. Jagabandhu Acharya, 'Oriya Migrants', pp. 95-140.
81. Pradipta Chaudhiri, 'Commercialization of Agriculture in Orissa 1900-1930', PhD thesis submitted in Jawaharlal Nehru University, 1984, pp. 1-235.
    The central theme of this thesis was published as 'The Impact of Forced Commercialization on the Pattern of Emigration from

Orissa 1901-1921', in K.N. Raj, N. Bhattacharya, Sumit Guha and Sakti Padhi (eds.), *Essays on the Commercialization of Agriculture*, Delhi, Oxford University Press, 1985, pp. 184-209.

82. According to the census the excess of wives was due to emigration rather than polygamy. *Census of India 1901*, vol. 6, pt. I, p. 251.
83. We have not come across references to this phenomenon in the decade 1911-21. But we have seen in chapter 3 that parents used to sell their minor daughters to prostitutes during the famine of 1866. Since the decade 1911-21 also faced a series of crop failures and epidemics, it is possible that daughters were given as second or third wives.
84. Recall that the actual famine is usually preceded by some months of food shortages when the rate of conception may have fallen.
85. K. C. Zachariah, *Historical Study of Internal Migration in the Indian Sub-Continent-1901-1931* . Bombay, Asia Publishing House, 1964.
86. Ibid., pp. 80-3.
87. Ibid., p. 85.
88. http://www.unescogym.org/wp-content/uploads/2015/05/Remittances-in-India-Facts-and-Issues-2011-C.Tumbe_.pdf (retrieved on 13 August 2019).
89. http://www.aajeevika.org/assets/pdfs/Orissa%20State%20Migration%20Profile%20Report.pdf (retrieved on 13 August 2019).
90. Priya Deshingkar ' Labour Migration and Policy Reforms in Orissa' https://www.odi.org/publications/3425-labour-migration-and-policy-reform-orissa-finding-pathways-social-inclusion-rural-development-edited
91. Ibid.

CHAPTER 11

Famines and Women, Past and Present
Some Concluding Reflections

In this work, an attempt was made to investigate the linkage of caste, class and gender as well as the state, in course of the frequent occurrences of food crisis for over a century and half, in a particular region of India. The cataclysmic experience of the Great Orissa Famine of 1866 has been taken as the base line for an intensive study. The social process and state policy around specific famines during 1866-1921 have been examined in-depth to pursue one central question. That is: who are the victims of food crisis and why? Is our understanding of the social consequences of past food crisis adequate even today? If the understanding is faulty, the response of state and social action groups will also be inadequate.

In particular, the objective is to find out who are the people who succumb first if famines and epidemics occur in a subsistence agrarian economy. We have studied the historical experiences, particularly under colonial rule. It is important to know this history to examine to what extent post-colonial states had evolved new policies based on the lessons from history. Our focus is on women to see how did they experience the famines and epidemics. There are many assumptions and beliefs about this question which needed scrutiny. It necessarily involved our looking at the caste composition and occupations and assets of various groups of affected people. Thus, gender, caste and class have been taken in their interconnection to analyse this process.

The gender issue has been examined in multiple dimensions, starting from mortality, fertility and migration to nutrition and other deprivations faced by women in general and girl child in

India. Thus the age composition data and migration data, together with mortality and nutrition data form a major basis of our study.

In this study, famine has been defined not only an *event* of a peak level food scarcity causing starvation and deaths, but a *process* thereby taking into account short-term as well as long-term factors. Short-term factors include extreme food shortage due to lack of adequate rain at the appropriate time, civil war or devastation of crops due to reasons such as prevalence of rats (north-east region of India) or economic blockade. The long-term factors refer to the decline of productivity resulting from factors such as land tenure, outbreak of war causing disruption of supplies (Bengal famine 1943-4), prolonged civil conflict (famines in Africa in the modern period) or a top down centralized policy regime where the centre was not aware of the gravity of the ground reality (Chinese famine in 1958-62), etc. Those factors would trigger famines and epidemics resulting in heavy mortality, decline of fertility and migration and other possibly unprecedented social, economic and political consequences. Some of those impacts have been discussed while taking Orissa's experience from 1860 to 1921 under colonial rule for a special study.

Even now, in spite of the so-called 'Fourth Industrial Revolution' characterized by artificial intelligence, rapid connectivity through Internet, decoding genes and many new achievements of modern science and even when world food production has reached a level adequate to feed the world's population and countries like India have achieved self-sufficiency in food production, the incidence of famines has not been erased from the face of the earth. It is particularly conspicuous in the context of African continent, but the phenomenon exists elsewhere as well. These famines are caused more by man-made factors such as civil war and economic blockade than by natural factors which may accentuate the distress further. It is important to stress that famine is not confined to Africa alone.

In many parts of contemporary India, vulnerability to food scarcity due to natural factors or policy failures, in inaccessible areas like hilltops or rain shadow areas, still persists, resulting in deaths, epidemics and migration. Still, like in the past, people are trying to devise various safety nets by adopting alternative patterns of production, distribution and migration. In so far as the production of alternative food crops is concerned, people are going back to growing so-called 'inferior' food grains such as *ragi*, *bajra* and new crops such as potatoes. As substitutes of food grains or supplementary food, many are rearing birds, crickets, and other edible insects including snakes and dogs, to alleviate their hunger when poor rainfall lead to crop loss. Some of these eating practices existed even otherwise.

With regard to the intra-family distribution of food, even now in many households, generally women and girl children are served less quantity of food grains or they are made to eat *ragi* or *bajra* while rice and vegetables are served to male children and adult men. Of course, one may argue that *ragi* and *bajra* are relatively more nutritious than rice. But in terms of taste, social value, rice and vegetables are considered as superior food grains. Besides, many of the substitutes have adverse impact on the digestive system. After eating such substitutes we know from history that often people suffer from severe dysentery and other forms of stomach disorder. Keeping that in mind, one must devise appropriate policy measures suitable for the present-day world.

It is a well-known fact that not much attention was paid to the gender question in the past. So no systematic data was available on the sex differential mortality, particularly in India. When gender data was collected for the first time perhaps, the Census commissioners of India in 1901 and 1911, made a categorical observation saying that the number of women who died during famine period were less compared to men because of favourable biological and sociological causes. According to them, the most important factors were that biologically, women apparently happened to be more resistant to various infectious diseases like cholera, dysentery, smallpox, malaria and plague. Besides, the conception rate would also decline during the famine period leading to less pregnancy. Finally, women required less food compared to men since they did less physical labour. Thus, according to the Census commissioners, these biological factors would help women to die less in number during the food crisis. In so far as the sociological factors were concerned, it was alleged that women would dispose off their ornaments and with that money would procure food and would share with the remaining family members. The officials also claimed that people would show tender feelings towards women and would offer them food or they would be employed in various unlawful activities. It was also observed that the women would stay home while men would wander around long distances in search of food and thereby be subjected to various epidemics. These sociological factors would help the women to survive the onslaught of famine mortality better in relation to men. This preconceived idea that women died less compared to men was partly due to the biased views of the colonial rulers who felt that Indian society was the replica of their own society. In the Western society the army tried to rescue women by risking their own lives. That example influenced the Western authorities. Hence they could not observe the extent of discrimination of women in Indian society, which made them vulnerable to much exploitation. Second, they were not aware of the fact that the female deaths were underestimates because the *chowkidars* felt women deaths did not count!

In our own research, in order to find out if biological factors really mattered, we examined medical evidence of various attack rates of the famine-related epidemics for both male and females separately. It was noticed that the resistance to different epidemics which prevailed during the famines, was not due to the biological factor but very much depended on the exposure to the pathogen. Similarly, it was true that the conception rate declined during the famine period, but in an agrarian economy a large number of women in the reproductive age group would have conceived already before the onset of famine. Thus the net result would not be that beneficial to women. Yet another factor which the commissioners cited was that women needed less food compared to males, since they did less physical labour. But women of low caste groups worked as hard as the men! But they had to eat less food because of scarcity of resources.

Now let us examine the sociological factors cited by the commissioners. It should be stressed that even in the contemporary world, women are discriminated a lot in terms of intra-family and inter-family distribution of food. Therefore it can be assumed that in the distant past they would be equally discriminated in terms of education as well as that of health care besides the distribution of food. The officials believed that women themselves ate more while distributing food. However, it should be noted that women were/are socialized in such a way that they always offered more food to their husbands and sons keeping the remnant for themselves. Second, as for disposing off their ornaments, one should add only if they had it to begin with. Women of low caste groups did not possess much ornaments, certainly not enough to sustain themselves for a long time. Yet another social factor that operated during the famines was the phenomenon of aimless wandering in search of food or work. Indeed, men had a propensity to wander in search of food in a larger number. In course of the migration they were exposed to various pathogens and in the process died in large numbers. Perhaps men wandered in large numbers in the beginning of the famine, but as the famine progressed, women also wandered in search of food and work because they had to look after the children and old people, though they may not have gone too far away from their village.

It should be remembered that initially there was poor resistance to certain diseases because of the sudden lowering of food intake. Moreover, because the food availability declined, famine victims started eating many roots, leaves, fruits and unknown grains as substitutes for their staple food thus becoming vulnerable to stomach disorders. This was happening when the public health measures had broken down during the famine years. Finally, famine generates considerable mobility of population and trade in food grains. In the process, famine victims also get exposed to various other diseases such as plague. It should also be mentioned that many other superintendents of the Census of different provinces did not share the above opinion with regard to sex differential mortality. Thus on the whole, the hypothesis put forward by the commissioners did not stand scrutiny.

The hypothesis on the impact of famine on women and men and the various groups in society was examined by closely looking at the agrarian system and the socio-economic process unfolding in the Orissa Division from 1860 to 1921. The focus on the famines and food crisis in relation to gender, caste and class governs this analysis. First of all, the characteristics of Orissa economy was discussed taking into account various factors such as land revenue system, nature of the cropping pattern, the demographic scenario and of course the occurrences of famines, droughts and floods. It was noticed that Orissa did not get any structural benefit out of the Industrial Revolution unlike the places like Bombay Presidency, Madras Presidency and a part of the Bengal Presidency. Cropping pattern changed towards cash crops in Bombay and in parts of the Bengal Presidency. Soil conditions and agricultural requirements were now looked after by farmers in Madras Presidency because it came under the *ryatwari* system. Orissa, on the other hand, remained as an appendage to Bengal Presidency with temporary land settlement. As we saw in some detail, periodically the rent on land kept on increasing as a consequence of the frequent renewal of the *zamindari*. The zamindars did not care for increasing the productivity of the land, partly because most of the big zamindars were absentee landlords from Bengal. Even Oriya landlords also proved to be no less exploitative. Orissa Division, in all the three districts, remained with mono-crop agriculture throughout the period. Even introduction of irrigation was not of much benefit to the bulk of the farmers of Orissa unlike that of Madras Presidency or United Provinces because of land tenure systems. The Division remained prone to droughts, famines and floods for the entire period. Population kept on decreasing even after 1921 even though rest of Indian population had started increasing.

In this backdrop, we have analysed the consequences Orissa suffered from the intense famine in 1866 in which she lost about one million people due to starvation and related epidemics. We also have examined both the long-term as well as short-term factors. This famine was so intense that members of all the castes ended up eating in the public relief centres and due to the complex consequences of the caste order a new caste group or rather a new community was formed called Chhatrakhias. They were placed low in the caste hierarchy and members of this 'outcaste community' still lived in poor conditions in many parts of the region.

These households can still be seen on the bank of the oldest canal – Taladanda-Machchagaon Canal – that was dug during the famine. Besides, a few village settlements were set up by the Christian missionaries to house many Chhatrakhias who converted to Christianity. They gradually improved their living conditions and were leading a relatively better life. My field study in these villages showed that economically they were better engaged than those who lived on the banks of the canal. I found that while a part of a family engaged in agriculture, others went for petty trade and government jobs and young people had high ambition in the life. But nobody marries outside the Christian community. Thus the role played by the missionaries during the famines had long-term effects on the life conditions of the affected people, especially the discriminated lot. The plight of the outcaste members have been documented in various novels, poems and autobiography, etc., that we have discussed. Sometimes the starving poor became a rebel instead of dying of hunger. In other words, the agony of the great famine still persists in the minds of the people though that intensity has declined over the years. But the most important point to note here is that the suffering of the intense famine has shaped the psyche of the Oriyas and their nationalism!

After 1866 there were other famines, which also seriously affected the people of Orissa, especially the famines in the years 1888-9, 1907-8 and 1918-19. Apart from that the region also suffered from a series of crop failures and floods. Floods became more frequent towards the end of 1921 because of various embankments and rail-roads.

All this caused a rapid increase in the incidence of malaria, which took a heavy toll. Orissa fortunately did not suffer from influenza in 1918-19. During the decade ending 1921, even though Orissa suffered from a famine only in 1918-19, because of a series of droughts and localized crop failures a lot of people died and the male death rate remained high, touching 40 per thousand for many years.

After assessing the impact of all the famines, we examined the evidence about who died during the famine years, taking all-India pattern as a test case. In this exercise, the evidence from the available studies showed that there was no uniform pattern of mortality. In some cases women died in larger number and in other cases more men died. Since the Census commissioners emphatically asserted that biological and sociological factors were responsible for the lower female death rates, we examined the medical evidence of the incidence of various epidemics which generally accompanied the famines, namely, cholera, dysentery and malaria. The evidence showed that females were not biologically resistant to all these diseases. The attack rates purely depended on the extent of exposure. Males suffered more from the epidemics of the first two because they were more exposed to the parasites. On the contrary, women died in larger numbers compared to males due to malaria because women usually lived in dark areas of the house and were more vulnerable to mosquito bite. Second, the beneficial impact of the decline in conception rate was offset because a large number of women were already in the conception stage.

The beneficial effects of the sociological factors were also discussed. The experience of Indian society and particularly that of Orissa revealed that women were discriminated with regard to distribution of food and health care because of their inferior position in the family. If the large-scale discrimination is visible even now, it would have been more so in the past when women were completely dependent on their male family members. Women were deeply entrenched with the patriarchal values, which morally compelled them to serve more food to the male family members at the cost of the women members. The historical and contemporary experiences of India as a whole and that of Orissa in particular indicated a somewhat different profile of the lower caste working women.

As in the case of the all-India experience, in Orissa too we did not notice any evidence to prove that male death rate was always higher than the female death rate. In order to examine this question, we conducted some qualitative tests as well as direct and some indirect tests, mentioned in Chapter 9. We briefly recapitulate the same here. First, we identified the high mortality years when the death rates touched 40 or more. The Famine Commissioner 1866 pointed out that lower castes died in larger number compared to higher castes. But regarding the sex composition of the deaths, the Commissioner was silent except saying more women attended the relief centres after the famine. For other famine years, annual male and female death rates had been documented by the Sanitary Commissioner's reports separately. It was well known that the *chowkidars* underestimated the female deaths. But it was assumed that the degree of underestimation would be more or less same in both famine and non-famine years. While trying to assess the impact of the famines on various castes it was noticed that no systematic data was collected by the officials on the caste composition of the famine victims. But some Census reports documented the sex ratios on the basis of castes. It was assumed that the lower castes such as Bauri, Kandara, Pana (all agricultural labouerers), Chasa (small farmers) and Tanti (weaver caste) were considered as the marginal castes. Members of these castes suffered more during the famine years. If the statements of the Census commissioners of 1901, 1911 were to be believed that less females died than males during famine years, then the sex ratio of lower classes/lower castes would increase at a faster rate compared to male rates in the decade ending in high mortality decades, compared to low mortality decades. We compared the rate of change of sex ratios of three lower castes, namely, Bauri, Kandara and Pan (proxy for agricultural labourers) with that of three high castes namely Khandayats, Karnas and Brahmins (proxy for landholding class). In Cuttack the sex ratio did rise for the lower castes faster, indicating higher male death rates at the end of the high mortality decades. In one of the high mortality decades at least the sex ratio of the Chasa and Tanti, the marginal castes, rose higher than that of the landholding castes. Hence the conclusion that keeping other things constant, the increase in female death rates were lower than that of males. But this statement must take into account the fact that during the famine years, out-migration increased considerably. Unfortunately, not much caste-specific migration data is available for Balasore and Puri, so no clear picture emerged.

Further, we also compared the phenomenon of increased sex ratio with respect to the various age groups at the end of the high mortality decades comparing it with the low mortality decades.

The age-specific death rates in the age groups of 15-60 increased at a higher rate than that of younger age groups with the exception of some higher age groups. These findings are contrary to the conventional findings which point out that people in the old and young age groups die in large numbers compared to adult age groups. Of course, the age data of India is always problematic.

Finally, the central question as to who died more, males or females. The hypothesis to test was whether increase in female death rate was higher than that of males in high mortality years in relation to low mortality years. Both indirect and direct tests were applied to find out the results.

The indirect test involved comparing the ratio of widows to widowers at the end of the high mortality decades with that of the low mortality decades. If the proposition that the increase in female death rate was lower than the increase in the male death rate in high mortality decades were true then the ratio of widows to widowers at the end of high death rate decades should have been higher than the low mortality decades, on the qualification of certain assumptions regarding remarriage and polygamy. This test yielded inconclusive results.

After that a direct test was conducted, known as 't' test. This test was conducted to find out whether the difference between the two death rates (male and female) increased in high mortality years compared to low mortality years. In this case it was noticed that the 't' test was significant. Moreover, the results for the other two districts were also significant. This supported the hypothesis that the increase in female death rates is lower than the increase in male death rate in high the mortality years. Two cautions have to be borne in mind. First, the 't' test is applied to a set of data collected on random sampling basis. When 't' test is done on time series data, it tends to overstate the statistical significance of the difference. Second, we have assumed that the under-enumeration of female deaths were constant in high and low mortality years. But in reality it might not always be so.

Finally, we turned to examining the role migration played in explaining the sex differential mortality rates since it was noticed that famines and crop failures generated a lot of migration of males. So the relationship of migration and sex ratio was taken up in-depth. It was noticed that male migration increased considerably after the introduction of the railways in 1901. The volume of out-migration increased considerably in Balasore and Cuttack but not so much in Puri district till 1921. In 1921 for example, as high as 18 per cent of the total male population of Cuttack, was enumerated outside the district. Thus the out-migration influenced partly the increased sex ratio.

Hence, the increased sex ratio of the Orissa Division especially after 1901 was partly due to sex differential deaths in high mortality years and partly due to sex selective out-migration.

In the end, one can ask the question, is the whole exercise like flogging a dead horse? We beg to differ, since even now women and girl children are discriminated against in terms of access to food and health care. So much so that the early life of the girl child has become uncertain. As for the occurrence of famines, the intensity and scale of such food crises might have reduced but widespread droughts srtill lead to mass migration and deaths due to food crisis and women and lower castes suffer the most.

Glossary

Aman: Winter paddy

Alekha Dharma: It is a reformist religion originating in the nineteenth century that does not accept idol worship and caste system.

Aghani: Winter rice

Abwabs: Illegal cess

Anna: Fraction of a rupee

Aus: Early paddy.

Ayurvedic: Indigeous medicine system of India

Bahaldars: Holders of revenue-free land

Bauri: A Dalit caste mainly engaged in agricultural labour

Bhadoi: Autumn rice.

Bhandari: Caste name of labourers

Bhata: Rice.

Bhima Bhoi: The mystic poet and also the founder of Alekh Dharm.

Bhois: Caste name of a section of Dalits

Biali: Autumn rice

Biri: Black gram

Bazyaptidars: Holders of resumed revenue-free tenure

Chasa: Cultivating Caste

Chakadars: Those who reclaimed land mostly for speculation

Chamar: A Dalit caste name, leather worker

Chandina: Homestead land for shopkeepers, artisans and those kind of labouring class who did not have arable land for which they paid rent.

Chhatrakhias: Persons who ate in the government relief centres.

Chandbali: Name of a port in northern Orissa coast

Chura: A kind of edible from husked paddy
Cess: A levy on tax generally illegally imposed by the zamindars
Cowries: Medium of exchange before the colonial rule in India
Dalits: Scheduled Castes
Dalua: Spring rice
Devadasi: Female servants of god, traditional singers in temples
Dharmsalas: Shelters for the pilgrims in religious places
Dhamra: Name of a port
Dhoba: Washerman
Dhotis: Long cloth worn by men.
Ekhrajat: Permanently settled land of Lord Jagannath
Gamcha: Small towel
Gaur: Caste name, palanquin bearers.
Gokha: Caste name: fish seller
Gudia: A caste that deals in parched rice
Gumastas: Record keepers in the court of the king and zamindars.
Gundicha ghar: A small temple where Lord Jagannath takes an annual journey from his own temple every year in June-July along with brother Balaram and sister Subhdra riding their chariots
Hari: Scavenger's caste
Jagannath Sadak: A road named after Lord Jagannath on which the pilgrims used to travel from Calcutta to Puri
Jagirdars: Persons holding land free of rent in consideration of their services
Jaishstha: The months of May and June, the second month of the Oriya lunar calendar
Jhuming: Shifting cultivation.
Kamar: Blacksmith
Kandara: Caste name, usually village chaukiders are recruited from this caste.
Karan: Writer's caste
Korta: Head of the household.
Kartik: Months of October and November, the sixth month of the Oriya lunar calendar

Kendu: A kind of fruit
Kewat: Fisherman
Kewat Shahi: The lane where fishing community inhabits.
Kilajat state: Princely States lying near sea belt or near the hills.
Khatian: A detailed record of each tenancy
Khandayat: Cultivating caste
Khas Mahal: Region where land rents were permanently settled.
Kharidadars: Purchasers of waste land
Kumbhar: Potter
Kulthi: Horse gram.
Lakhraj or *bahaldars*: Property owners holding their land free of revenue in perpetuity
Langar-Khana: Indigenous relief centre where food is distributed free of cost
Lohar: A person from blacksmith caste
Lion's Gate: *Singha Dwar*, the entry door of Lord Jagannath
Mahaprasad: Food offered to lord Jagannath considered to be sacred
Mali: Gardener
Mahajan: A moneylender and merchant
Mahima Dharma: Same as Alekha Dharm
Masala: Spices.
Mandia: A small millet grown in Orissa both as autumn and spring crop
Mandia jau: Gruel made out of small millets.
Math: A religious institution resembling a monastery
Madaranga: A kind of leafy vegetable that grows in damp places.
Molongis: Salt workers from Madras Presidency
Maund: Indian measure for paddy
Manusmriti: The religious book written by Manu (the first man) narrating various social and religious rules and regulations which should be observed by the members of the society
Murrimurki: Parched grain
Muthi sag: A kind of leafy vegetable that grows in drought conditions
Muqaddam: A class of proprietary tenure holders

Na'anka: The ninth year of the rule of Puri king.
N'ank Durbhikhya: Another name of the great famine of 1866 in Orissa
Pahi: Raiyats whose land rent were not fixed for the period of the settlement
Pan: Dalit Caste name: Drum beater
Parganas: Name of fiscal division of Mughal period
Pandas: Temple priests
Panchak: A festival in the month of November
Pandits: Learned Brahmins
Paik: Local militia caste who performed duties as soldiers in war time and cultivated land during peace time
Peja: The hot liquid separated from boiled rice
Polygamy: A man marrying too many women
Pradhan: A class of proprietary tenure holders
Proclaimed clans: Members of certain castes which habitually committed thefts and other minor crimes, were declared as proclaimed clan by the colonial rulers
Purdanashin: women in veils
Rabi: Spring crop
Raiyat: tenant
Raiyatwari: A system where the peasant pays revenue directly to the government
Ristedari: Family relationship.
Quinquennium: A length of five. It is a mathematical measure for the length of five months and years, etc.
Sarad: Winter rice
Sahibs: Englishmen
Savars: Name of a tribe.
Sarbarakar: Originally a collector of revenue
Santhals: Name of a tribe
Seer: Indigenous measure to weigh goods
Singhadwar: The main entry door to the temple of Lord Jagannath
Sirdar: Persons who were employed by factory and plantation industries
Sitala: Goddess of smallpox
Swan: A variety of supposedly inferior grain

Taccavi: Official advance payment to cultivator from public funds for agricultural purposes

Tanti: Weaver caste

Talukas: An administrative division of the district

Thana: Police division of a district

Thani: *Raiyats* resident in the villages where rents were fixed for the period of settlement

Teli: Oil pressing caste

Telenga Koomtees: Trading caste from Andhra region of Madras Presidency

Unani: Traditional medicine of Islamic countries

Zamindars or Malguzars: Proprietors directly responsible to the colonial government for payment of revenue for the region under their control where tenants cultivated land and paid revenue to them

Index

30 year settlement 82

age-specific death rates 406
Agricultural labourers 56-7; buyers of land and the state of agriculture, social composition of 57; Famine Commissioner of 1866 56; farm servants were better off 56; restructured land system 57
Alekha Dharma 142, 158, 164
Anderson, Rodney J. 244

Balasore 32, 36, 37, 39, 41-3, 45-6, 52-5, 111-12, 122, 185, 190-1, 298, 351, 359-61, 365-7, 378, 385
Banerjee, N.N. 358
Bangladesh Famine of 1974: *langar-khanas* 227-8; sex differential mortality 227
Barlow, G.N. 84
Bauri 154; relief centers 153
Bengal famine of 1943 18, 223-7; Patnaik, Utsa analysis of 18-19, 196; sex- and age-specific death rates 225
Bengal Presidency: Permanent Settlement 31
Bengal-Nagpur railway 61
bhaata Christians 163
Bhoi, Bhima 164
Bihar Famine 1966 14
Birth place statistics, accuracy of 350; famine emigration, extent of 350; permanent or semi-permanent emigration 350; short-term migrants 350
Brahmo Samaj 164
Burrows, William 243-4

Car Festival 43, 149, 150-1
Chaudhuri, B.B. 52
Chhatra Bazar 145-6, 162, 172
Chhatrakhia 119-20, 141-2, 158, 402-3; cluster of differentiated social groups 159; many people had kept the destitute of this 'caste' as servants 120
Chhatrakhia caste: destitutes as servants in their homes 159-60
Chhatrakhia Community 141-73: Brahmin priests and the upper-caste landlords resisted the *raiyats* 160; caste system, rigidity of, 173; Christian converts 163; famine period, land transactions increased considerably 160; grain robbery 154; Khandayat caste, surnames of 171; new caste, formation of 158-64; relief seekers, caste, class, age and gender of 153-7; settlement of tribals in the same colony as the non-tribal people 162; social behaviour 172; social order, new trends in 157
Chhatrakhia phenomenon, cultural impact of 162

Chilika lake 36, 59, 64, 91, 117-18, 119, 155, 183
China, famine in, cause of 18
Cholera 47, 98, 102, 106, 185, 186, 242-3, 247-8, 260-1
Cropping pattern 402

Das, Ananta 157
Das, Bichitranand 120, 160
Das, Gopabandhu 186, 190, 311, 368, 373
deaths, sex composition of 405
Dyson, Tim 230, 269, 370

East India Irrigation Company 60, 123, 148, 152
embankment, canals and railways and their impact, 1866-1921 59-62

Flood Committee Report of 1928 62; Orissa undertaking 60; rail roads led to the expansion of the market 61; *zamindari* embankments in Cuttack 59
Englishman, The 95
Fakir Mohan Senapati 22, 120, 149, 166-7, 358
Famine and Oriya literature 165-70; *Amar Chita* (Eternal Pyre) 167; *Anandamath* 165; Bengali film *Ashani Shanket* (Distant Thunder) 165; *Bhasha Kosha* 165-6; 'Ebe Madhya Banchichhi' 168; *Ha Anna* (O' Rice) 169; *Hunger* 169; *Muktagarhara Khyudha* (Hunger in Muktagarh) 167; *N'ankia* 165-6; *Naba Abhidhan* (New Dictionary) 166; Radhamohan Gadanayak's poems 168-9; *Sanatan in the truck carrier as a labourer* 168; Sanatan, character of 168-9; *Shasti* (Punishment) 169-70
Famine Commission Report 26, 74-5, 77, 113, 226
Famine Commission 1866, 56, 70, 83-5, 88, 91, 98, 99, 104, 105-6, 118, 149, 154, 156, 170
Famine Histories 78, 82-6, 88, 99, 102
Famine History 88
Famine: categories 17; impact on women 401-2
Famine of 1866, relief administration and caste question 142-53; Balasore district, regular roadside rest houses for pilgrims or *dharmshalas* 146; caste consciousness 146-7; East India Irrigation Company 152; Ganjam district, 146; government relief centres, relief and caste in 142-8; missionaries, relief and caste in 149-50; Orissa Division, relief centres, chaotic 147; private initiatives, relief and caste in 148-57; relief committees reluctant to distribute cooked rice to the famine-affected people 144; relief committees, activities of 143; zamindar of Parikud estate 153; zamindars of Kendrapara subdivision 153; zamindars, role of 153
Famine of 1888-9 181-4; agricultural labourers, plight of 181-4; Khorda in 1887-8, scarcity condition, 182; Khorda sub-division, agricultural labourers 182-4; *raiyats* especially in Khorda sub-division (including Puri) 181
Famine of 1907-8 184-93; agricultural labourers 184-5; Agriculturalists' Loans Act XII of 1884 187-8; composition of food grain, change of 189; government tried help the *raiyats* in very small measure 188-9; Land Improvement Loans Act XIX of 1883 187; press, role of 185-7; *raiyats* of the unprotected

areas 187-91; revision settlement operation 188; *taccavi* loans 189; weavers, condition of 191-3
Famine of 1918-19 193-8; agricultural labourers, effect on 194-5; *raiyats*, effect on 195-7; weavers, effect on 197-8
Famine of 1974, deaths in Matlab Thana 229-33; adult sex ratio increased 230; patterns of mortality in various famines all over the world 230
famine *per se* 17-18
Female mortality in famines, 1866-1974 205-34; Bengal Famine of 1943 223-7; biological and sociological factors, official views 216-20; biological and sociological factors, perspective of scholars 220-2; famines on the sex ratio (SR) 205; female and famine mortality, census views on 213-16; narrower sex differential mortality 211; SR and sex differential mortality between 1881 and 1921 206-13; SR influenced by sex-selective out-migration 212
Food and health care, gender discrimination in 268-86; access to food 272-7; anthropometric measures 280-3; Census commissioners 286; discrimination persisted 286; economic causes of 283-5; famine period, social factors affecting women during 269-70; general bias against women 268-72; Harvard Standard Measure 280-1; health care 277-80; social discrimination during normal period 270-2
Food: intra-family distribution of, 399; scarcity, vulnerability to 398-9
Fourth industrial revolution 398
Ganjam famine 124, 146
Great influenza of 1918-19 (war fever) 194
Great Irish famine of 1845-52 26, 93, 141
Great Orissa Famine of 1866 19, 26, 74-125; adult units 86-8; agriculture, organization of 122-3; area under *thani* cultivation declined 121; canal irrigation, introduction of 122-3; causes as per the Famine Commission reports 74-5; condition factor 83-4; consumption, per capita requirements 84-6; crimes and protests 92-5; press, role of 94-5; currency notes, introduction of 76; Dalit agricultural labourers or Kandaras 106; Deputy Magistrate of the Relief Committee 94-5; Disaster Relief International (DRI) 94; employment opportunities for agricultural labourers, decline in 113-14; estimates of output 81-8; Famine Commission Report of 1880 74; famine victims 118-20; famine victims, occupational structure of 105-11; famine, sex-differential mortality and out-migration 103-5; fishing community, situation of 117-18; free press 94; government, role of 96-9; identified the 'bona fide laboring class' as Panas, Kandaras, Bhois 110; immediate as well as long-term causes 77-81; Khorda subdivision of Puri 110-11; *laissez-faire* policy, expanding practice of 78; land settlement, nature of 76; land tenure 75-6; large-scale out-migration, due to scarcity conditions 119; long-term consequences 119-22; minor

revolts against zamindars 93; mortality, different estimates of 99-103; Oriya nationalism, nascent birth of, 121; output decline due to rain failure 77-8; *pahi raiyats* 109; post-famine money wage rates 123; post-famine wages and prices 123; production relations, changes in 121-2; *raiyats* who suffered in the hands of zamindars 114-16; *raiyats* 105; rent-free holdings changed hands 122; rents determined according to the caste rank in the Parikud *pargana* of Puri 121; rice, export of 79-81; social behaviour of people, deep impact on 124; standard yield 82; *thani* peasants 81; *thani raiyats*, rents paid by 114-15; times of price rise, expectations and anxieties during 88-91; *Utkal Dipika* 95; violence and protests, famine-time incidents of 92; wages of the labourers, fall in 111-13; weavers, distress of 116-17; zamindars reduced the *pahi* rent 122

Greenough, Paul 119, 219, 226-7, 271

Hen Christians 163

Hunter, W.W. 38, 44, 45, 54, 74, 85, 103-4, 109, 118, 121, 122, 150, 154, 358

India: drought-stricken areas 19; starvation conditions and acute distress 19; sex differential mortality 399

Infectious diseases, gender and class incidence of 241-62; cholera, sex-related innate immunity 247-8; diarrheal diseases 252-4; gender dimension in official reports 249-50; influenza, sex-related innate immunity 249; influenza, vulnerability by age groups 257-8; malaria, sex-related innate immunity 248-9; malaria, vulnerability by age groups 255-6; malnourishment and sex incidence of diseases 258-9; medical component 243-5; newborn infants 255; plague, sex-related innate immunity to infectious diseases 246-7; Punjab, age- and sex-specific incidence of plague mortality 246-7; sex-related innate immunity 244-54; victims of different diseases, sex composition of 243-6; victims of diseases, class composition of 259-61; vulnerability by age groups 254-8; Western medicine, efficacy of 242; women, children and the poor, sufferings of 261-2

Influenza outbreak 46, 47, 216, 222, 241, 243, 249, 250-3, 257-8, 260-1, 293-4

Inundation Committee Report of 1869 88, 116

Jagannath Temple 150-2; Car Festival 150-1; *Lakshmi Panchali* 151; *Lakshmi Purana* 151; organizing famine relief activities 152; role of *maths*, 45, 148, 150, 151-2, 358

Kalahandi 168, 186-7, 363

Kayastha, Karan 161

Kendrapara Canal 144

Keynes, John Maynard 18-19; profit inflation, policy of 19

Khandayat, Chasha 171

Khandayats 142

Khordha sub-division, cultivators of 34; *raiyatwari* settlement 34

Klein, Ira 97, 260

Kurmis in Bihar 142

Lady Christians 163

Maddox Report 57, 375
Madras Famine of 1876-8 147; shelter houses 147
Madras Presidency, *raiyatwari* system of land revenue 34
Mahapatra, Jayanta 156, 170
Maharatna, Arup 364
Mahima Dharma 142, 164, 173
Malaria 62, 215-16, 255-6, 260-1
Mansingh, Mayadhar 155, 157, 175
Maritime trade 58, 75
Marx, Karl 121
McAlpine, M. 61, 218, 220-2
Missionaries 105, 106, 120-1, 148-9, 156, 160, 163, 404
modern global era, relevance of famine studies 25-7; coping strategies 25; Famine Commission Report, 26
Mohanty, Kanhu Charan 169
Mukherjee, Prabhat 12

N'anka Durbhikhya 151
Nanda, Ramakrishna 169
Naoroji, Dadabhai 121
Narendra, the king 153

O'Grada 25, 92, 230, 231, 364
Orissa demographic situation from 1872 to 1921 46-9
Orissa division, cash crops in 38-40; absentee zamindars staying in Calcutta kept on demanding various types of cess 39; Banking Enquiry Committee Report of 1929-30 40; irrigation facilities and railroads, development of 39; jute 39-40; tobacco 40; winter rice 40
Orissa division, land revenue and land tenure systems 49-57; *Chandina* 51; *Jagirdars* 51; *kharidadars* 51; Khordha, revenue system of 52; Kilajat estates 49-50; *lakhiraj* or *bahaldars* 51; *muquaddams, padhans* (*pradhans*) and *sarabarakars* 51; *Pahi raiyats* 51; Paik rebellion 52; proprietors 50; *rayatwari* or *khas mahal* system 50, 52; revenue-free tenures or *bazyaftidars* 51; settlement, types of 49-50; *thani raiyats* 51; *zamindars* or *malguzars* 50
Orissa division, physical configuration of 35-40; agrarian scene 37-8; arable land 36; arable tract 36; Banki Government estate, *raiyats* of 38; Flood Committee Report of 1928 38; Settlement Report of 1906-9 37-8
Orissa Famine of 1866 19-21; colonial regime's policies 20; gender neglected both by policy makers and analysts 23; gender matters 23-5; impact of 20; *n'anka durbhikshya* 19-20; Oriya nationalism 20; plight of girls trying to get education 22; T.E. Ravenshaw, responsibility of 21-2
Orissa, 1860-1921, political economy of 31-64; British colonized four districts 32; canal irrigation 35; capital formation 35; *chakdars* 42; colonial misrule 35; cultivation, extension of 40-3; Industrial Revolution in Europe, no visible impact of 35; influenced economic structure of Cuttack and Balasore indirectly 45; Jagannath temple, priests given rent-free land to serve deities 43; Jagannath temple, role of 43-6; *jhum* (shifting) cultivation 42; Khordha sub-division, cultivators of 34; Orissa division, physical configuration of 35-40; Orissa, post-famine period 34-5; *pahi raiyats* (temporary

cultivators) 33; pilgrims visited other sacred places of Balasore and Cuttack 45-6; *raiyatwari* settlement 34; *thani raiyats* (permanent cultivators) 33; Yield Per Acre 42
Orissa, demographic situation from 1872 to 1921 46-9; Census Commissioners wrote extensively regarding the social systems 47; female-dominated occupations, sex ratio of 49; First Census of 1872 46; Pati, Biswamoy 49
Orissa's agrarian economy, vulnerabilities of 62-4; Jagannath Temple in Puri 64; *zamindari* estates 63
Oriya zamindars 52
Out-migration from Orissa division, classification of 350-64; and increasing sex ratio: statistical indicators 376-85; Balasore, famine situation 367; distress migration 365; famine emigration, other indicators of 368-76; famine migration between 1866 and 1921, quantitative evidence of 364-8; famine of 1919, migration to Calcutta and Assam 368; famine situation of Puri 367; Hugli and Howrah, relief centres 366; 'Madras Famine' or 'Temple Famine' 364; migrants to Calcutta 360; migrants to other places, characteristics of 361-4; migrants, occupational structure of 359-60; migration and its relationship with sex ratio 386-8; migration of men in prime of life, age distribution of emigrants 353-5; Oriya emigrants in Calcutta City, caste and occupational structure of 356-9; pattern of emigration through birthplace data 380-5; recent trends 385-6; salt tract, destitute of 366

Paddy Christians, 163
Pahi raiyats 53-4
Paik rebellion of 1817 33
Pandas, of Puri Temple 118, 164
Parikud 117, 121, 153, 155
Patamundai canal 171
Pen Christians 163
Permanent settlement 31, 33, 50, 76
Pilgrim Road 151
Pilgrim tax 44, 68
Poor Law 97
'Potato Eaters' 141
Praharaj, Gopal Chandra 165, 166
Preston, Samuel H. 244-5

raiyats of Orissa: indebted to the local moneylenders and the zamindars 54; small size of the holding, 55
Raiyats 53-4; indebtness of 54-6; pahi *raiyats* 53
Raiyatwari 33, 34, 50, 52, 402
Ravenshaw College 22
Ravenshaw, T.E. 21-2, 63, 78, 82-6, 91, 93, 96, 109, 117
Royal Commission on Agriculture 54, 368

Salt manufacture since 1860, decline of 58-9; cheap Liverpool salt 58; employment situation, impact on 58-9; Madras-made salt 58; manufacturers employed working parties of *molongis* 58; Orissa salt 58
salt monopoly 33-4
Salt production 33, 50, 52, 58, 63, 75, 84, 109, 113, 117, 122, 183
Sambad Bahika 190
Sambalpur Hiteishini 195

Sanitary Commission of 1868 103
Sanitary Commission Reports 25, 194, 320
Saryuriyas 158
Sebayats 43
Sen, Amartya 18, 94, 225, 232-3, 275, 276; famine as an entitlement failure 19
sex differential mortality rates, role of migration 406-7
Sex ratio: causes of fall 283, 285, 293; definition, 205; official view 216-20
Sex ratio, rise and fall of 293-315; caste and sex ratio 306-9; conception rate 302-6; discriminations against women and economic role 313-15; food, intra-family distribution of 310-11; high mortality and low mortality decades, age-specific SR's (ASR) in 295-306; medical treatment, differential access to 312-13; relative ratio of widows to widowers 298-300; rise in 315; social factors 310-13; T tests 300-2, 406
Singh, K. Suresh 158, 163
Sobieski, Dean A. 244
sociological factors, beneficial effects of 404

Taladanda-Machchagaon canal 403
Temporary settlement 50, 77
thani peasants 81
thani rayat 33, 50, 53, 114, 122
True famine 17

Utkal Dipika 12, 22, 88, 95, 120, 148, 150, 159-60, 164, 169, 186, 190, 192, 195, 196, 368

Visaria, Pravin 209, 210, 212-13, 220

Waldron, Ingrid 245
Women of low-caste groups 401

Zamindari 59, 63, 402
Zamindars responsible for collection of revenue 51; Sunset laws' imposed by the British 52-3